ARCHITECTURE IN ANCIENT EGYPT
AND THE NEAR EAST

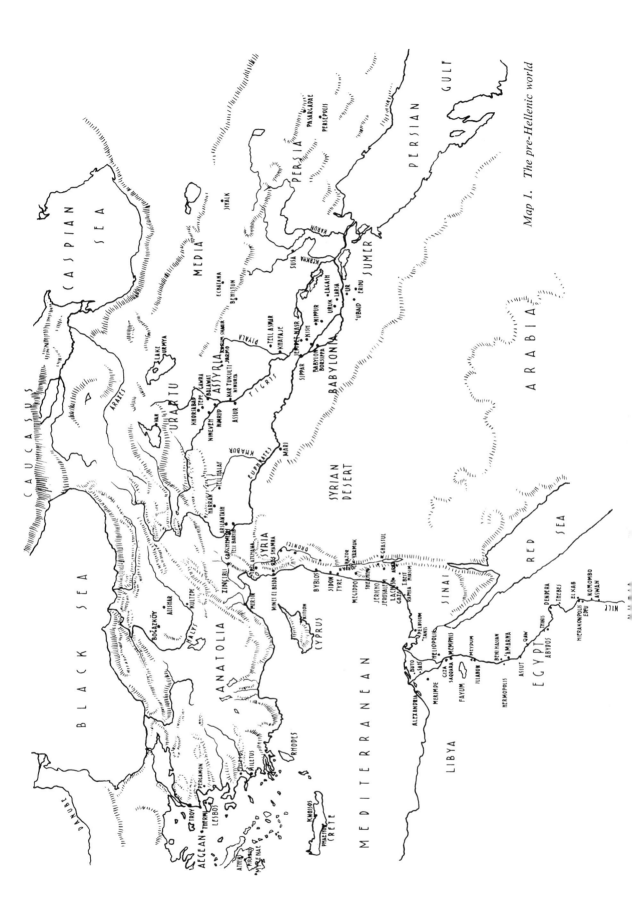

Map 1. The pre-Hellenic world

ARCHITECTURE IN ANCIENT EGYPT
AND THE NEAR EAST

by ALEXANDER BADAWY

THE M.I.T. PRESS

Massachusetts Institute of Technology
Cambridge, Massachusetts, and London, England

Copyright © 1966 by
The Massachusetts Institute of Technology

All rights reserved. This book may not be reproduced in whole or in
part, in any form (except by reviewers for the public press), without
written permission from the publishers.

Second printing, June 1972

ISBN 0 262 02 020 3
Library of Congress Catalog Card Number: 66–22351
Printed in the United States of America

Preface

This book presents students of pre-Hellenic architecture and archaeology with information in a clear and condensed form about the historical development of architecture, the most essential and noblest of the arts of mankind and the truest expression of culture. It is in this light and with an eye to human values that the information should be transposed into our own sphere of creative architecture. "Modern" architecture, admittedly, started on a sound basis but has since, more often than not, ignored this human scale. Some architects have gone so far as to turn the concept of the home into a "machine for living" and to ignore symmetry in religious architecture, which has consequently become grotesque. Yet the architectural aspirations of man after the industrial revolution do not differ essentially from those of the forefathers of the urban revolution. The astronaut returning home from a trip to the moon will hope for much the same home comfort, though interpreted in new media, as those settlers at Haçilar who nine millennia ago burnished the red plaster on the walls and floors of their houses to combine beauty and function. Even then, men had adopted for their place of worship the idea of symmetry, that irreplaceable aesthetic norm copied from the design of the animal figure.

This is not the place for an apology of the history of architecture of the pre-Hellenic world. But since the ideology of architecture is based on parallel achievement of both function and aesthetics, it is good to remember that it can be developed only through an investigation of the architectural contributions of the various cultures in terms of their respective environments. It is only through the experience acquired by generations of master builders, which is manifested in their achievements, that modern architects will be able to proceed successfully. Now that it has become usual for practicing architects to publicize their theories, one comes across some of their enthusiastic discoveries of a "modern" sense of function allied to beauty in ancient styles such as the modern lines of Egyptian façades, the ideal design of the typical villa at ᶜAmarna, the impressive architectural statuary in the Khorsabad palace, or the lively chromatic charm of the murals on the processional street at Babylon.

No one can miss the obvious differences between the eclectic refinement of Darius' palace at Persepolis and the primeval house at Haçilar. But the alert student will readily recognize from a perusal of the illustrations in this book the extremely subtle evolution in various architectural types and styles, even before he turns to the text for more substantial information about their sociology and history. The book is so designed as to give a clear account of each category of buildings in vertical cross sections through space and time. Based on these cross-sectional views, the synthesis in the final chapter reconstructs the architectural views of the pre-Hellenic world, with special emphasis on the underlying currents of cultural interconnections in the third, second, and first millennia B.C. up to the eve of the Hellenic revolution. Care has been taken to provide a comprehensive pictorial documentation, obtained from often inaccessible publications, in the form of about 400 line drawings. A brief glossary of special terms has also been compiled.

This survey is based on a mass of published material made accessible to the author at the Oriental Institute of the University of Chicago, where he was invited in 1955–1956 to be a Fulbright Visiting Professor by Professor John A. Wilson, the director of the Institute. It is a pleasure to acknowledge this help, as well as that of colleagues and the former librarian Miss J. Vindenas and her staff.

Los Angeles, California   ALEXANDER BADAWY
April 1966

Contents

PART I. ANCIENT EGYPT   *1*

Egypt   *3*

The Physical Environment   *3*

The Religious and Social Background   *6*

The Historical Background   *8*

The Prehistoric Settlements   *10*

Towns of Historical Egypt   *15*
    Orthogonal Layouts
    Axial Layouts
    Irregular Layouts
    Mixed Town Plans

Houses   *21*
    The Old Kingdom
    The Middle Kingdom
    The New Kingdom

Palaces   *28*

Temples   *33*
    Cult Temples
    Sun Temples
    Mortuary Temples

Tombs   *46*
    The Development of the Mastaba Tomb
    The Development of the Pyramid
    The Development of the Rock-Cut Tomb

Forts   *56*

Materials and Methods of Construction   *59*
    Materials
    Techniques
    The Construction of the Pyramids
The Style   *64*

PART II. THE ANCIENT NEAR EAST   *73*

Mesopotamia   *75*

The Physical Environment   *75*

The Social Environment   *76*

Religion   *77*

History   *78*

Towns   *80*

Houses   *85*

Palaces   *89*

Temples   *97*
    The Predynastic Period
    The Early Dynastic Period
    Akkad and Gudea of Lagash
    Dynasty III of Ur
    Isin-Larsa (1970–1698 B.C.)
    Babylon and the Kassites
    The Assyrians
    The Neo-Babylonians

Tombs   *108*

Fortifications   *111*

The Style   *116*

Asia Minor and North Syria   *120*

The Physical Environment   *120*

The Social Environment   *121*

Towns   *122*
    Haçilar
    Troy
    Boğazköy
    Alishar
    Kültepe
    Samʾal
    Carchemish
    Hadattu

Houses   *128*

Palaces   *130*

Temples   *133*

Tombs   *137*

Fortifications   *138*

The Style   *144*

The Levant   147

The Setting   *147*

Towns   *150*
  Jericho
  Gezer
  Megiddo
  Byblos
  Sidon
  Tyre
  Ugarit

Houses and Palaces   *157*

Temples   *163*

Tombs   *168*

Fortifications   *172*

Construction and Style   *176*

Elam and Persia   179

The Environment   *179*

Towns   *180*

Houses and Palaces   *182*

Temples   *184*

Tombs   *185*

Fortifications   *187*

Construction and Style   *187*

Cyprus   190

The Environment   *190*

Towns   *192*

Houses and Palaces   *192*

Temples   *195*

Tombs   *197*

Fortifications   *200*

Construction and Style   *201*

PART III.   ARCHITECTURE IN THE ANCIENT WORLD   *203*

The Ancient Orient and the Aegean   *205*

A Chronological Synopsis   *211*

Before the Third Millennium B.C.   *211*

Third Millennium B.C.   *214*

Second Millennium B.C.   *218*

First Millennium B.C.   *222*

Chart 1. Chronological Appearance of Various Architectural Characteristics Throughout the Ancient World *226*

Chart 2. Suggested Filiations from Egypt and the Near East to Greece   *228*

Glossary of Technical Terms   *229*

Index of Authors   *230*

Historical Index   *230*

Geographical Index   *235*

Subject Index   *240*

Index of Foreign Architectural Terms   *246*

PART I

ANCIENT EGYPT

Egypt

The Physical Environment

When the Greek historian Herodotus described Egypt in about 450 B.C. as "a gift of the river,"[1] he could also have mentioned the sun, for both the Nile and the sun have created the land of Egypt and are the sources of its animal and plant life. The gradual process of desiccation that had begun in the Sahara in the Quaternary Period spread also to eastern Africa. Some million years ago the valley of the Nile lay below the sea. After the waters retreated, the river proceeded to cut its bed and deposit silt layers annually. This alluvial deposit, 6 to 11 meters thick, forms a plain 10 to 20 kilometers wide and 900 kilometers long on both sides of the river, from the First Cataract to the apex of the Delta. This green triangle fanning out between the two main arms of the Nile to the Mediterranean was so named by the Greeks because its shape resembled their letter *delta*. In antiquity there were several secondary branches of the river in the Delta, and even at the beginning of our era the geographer Strabo mentions seven mouths of the Nile.[2]

As if it had pledged to maintain life in the plain that it had created, this providential river swells at a fixed date each year and, till the turn of the present century, before the irrigation projects, inundated the low-lying lands during the three months from July to September,[3]

---

[1] Herodotus, *Histories*, Bk. II, par. 5.
[2] Strabo, *Geography*, Bk. XVII, Chap. I, pars. 4, 18.
[3] *Ibid.*, par. 4. Strabo mentions forty days of flood and sixty days of gradual emergence and drying up. Cf. Herodotus, *Histories*, Bk. II, par. 20.

leaving a deposit of rich black silt. The inhabitants therefore called their valley "The Black" (*Kemet*) in contrast with the surrounding desert, "The Red" (*Desheret*), which was the land of the god of evil. Cultivation was relatively simple, because little plowing was needed before the inundation; but when the waters withdrew, grain was sown and trampled down into the wet alluvium by animals.[4] The Egyptian year was accordingly that of an agricultural people, with three seasons: "Inundation" (*Akhet*); "Winter" (*Peret* , literally "emergence"); and "Summer" (*Shemw* , literally "heat" or possibly "deficiency of water"). Since rainfall was negligible, as it still is today, agriculture had to rely entirely on the Nile and its beneficent inundation, deified as Haᶜpy. The agriculturist's year of $365\frac{1}{4}$ days, determined by the regular rise of the Nile and the succession of the seasons, was more accurate than the official solar year of 365 days, and even today the peasants use the Coptic months derived from the Egyptian ones.

Besides this immediate relationship of the Nile to rural life in Egypt, several other aspects of civilization and particularly architecture were also influenced by the river. In a land deprived of rain or springs, settlements grew up along the river and the canals, because water meant life as well as ease of communication and even accommodation for houseboats. Later, villages and towns grew in oblong settlements near the water, and since the river was the main artery, the official buildings such as temples and palaces were laid out perpendicularly to the riverbank and connected to its quay by a monumental approach, a basic pattern for urban layout that was noted by Vitruvius.[5] Structures in these towns had to be erected on mounds out of reach of the highest floodwaters, and this picturesque scene was still evident at the turn of the century. It was described in graphic terms by Herodotus: "When the Nile overflows, the whole country is converted into a sea, and the towns, which alone remain above water, look like the islands in the Aegean."[6] Through the centuries the silting process gradually raised the level of the inundation higher than the quays and pavements of early structures, and during the Late Period the temple of Amun at Luxor was more than once invaded by the waters. An elaborate system of dikes and canals had been devised and developed since protodynastic times to regulate the flood and supply water to the urban settlements lying inland at some distance from the river.[7] The hieroglyphs that stand for the words "garden, estate, nome," , and "canal, river, irrigated land,

[4] Herodotus, *Histories*, Bk. II, par. 14.
[5] Vitruvius, *Architecture*, Bks. IV, V.
[6] Herodotus, *Histories*, Bk. II, par. 97.
[7] *Ibid.*, par. 108.

boundary, season,"[8] ⚏ ⚎, actually represent either an orthogonal or parallel system of canals or one single watercourse. As Herodotus remarks, "this was perhaps the way in which geometry was invented,"[9] from the necessity of checking the position of the boundary stelae and surveying land property anew after the annual inundation. The regularity of the inundation and the early invention of geometry underlie the sense of order and regularity pervading Egyptian culture and particularly the rhythm and harmony in its art.

The neolithic Egyptians had lived on boats even before they settled on the riverbanks, sailing upstream with the north winds swelling their sails and downstream, following the current throughout the year. During inundation "water transport is used all over the country, instead of merely along the course of the river."[10] Egyptians took advantage of this extended facility of communication when field labor was free to transport materials of construction. Granite from far-off Aswan, alabaster from Ḥatnub near ʿAmarna, red sandstone from Gebel Aḥmar opposite Heliopolis, and the "beautiful white limestone" from Tura and Maʿsara opposite Memphis were carried on barges from the quarries to the building fields. The elaborate waterways and the Nile artery contributed to the cultural unity, for craftsmen and laborers could be shifted to various points, artifacts traded, and social contacts established. These are some of the environmental factors that contributed to the racial and cultural unification of ancient Egypt.

The annual inundation did not mean a spell of idleness, for the available manpower was recruited to work on the large monuments of the kings or the temples, probably being drafted under the *corvée*,[11] similar to the compulsory work on dikes and canals.

Another bountiful aspect of the Nile was its provision of the cheapest materials of construction. Reeds and plants that grew freely along the banks of the canals and in the marshes of the northern Delta were used to build the earliest boats and subsequently the earliest huts. The silt deposited by the river was found to be a valuable material, which was used extensively for daubing party walls in wattlework or building massive walls and ultimately for striking brick.

The radiant sun of Egypt, seldom obscured by a cloud, was called Reʿ, the most important among the cosmic gods, whose light and heat imparted life to people, animals, and plants alike. Thus in houses small windows set high in the walls sufficed for adequate lighting, while the large central hall in the mansion or in the temple could be

[8] A. H. Gardiner, *Egyptian Grammar*, 3rd ed. (Oxford, 1957), pp. 488, 491.
[9] Herodotus, *Histories*, Bk. II, par. 109.
[10] *Ibid.*, par. 97.
[11] J. Wilson, *The Culture of Ancient Egypt* (Chicago, 1958), p. 84.

lit by clerestory windows. This bright lighting accounts for the lavishness of color decoration and the contrasting use of sunk relief for directly sunlit areas and low relief for shaded ones in mural art.

Among the amenities that life in the open allowed in domestic architecture were a courtyard, a garden often with a pond in the country estate, and columned porticoes facing north to take advantage of the "cool, sweet breeze" so praised by the literary texts. The columned portico, one of the basic elements among the planning units, always faced north independently from the orientation of the house. Towns as a rule also grew northward because of the prevailing north breeze. To evade the loathsome heat during the long summer, people sought on their terraces the cool shade of an awning or a columned portico and slept under the wonderful ceiling of a starry sky. Ventilators consisting of slanting intake channels that opened north in the terrace conveyed fresh air to the hot rooms below. This system was still used at the turn of the century, as exemplified by the *mulqafs* in Islamic architecture. Similar devices were found in Elamite houses and later in the roofing tiles of Roman homes.

The exceptionally dry climate permitted the use of a very cheap building material, sun-dried brick set with mud mortar and plaster. Also because of dryness, the unpaved narrow lanes were sprinkled with water during the hot hours of the day to facilitate the circulation of people in the cool shade. Finally, since there was no need for rainwater disposal in such a climate, no public drainage system was deemed essential, and waste waters from the few sanitary installations in palaces or mansions were led to soak into the sand outside the buildings. However, in preplanned towns and fortresses in Nubia and the Sudan public drains ran along the axis of the streets and issued from the gateways.

Egypt has an exceptional geographical situation at the crossroads between Africa and Asia at no great distance from Europe, bordered by the Mediterranean to the north and the Red Sea to the east. Records of very early trade relations with Lebanon mention the import of the tall cedar and pine trunks essential to monumental architecture and boat construction. Trade resulted in direct and indirect exchanges of cultural influences, as early as the prehistoric period, with the countries to the north and southeast.

The Religious and Social Background

The extreme religiosity of the Egyptians, described by Herodotus, is characteristic of all epochs, beginning with predynastic carved labels, representing primitive wattle-and-daub shrines. It would be safe, indeed, to describe religion as the strongest stimulus in the life of the ancient Egyptian. Most architectural monuments still extant are religious or funerary, because the best location, the largest scale, and the most durable materials of construction were selected for religious programs.

A basically monotheistic creed was shrouded by associations with myths in which numerous gods appeared in human or animal forms, probably representing aspects of the forces of nature. There were universal gods of the cosmic elements such as Re^c ("Sun"), Nut ("Sky"), Geb ("Earth"), and local deities such as Sobek (the crocodile) and various ram gods. Some of the local gods such as Amun ("The Hidden") of Thebes, Osiris ("Resurrection"), and Horus ("The High One") attained the status of universal gods.

In order for a god to receive a cult and dwell on earth he allowed himself to be embodied in a small statue of wood set in a naos at the rear of the temple, to be serviced by the king or his delegate priest. The cult aimed at providing this god with prayers, offerings of food, ablutions, and clothing according to a regular schedule. The temple was actually "the house of the god" (r^3-pr 〒 〒) or his "castle" ($ḥ.t$-$nt̲r$ ¶ 𝕚). Re^c and later Aten were worshiped in the shape of the sun in the sky, and their temples had no cult statue or sanctuary, but instead an altar set near an obelisk (for Re^c) or simply one or two main altars with a stela in the open courtyards (for Aten).

The Egyptian pictured an eternal afterlife of happiness for the person whose soul had been justified and whose body could be preserved from corruption. This accounts for the design of the tomb as an underground abode where the mummy could dwell and a superstructure with a chapel where the funerary offering ritual would be performed by the assigned priest. Cities of the dead grew in the arid desert west of the Nile in an orthogonal pattern of streets around the royal pyramid. The location of the necropolises on the western plateau reflected the solar destiny of the deceased as determined by the setting of the sun in the west. To the individual and to the ruler alike, the most important achievements during a lifetime were to build a tomb that could defy time and violators and to secure a funerary service.

Apparently this strong religious emphasis implied high ethics. Pharaoh, who represented God, was himself a deity and acted as an autocratic ruler who strove to obtain the welfare of his people and to establish Truth ($Ma^c t$). He often showed his personal concern about one of his retinue, the building of a preplanned town for the craftsmen who worked on his tomb, the provision of drinking water for the quarry gangs in the desert, or the erection of colossi as intermediaries to which the needy could pray. Pharaoh often boasted that he was the "shepherd" of his people, a title probably originating from the dawn of history.

As might be expected under autocratic rule, the administration was entrusted, though not exclusively, to the nobles. But as a result of the social upheavals during the First and Second Intermediate Periods, the middle class gradually obtained leading posts. The slaves were foreigners, often prisoners of war, who formed the regular troops of laborers. Compulsory work on public projects also may well have provided relief to the masses of idle husbandmen during the inundation.

Arts and sciences flourished, though they conformed to the strict traditions of the educated priesthood. Moreover, Egyptian culture closely reflected the political ebbs and tides of history.

The Historical Background

It is only with the Neolithic Period (*ca.* 5000–3000 B.C.), when man settled down to become a food producer, that the building process appears. The Egyptian race seems to have been autochthonous, although its language had Hamito-Semitic origins. It is indeed remarkable that the foreign elements with which the Egyptian race and culture came into contact through the ages were so completely assimilated.

Manetho, the Egyptian priest who was commissioned by King Ptolemy I or II to write a history of Egypt, divided it into thirty dynasties, which were grouped by Egyptologists into the following periods:

Old Kingdom (Dynasties I–VI: 3200–2280 B.C.)
First Intermediate Period (Dynasties VII–XI: 2280–2131 B.C.)
Middle Kingdom (Dynasties XI–XII: 2131–1785 B.C.)
Second Intermediate Period (Dynasties XIII–XVII: 1785–1580 B.C.)
New Kingdom or Empire (Dynasties XVIII–XX: 1580–1085 B.C.)
Period of Decadence (Dynasties XXI–XXIV: 1085–715 B.C.)
Late Period (Dynasties XXV–XXX: 730–341 B.C.)
Persians (341–332 B.C.)

The beginning of the historic period was marked by the ultimate unification of Upper and Lower Egypt under one king (*ca.* 3200 B.C.), the invention of hieroglyphs, and the organization of an elaborate system of administration. Under the Third Dynasty the capital was established at Memphis, and stone was extensively used for the first time in the complex of the pyramid of Pharaoh Neterikhet Djeser (2778 B.C.), imitating reed construction. Quarries and mines were exploited regularly in Sinai and Nubia to provide stone, gold, and copper. Egyptian civilization attained its first and highest climax during the Fourth Dynasty (2723–2563 B.C.), when huge pyramids and elaborate tombs were built with astonishing skill to meet the requirements of the hereafter. But decline began under the Sixth Dynasty (2423–2270 B.C.) with the decentralization of royal power resulting from extensive royal donations to the nobility and the clergy, the transfer of privileges and power to the governors of districts or nomarchs, intrigues at the court, and especially the long and ineffectual reign of Pepy II for 94 years.

The First Intermediate Period (2280–2131 B.C.) was a dark period of civil war and of struggles between petty kings and later against the Asiatics. The rulers of Thebes, who at first recognized the dynasties at Herakleopolis (IX–X), later superseded them and governed the whole country (end of Dynasty XI).

During the Twelfth Dynasty (2000–1785 B.C.) prosperity resulted from excellent administration and irrigation projects created in the Fayum. Egypt gradually annexed Nubia in order to exploit its gold mines and caravan trade, and a chain of elaborate fortresses were built there along the Nile.

A Second Intermediate Period followed starting with the Thirteenth and Fourteenth Dynasties (1785–1680 B.C.). At this time the Asiatic Hyksos who infiltrated the eastern Delta succeeded in conquering Lower Egypt and part of Middle Egypt, thanks to their horse-drawn chariots and composite bows. It must be conceded to their credit that they tried to adapt themselves to Egyptian civilization. Again it was from nationalistic Thebes that rescue came, and the last rulers of the Seventeenth Dynasty freed the country from the invaders.

The New Kingdom (1580–1085 B.C.) saw the establishment of an empire whose capital was located at Thebes. Stretching east as far as the Euphrates and south into Nubia and the Sudan, it was based on military power and internal prosperity. Pharaohs married Mitannian princesses and struggled to maintain a balance of power between the Hittites, the Mitannians, and the Kassites of Babylon. A unique episode, perhaps related to these foreign contacts, occurred when Pharaoh Akhenaten left Thebes and its god Amun, founded a new capital in Middle Egypt at ʿAmarna, and developed the religion of the sun disk Aten. This ephemeral attempt (1364–1352 B.C.) marks an acute crisis that grew out of the latent antagonism between the pharaohs and the ever-increasing power of the god Amun and his clergy. At Thebes huge cult and funerary temples were built with all the lavishness and refinement of art allowed by financial prosperity and foreign imports. A number of decorative elements seem to have been introduced from Crete. But Egypt had already reached more than once the apex of its civilization, and decline again set in as a result of the harassing wars in Asia under the Ramessids, corruption in an intricate bureaucracy, and intrigue at the court. The tombs that the pharaohs cut deep in the cliffs of Western Thebes were desecrated by tomb robbers.

The Period of Decadence (1085–715 B.C.) saw the succession of a Libyan Dynasty (XXII) at Bubastis in the eastern Delta, obscure kinglets (Dynasties XXIII and XXIV), an Ethiopian or, rather, Kushite Dynasty (XXV), and several invasions by the Assyrians, who sacked Thebes (667 B.C.).

From the chaos there emerged at Sais in the northern Delta a dynasty of native rulers (XXVI) who imitated the Old Kingdom culture, especially its artistic style, in a vain attempt to re-establish its power. Two conquests by the Persians (525–404 B.C. and 341–332 B.C.) proved the incapacity of the later Egyptian rulers. The Macedonian Alexander the Great was welcomed as a savior (332 B.C.) and acknowledged as a native pharaoh by the god Ammon of Siwa Oasis.

The Prehistoric Settlements

The wind screens in the shape of a curving series of stones erected by the Paleolithic hunter[12] to protect his fire while he roamed the plateaus bordering the Nile can hardly be regarded as pertaining to architecture. True architecture began with the Neolithic settler in the valley who tried his hand at growing wheat and barley, though still actively hunting and fishing, and who learned to domesticate some of the meeker animals like cattle, sheep, goats, pigs, and dogs. Only those settlements located on the edge of the flood plain have been recovered, though there must have been numerous others, now buried deep beneath the layers of silt deposited through the ages. Sites were deliberately chosen on sandy Nile gravels for the wattle-and-daub structures[13] half sunk below ground level as protection against the elements and marauding animals.

The earliest settlement known is at Merimde,[14] on the margin of the southwestern Delta. Dating from about 5000–4000 B.C., it seems

[12] K. S. Sandford and W. J. Arkell, *Paleolithic Man and the Nile Valley in Nubia and Upper Egypt* (Chicago, 1933). Sandford, *Paleolithic Man and the Nile Valley in Upper and Middle Egypt* (Chicago, 1934). Sandford and Arkell, *Paleolithic Man and the Nile Valley in Lower Egypt* (Chicago, 1939). Et. Drioton and J. Vandier, *L'Égypte* (Paris, 1952), pp. 121 ff.

[13] K. W. Butzer, "Archaeology and Geology in Ancient Egypt," *Science*, Vol. 132 (Dec. 1960), pp. 1617–1624.

[14] H. Junker, "Vorläufiger Bericht über die Grabung der Akademie der Wissenschaften in Wien auf der neolithischen Siedlung von Merimde-Benisalame," *Anzeiger der Akademie der Wissenschaften in Wien, Phil.-Hist. Klasse* (Vienna, 1929), Vols. XVI–XVIII, pp. 156–250; (1930), Vols. V–XIII, pp. 21–83; (1932), Vols. I–IV, pp. 36–97; (1933), Vols. XVI–XXVII, pp. 54–97; (1934), Vol. X, pp. 118–132.

to have lasted for several centuries. Merimde covers about 180,000 square meters and is one kilometer from the Rosetta Nile, with a layer of debris two meters in thickness. It may have accommodated a population of 16,000. Two types of structures are found: houses for night quarters and shelters for daytime life. Oval huts surrounded by a low wall of irregular clay blocks were used by individuals (1 × 1.5 m.) or groups (3.2 × 2 m.) who slept in a crouching position (Fig. 1, bottom left). Their floor, which was sunk below ground level, was plastered with mud and had at one end a drainage aperture leading to a buried vessel. The shelters were larger oval and domed huts open to the southeast (Fig. 1) and were made of reeds woven on a framework of wooden posts set in holes in the ground. The discovery of baskets and vessels in these shelters suggests that these were living rooms also used as workshops and cattle enclosures. Near by were baskets and jars sunk in the ground for the storage of grain, holes for mortars, and circular threshing floors also sunk in the ground (4 m. in diameter). The occasional arrangement of several houses in two rows along a curving alley or street (Fig. 1, top left) may be an early attempt at communal layout. Graves were located near the huts.

Similar though much smaller settlements were found at El ʿOmari, which was south of Cairo, and in Upper Egypt at Ṭaṣa, Badari,[15] and Ḥemamiya. The huts were circular (1–2.3 m. in diameter), with walls made of blocks of clay and stone, lined internally with straw or reeds, and a floor below ground level. Unlike settlements in Lower Egypt, the graves were grouped into cemeteries on the outskirts of the desert.

From the late Neolithic or so-called Gerzean Period (3700–3200 B.C.), numerous sites have been found in Upper Egypt. Hierakonpolis, a city of religious significance in historic times, covered then 50,800 square meters and had a population of 4,700 to 10,000. Naqada was about half that size. Many of the sites remained as urban nuclei well down to the Dynastic Period. Though no actual evidence of a development in town planning is available, there were several basic stages in the evolution of houses and their construction. Among the most important is the appearance of a quadrangular plan in a structure of wattle-and-daub (Maḥasna)[16] and the invention of brick dried in the sun. Ovens are now built of two rows of 17 or 18 earthenware vessels plastered externally with clay and set between two brick walls (Maḥasna, Abydos).[17]

---

15 G. Brunton and G. Caton-Thompson, *The Badarian Civilisation and Predynastic Remains near Badari* (London, 1928).

16 J. Garstang, *Mahasna and Bet Khallaf* (London, 1902), pp. 6–7, pl. IV.

17 E. Peet, *Cemeteries of Abydos*, Vol. II (London, 1914), pp. 7–10, pl. I; Vol. III (London, 1913), pp. 1–7, pl. I.

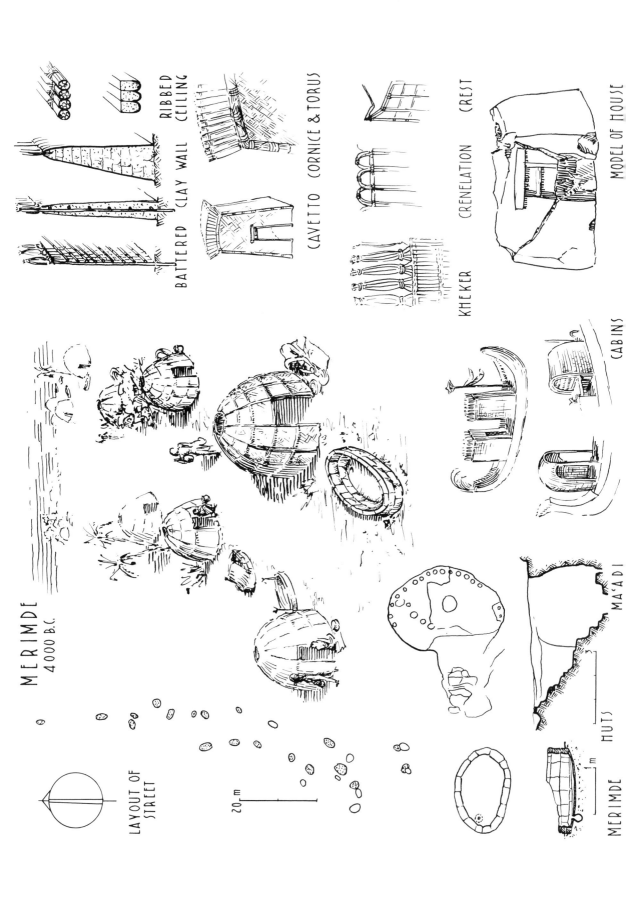

RIBBED CEILING

BATTERED CLAY WALL

CAVETTO CORNICE & TORUS

CRENELATION CREST

KHEKER

MODEL OF HOUSE

CABINS

MA'ADI

HUTS

MERIMDE
4000 B.C.

LAYOUT OF STREET

20 m

MERIMDE

1 m

3 m

The settlement at Maʿadi,[18] south of Cairo, dates probably from the Protodynastic and even the Dynastic Period. The huts have deep excavations in alluvial soil or sand in an irregular form (2.5 × 4 m.), with a row of post holes along the slanting curved sides and a series of steppingstones descending to the floor (Fig. 1, bottom left). The wooden posts once formed a framework to support the domed roof. Sunken magazines in a rectangular shape (3.8 m. long) have retaining walls made of large clay blocks set on stone rubble. Shelters or cattle enclosures (3 × 4.8 m.) on a rectangular plan were also built with walls of reeds and a doorway in the south end of the eastern side. The versatility in types of plans and in methods and materials of construction shows definite evolution toward standard architecture in historic times.

The evidence for the construction of houses can be complemented from sketchy paintings representing boats on the pottery of the Gerzean Period. In the middle of the wickerwork and papyrus boat one or two cabins with flat, slanting, vaulted, or domed roofs are erected (Fig. 1, bottom middle). The upper edge of the cabin is decorated with a row of semicircular or upright elements formed from the upper ends of the vertical reeds of the wall bent into a crenelation of loops or bound into bundles (Fig. 1, middle right). The latter shape was the basis for the standard decorative frieze painted or carved along the top of the walls and called in Egyptian *kheker*, meaning "adorned, ornament" (Fig. 1, middle). There is good reason to believe that a large part, if not most, of the life of the Neolithic Egyptian was spent on boats, either fishing or trading.[19] The types of cabins on these boats are reminiscent of early dynastic structures represented on contemporaneous labels and cylinders, and it is safe enough to picture the shelters, huts, and even shrines erected on both banks of the Nile as having been derived from these cabins.[20]

A unique clay model from El ʿAmrah[21] represents a house built on a squarish plan with battered walls probably of clay rather than brick, which have one doorway featuring a lintel and two windows with protruding sills set high up in the opposite wall. The roof was

[18] O. Menghin and M. Amer, *The Excavations of the Egyptian University in the Neolithic Site at Maadi*, Vols. I–II (Cairo, 1932, 1936). O. Menghin, "Die Grabung der Universität Kairo bei Maadi (III Grabungsjahr)," *Mitteilungen des deutschen Instituts für ägyptische Altertumskunde in Kairo*, Vol. V (Berlin, 1934), pp. 111–118. J. Vandier, *Manuel d'archéologie égyptienne*, Vol. I (Paris, 1952), *Les Epoques de Formation: La Préhistoire*, pp. 508–518.

[19] C. Boreux, *Études de nautique égyptienne*, *Mémoires publiés par les Membres de l'Institut français d'Archéologie Orientale du Caire*, Vol. L (Cairo, 1924–25), p. 21.

[20] W. Edgerton, *Journal of Semitic Languages and Literatures*, Vol. 39 (1922–23), pp. 109–135. Alexandre Badawy, *La dessin architectural chez les anciens Égyptiens* (Cairo, 1948), pp. 4–8.

[21] D. Randall-MacIver and A. C. Mace, *El Amrah and Abydos, 1899–1901* (London, 1902), p. 42, pl. 10.

←*Fig. 1*

probably a flat terrace of brushwood or reeds on beams (Fig. 1, bottom right).

About the temples little is known, except for the large square terrace (50 m.) beneath the archaic temple at Hierakonpolis,[22] which had rounded corners and was enclosed by a stepped retaining wall. Some representations of a wattle-and-daub domed or vaulted structure with four corner posts have been identified as the national sanctuary of Lower Egypt (*pr-nw*[23] ⌂).

The remains of cemeteries are far more numerous than are those of settlements, a fact which proves, if need be, that the latter lie buried beneath the layers of silt in the flood plain. The grave is a round, oval, or rectangular pit used for one individual. The walls of the excavation are lined, in the later stage, with mats and brickwork. A transverse party wall sometimes subdivides the room into a burial area and one or two compartments for the funerary equipment (El ꜤAmrah). The very early tombs at El ꜤOmari were each covered with a round tumulus (7 m. in diameter) of stone chips, and it is fair to assume that the superstructure remained a regular feature down to the Archaic Period, when it is substantiated by actual monuments.

Protodynastic slate palettes for grinding pigments are carved in low relief representing the square plans of forts with external bastions, either rounded or square or triangular.

These finds, which cover a period of about two millennia, are more significant than would appear at first, for they bring out the basic elements that influenced later techniques and styles. We have seen how the basic architectural plan evolved from oval to rectangular shape. We have also noted achievement in various fields of architecture: domestic, religious, funerary, and military. The battered clay wall is probably the result of the gradual increase in the thickness of plaster applied to a wattle-and-daub wall till the inner framework becomes superfluous (Fig. 1, top right). The batter is used to achieve stability in a massive wall built of slippery clay blocks. Pliable sticks are set upright in the ground and bent so that their top ends meet to form arches, vaults, or domes, later imitated in brickwork even to the semicircular reinforcing ribs protruding from the intrados at regular intervals (Fig. 1, top right). The ceiling, made from bundles of reeds set side by side, is copied in stone ceilings in the Old Kingdom with semicircular ribs (Fig. 1, top right).

As we trace the stylistic development, we shall say more about the origin and evolution of the standard cavetto cornice and torus

[22] J. E. Quibell, *Hierakonpolis*, Vol. II (London, 1902), pp. 3 ff., pl. LXXII. Vandier, *Manuel*, Vol. I, pp. 521–522.

[23] Vandier, *Manuel*, Vol. I, pp. 577–578. Alexander Badawy, *A History of Egyptian Architecture*, Vol. I (Cairo, 1954), p. 24, Figs. 12–13.

molding (Fig. 1, middle right), as copied from earlier plant structures. In the cabins of boats the upper ends or tufts of the uprights in the shape of series of semicircular loops or vertical bundles are the prototypes of the merlons and *kheker* frieze respectively (Fig. 1, middle right). The curious prismatic elements that appear at the top corners of some boat cabins are the prototypes of similar ones set at the top of the predynastic model of a house from El ʿAmrah and of the enclosures of granaries in the Old Kingdom (Fig. 1, lower right). The tradition of Egyptian architecture is deeply rooted in the earliest civilization, which dawned far back in the Neolithic Period.

Towns of Historical Egypt

Community life began in the Neolithic Period in such settlements as Merimde, Hierakonpolis, and Naqada. Though they cannot be described as towns, they formed the embryos of the later urban settlements that were enclosed within walls and governed by a representative of the central authority. They began on the Nile or a canal at a location significant for trade and military activities.

The plans carved on protodynastic palettes represent square forts or fortified cities with blocks of buildings set in rows along streets on an orthogonal layout. When an animal is shown outside the bastioned enclosure hacking at the wall with a hoe, we are to understand that it symbolizes the besieger attacking an autonomous city-state, whose emblem, often another animal, is shown *intra muros*. This concept of a politico-urban entity, similar to that of the Sumerian city-state, is corroborated to a certain extent in the early hieroglyph for "town" that shows a circular enclosure surrounding an orthogonal system of streets (Fig. 2, top left) or two arteries crossing at right angles (Fig. 2, top left). We know that there was an Egyptian title for "governor of the town" (ḥȝtj-ʿ) in the Middle Kingdom. We know also that Pharaoh Waḥkareʿ (Dynasty X, 2100 B.C.) advised his son to build "new towns" in the Delta to form nuclei each having 10,000 colonists loyal to the throne, and we know that there was a title "ruler of new towns."[24]

The figures for the periphery of large cities as given by the Greek writers should not be discarded as fantastic, though 150 stades (27.75 km.) given by Diodorus for Memphis and 80 stades (14.4 km.) for Thebes given by Strabo seem quite large. They could refer to the total length of a double enclosure such as the ones around many fortified towns in Egypt. They also agree closely with the known periphery of Nineva and Babylon.

---

[24] Alexander Badawy, "Orthogonal and Axial Town Planning in Egypt," *Zeitschrift für ägyptische Sprache und Altertumskunde*, Vol. 85 (Berlin, 1959), pp. 1–12.

There are actual remains of towns from the Archaic Period. At Hierakonpolis[25] there is a rectangular enclosure of brick (210 × 300 m.) that is oriented to the cardinal points by the corners, with its longer side parallel to the Nile. The massive rectangular enclosure at El Kab (512 × 600 m.) is of uncertain date, though the circular double wall (390–400 m.)[26] is from the Archaic Period (Fig. 2, top).

Orthogonal Layouts. Pyramid cities were preplanned settlements built in the desert for the laborers and craftsmen working on royal tombs or for the funerary priests. They always feature blocks of single or double rows of houses of a uniform attached type in each block. The town is surrounded by a massive wall of brick forming a square that is oriented to the cardinal points. The layout of the streets is orthogonal, with main streets running north–south and secondary ones east–west. Houses are grouped according to types into quarters, conforming to a system of zoning. One house of a different plan set in a corner of a quarter must have been intended for the official in charge. Near the tomb of Queen Khentkawes (2563 B.C.) at Giza a row of eleven large brick houses bordered on the north and south sides by a street running east–west, with an underpass beneath it for a transverse street servicing a group of subsidiary buildings, may have been part of a pyramid city for the funerary priests. The extensive town for the priests and artisans of Sesostris II (1906–1888 B.C.) at El Lahun[27] is by far the most interesting, though only half of its area could be excavated. This town is enclosed within a square wall (740 cubits, or 387 meters, to a side), oriented to the cardinal points, and divided into two unequal areas by a wall running north–south, the western area being about one third the eastern one. The main streets run north–south, crossing secondary ones at right angles and forming rectangular blocks of double rows of attached houses side by side and back to back. There are at least four types of house plans, besides the large mansion type along the northern street. The discovery of Syrian and Minoan Kamares pottery at El Lahun implies the existence of artisans of foreign origin, perhaps Syrians.[28] The town was inhabited by the funerary priests till the Thirteenth Dynasty, on the evidence of contemporaneous papyri. It can easily be confirmed that the town's population

[25] Quibell, *Hierakonpolis*, Vol. II, pls. LXXII, LXXIII.

[26] S. Clarke, "El Kab and the Great Wall," *Journal of Egyptian Archaeology*, Vol. VII (London, 1921), pl. X.

[27] W. Fl. Petrie, *Illahun, Kahun and Gurob, 1889–90* (London, 1891), p. 5; *Kahun, Gurob and Hawara* (London, 1890), p. 23. Alexandre Badawy, "La Maison mitoyenne de plan uniforme dans l'Egypte pharaonique," *Bulletin of the Faculty of Arts, Cairo University*, Vol. XVI (1953), pp. 15–21.

[28] C. Schaeffer, *Stratigraphie comparée et chronologie de l'Asie Occidentale* (Oxford, 1948), p. 19.

Fig. 2→

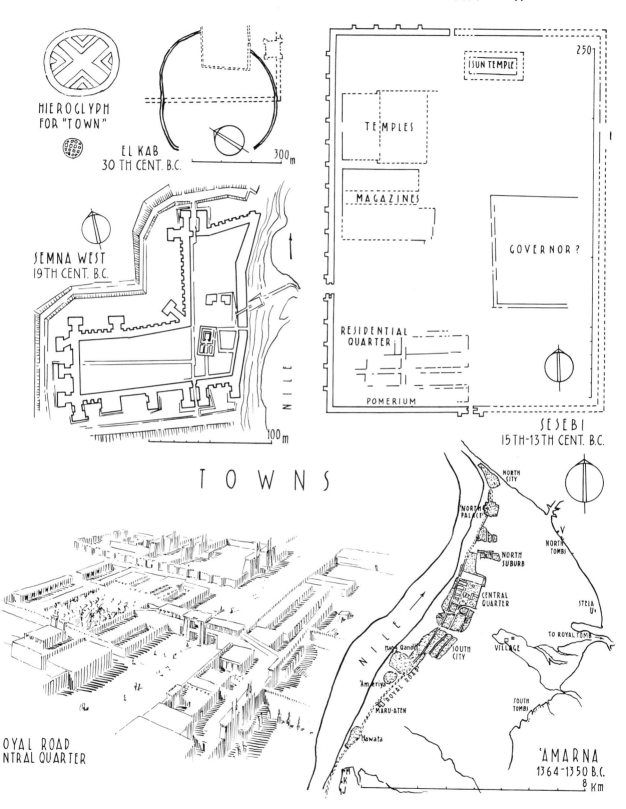

HIEROGLYPH
FOR "TOWN"

EL KAB
30 TH CENT. B.C.

300 m

SUN TEMPLE

250

TEMPLES

MAGAZINES

GOVERNOR ?

SEMNA WEST
19TH CENT. B.C.

RESIDENTIAL
QUARTER

POMERIUM

NILE

100 m

SESEBI
15TH-13TH CENT. B.C.

T O W N S

NORTH CITY

NORTH PALACE

NORTH SUBURB

NORTH TOMBS

CENTRAL QUARTER

STELA U

TO ROYAL TOMB

VILLAGE

Hagg Qandil

NILE

SOUTH CITY

'Ameriya

ROYAL ROAD

MARU-ATEN

Hawata

SOUTH TOMBS

M K J

'AMARNA
1364-1350 B.C.

8 Km

OYAL ROAD
NTRAL QUARTER

was about 10,000, as estimated by Pharaoh Waḥkareᶜ when he advised his son Merikareᶜ to build new cities in the Delta. From the workmen's town built by Pharaoh Aḥmes I at Abydos there are remains of some attached uniform houses. The small artisans' town in Akhetaten (ᶜAmarna East), dating from 1364 B.C.,[29] is the best preserved (Fig. 3). Its enclosure wall is a perfect square oriented to the cardinal points (70 m. to a side), with one gateway in its south side next to a shrine. The area is also divided by an inner wall running north–south into a larger eastern quarter and a smaller western one (2/5 of the eastern). All the streets run north–south, servicing single rows of attached houses of uniform type (5 × 10 m.). It may be surmised that the lesser eastern quarter was for the craftsmen of foreign origin, who were perhaps even subjected to compulsory labor. In the capital itself at ᶜAmarna several blocks of attached houses belonged to officials. The seclusion and easy control of these self-contained towns was necessary because some of the workmen were foreigners and their work on the pyramids or tombs had to be kept secret.

Axial Layouts.[30] Though such towns could have existed earlier in Egypt itself on the evidence of the hieroglyph for "town," the only archaeological remains are those of the series of forts built along the Nile in Nubia by the pharaohs of the Twelfth Dynasty. The forts that were located on rocky ground have an irregular outline following the contour lines of the terrain; others, situated on flat banks, are rectangular. From the strong outer wall project bastions and long spur walls. Two main streets crossing at right angles and a street running along the inner periphery of the wall, or pomerium, connect two gateways at the smaller opposite ends. Inside the public buildings, granaries, a temple, and barracks in regular blocks for the garrison, as well as a mansion for the commandant, are laid out according to a zoning system. Such forts occur at Semna (Fig. 2, middle left), Kumma, Uronarti, and Askut. Those on flat land at Buhen, Kuban, and Ikkur are rectangular, with two arteries crossing at right angles along the two main axes and connecting the opposite pairs of gateways, much like a Roman castrum. At Buhen the two main streets are paved with stone, and a drain runs along the middle of each, the east–west street terminating at a well-preserved water gate. At Askut the main street is paved with terra-cotta tiles covering a drainage system that issues through the gateway.

A modest settlement of workmen in Western Thebes at Deir el

[29] T. Eric Peet and C. Leonard Woolley, *The City of Akhenaten*, Vol. I (London, 1922), pl. XVI, pp. 51 ff. Badawy, "Maison," pp. 25–30.

[30] Badawy, "Orthogonal and Axial Town Planning," pp. 5 ff.

Fig. 3→

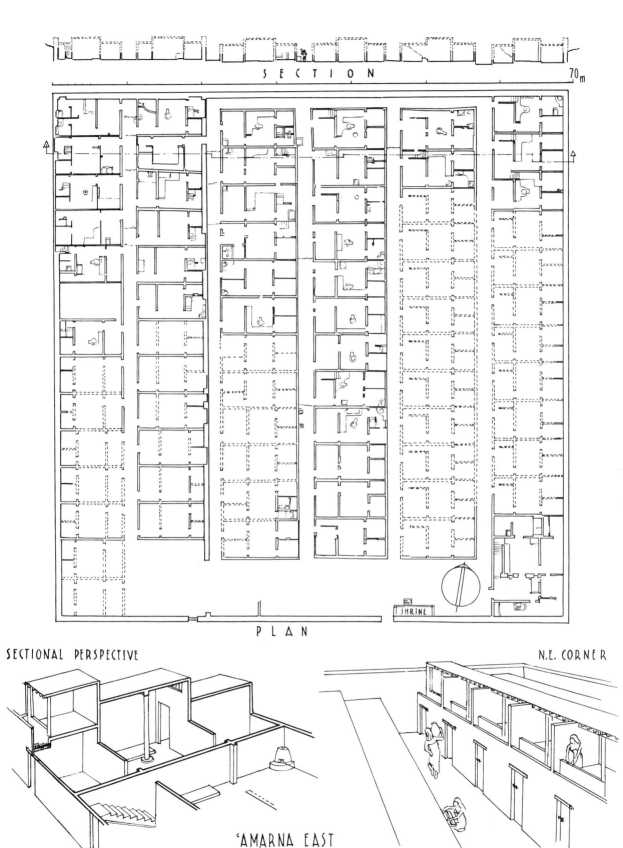

SECTION

70m

PLAN

SHRINE

SECTIONAL PERSPECTIVE

N.E. CORNER

'AMARNA EAST

Medina, dating from the reign of Tuthmosis I (1528–1512 B.C.), features a central artery flanked by two rows of attached houses, narrow and deep. Though the settlement was inhabited during four centuries, the streets and houses were clean to the bedrock, which indicates the existence of ordinances enforced by a responsible authority or by the inhabitants themselves. Furthermore, the houses are decorated with paintings that are a credit to the good taste and love brought to their homes by these modest craftsmen.

Sesebi in the Sudan (Fig. 2, top right), a large garrison town of the Eighteenth Dynasty, presents a perfectly oriented axial layout that is zoned into residential quarters (southwest), magazines (west), temples (north), and a large building, presumably the governor's quarters (east), all enclosed by a rectangular wall.

Irregular Layouts. In the Orient the urban settlement has always grown organically, one house being added to an earlier one along narrow streets according to an arbitrary alignment. This was probably the process followed in the villages and the smaller rural towns in Egypt. In larger cities and in the capitals a master plan must have defined a zoning system that was co-ordinated with a network of main streets leading to the temples. Evidence of such a plan is found in the only city we know, the capital at ʿAmarna (Fig. 2, bottom right). Bordered by a cirque of mountains to the east, it has three main streets running parallel to the Nile bank, which forms its western border for 12 kilometers. Transverse ravines divide the built-up area, 3.5 kilometers long and 1.3 kilometers wide, into quarters that conform to a zoning plan. The central quarter (Fig. 2, bottom left) contains the royal palaces, temples, and government buildings. In the residential quarters the houses are not very regularly distributed within the blocks. A palace and a reserve for animals at the north end of the capital and a religious complex at its south end form the two terminal poles of the layout.

At Memphis there were two rectangular enclosures oriented north–south, the northern one for the palaces and the southern for the temples. Since no trace of the city itself has been found, we assume that it disappeared after many centuries of flooding and cultivation. At Thebes a processional avenue about three kilometers long, bordered by sphinxes and connecting the temple of Amun at Luxor to that of Amun at Karnak to the north, ran parallel to the Nile. It is presumed that the town itself extended south of Luxor temple.

Mixed Town Plans. Some of the towns from the Late Period and the Greco-Roman towns were enlarged or even superseded by Greek settlements. At Naukratis the earlier type of layout stretching to the south and west, possibly an Egyptian or Cypriote–Phoenician town, was later connected to the Greek quarters that expanded north. The irregularity of the blocks at Tebtynis comes from the fact that the later town was built on the remains of the one from the Twelfth Dynasty.

Houses

In the Protodynastic Period the typical house plan had evolved from the oval to the quadrangular outline. Among the hieroglyphs representing buildings the commonest one represents the plan of a simple rural homestead in the shape of a rectangular courtyard surrounded by an enclosure wall, and it determines the word "house" (*pr* ⊐). Other hieroglyphs represent in elevation: a wickerwork partition (▥) or a stockade (𝔪), or the façade of a columned portico (▦), or the cross-sectional elevation of a flat-vaulted hypostyle hall (⋒), or the domed room for the women of the *ḥarim* (⌂), or beehive granaries (⋀⋀⋀). Most of the forms and undoubtedly some of the materials used are derived from reeds and other plants, though brickwork must have been the most common material.

The Old Kingdom. A few texts describe "ideal" houses and thus are too subjective to be useful; all emphasize the importance of a garden with fruit trees and a pond surrounded by a high wall. Such a setting was usual for suburban houses of the middle class in all periods.

Actual remains from Third Dynasty houses are found at Hierakonpolis and at Saqqara. The latter type of house is a small rectangular structure (5.4 × 4 m.) divided longitudinally into two strips, with an entrance facing north, and a vestibule[31] from which open a small closet (latrine?), a hall, and a living room with bedroom. The house bears a striking resemblance to the so-called royal pavilion in the funerary complex of Djeser located near by (Fig. 5, middle left), both in the presumed use of the rooms and in their arrangement into two groups, one for reception and the other for private quarters.

In the unique remains of a pyramid city near Queen Khentkawes' tomb at Giza (Fourth Dynasty),[32] houses of a uniform plan are attached side by side in one row (11.4 × 14.4 m., making 164 sq. m. per unit; Fig. 4, top left). The brick walls are rather thick, and the arrangement of the rooms, a few of which are L-shaped, is somewhat like a labyrinth. Each house has two doorways, the service entrance

---

[31] Badawy, *Egyptian Architecture*, Vol. I, Fig. 39, p. 54.

[32] S. Hassan, *Excavations at Giza, 1932–1933* (Cairo, 1943), Fig. 1, pp. 35 ff. Badawy, "Maison," pp. 8 ff.; *Egyptian Architecture*, Vol. I, pp. 54–55.

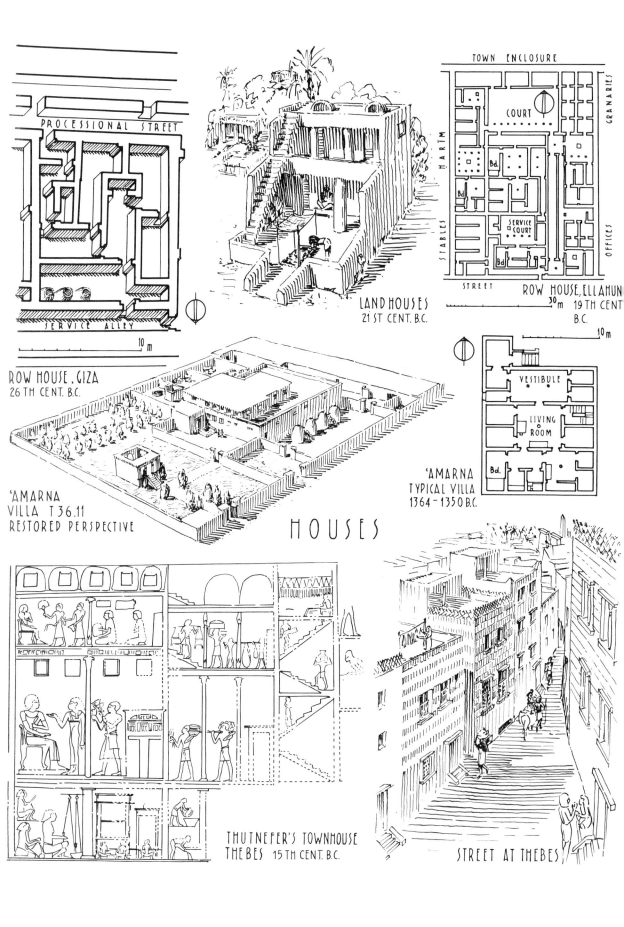

PROCESSIONAL STREET

SERVICE ALLEY

10 m

ROW HOUSE, GIZA
26TH CENT. B.C.

LAND HOUSES
21ST CENT. B.C.

TOWN ENCLOSURE

HARIM

STABLES

COURT

Bd.

SERVICE
COURT

Bd.

GRANARIES

OFFICES

STREET

ROW HOUSE, EL LAHUN
19TH CENT.
B.C.

30 m

10 m

VESTIBULE

LIVING
ROOM

Bd.

'AMARNA
TYPICAL VILLA
1364–1350 B.C.

'AMARNA
VILLA T 36.11
RESTORED PERSPECTIVE

HOUSES

THUTNEFER'S TOWNHOUSE
THEBES 15TH CENT. B.C.

STREET AT THEBES

on the north street and the main one on the south processional
street. Inside the south entrance there are a lobby with screen wall, a
corridor leading to the reception room, and a courtyard. On one side
of the courtyard are two bedrooms and to the north a magazine
with silos and a smaller storage room on either side of the north
entrance. The long narrow shape of the rooms suggests that they
were roofed over with brick vaults. Numerous small models of
houses[33] found in tombs (Dynasties VI–XII) were intended to replace the actual house of the deceased in the afterlife. They represent
a variety of types. The simplest is a rectangular enclosure that has at
its rear an awning or a columned portico in front of several rooms.
Another type is a two-storied house fronted by a columned portico
on each floor and a stairway ascending to the terrace (Fig. 4, top
middle). In the front courtyard there are a small water basin, an
oven, and grain bins. Rooms are roofed with vaults and half vaults,
while awnings simply have a flat ceiling of branches or bundles of
reeds. Windows open high in the lateral or rear walls. From the
terrace protrude half cupolas that face north and form ventilating
channels to the rooms below.

Data available from houses of the Old Kingdom, mostly from
murals in tombs, conjure up a picture of the dependencies, storerooms, and granaries. Large jars for storing grain are set in the magazines, as in the pyramid city at Giza or in the court. According to
paintings and models, a large granary consists of a row of domed
mud bins or wooden compartments with four corner posts set on a
low platform along two or three sides of a rectangular court.[34] The
bins are filled through an opening at the top, and grain can be with-
drawn from a trap door sliding vertically at the lower part of the
façade. Sometimes a sophisticated rich landowner or a government
institution would build an elegant portico on slender lotiform
columns of wood painted in gaudy colors in front of the bins to
provide cool shade for the scribes who recorded the transport of
grain.

To the west of the pyramid of Chephren at Giza[35] a row of deep
narrow rooms roofed with brick vaults runs along three sides of a
long narrow courtyard. This is presumed to be a large magazine for
all of the supplies and equipment required during the construction,
rather than barracks for the workmen.

Although there has been no discussion of water supply and drainage systems, they were not unknown. As a matter of fact, a latrine

[33] W. Fl. Petrie, *Gizeh and Rifeh* (London, 1907), pp. 14–20, pls. I, XIV–XXII.
Badawy, *Egyptian Architecture*, Vol. I, pp. 55–59.
[34] Badawy, *Dessin architectural*, pp. 116–121.
[35] W. Fl. Petrie, *The Pyramids and Temples of Giza* (London, 1883), p. 213.

←*Fig. 4*

was certainly installed in the better houses, for there is a copy of one in the substructure of Ruaben's tomb at Saqqara (Dynasty II).[36]

Walls plastered with mud or white stucco were sometimes painted to look like hangings of brilliantly colored mats or rugs, and sometimes the walls were actually covered with these rugs. Superstructures of tombs as well as stelae and sarcophagi which imitated houses were often painted or carved to represent such mats cleverly stretched in the recesses between wooden posts.

The Middle Kingdom. Our main source of information about houses during the Middle Kingdom is the workmen's town at El Lahun in the Fayum,[37] one of those preplanned towns that were never remodeled and on account of their location on the edge of, or in, the desert were spared the oblivion that was the fate of urban settlements in the valley. Of the several types of houses at El Lahun let us first examine in detail the large mansion type (Fig. 4, top right), set along the northernmost street running east–west. Its rectangular plan (40 × 60 m., making 2,400 sq. m.), with the entrance facing either toward the north or toward the south, is divided into two main sections, each accessible from one of the two long corridors running side by side from the entrance lobby. The eastern area is a strip directed north–south, much narrower than the other one, and it features three courts surrounded by offices and, at the rear, a set of granaries. The residential part of the house is accessible from the other corridor, leading onto the main courtyard near the back, which has a columned portico facing north. Behind this portico stretches the central strip running north–south, with the master's apartments, which consist of a broad hall, a hypostyle hall, a bedroom, and farther behind it a small court with its portico and various rooms. The last strip to the west contains the workmen's quarters on one side and the servants' premises on the other. Near the front of the house and accessible from the entrance doorway are stalls. The plan is extremely ingenious and avoids wasteful corridors. Its various components are skillfully patterned around courts, large or small, which provide light and air and always contain a portico along their south side to take advantage of the "sweet breeze of the north," so highly praised in Egyptian literature. Whether the house is to the north or to the south of the street, it is planned so as to have all its porticoes set along the south side of the courts. It is also noteworthy that the architect succeeded in isolating each type of quarter (offices and granaries to the east, master's apartments in the middle, women to the west, stalls with separate approach), though he

[36] Badawy, *Egyptian Architecture*, Vol. I, p. 40, Fig. 30.
[37] Badawy, "Maison," pp. 17–21.

allowed only one entrance, probably as a security measure for the
whole complex. The typical arrangement of the two bedrooms
consists of an alcove at their south end, raised one step and slightly
narrower than the room itself. Above the alcove is one of the roof
ventilators already encountered in the house models from the First
Intermediate Period. There is a bathroom in the vicinity of each
bedroom. Such a large house of a high official usually had five
courts and not less than forty rooms and could have accommodated
forty to sixty persons.

Smaller houses at El Lahun measure 9.9 by 9.6 meters, making
95 square meters, with four rooms, an area equivalent to 1/25 that of
a mansion, or 10.5 by 16 meters, making an area of 168 square
meters, with six to twelve rooms. In all cases only one entrance
gives access from the street through a corridor to the main hall.
Connected to the court are two rooms on the street side for reception, and beyond the court there are bedrooms. The small closet
set just inside the entrance could well have been a latrine.

In the fort at Uronarti in Nubia (Dynasty XII)[38] there are two
groups of attached houses side by side and back to back on either
side of the main street. The housing unit (9 × 5 m.) features a front
room or court and two narrow deep rooms at the rear.

The columned portico, which forms a basic element in Egyptian
houses, is accurately represented in a small wooden model found in
the tomb of Meketreᶜ (Thebes, Dynasty XI).[39] Two rows of slender
bundle columns, papyriform and lotiform, painted with horizontal
stripes carry an entablature imitating the ends of rafters surmounted
by three rain spouts. Behind these columns, in the rear wall, are the
doorways to the house. A similar portico is copied in stone in
the façades of the rock-cut tombs at Beni Ḥassan (Dynasty XII). The
hypostyle hall of these tombs is probably a copy of the hypostyle
hall of the contemporaneous house. It features four or more columns
in two rows carrying beams that support a flat gabled or vaulted
roof; on the roof are painted ornamental patterns deriving from the
mats that formed the roof of the original hall and the ventilator
opening above its nave.[40]

The New Kingdom. For the New Kingdom much information can
be derived from the capital of ᶜAmarna, the fortified city of Sesebi,
houses in the temple of Medinet Habu, the artisans' village at Deir el
Medina, and numerous representations of houses in private tombs
in Western Thebes. The housing unit in the artisans' village at

[38] W. S. Smith, *The Art and Architecture of Ancient Egypt* (Baltimore, 1958), Fig. 43.
[39] H. E. Winlock, *Models of Daily Life in Ancient Egypt* (Cambridge, Mass., 1955).
[40] Alexander Badawy, "Architectural Provision against Heat in the Orient," *Journal of Near Eastern Studies*, Vol. XVII (Chicago, 1958), p. 123, Fig. 1.

ᶜAmarna East[41] (Fig. 3) is about 5 by 10 meters, making an area of 50 square meters, and is oriented east–west. Its tripartite plan features a western front courtyard, a hypostyle hall with a bench along one or two walls, and at the rear a bedroom and a kitchen. A staircase rises from the kitchen to the terrace, which is probably provided with an awning. The construction is extremely economical, and the orientation of the bedroom to the east and that of the front courtyard or room to the west are ideal for providing maximum sunlight in the bedroom at sunrise and again in the front apartment when the artisan returns home at sunset. Similar attached houses on a more elaborate plan are used for officials in the capital itself.

The typical house at ᶜAmarna is the villa[42] set on a large independent plot and surrounded by outbuildings consisting of granaries, storerooms, kitchens, chariot house, and chapel, as well as a garden within an enclosure (Fig. 4, middle right). The house proper is square and is approached from a porch leading to a north hypostyle hall or loggia in the front. Beyond is a central hypostyle hall rising higher than the other parts of the structure and lit by clerestory windows, flanked by a western hypostyle hall or loggia and the staircase (Fig. 4, middle right). This squarish hall is the nucleus of the house since it is used as a living room and contains a brick bench or divan along the rear side, a small platform for the water jars, and a small shrine for the worship of the sun disk with a stela representing the pharaoh at this service. The walls are painted and topped by a frieze with plaster garlands in high relief. Beyond are the private quarters arranged around a central lobby, with the master's bedroom, a bedroom for the ladies and children, and a bathroom. The characteristic alcove for the bed is recognizable at the south or west end of the bedroom. The upper floor stretches only on the front with an open loggia facing north and west, the two directions from which a cool breeze blows at ᶜAmarna. Brick walls and wooden columns and ceilings are stuccoed and painted in vivid colors. In this type of villa the plan is also tripartite: front reception rooms, a central living room, and rear bedrooms. Water was carried from the Nile or drawn from private wells, and waste waters were led outside the houses to soak into the desert soil. The plan conforms to both a harmonic design and a modular system.

In the southwest part of the town at Sesebi in the Sudan (Fig. 2, top right) there are four blocks of attached houses set in two rows running east–west. They do not conform to a uniform plan or width, though the depth is the same for all the houses in one block. A special

---

[41] Peet and Woolley, *The City of Akhenaten*, Vol. I, pl. XVI.
[42] H. Frankfort and J. D. S. Pendlebury, *The City of Akhenaten*, Vol. II (London, 1933).

alley in the middle of the southernmost blocks seems to be the way of access to the houses since the pomerium must have been reserved for rapid access to the walls in case of attack.[43]

Attached uniform houses are a favorite solution to housing accommodation, extending from temples (Ramses III at Medinet Habu, Dynasty XX, 1198–1166 B.C.) or palaces (Ramses III at Medinet Habu). The suites for the *harim* ladies were also planned in this way: front columned hall, hypostyle hall with rear throne, bedroom closet, and robing room (tripartite plan, 8.5 × 22 m., palace of Amenhotep III at Malqata).[44]

Dating back to the reign of Tuthmosis I (1530–1515 B.C.),[45] the small village for artisans in the desert valley at Deir el Medina was enlarged twice and occupied for about four centuries, till the end of the Twentieth Dynasty. The earlier houses are long, narrow, and rather irregular in shape (5 × 15 m.), and are oriented east–west. Their tripartite plan consists of a front room with an altar; a hypostyle hall with one central column, a bench, a false-door, and a stela; and at the rear a bedroom and a kitchen in which a staircase rises to the terrace. One or more small cellars were cut from the bedrock beneath the floor or at the back. As a measure to ensure privacy the entrances of houses facing each other seldom open on the same axis. Later houses are more regular in shape and broader, and are provided with stables and silos. Water was brought from a canal on donkeys and stored in a large open tank outside the north gateway of the village. The mural paintings representing lively scenes with either religious or lay motifs are evidence of the sensitive taste of the artisans.

It will be observed that nearly all the houses studied so far were those of preplanned villages except the villas at ʿAmarna. Much additional information can be derived about the townhouse from the wall paintings in private tombs at Thebes.[46] A cross section of the three-storied house of Thutnefer, scribe of Tuthmosis III, presents a unique scene (Fig. 4, bottom left): a basement with weaving looms, a loftier first floor featuring a front room with two columns and a larger and higher hypostyle hall with clerestory windows, a second floor with living rooms surmounted by a terrace with grain bins. A stairway rises independently in its own well at one end of the house. A comparison with a contemporaneous model of townhouse may prove interesting: the basement is lit through horizontal slots at ground level; the doorway opens on the side; each of the first-floor windows has a mullion and transom and has tracery in its lower

43 Badawy, "Orthogonal and Axial Town Planning," p. 8.
44 Badawy, "Maison," pp. 38 ff.
45 *Ibid.*, pp. 35 ff.
46 Badawy, *Dessin architectural*, pp. 76–95.

half; and a columned loggia probably open to the north is built to the rear of the terrace. Several paintings convey a similar impression about the external aspect of the façade, which is by no means as drab as one might imagine. Some even have colored patterns resembling those on Cretan houses and are topped with balustrades of interwoven palm fronds (Fig. 4, bottom right). Occasionally a row of palm trees alternating with fruit trees in brick containers enlivens the façade of the townhouse with a cheerful touch of countryside color.

Suburban houses are set sparsely in the countryside, scarcely showing behind their high outer walls, which were sometimes topped with an undulating crenelation (house of the architect Ineny). The house proper is a two- or three-storied structure painted to imitate ashlar masonry, and it is surrounded by beehive granaries, vaulted magazines, and a lovely formal garden around an artificial rectangular pond. Smaller landhouses or resthouses, where the owner of an estate could reside during an inspection, are cubical one-storied structures sometimes set on a small podium with windows opening high in the wall and often richly decorated with a pattern of colored circles and tracery in their lower part. On the terrace emerge the triangular funnels of the ventilators.

Evidence about the Late Period can be found in the successive layers of houses around the temple at Medinet Habu.[47] The typical plan consists of a tripartite arrangement, which persists well into the Saitic Period except for a period of decline (Dynasties XXII–XXIV). The simpler type is strongly reminiscent of the attached deep house in the preplanned villages at ᶜAmarna East and Deir el Medina. This type has a vestibule, a square hall with dais, and two rear rooms from which rises a staircase. Most of the houses have more than one story. The larger ones are squarish and are fronted by a court containing an underground cellar; they also have a front lobby, a staircase, and two halls.

Palaces

A perusal of the earliest hieroglyphs for "castle" is quite rewarding, since they clearly indicate the typical design. A castle may be a rectangular enclosure with one gateway in a corner and plain walls (⬚), or it may feature a deep narrow passageway along one side (⬚), often buttressed externally or topped with a row of *kheker* elements (⬚). The purpose of the long passageway is obviously strategic: to

---

[47] U. Hölscher, *The Excavation of Medinet Habu*, Vol. V (Chicago, 1954), Figs. 3–20, pp. 4–16.

provide a control of the entrance from the top of its flanking walls in case of attack. A hieroglyph often shows in its farthermost corner from the entrance the castle tower or "dungeon" ($^c h$ 🏰). This three-storied tower is set on low horizontal courses, perhaps on wooden beams, with the diagonal wooden framework of the staircase showing, and two upper windows and a *kheker* topping the edge of the terrace. Two terms for "palace"—*pr*-$^c_3$ 🏛, meaning "the great house" (used for the title pharaoh) and *pr-nswt* 🏛 (literally, "king's house")—indicate that the protohistoric palace of the king was actually the largest house in the settlement.

Three rectangular fortified enclosures in brick, assumed to be royal citadels from the Second Dynasty,[48] feature double walls with one (Hierakonpolis 76 × 67 m.) or more entrance gateways with towers (Abydos about 14.5 m. long). In the two enclosures at Abydos a building near the southeast gateway could be identified as the palace proper (Fig. 5, top left). Its façade and its inner wall both have recessed paneling. This characteristic of palace architecture has been explained as an imitation of the actual palace doorways flanked by bastions or towers (Fig. 5, middle right). This typical façade is represented in elaborate detail on the sides of the sarcophagi and archaic mastaba tombs, the lower part of the stelae, and the *serekh* that frames one of the five names forming the royal titulary. The original structure must have been a visible wooden framework with brick party walls, topped either by a frieze forming a rectilinear skyline or by projecting towers resulting in a battlemented skyline (Fig. 5, middle right).[49] The beautiful colored mats and rugs that are represented in paintings as hanging from the wooden frame along the recesses of the walls are presumably on the inner faces of the structures.[50]

The so-called "Pavilion" in the mortuary complex of Djeser at Saqqara (Fig. 5, middle left) is thought to be a copy in stone of one of the minor palaces of that pharaoh. Beyond a columned entrance vestibule is a central hypostyle hall connected with a throne room set on the same axis behind and onto which open two lateral rooms. The bedroom is at the rear of the structure.

At Memphis the northern rectangular enclosure within which Pharaoh Apries later built his palace is probably the royal citadel (300–320 × 440–500 m.). Oriented north–south and resembling in many ways the enclosure with recessed paneling of the funerary complex of Pharaoh Djeser (277 × 544.9 m.), it has been interpreted

---

[48] Badawy, *Dessin architectural*, pp. 141–143; *Egyptian Architecture*, Vol. I, pp. 46–47.
[49] Badawy, *Egyptian Architecture*, I, pp. 30–31.
[50] *Ibid.*, pp. 60–61.

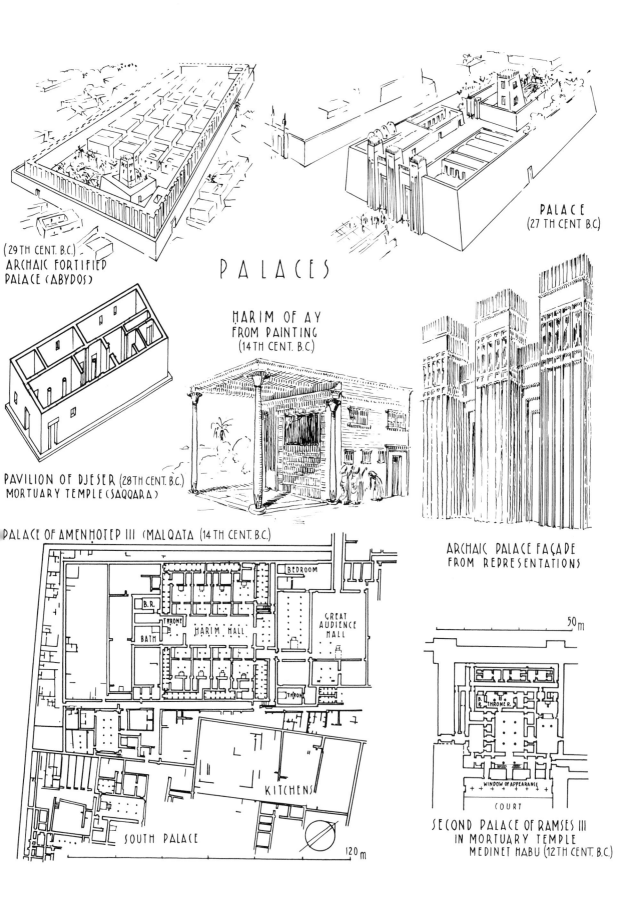

(29TH CENT. B.C.)
ARCHAIC FORTIFIED
PALACE (ABYDOS)

PALACE
(27TH CENT B.C)

PALACES

HARIM OF AY
FROM PAINTING
(14TH CENT. B.C.)

PAVILION OF DJESER (28TH CENT. B.C.)
MORTUARY TEMPLE (SAQQARA)

ARCHAIC PALACE FAÇADE
FROM REPRESENTATIONS

PALACE OF AMENHOTEP III (MALQATA (14TH CENT. B.C.)

BEDROOM

B.R.

THRONE

BATH

HARIM HALL

GREAT
AUDIENCE
HALL

THRONE

KITCHENS

SOUTH PALACE

120 m

50 m

B.R. THRONE R.

WINDOW OF APPEARANCE

COURT

SECOND PALACE OF RAMSES III
IN MORTUARY TEMPLE
MEDINET HABU (12TH CENT. B.C.)

as a smaller copy of the "White Wall" of Memphis.[51] This enclosure has only one actual doorway, though fourteen bastions are treated as dummy doorways in the pattern of the palace façade.

It is not until the early New Kingdom that actual remains of palaces are again found as the two complexes at Deir el Ballas[52] (about 167 × 334 m. and 109 × 48 m.). Each is reminiscent of a castle with a dungeon, being surrounded by large columned halls of the later Persian apadana type and decorated with mural paintings of military scenes.

The ruins at ʿAmarna and Thebes give some idea about the splendor of royal palaces, even though they are always built of brick and wood with some stone elements and lining in the bathrooms. The palace complex of Amenḥotep III at Malqata in Western Thebes (Fig. 5, bottom left), which is about 350 by 270 meters, consists of four palaces with subsidiary buildings[53] and a huge lake, probably T-shaped and connected to the Nile. In the so-called palace of the king the official quarters feature a few columned audience halls, each with a throne on a dais along the east wall, a staircase to the upper floor or terrace, a large central hall with two rows of columns arranged symmetrically with four separate suites for ḥarim ladies on each side and a royal suite at the rear (south). The kitchens are in a separate block between this palace and another one to the south. Paintings and decorative moldings in appliqué lavishly cover the walls with scenes from official life or with images of the household genius Bes; floors are decorated with the representation of pools, plants, and birds, and ceilings have rows of flying vultures and geometric patterns. Each suite in itself forms a complete dwelling based on the tripartite plan and featuring a front columned vestibule, a central hypostyle hall with a canopied throne, a closet, a bedroom, and a robing room.

At ʿAmarna,[54] Akhenaten, the former Amenhotep IV, had two palaces on opposite sides of the Royal Road connected by a bridge with a "window of appearance" from which he distributed gifts to his retinue. The official palace to the west has vast courts bordered by colossal statues of the pharaoh and the queen in front of the large halls. One of these halls forms a perfect square, with 540 pillars in rows, an arrangement similar to that of the later apadana in Persia. It is approached through doorways by means of two ramps rising in opposite directions on either side of the threshold, a device that

[51] H. Kees, *Das alte Ägypten, Eine kleine Landeskunde* (Berlin, 1958), p. 84. E. Egli, *Geschichte des Städtebaues* (Zurich, 1959), pp. 36–38, Figs. 2–5. Badawy, *Egyptian Architecture*, Vol. I, p. 69.
[52] Smith, *Art*, pp. 156 ff.
[53] *Ibid.*, pp. 160–172, pls. 120–122.
[54] J. D. S. Pendlebury, *The City of Akhenaten*, Vol. III (London, 1951).

←*Fig. 5*

permits movement of wheeled vehicles, like that used in Assyrian palaces. Along the road a series of suites and a sunken garden for the *harim* ladies form an aisle to the official palace. The complex faces the Nile with a quay that is probably decorated by an elegant portico, as represented in the tomb of May. The second palace or "King's House," on the opposite side of the Royal Road, is much smaller and comprises the king's and queen's apartment and nurseries for the children, all decorated with painted murals representing delightful uninhibited scenes of family life. There is a garden in front of the north façade of this residence. Farther north are blocks of storehouses and the Great Temple, while to the east are government offices as well as military and police quarters and to the south the Smaller Temple. The palaces were actually planned as the focal point of the Central Quarter of the capital. The rubbish from the palaces was burned in heaps south of the area. A painting in the tomb of Neferhotep at Thebes represents a smaller residence, probably that of the *harim* of Pharaoh Ay (Fig. 5, middle). One side features a wide royal balcony of appearance with a lofty porch elaborately decorated in a glitter of variegated colors, possibly in enamel inlays.

At Memphis the remains (about 30 × 105 m.) of a palace of Merneptaḥ (1232–1224 B.C.) outside the enclosure of the temple of Ptaḥ are oriented north–south, and a large audience hall is still recognizable.[55] The later palace of Apries (588–568 B.C.)[56] in a ruined state has been compared to the type of mansion built at El Lahun some 1,300 years earlier. Its plan seems to feature a long passage running north–south from the drawbridge through a central area, perhaps a peristyle court, to a north court.

A third type of palace is the temple-palace whose façade extends along the left side of the front courtyard in the funerary temples of the pharaohs of the New Kingdom in Western Thebes,[57] such as those of Ay, Merneptaḥ, Ramses II, Ramses III at Medinet Habu, Seti I at Abydos, and Ramses III at Deir el Medina. They were meant to provide accommodation for the pharaoh and his retinue when they came to the funerary temple during the yearly visit of the statue of Amun of Karnak to Western Thebes. The façade of the palace features a central window of appearance looking onto the front court of the temple and accessible by a flight of steps from

55 Vandier, *Manuel*, Vol. II, p. 1006, Fig. 476.

56 W. Fl. Petrie, *The Palace of Apries* (*Memphis II*) (London, 1909), pp. 1–5, pls. 5, I, XIII A.

57 U. Hölscher, *Medinet Habu*, Vol. II (Chicago, 1939), pp. 81–82; Vol. III, Figs. 52–53, pp. 77–78 (Ramses VI). W. Fl. Petrie, *Six Temples at Thebes* (London, 1897), pl. CCV (Merneptaḥ), U. Hölscher, *Das hohe Tor von Medinet Habu*, Fig. 51, p. 54. B. Bruyère, *Fouilles à Deir el-Medineh*, Vol. VIII (Cairo, 1933), pp. 72–79, 85–89, Fig. 36 bis (Ramses III at Deir el Medina). Hölscher, *Medinet Habu*, Vol. III, pp. 44–48 (Ramses III at Medinet Habu).

the main hypostyle hall of the palace behind it. The palace is strictly symmetrical (Ramses II: 32 m. square), or nearly so (Ramses III; Fig. 5, bottom right). Behind the hypostyle hall is a smaller columned throne room flanked by residential apartments. Outside this massive vaulted structure is a row of three or four attached tripartite suites to accommodate the retinue. It was the fashion to line prominent elements such as doorways with decorative glazed tiles partly in relief.

Temples

It is probable that there were shrines among the buildings represented on the protodynastic palettes such as a domed wattle-and-daub structure on a round plan with four corner posts.[58] The earliest names for the temple—"castle" ([glyph] *ḥt*), "great castle" (*ḥt ʿȝt*), and "castle of the god" (*ḥt nṯr* [glyphs])—imply that gods lived in castles similar to that of the pharaoh. The cult ritual corroborates this interpretation, for the god was actually believed to be living in the cult statue in the naos, and the cult ritual was performed thrice daily by a priest who washed the statue, anointed it, dressed it, and offered it food, incense, and prayers. No wonder, then, that the temple derived many of its features from domestic architecture, mainly the concept of the tripartite plan.

The name *itrt*[59] for the national sanctuary of Upper Egypt ([glyph]) and of Lower Egypt ([glyph]) would suggest that it had some connection with the Nile (*itrt*), a connection quite possible in a country where the earliest architecture was obviously influenced by, if not derived from, the cabins of the predynastic Nile boats. The forms of the shrines unmistakably imply a wattle-and-daub technique. This is also true of the other shrines represented on early dynastic labels, such as the theriomorphic shrine of Anubis or those of Neith (Fig. 6, top left) and Khnum and the pavilion for the jubilees of the pharaoh called *ḥeb-sed*.[60] It is noteworthy that some of the commonest stylistic elements such as the cavetto cornice, the torus, and the hunchback vault were invented at that early date and recurred thereafter, produced in stone, wood, or stucco.

The earliest remains of a temple, that of Khentiamentiw, "The Foremost of the Westerners (the deceased)," at Abydos already feature the tripartite plan similar to that of the house with a forecourt, a central room, and a rear sanctuary flanked by two chambers. The doorways are definitely offset in the transverse brick walls to

---

[58] Badawy, *Dessin architectural*, pp. 16–17.
[59] A. Erman and H. Grapow, *Wörterbuch der Aegyptischen Sprache*, Vol. I (Leipzig, 1926–1950), p. 147.
[60] Badawy, *Dessin architectural*, pp. 10–27; *Egyptian Architecture*, Vol. I, pp. 34–36.

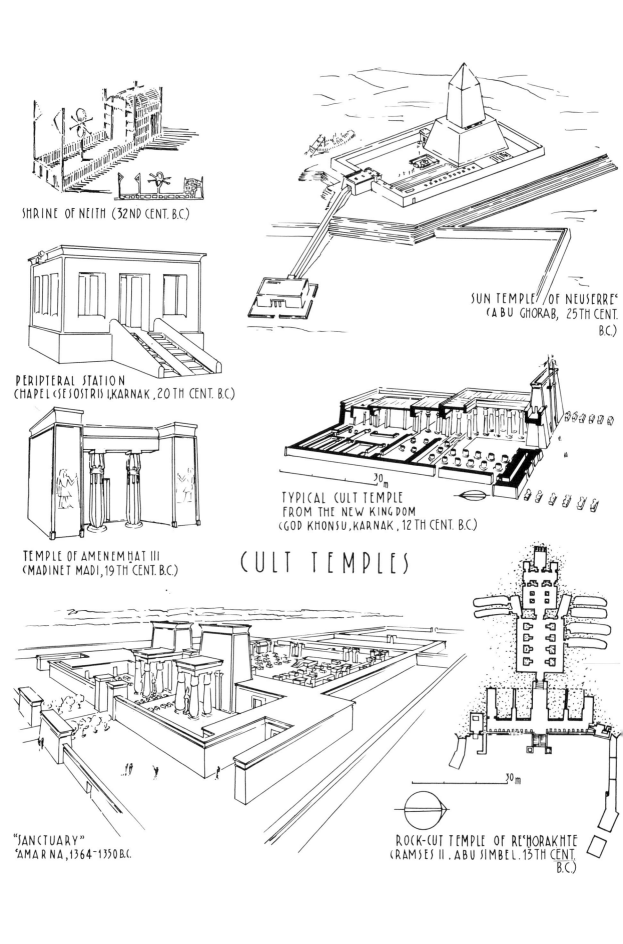

SHRINE OF NEITH (32ND CENT. B.C.)

PERIPTERAL STATION
CHAPEL (SESOSTRIS I, KARNAK, 20TH CENT. B.C.)

TEMPLE OF AMENEMHAT III
(MADINET MADI, 19TH CENT. B.C.)

SUN TEMPLE OF NEUSERRE
(ABU GHORAB, 25TH CENT.
B.C.)

TYPICAL CULT TEMPLE
FROM THE NEW KINGDOM
(GOD KHONSU, KARNAK, 12TH CENT. B.C.)

30 m

CULT TEMPLES

"SANCTUARY"
AMARNA, 1364-1350 B.C.

ROCK-CUT TEMPLE OF RE-HORAKHTE
(RAMSES II, ABU SIMBEL, 13TH CENT.
B.C.)

30 m

prevent an axial view into the sanctuary, a search for privacy that will be achieved later by means of screening the doorways with wooden porches.

At this point in our investigation it would be helpful to study separately the three types of temples, grouped according to their function into cult temples, sun temples, and mortuary temples.

Cult Temples. The cult temple (Fig. 6, middle right)[61] is dedicated to the god embodied in a small cult statue usually made of gilded wood that is kept in the naos at the rear of the temple. Its plan is rectangular, symmetrical, and tripartite with the most essential element being a naos set on the longitudinal axis, approached through one or more courts and hypostyle halls. It had become a custom with pharaohs to satisfy their religiosity and prove their loyal allegiance to a god by enlarging his temples, adding a court and a pylon or a hall in front of the existing structure. This accretion method of construction, which persisted through the centuries, resulted in the growth of the temple complex according to set rules of harmonic proportions, with a series of courtyards fronted by pylons, each court being larger than the former one so as to embrace it. The orientation of the temple, except for those dedicated to solar deities, is not cosmic but local since its layout is perpendicular to the Nile or to the watercourse that flows along its façade.

The tripartite plan of the temple and that of the house show the following similarities:

Temple	House
pylon and courtyard	entrance vestibule for reception
hypostyle hall	columned hall as living area
sanctuary	bedrooms as private quarters

Since the temple is the abode of the god, it is built of "materials of eternity," either soft stone (limestone, alabaster, sandstone) or hard stone (granite, basalt, diorite). The naos has only one door, opened and resealed three times daily by the priest or "servant of god," who performs the cult ritual as a representative of the pharaoh. In the sanctuary the various rooms such as a sacristy and the storerooms for sacred utensils are arranged around the naos. Occasionally in later temples there is also a crypt beneath the sanctuary where the most valuable treasures are hoarded. In the New Kingdom a sacred boat that carries the statue of the god in processions is kept in a special room in front of the naos.

[61] Drioton and Vandier, *L'Égypte*, pp. 90–93. F. Daumas, *Les Mammisis des temples égyptiens* (Paris, 1958), pp. 144, 158. T. Dombart, "Der zweitürmige Tempel-Pylon altaegyptischer Baukunst und seine religiöse Symbolik," *Egyptian Religion*, Vol. I (New York, 1933), pp. 87–98, 135. L. Borchardt, *Tempel mit Umgang* (Cairo, 1938).

←*Fig. 6*

The hypostyle hall has been compared to a basilica. It has the loftiest ceiling in the temple carried on rows of columns of the open papyriform type bordering the central nave and columns of the bundle papyriform type in the two aisles. The papyriform columns symbolize "youth," while those in the shape of the handle of the musical instrument called a sistrum indicate the "joy" dispensed by the goddess Ḥathor. Through the clerestory windows between the ceiling of the nave and the lower ones on the aisles the light penetrates to bring to life the low-relief scenes on the walls and columns representing the ritual performed in the hypostyle. Only the highest class had access to this hall.

Along one or more of the sides of the courtyard there is usually a columned portico. Anyone who had been "purified four times" could enter the court. The façade of the temple is in the shape of a pylon consisting of two rectangular towers with battered faces, topped with the cavetto cornice and torus, on each side of a central doorway. This pylon symbolizes the sunrise mountain, and the god was supposed to "appear" between the two towers as does the sun on the luminous mountain horizon. In the New Kingdom large scenes in sunken relief on the pylon and on the external walls of the temple represent the war glories of the empire, victories awarded by Amun to Pharaoh over Asiatic cities and prisoners, always presided over by a heroic-sized figure of Pharaoh striking a group of prisoners with his mace. An inner staircase rises inside one tower, extends over the doorway, and proceeds through the other tower to the terrace. Later pylons have two staircases (Edfu). Brackets project from the top front of the towers to hold flagstaffs made of pine trunks, which are set on stone bases and have glittering metallic sheaths at the top to carry the colorful flags of the god. These flags evolved from the earliest emblem for the deity, a flagstaff (called *ntr*, meaning "god") that was set upright in front of the predynastic shrine.

One important characteristic of the temple's design is the gradual rise in the levels of the floors from the outer court to the rear and the corresponding decrease in the heights of the ceilings and in the intensity of the lighting, so that there was total darkness in the sanctuary. This very subtle combination of factors induced religious awe in the worshiper, enhanced as it was by the mystery of the dimly lit painted reliefs and inscriptions on every single wall, ceiling, and column. Sometimes this mystical atmosphere is brought to a climax by the harsh contrast between the subdued colors and the god's figure glittering in a beam of rays coming through a slot in the ceiling of the naos or from reflection through the doorway. Color is lavishly used on all the reliefs, and gold sheet lines certain especially sacred figures of deities. The floors and doors are partly covered with electrum, an alloy of gold and silver. In the courts, statues of pharaohs and later those of private people were erected in the hallowed neighborhood of the deity. Colossi of pharaohs set in front of the pylons during the Empire were used not only as mediators, to listen to the prayers of the populace, but also as a means of political propaganda. Such a purpose can be clearly assigned to the rock-cut temples in Nubia, which were intended to impress the natives with the ubiquitous power of Pharaoh.

Various structures that are not essentially connected to a cult are found, however, within the temple precincts. The jubilee pavilions derived from the early dynastic awnings erected on a podium evolved into peripteral chapels built sometimes of stone that was elaborately carved with fine scenes in low relief (Sesostris I at Karnak; Fig. 6, upper left). In some temples there are four stairways branching off the sides of the square podium toward the four cardinal points (at ʿAmarna; Osorkon at Bubastis) in a cosmogonic symbolism of the world power of the pharaoh. Station chapels or repositories for the bark of Amun are built along the processional avenue between Luxor and Karnak in the style of peripteral structures on podiums with a central stand for the bark (jubilee chapel of Sesostris I as altered), or a central cella (Ḥatshepsut at Medinet Habu; El Kab; Elephantine).

In the Late Period the *mammisi*[62] is a chapel symbolizing the birth of the god's son and his ascent to the throne of his father, correlated to the reigning pharaoh as successor of the god. It is built near the front of a cult temple, transversely to its main axis (Nektanebo at Dendera), and evolves from a chapel into an elaborate temple in the Ptolemaic and Roman Periods (Philae, Edfu, Hermonthis, Dendera).

Only a few remains of cult temples can be ascribed to the Old Kingdom. One is a unique layout with two shrines buried under two mounds that could have been an Osireion at Medamud.[63] Other examples are the temple of Khentiamentiw at Abydos, the temple of the Great Sphinx at Giza,[64] and the only two uncovered sun temples from the Fifth Dynasty at Abu Ghorab and Abusir.

From the Middle Kingdom the two temples of Amenemḥat III in the Fayum are essentially three contiguous cellae fronted by a transverse vestibule (Medinet Madi,[65] Fig. 6, middle left) or even seven

[62] Daumas, *Mammisis.* Borchardt, *Tempel mit Umgang.*

[63] C. Robichon and A. Varille, *Description sommaire du temple primitif de Médamoud* (Cairo, 1940). Badawy, *Egyptian Architecture*, Vol. I, pp. 115–116.

[64] S. Hassan, *The Great Sphinx and Its Secrets* (Cairo, 1953), pp. 25–29, pl. XVI. Badawy, *Egyptian Architecture*, Vol. I, pp. 115–117.

[65] R. Naumann, "Der Tempel des Mittleren Reiches in Medinet Madi," *Mitteilungen des Deutschen Instituts für ägyptische Altertumskunde in Kairo*, Vol. VIII (Cairo, 1939), pp. 185–189, Abb. 1, pl. 30.

cellae (Qasr el Sagha).[66] At Medamud[67] the temple that was built on the site of an earlier one from the Old Kingdom has an unusual plan.

When the building activity of the pharaohs during the Empire became concentrated in Thebes, the temples of Amun grew by a process of accretion into huge complexes. The temple of Amun at Luxor and the funerary temple of Ḥatshepsut at Deir el Baḥari seem to be oriented toward that of Amun at Karnak. A processional avenue bordered with sphinxes, which is now being excavated, connected Luxor to Karnak. As to the scale, let us mention that the temple of Amun at Luxor (Amenḥotep III–Ramses II) is 265 meters long, while the one at Karnak, built from the time of the Middle Kingdom till the Kushite Dynasty (2060 B.C. to seventh century B.C.), is enclosed within a temenos (470 to 560 m. × 470 m.) and has a rectangular outline (325 × 90 to 100 m.).[68] To it are connected a sacred artificial lake (70 × 110 m.) where the barge of Amun was sailed on certain festivals, a temple of Ramses III, a triple chapel of Seti I, and outside its precincts a temple of Khonsu, son of Amun, and another temple of Mut, wife of Amun. As a result of the accretion process there are successive courtyards fronted by pylons of increasing dimensions. In front of the Great Temple of Amun at Karnak are six such pylons, the foremost and largest of which dates from the Kushite Dynasty and was left incomplete (124 × 19.5 m. and 47.5 m. high). No less than four courts, four pylons, and an avenue of sphinxes connect the central court of Amun to the complex of Mut. The great hypostyle hall in the temple of Amun at Karnak (*ca.* 113 × 53.5 m., covering an area of 6,045 sq. m.) has twelve large open papyriform columns flanking the nave, each column 26.4 meters high, and 122 smaller bundle papyriform columns in the aisles.

In the temple of Seti I at Abydos seven sanctuaries in one row are dedicated to six deities and the Pharaoh himself. The original plan was probably symmetrical, but the rear part had to be built to one side to avoid the so-called cenotaph in the same axis at a lower level behind it. This abnormal shift in the plan was made, however, to conform to the rules of harmonic design.

The later temples in the Ptolemaic and Roman Periods are the best preserved, some having still retained their stone ceilings. A new element was introduced in the Late Period and became a constant feature in the Ptolemaic temple. This was the open front of the transverse vestibule that was designed with columns and low intercolumnar walls (Edfu, Dendera, Kom Ombo). There also appear to be several variants of the composite capital derived from the open

[66] O. Menghin and K. Bittel, "Kasr el Sagha," *Mitteilungen des Deutschen Instituts in Kairo*, Vol. V (Cairo, 1934).
[67] Robichon and Varille, *Description*, Fig. 2.
[68] G. Steindorff, *Egypt* (Baedeker series; Leipzig, 1929), pp. 277–292.

papyriform one, as rows of floral elements were added in high relief around the campaniform capital.

Sun Temples. Since the sun temple has no cult statue, its design differs from that of the typical cult temple, for there is no need for a naos and the entire layout is open to the sky to allow the ritual to be performed at an altar with an obelisk (Abu Ghorab) or without one (ᶜAmarna). Little is known about the temple of the sun called "Horus-of-the-Eastern-Horizon" (Reᶜ-Ḥorakhte) at Heliopolis except that it presumably had three courts, with an altar in the rearmost one surrounded by cells and an upright stone inside a chapel, which was perhaps hypaethral.[69] The sun temple built by Pharaoh Neuserreᶜ (2500 B.C.) on the western plateau at Abu Ghorab[70] features a valley portal forming the entrance along a canal, from which a causeway rises to the temple proper (Fig. 6, top right). An oriented temenos wall surrounds a court, within which are a central altar of alabaster consisting of five blocks in the shape of the hieroglyph ($\triangle$ *ḥtp*) meaning "offering," oriented to the four cardinal points around the sign *Reᶜ*, and beyond it a massive obelisk built of stone masonry on a base represented in contemporaneous hieroglyphs as $\triangle$. A chapel at the entrance to the obelisk and two slaughter areas with drains and magazines are also located within the enclosure, and a large sun boat of brickwork is situated outside it. The obelisk, perhaps a derivative from the benben stone at Heliopolis, is a symbol of the sun's rays and functions as the connecting link between the sun and the worshipers. Of the five other temples built to the sun by the pharaohs of the Fifth Dynasty only the ruins of that of Userkaf have been excavated. The sun temple seems to have been the special place for worship of the sun as the potent creator by his son the pharaoh during his life and after his death.[71] Akhenaten built a temple called "Life-of-Reᶜ" at Heliopolis, another called "The-House-of-the-Benben" at Karnak,[72] three others to the Aten at ᶜAmarna, one at Sesebi in the Sudan, and others. Two of the temples at ᶜAmarna, "Castle-of-the-Aten" and "Mansion-of-the-Benben,"[73] are of the same type: a symmetrical temple facing west, enclosed within a large temenos, and composed of a front court and the court of the great altar. A party wall screens the entrance to the second court, which is surrounded by cells (Fig. 6, bottom left). Both courts are filled with rows of small offering tables

[69] H. Ricke, "Eine Inventartafel aus Heliopolis im Turiner Museum," *Zeitschrift für ägyptsiche Sprache und Altertumskunde*, Vol. 71, pp. 119–133.

[70] W. von Bissing, *Das Re-Heiligtum des Königs Ne-Woser-Re (Rathures)*, Vol. I, pp. 117–121.

[71] E. Winter, "Zur Deutung der Sonnenheiligtümer der 5. Dynastie," *Wiener Zeitschrift für die Kunde des Morgenlandes*, Vol. 54 (Vienna, 1957), pp. 222–233.

[72] Badawy, *Dessin architectural*, p. 198.

[73] Pendlebury, *City of Akhenaten*, Vol. III, pl. XVI.

in brickwork. One odd feature is the pair of blank walls in the shape
of arms protruding along both external sides of the front court. I
have interpreted[74] this unique element as a device for expressing the
location and the dimensions in cubits of one of the basic squares in
the constructional diagram for the harmonic plan. It is noteworthy
that some of the best chapels in the gardens of the villas at ʿAmarna
contain similar protruding arms, and the length of their sanctuary
forms the module used in the design of the whole villa complex. The
Great Temple called Per-Ḥai/Gem-Aten[75] ("House-of-Rejoicing/
Meeting-Aten") also has a unique layout in the narrow rectangular
enclosure running east–west that is fronted by a hall with two
columned aisles and divided by transverse walls into six successive
courts. The whole area is covered with parallel rows of offering
tables, while a large altar is set in the fifth court and another in the
sixth court. The total number of offering tables on either side of the
longitudinal axis for the first five courts is 365, and for the first four
courts plus the sixth is 366 (?), which would correspond to the number of times that the daily ritual was performed during one normal
year and during a leap year, respectively. This is an interesting example
of calendric symbolism.[76] Also at ʿAmarna is the Northern Palace,
which seems to be a reserve for animal life, with quarters for the
animals, a pond for fish, and an aviary. It is dedicated to the sun disk
Aten. The religious complex in the front subdivision of the court and
the paintings on the walls of the aviary would corroborate this interpretation. The complex called Maru-Aten ("Sighting-the-Aten")[77] at
the south end of the river front offers another instance of calendric
symbolism in its layout of eleven T-shaped basins and a chapel,
representing the twelve monthly festivals of Aten in honor of his
power as creator of plant life. Thus there is evidence for the existence
of calendric, harmonic, representational, and cosmic symbolism in
the design of the sanctuaries at ʿAmarna.

At Abu Simbel in Nubia, Ramses II cut from the rock of the
western cliff two unique temples that he dedicated to Reʿ-Ḥorakhte
("Reʿ-Horus-of-the-Eastern-Horizon") and to Ḥathor (Fig. 6,
bottom right).[78] In the larger temple abutting on the façade of a one-
towered pylon carved in the rock face and looking due east across the
Nile are four seated colossi of Ramses II (21.3 m. high). The hawk-
headed god Reʿ-Ḥorakhte stands in a niche above the doorway.

[74] Alexander Badawy, "The Harmonic System of Architectural Design in Ancient
Egypt," *Mitteilungen des Instituts für Orientforschung*, Vol. VIII (Berlin, 1961), pp. 1–14.
[75] Pendlebury, *City of Akhenaten*, Vol. III, pp. 5–20.
[76] Alexander Badawy, "The Symbolism of the Temples at ʿAmarna," *Zeitschrift für
ägyptische Sprache und Altertumskunde*, Vol. 87 (Berlin, 1962), pp. 79–95.
[77] Alexander Badawy, "Maru-Aten: Pleasure Resort or Temple?" *Journal of Egyptian
Archaeology*, Vol. 42 (Oxford, 1956), pp. 58–64.
[78] Steindorff, *Egypt* (Baedeker), pp. 431–435.

The layout is symmetrical, consisting of a hypostyle hall with one nave flanked by Osiride colossi, supported by pillars, and two narrow aisles, then a second pillared hall, a transverse chamber, and the rear sanctuary with the seated statues of three deities and Ramses II. On the walls are scenes in low relief representing the battle of Qadesh. Magazines branch off on either side. The only source of light is the doorway; here, as in the typical cult temple, lighting decreases toward the rear, and at the same time the heights of the ceilings become lower. It has been reported that at sunrise on certain days of the year the rays of the sun penetrate through the doorway to light the innermost statues. To the north end of the façade is a small court with an altar fronted by a miniature pylon. Between both towers of the pylon the sun could be sighted and worshiped at sunrise. Calendric symbolism exists in the layout of both the large temple and the small chapel. The smaller temple to Ḥathor, located at a short distance to the north, has standing colossi carved in niches on its façade. The fashion for colossal architectural statuary reached its climax with Ramses II. It was built to impress the populace of the Nubian colony with Pharaoh's ubiquitous power. The 21.3-meter colossi at Abu Simbel and the 100-meter ones at Gebel Barkal[79] are clear instances of this purpose.

Mortuary Temples. The mortuary temple developed from the chapel that was built on the east face of the superstructure of the mastaba tomb and used for the performance of the funerary ritual. Since the soul depended in the afterlife upon the preservation of the body, it was deemed essential to provide for a food offering, which was secured through an "eternal" funerary service performed by the priests of the necropolis and financed by a special endowment.

The funerary chapel of the mastaba tomb[80] in the Old Kingdom abuts on the south end of the east face of the superstructure; later, the chapel is built within it. Its important element is the false-door facing east and just behind an offering table (Fig. 7, top left). To one side or behind the false-door is a small room for the statue of the deceased, often with slots or peepholes in front of its eyes so that it could benefit from the funerary ritual, while the soul would come through the false-door. In the Fifth Dynasty, the chapel evolves into a complex of many rooms around a pillared hall, with murals usually carved in low relief and painted to represent the daily life of the deceased, probably a device to provide him by magic with food in case the funerary service is discontinued.

[79] H. N. Chittick, "An Inscription on Gebel Barkal," *Journal of Egyptian Archaeology*, Vol. 43 (Oxford, 1957), p. 42. Alexandre Badawy, "Politique et Architecture dans l'Égypte Pharaonique," *Chronique d'Égypte*, Vol. XXXIII (Brussels, 1958), p. 180.
[80] Badawy, *Egyptian Architecture*, Vol. I, pp. 114, 157 ff.

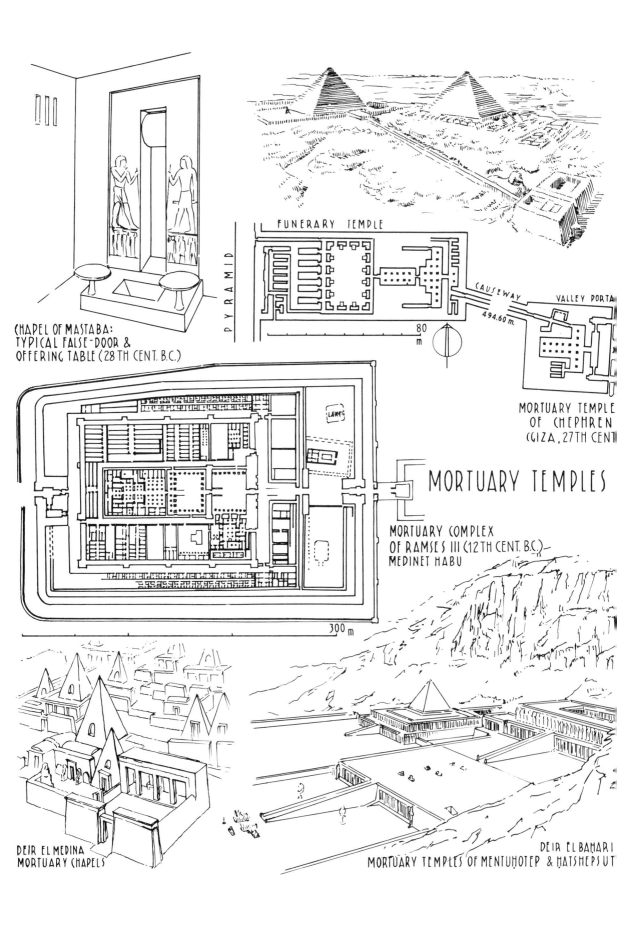

CHAPEL OF MASTABA:
TYPICAL FALSE-DOOR &
OFFERING TABLE (28TH CENT. B.C.)

FUNERARY TEMPLE

PYRAMID

CAUSEWAY
494.60 m.

VALLEY PORTA

80
m

MORTUARY TEMPLE
OF CHEPHREN
(GIZA, 27TH CENT

MORTUARY TEMPLES

LAKE

MORTUARY COMPLEX
OF RAMSES III (12TH CENT. B.C.)
MEDINET HABU

300 m

DEIR EL MEDINA
MORTUARY CHAPELS

DEIR EL BAHARI
MORTUARY TEMPLES OF MENTUHOTEP & HATSHEPSUT

In the royal pyramids the funerary chapel is on the north side (Dynasty III) and later in the middle of the east side of the pyramid base (Dynasty IV). The mortuary temple on the north side of Djeser's pyramid features twin courtyards symbolizing the ubiquitous duality of kingship for Upper and Lower Egypt. This complex is also unique in having a series of contiguous chapels in dummy construction along the two sides of a courtyard and a palace façade on the north side of each of two other courts. A pavilion, possibly for the celebration of the jubilee festival, is the only normal structure with several rooms. In the Fourth Dynasty, because the mortuary temple was located at the edge of the plateau at Giza, it developed into a large complex with a lower valley temple along the canal, a slanting causeway, and a funerary cult temple—a tripartite design seemingly initiated at Dahshur in the early years of the dynasty under Snefru. Built in massive masonry lined with granite, each element is on a symmetrical plan and strictly oriented. There are T-shaped (Chephren; Fig. 7, top right) or steplike pillared halls (Mykerinos), a court with a pillared portico surrounded by statues of the pharaoh (Chephren), or a peristyle court with palmiform columns (Saḥureꜥ) and five rear contiguous cellae, sometimes duplicated. The design of these elements was adapted to the performance of the rites in each area and accordingly symbolized the various regions from which these rites originated.[81]

A design closely conforming to the terraced cliff of the western mountain characterizes the unique mortuary temple of Pharaoh Mentuḥotep at Deir el Baḥari (Western Thebes, Fig. 7, bottom right).[82] While the lower terrace has only a pillared portico in front of it, the upper one has a peripteral gallery surrounding the core of the base carrying a pyramid. Farther on the longitudinal axis of symmetry are a peristyle court and a hypostyle hall leading to a rock-cut chapel. The total of 250 columns and 172 pillars forms a stupendous achievement. The actual layout of excavations filled with humus for trees planted in a formal park in front of the temple can be checked with that given by a contemporaneous sketch plan. A symbolic implication may have been attached to the shape of the earlier enclosure wall, which strikingly resembles that of a Theban shield, perhaps in honor of the final victory of the Thebans over Herakleopolis.

Two terraced mortuary chapels of the princes of the Twelfth Dynasty at Qaw,[83] also partly cut from the cliff, are still connected

[81] H. Ricke, *Bemerkungen zur ägyptischen Baukunst des Alten Reichs, II* (Cairo, 1950). S. Schott, *Bemerkungen zum ägyptischen Pyramidenkult* (Cairo, 1950).

[82] H. E. Winlock, *Excavations at Deir el Baḥri, 1911–1931* (New York, 1942); *The Rise and Fall of the Middle Kingdom at Thebes* (New York, 1947).

[83] H. Steckeweh, *Die Fürstengräber von Qaw* (*Veröffentlichungen der Ernst von Sieglin-Expedition*, Vol. 6), (Leipzig, 1936).

←Fig. 7

to their valley portal by a long slanting causeway, a style reminiscent of the Old Kingdom. The layout is impressive, with two terraces, porticoes, and halls, some cut into the cliff but most built of brick. The mortuary temple of Sesostris I at Lisht abuts on the middle of the east side of the pyramid and copies the mortuary temple of Pepy II (Dynasty VI) in both its plan and its decoration.[84]

The rock-cut tomb of the nobles of the Twelfth Dynasty in Middle Egypt (Beni Ḥassan, Meir, Bersha) and in Upper Egypt (Aswan) consists of a rock-cut chapel connected to the burial chamber below it. This chapel opens high up in the cliff and features a symmetrical columned hall with a niche for the statue of the deceased carved in the middle of the rear wall. It has already been noted that its roof resembles a flat gable or vault supported by beams set on two rows of palmiform polygonal or bundle lotiform columns. The front façade has a portico with two polygonal or fluted cylindrical shafts without capitals, which are of the so-called proto-Doric style, a forerunner of the Doric. Above is an architrave and a soffit of rafter ends carved from the rock (cf. Greek mutules). A courtyard stretches in front of the chapel. The troubled times marked by civil war before the Eleventh Dynasty are reflected in painted murals representing besieged forts in Middle Egypt and intricate groups of wrestlers. These murals were later superseded by the old repertory of scenes from daily life on the walls, while geometric patterns imitating mats decorated the roof.

Perhaps the most impressive mortuary temple dating from the beginning of the New Kingdom is that of Queen Ḥatshepsut (Dynasty XVIII) at Deir el Baḥari just to the north of that of Mentuḥotep and inspired by it (Fig. 7, bottom right). It seems to be oriented toward Karnak, and its design illustrates a well-developed stage of the terraced type, since it is an obvious and quite successful attempt to integrate the architectural style with the impressive mountain cirque behind. The three horizontal stages of the background—the lowest expanses of sand, the middle bastionlike projections, and the upper clefts of the rock—are paralleled by the three terraces of the temple, each fronted by a retaining wall treated as a long portico. Compared with the temple of Mentuḥotep near by that is designed to be seen in perspective from all sides, that of Ḥatshepsut emphasizes the frontal approach, which is enhanced by the axial ramps connecting the terraces. The porticoes have an outer row of pillars and an inner row of columns at the lowest level or pillars at the middle level. A chapel of Anubis (north) and a shrine of Ḥathor (south end) flank the middle porticoes. In front of the uppermost portico were Osiride pillars of the queen. Evidence from current excavations favors the interpreta-

---

[84] Smith, *Art*, p. 100, Fig. 41, pl. 64A.

tion of the so-called peristyle court as a hypostyle hall,[85] beyond which is a deep sanctuary with lateral niches containing statues of the queen. Scenes in low relief cover the walls of the porticoes, some of which represent the theogamy of the queen mother Aḥmose with Amun and the trade expedition by sea to Pwēne (Somaliland). The tomb itself is dissociated from its mortuary temple and cut far behind in another valley.

The royal mortuary temples of the Empire at Thebes are set in a row on the edge of the desert perpendicularly to the riverbank, the later temples inserted between the earlier ones. Love of the colossal is conspicuously displayed in the mortuary temple of Ramses II and the similar one of Ramses III at Medinet Habu (Fig. 7, middle left). The temple itself is a large structure surrounded by a whole complex of administrative offices, magazines, workshops, and priests' dwellings; and even outside its own enclosure there are houses for foreign artisans. Appended to the front court of the temple is a temple-palace where the pharaoh and his retinue reside when Amun of Karnak visits the mortuary temple. A lateral courtyard and an altar near the sanctuary are dedicated to Reᶜ-Ḥorakhte. The façade of the palace has a monumental window of appearance, and on the opposite side of the court runs a portico with Osiride pillars so set as if they were greeting the pharaoh as he looks from the window. The temple of Ramses III embodies elements of military architecture, mainly a massive buttressed enclosure with two fortified gateways in the shape of double towers connected by a bridge at three levels, perhaps reminiscent of the Syrian fortresses destroyed by the Egyptians during their expeditions. Under the late Ramessids this temple became the seat of administration of Western Thebes. One of the subsidiary purposes of the colossi, Osiride pillars, and the repertory of scenes in relief on the outer walls of the temples was, of course, to publicize the political influence of Pharaoh. Let us also mention that the gateways of the temple of Ramses III were so designed and ornamented with statuary groups applied in high relief as to achieve illusionism by creating the impression of greater depth to the front passageway and the existence of two sets of double towers flanking it.

The mortuary chapels of private individuals became integrated into the rock tombs to an even greater degree than in the Middle Kingdom. There could, however, have been independent chapels on the edge of the valley. The walls of the inner corridors are covered with paintings of scenes from daily life, while those in the extensive royal tombs often in low relief and painted show aspects of the

---

[85] Leszek Dabrowski, "A Famous Temple Re-examined: Queen Hatshepsut's Temple at Deir el Bahari—and a Hitherto Unknown Temple," *The Illustrated London News*, Sept. 19, 1964, pp. 413–415.

afterlife with its genii and gates. At ᶜAmarna and Deir el Medina (Fig. 7, bottom left) the superstructure imitates the standard shrine (⌂ sḥ), its internal chambers being vaulted, often topped with a brick pyramid, and sometimes fronted by a columned portico. The royal tomb at ᶜAmarna and the private ones, only one of which is finished, are cut from the rock of the eastern cliff. Their inner walls, daubed with thin or thick layers of plaster, are covered with realistic scenes of daily life in a sensitive, though often sketchy, naturalistic style. There is no evidence of funerary chapels or superstructures.

This type of *sḥ* chapel lives on beyond the end of Egyptian dynasties in Hellenistic and Roman cemeteries (Hermopolis West), as one- or two-storied structures with vaulted rooms in which scenes from the netherworld and from daily life are painted in a mixed style. In the Late Period a private funerary chapel can assume a stupendous scale like that of Mentuemḥat (end of the seventh century) in Western Thebes, which has a huge pylon of brick with an arched entrance.

Tombs

Nowhere in the ancient world has the tomb been given such importance as in Egypt, a direct outcome of the essential concept of the afterlife. Egyptians believed that the soul could live only if the body was preserved from corruption and depredation. Mummification was accordingly invented at the dawn of history, and the tomb evolved as a function of the various destinies of the deceased as defined by corresponding ideologies. Although, with the intermingling of various theological systems and the differentiation between royal and private deceased, these destinies became confused, one can theoretically isolate three types of destinies:

1. Stellar, where Pharaoh "goes to his ka" or "goes to the sky."[86]
2. A netherlife, similar to an enjoyable life on earth, in a well-equipped tomb after the "justification" of the deceased by Osiris.[87]
3. Solar, where one accompanies the sun in his boat across the sky and becomes part of the retinue of that god or even merges with him.[88]

These beliefs already seem to be mixed in the Pyramid Texts of the Fifth Dynasty, where Reᶜ is correlated with Osiris. One of the important results of the democratization process at the end of the Sixth Dynasty was that some royal prerogatives become available to the people. The evolution of the tomb follows that of the types of destiny.

[86] Pyr. 1431, 882, 820. Cf. J. H. Breasted, *Development of Religion and Thought in Ancient Egypt* (New York, 1959), pp. 53, 137.
[87] Breasted, *Development*, p. 60.
[88] Pyramid Texts 334.

The tomb in the Fifth Dynasty is a rectangular superstructure called a *mastaba* (Arabic "bench"), oriented north–south with battered walls enclosing a central room surrounded by a row of other compartments without connection to the exterior (Djer, Fig. 8, top left). The proportions of the plan of the superstructure at Saqqara are about 1:2, and the faces are articulated into recessed paneling, presumably imitating the façade of the palace of Lower Egypt. Soon, however, the main room is excavated deeper under ground level, and a stairway or ramp descends to it from the north (Qay‘a; Fig. 8, top middle), probably symbolizing the northern circumpolar stars to which the deceased was supposed to fly. Even in the pyramid of Djeser (Dynasty III at Saqqara) or in the so-called stairway type of tomb the substructure is accessible through a passage from the north.[89] This idea of ascension is expressed in the early names of the tomb: "ascension" (?)[90] and "place of ascension" (*m‘ḥt*). During the First Dynasty the location of the stairway shifts from the north end to the east, toward the sunrise, an architectural expression of the shift from stellar to solar destiny.

The burial apartment underground sometimes copies the plan of a house cut from the rock with several rooms about a central corridor, a latrine, and a water-storage niche (Ruaben at Saqqara).[91] The mastaba superstructure imitates the external aspect of the palace, its walls being covered with recessed paneling to imitate the façade of an early palace in wood and brick. Often they were painted with geometrical patterns in gaudy colors to represent mats or rugs hanging from the wooden framework (Ḥesire‘, Djadjaem‘ankh)[92] such as those which were actually hung on the inner walls of palaces and mansions. The correlation of the tomb with a house is illustrated in its name, "castle of eternity" (*ḥt nḥḥ*), "house of eternity" (*pr n ḏt*), or "castle of the ka" (*ḥt k3*).[93] The sarcophagus itself in wood or stone is called the "lord of life" (*nb ‘nḫ*) and is also a diminutive copy of a house with a flat vault and recessed paneling on the walls. To complement this parody of life, funerary furniture and food ("all things good and pure on which a god lives," according to the formula of offering)[94] are provided as "equipment" of the deceased.[95]

Some of the pharaohs even from the First Dynasty had more than one tomb, and it is surmised that one tomb was built as a cenotaph,

[89] Badawy, *Egyptian Architecture*, Vol. I, p. 127, Fig. 87; pp. 158–159, Fig. 102–103.

[90] Alexander Badawy, "The Ideology of the Superstructure of the Mastaba-tomb in Egypt," *Journal of Near Eastern Studies*, Vol. XV (Chicago, 1956), pp. 180–183.

[91] Badawy, *Egyptian Architecture*, Vol. I, p. 40, Fig. 30. A. Scharff, *Das Grab als Wohnhaus in der ägyptischen Frühzeit* (Munich, 1947).

[92] W. B. Emery, *Great Tombs of the First Dynasty*, 2 vols. (Cairo, 1949; London, 1954).

[93] Erman and Grapow, *Wörterbuch*, Vol. I, p. 514, Vol. III, pp. 2, 5.

[94] Gardiner, *Egyptian Grammar*, p. 170.

[95] Breasted, *Development*, p. 62. Pyr. 1559.

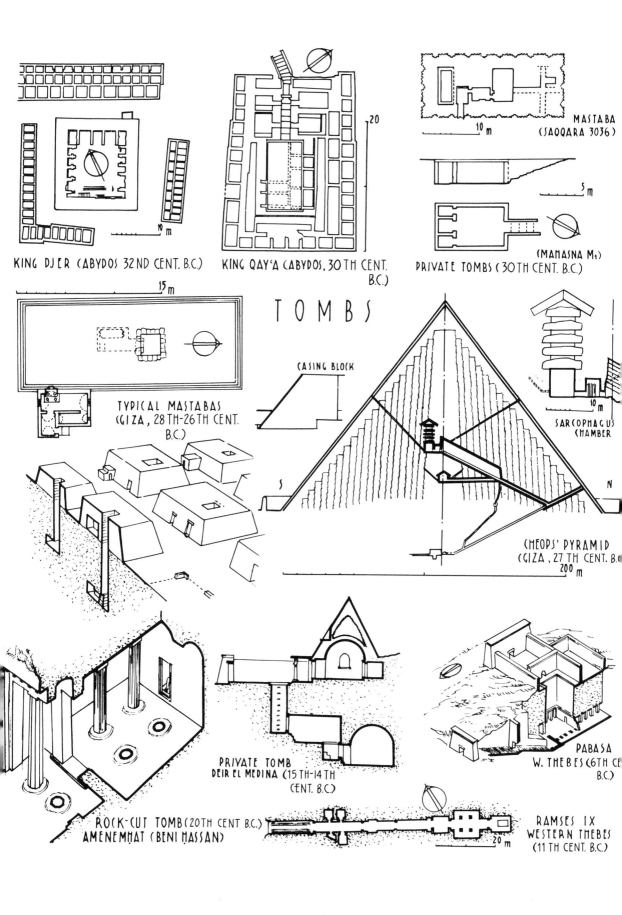

KING DJER (ABYDOS 32ND CENT. B.C.)

KING QAY'A (ABYDOS, 30 TH CENT. B.C.)

20

MASTABA (SAQQARA 3036)

10 m

5 m

(MAHASNA M₁)

PRIVATE TOMBS (30TH CENT. B.C.)

15 m

TOMBS

TYPICAL MASTABAS (GIZA, 28TH-26TH CENT. B.C.)

CASING BLOCK

SARCOPHAGUS CHAMBER

10 m

S

N

CHEOPS' PYRAMID (GIZA, 27 TH CENT. B.C)

200 m

ROCK-CUT TOMB (20TH CENT B.C.) AMENEMHAT (BENI HASSAN)

PRIVATE TOMB DEIR EL MEDINA (15TH-14TH CENT. B.C.)

PABASA W. THEBES (6TH CE B.C.)

RAMSES IX WESTERN THEBES (11 TH CENT. B.C.)

20 m

especially when it was located at Abydos near the "tomb of the great god" (Osiris). We have some evidence that private mastaba tombs, like royal ones, connote the solar destiny when their stairway descends from their eastern face; this is clearly expressed in the shape of the royal pyramid symbolizing the sun's rays slanting toward each of the four cardinal points, as early as the Third Dynasty (Djeser and Sekhemkhet at Saqqara), if not before[96] (two pyramids at Zawiyet el ʿAryan?). The pyramidal form is derived from the pyramidion topping the obelisk and is called "benben" after the upright stone dedicated to Reʿ in the "Benben House" at Heliopolis.[97] Every pyramid was given a name composed from that of its royal owner, such as "Snefru-gleams," "Cheops-is-belonging-to-the-horizon," "Great-is-Chephren," "Mykerinos-is-divine," or "Sesostris-is-strong."[98]

The Development of the Mastaba Tomb. The superstructure of the mastaba tomb originates from the artificial mound covering the prehistoric grave. It is natural for the royal tombs to be larger and more elaborate than those of private people. In the Archaic Period the superstructure of massive brickwork is rectangular and oriented north–south, with battered walls, plain or recessed faces (Men), surrounded by an enclosure. The walls of the burial chamber, which is roofed with reeds plastered with mud, may be given a lining. It later evolves into a larger underground substructure made of brick and lined internally with wood, with party walls or a mud floor covered with a wooden framework (Djet). Around the central burial chamber are compartments for storage to which correspond the niches in the recessed external faces (Neithotep, Hor ʿAha). After the burial, there was no access to the tomb.

Later the substructure is cut deeper underground, and a stairway or ramp starting in front of the north side descends to the main chamber, but is sometimes blocked by a portcullis that slides vertically (Udimu, ʿAdjib, Semerkhet). The number of magazines increases (Qayʿa, Hemaka, Nebetka) so that their area surpasses by far that of the central burial chamber (Khaʿsekhemwy: total area 1,000 sq. m., burial chamber 17.55 sq. m.), which is roofed with a corbel. Since the Second Dynasty, the substructure at Saqqara was cut from the rock, a process that spread to other necropolises in the Third Dynasty. The substructure of Ruaben is unique in that it imitates a dummy apartment, even including a latrine.

The early superstructure shows two niches on the east face that

[96] Badawy, *Egyptian Architecture*, Vol. I. pp. 126 ff. The layer pyramid at Zawiyet el ʿAryan is dated by Smith, *Art*, p. 31, to Khaʿba, after Sekhemkhet and Djeser.
[97] Breasted, *Development*, p. 71.
[98] I. E. S. Edwards, *The Pyramids of Egypt* (London, 1961), pp. 241 ff.

later in the Old Kingdom develop into the large standard niche with false-door and offering table at the south end, fronted by a chapel, and the subsidiary niche at the north end of the same east face. In some of the larger mastabas all the faces have recessed paneling, the so-called "palace façade" motif imitating the walls of the royal palace of the north (Fig. 8, top right). Beginning with the Third Dynasty only private people are buried in mastabas, which are laid out in rows around the royal pyramid. The superstructure of the mastaba is still of brick with recessed paneling, sometimes encasing wooden panels carved in low relief (Ḥesireᶜ) or two niches. A stairway descends to the underground apartment (Mastaba T at Giza), often ending with a vertical shaft to the burial chamber. Later, instead of this compound access, there is only a vertical shaft opening on the flat roof of the stone superstructure, with plain battered or stepped faces around a masonry core. This vertical shaft to the burial chamber was filled in after the funeral (Fig. 8, middle left).

During the Fourth Dynasty the mastabas are laid out in the western desert on an orthogonal system of streets oriented north–south around the royal pyramid in the district of Memphis, between Abu Roash to the north and Dahshur to the south. Each mastaba, originally designed for only one person, later features two or more shafts leading down to two burial chambers. At the south end of the east face the funerary chapel, looking toward the valley at sunrise, soon develops into a corridor running along the east face (Ḥesireᶜ, Ḥemiwnw) or is built within the superstructure (Duwanḥor) as an apartment on an L-shaped or cruciform plan. Sometimes it even spreads into a larger complex with several rooms fronted by a columned portico (Seshemnefer at Giza, Sixth Dynasty; Ti, Ptaḥḥotep, and Akhethotep at Saqqara). The walls of the pillared hall, storeroom, and chapel proper are then carved and painted with scenes of daily life, such as work in the fields or in the granary, kitchen, or workshops and leisure-time activities like dancing, music, hunting or fishing in the marshes, and playing chess or the serpent-game. The purpose of the murals was to provide the deceased by magic with an everlasting source of food and enjoyment[99] rather than to enhance his social status. The mastaba in the Sixth Dynasty, and even before then, serves for the burials of a whole family.

It is also in the Fourth Dynasty that the earliest rock-cut tombs appear at Giza. This type, favored wherever the cliffs are near enough to the city, came into fashion probably because of its relative efficacy against tomb robbers. In the alluvial flat country, however, during the Twelfth Dynasty (El Lahun, Lisht) mastabas are still built around the royal pyramids. Elsewhere (Hawara, Abydos,

[99] Drioton and Vandier, *L'Égypte*, pp. 126–127.

Dendera) they are large structures built usually of brick. The inner apartments employ a number of devices borrowed from the pyramid to delude robbers, such as a "doubling-back" plan, portcullises sliding sideways, false burial chambers (Inpy), or a vertical shaft filled with sand and ending at the entrance passage, which slopes from the north (Senusertʿankh).

In the New Kingdom the mastaba becomes rare, being largely superseded by the independent pyramid chapel above a burial chamber (ʿAniba in Nubia). In the Late Period there occur huge complexes with elaborate brick superstructures in the shape of tombs. These structures, which contain the burial chambers, are arranged around a large central well accessible from a broad staircase (Pabasa, Fig. 8, lower right; Pedamenopet at Thebes), or they have a huge shaft at the bottom of which a vaulted burial chamber is built (Saqqara).

The Development of the Pyramid. The earliest pyramids[100] at Zawiyet el ʿAryan and those of Djeser and Sekhemkhet at Saqqara are stepped superstructures built on the desert plateau in layers of rubble inclined at a 75-degree angle. These so-called "accretion layers" abut a core on either a square plan (Zawiyet el ʿAryan, 88 m.) or a rectangular plan (Djeser, 125 × 104 m., 61 m. high). The underground burial apartment is accessible from a stairway or ramp starting in front of the middle of the north side. A wall with recessed paneling surrounds the pyramid (Sekhemkhet) or its complex (Djeser). The sarcophagus is set at the bottom of an underground vertical shaft in the vertical axis of the superstructure. In the pyramid of Djeser the chambers to the east are lined with blue glazed tiles imitating wattlework, or they have scenes of the pharaoh performing the rites during his jubilee festival, similar to those in the south mastaba.

Two elements appear for the first time in the pyramid of Ḥuny, which was finished by Snefru at Meydum:[101] The corbeled burial chamber is at ground level accessible through an inclined corridor opening in the north face somewhat above ground level, and the outline of the casing assumes a true pyramidal shape with smooth triangular faces (51° slope). The mortuary temple abuts on the middle of the east face. Snefru built two pyramids at Dahshur, the south one with a flat angle of incline and the other with a unique rhomboidal outline (two-sloped), its two burial apartments opening from the north and from the west faces.[102] Two questions remain:

[100] Badawy, *Egyptian Architecture*, Vol. I. pp. 176–179, Figs. 86–87. Edwards, *The Pyramids of Egypt*. A. Fakhry, *The Pyramids* (Chicago, 1961).
[101] Badawy, *Egyptian Architecture*, Vol. I. pp. 179–181, Fig. 88.
[102] *Ibid.*, pp. 131–133, Fig. 89.

Was the change to a flatter incline in the upper part caused by financial difficulties? Were the apartments duplicated as a device to delude robbers?

There is no doubt that pyramid design and construction reach a climax at Giza. The great pyramid of Cheops was, indeed, one of the seven wonders of the ancient world (Fig. 8, middle right). Still built with inner accretion layers and faces (5.25 m. thick) of huge blocks of limestone, it has a geometric pyramidal shape on a square plan 400 cubits long (*ca.* 230 m.); it is accurately oriented and faced with prismatic blocks (51° 52′ incline; Fig. 8, middle), originally reaching a height of 280 cubits (146.6 m.). The internal apartments show three stages of construction: an earliest underground chamber to which a sloping corridor descends from the middle of the north face at some height above ground; an intermediate chamber reached from a corridor rising from the earlier one and turning horizontally; and the third chamber farther up reached through a high corbeled gallery (16 m. high, 2.09 m. wide). This burial chamber, set slightly south of the vertical axis through the apex, contains the granite sarcophagus along its west wall. It is lined with polished pink granite and has two square shafts rising toward the north and south faces, to provide a passage for the soul to the circumpolar stars and to the Orion constellation, respectively. Five superimposed ceilings of large horizontal blocks alternate with relieving chambers topped by a gable (Fig. 8, middle right). The doorway to the chamber was to be blocked by three granite portcullises sliding vertically in lateral grooves in a small antechamber. The technical excellence of the masonry owes more to the ability of the craftsmen than to the use of mechanical devices more elaborate than sledges hauled up ramps, windlasses and pulleys for lifting and transporting, adzes, chisels, saws, drills, and polishing stones for dressing and finishing the stone blocks. The court of the pyramid was paved in stone and contained the funerary temple on the middle of the east side. Sun boats of cedar wood were set in excavations at some distance from the eastern and southern faces.

The pyramid of Chephren is slightly smaller than that of Cheops, still covered at the top by its casing. Its burial chamber at ground level is accessible from a horizontal corridor.

While the pyramids of the Fifth and Sixth Dynasties are considerably smaller and poorer technically than the earlier ones, these deficiencies were supposedly compensated by the ritual texts inscribed on the walls of the burial chamber which "insured the king felicity in the hereafter."[103] The burial apartments assume a standard

---

[103] Breasted, *Development*, p. 88. S. A. B. Mercer, *Literary Criticism of the Pyramid Texts* (London, 1956), pp. 8–9.

type. A horizontal corridor at, or slightly below, ground level (Sixth Dynasty) leads to a lobby flanked to the west by the burial chamber roofed over with a double or triple gable, and to the east by a small room for statues (Sixth Dynasty). Granite portcullises block the horizontal corridor, and between these and the entrance large granite plugs were slid in.[104]

After the First Intermediate Period the pyramid is dissociated from the tomb and becomes a symbolic small brick structure above the rock-cut tombs of the Intefs (Western Thebes)[105] and on the mortuary temple of Mentuhotep (Nebḥepetreᶜ), but the true pyramidal tomb reappears in the Twelfth Dynasty near the contemporaneous capital at Dahshur, Lisht, and El Lahun. Built of brick, it is not as large as the pyramids at Giza, and its inner apartments are equipped with a host of devices to protect the contents against tomb robbers. There are no texts on the walls since these texts are now painted on the sides of the coffin (so-called Coffin Texts). The plan features a long corridor leading down from a hidden entrance, with some stretches winding at right angles, and running at various levels to end ultimately in the vicinity of its starting point according to the so-called "doubling-back" layout. Also to delude robbers, false burial chambers are ingeniously arranged, trap doors to the farther stretches of the corridors are blocked by heavy portcullises hidden in the ceiling, and the royal coffin is enclosed beyond reach within huge sarcophagi of granite or quartzite. The ceiling of the burial chamber is a pent roof (pyramid of Amenemḥat III at Dahshur). To compensate for the looseness of the core, a framework of retaining walls radiates from the center toward the corners and the middle of each face (Senusert I at Lisht, Amenemḥat II at Dahshur, Senusert II at El Lahun). The substructure of the pyramid is built in a huge excavation.

In the New Kingdom the pyramid is no longer a royal prerogative. In Western Thebes pharaohs have rock-cut tombs, while other people give the superstructures of their tombs the shape of small brick pyramids with steep incline, which are entered from a portico along the east face (Deir el Medina).[106] At the top is a painted pyramidion and beneath it on the east face a niche containing a stela, sometimes held by a kneeling statue of the deceased. The burial is in an underground chamber accessible through a shaft. At Abydos[107] a hollow

[104] Badawy, *Egyptian Architecture*, Vol. I, pp. 145–151.

[105] H. E. Winlock, *The Rise and Fall of the Middle Kingdom in Thebes* (New York, 1947), pp. 11 ff. W. C. Hayes, "The Middle Kingdom in Egypt," *Cambridge Ancient History* (Cambridge, 1961), pp. 54–55. Edwards, *The Pyramids of Egypt*, pp. 168 ff. Smith, *Art*, pp. 88–90, 95 ff.

[106] Bruyère, *Fouilles à Deir el-Medineh*, Vol. VIII.

[107] T. E. Peet, *The Cemeteries of Abydos*, Vol. II. (London, 1914), pp. 84–91, Figs. 46–51.

pyramid forms the superstructure, integrated with the substructure since the Twenty-Fifth Dynasty.

The later pyramids (7th century) of sandstone in far-off Kush are different in that they are massive superstructures; at the east face a chapel is erected above an underground burial apartment accessible from a ramp opening at some distance east of the superstructure.[108] The latest pyramids at Meroë (A.D. 3rd–4th centuries) are similar.

The Development of the Rock-Cut Tomb. The rock-cut tomb appears toward the end of the Old Kingdom and becomes a favorite with the nobles during the First Intermediate Period in Middle Egypt. They have their tombs carved in the cliff above their cities at Asyut, Meir, Bersha, and Beni Ḥassan. So do those at Qaw and Aswan as well as the pharaohs of the Eleventh Dynasty at Thebes. The pharaohs' large tombs have wide porticoes (80 m., Seḥertawy Intef I; 180 m., Waḥꜥankh Intef II) in front and descend deep into the mountain. The courtyard of the tomb is flanked by the rock tombs of the retainers.[109]

When the pharaohs of the Twelfth Dynasty reverted to the pyramidal tomb, some of the nobles at the court chose to have their mastaba tombs around it, following the tradition of the Old Kingdom. The majority, however, still "went to rest" in their rock-cut tombs above their city. It became a tradition about which they boasted. "My chief nobility was: I executed a cliff tomb [for] a man should imitate that which his father does," said Prince Khnumḥotep II of Beni Ḥassan under Senusert II. The chapel (Fig. 8, bottom) is so well integrated with the burial apartment, which is accessible from a slanting passage or shaft opening in the court or in the floor of the chapel itself, that it is hard to dissociate them for study.

There is no doubt that the rock-cut tomb offers more security than the mastaba. Yet the tradition, appearing toward the end of the Old Kingdom, that allowed a whole family to use a mastaba is carried on in the rock tomb. Sometimes as many as six burial shafts descend from the chapel (Remushenti at Beni Ḥassan). At Bersha the shaft descends from the floor of the front portico to a horizontal passage running a short distance to a small room with a niche for the coffin, just beneath the shrine in the chapel (Djeḥutiḥetep).

In the impressive terraced tombs at Qaw the burial apartment consists of two small chambers accessible through two sloping passages, originally plugged, from the floor of two side chambers (Waḥka I) or through six shafts from the inner hall (Waḥka II).

At Aswan two staircases descend from the rearmost hall to two

---

[108] D. Dunham, *The Royal Cemeteries of Kush*, 2 vols. (Cambridge, 1950–1955).
[109] Winlock, *Rise and Fall.*

chambers one of which is connected by a vertical shaft to a gallery, which has two other shafts (Sirenput I). The system is sometimes even more complex, with interconnected shafts and as many as four shafts (Sirenput II), in order to delude robbers.

In the New Kingdom the royal tomb is cut from the rock in the Valley of the Kings in Western Thebes. It consists of a slightly slanting corridor with three offset stretches flanked by niches; passing through an antechamber, the corridor is intercepted by shafts and ends in a sarcophagus chamber (Fig. 8, bottom right). This corridor, sometimes as long as 234 meters (Ḥatshepsut), starts at an angle to the entrance façade and turns to the right (Amenḥotep I, Ḥatshepsut, Ramses II) or, at a later period, left (Tuthmosis I, Tuthmosis III, Amenḥotep II). A new feature in the floor of the room is the stairway, which is a continuation of the corridor. The sarcophagus chamber called "House-of-Gold" has rounded corners and perhaps symbolizes the shape of the world or the royal cartouche. Later it is rectangular, with six pillars, and is preceded by a pillared vestibule. This type of plan is an ultimate effort to preserve the secrecy of the burial. Ineny, the architect of the Tuthmosis I tomb, puts it this way: "I inspected the excavation of the cliff tomb of his majesty, alone, no one seeing, no one hearing." The entrance is inconspicuous, and after the funeral it is blocked with a small wall, sealed by the priests of the necropolis, and buried beneath sand. In contrast with the private tombs, the subjects of the painted or occasionally carved murals in the royal tombs are religious, derived from three main groups of ritual texts called "books" and two minor ones. Only at ᶜAmarna are the walls of Akhenaten's tomb and the private tombs covered with realistic scenes in low relief from court life, to the exclusion of scenes from the life of the owners of the tombs. One picture shows the royal pair mourning the death of their little daughter. The private tomb at ᶜAmarna is axial, as if to allow the sun's rays to penetrate it, and is built on a cruciform plan with a deep hall preceding the broad hall, both rectangular and columned. A niche for one or more statues is cut in the rear wall. The connection to the burial chamber beneath the shrine is through one or more shafts or sometimes even a curious spiral (Paneḥsy). The fact that the repertory of scenes features almost exclusively Akhenaten has led to the surmise that the tombs were prepared at the king's orders for his faithful courtiers.

At Thebes[110] the private tomb is a long corridorlike chapel behind a columned portico surmounted by a brick pyramid. The burial chamber consists of two or three rooms reached through a shaft or

---

[110] G. Steindorff and W. Wolf, "Die Thebanische Gräberwelt," *Leipziger ägyptologische Studien*, No. 4 (Glückstadt, 1936).

stairway from the rear room or from the court (Deir el Medina; Fig. 8, lower middle).

Forts

Primitive man had to defend himself and his property against beasts and his fellow men, and this search for security became an abiding element in Egyptian society. Every settlement, whether sacred or lay, and every private home was surrounded by a protective enclosure. Protodynastic and early dynastic labels represent fences and palisades, which were entered in the repertory of hieroglyphs. We have seen how the house, castle, and shrine are always set within an enclosure. Archaic pictures of forts or fortifications show a wall on a square plan with rounded corners, bordered with protruding rectangular or triangular projections, representing buttresses or bastions, rather than crenelations.[111] Two typical fortified towns, possibly the capitals of city-states, have an orthogonal layout of blocks of houses along streets (Fig. 9, top left). Oval or rectangular walls with rectangular or semicircular bastions also occur[112] as strongholds (*wnt* ⬚). Other fortifications from the Archaic Period are in the shape of isolated towers (*swnt* ⬚), round in area, with battered sides; topped by a crenelated balcony and probably machicolated, the tower could be reached by means of a rope ladder hanging from an aperture just beneath the balcony (Fig. 9, top left).[113]

The Archaic palace is enclosed within a double rectangular wall. It was accessible from a protruding gateway (Hierakonpolis fort) or from two entrances flush with the face (Shunet el Zebib at Abydos), where a winding approach was devised by means of two doorways not on the same axis or at right angles with an intermediate anteroom in the form of a shaft, very likely guarded by sentries on the top of its walls (Fig. 9, top middle).[114] Two towers flank the doorway; a feature also found in the Syrian fort represented in an Egyptian tomb from the Sixth Dynasty at Deshasha.[115]

With the social upheavals of the First Intermediate Period and a raging civil war between Thebes and Herakleopolis, military architects perfected a type of small local fortress which was manned by a garrison and could occasionally become a citadel and a refuge to the

---

[111] Badawy, *Dessin architectural*, Figs. 10, 15, 55a; p. 28, Fig. 38; *Egyptian Architecture*, Vol. I, p. 48, Fig. 36.

[112] Badawy, *Egyptian Architecture*, Vol. I, p. 177, Fig. 120.

[113] Badawy, *Dessin architectural*, pp. 61–64; *Egyptian Architecture*, Vol. I, Figs. 36, 120.

[114] Badawy, *Dessin architectural*, pp. 141–142, Figs. 166a, 166c; *Egyptian Architecture*, Vol. I, p. 46, Fig. 35.

[115] Badawy, *Egyptian Architecture*, Vol. I, p. 178, Fig. 121.

Fig. 9→

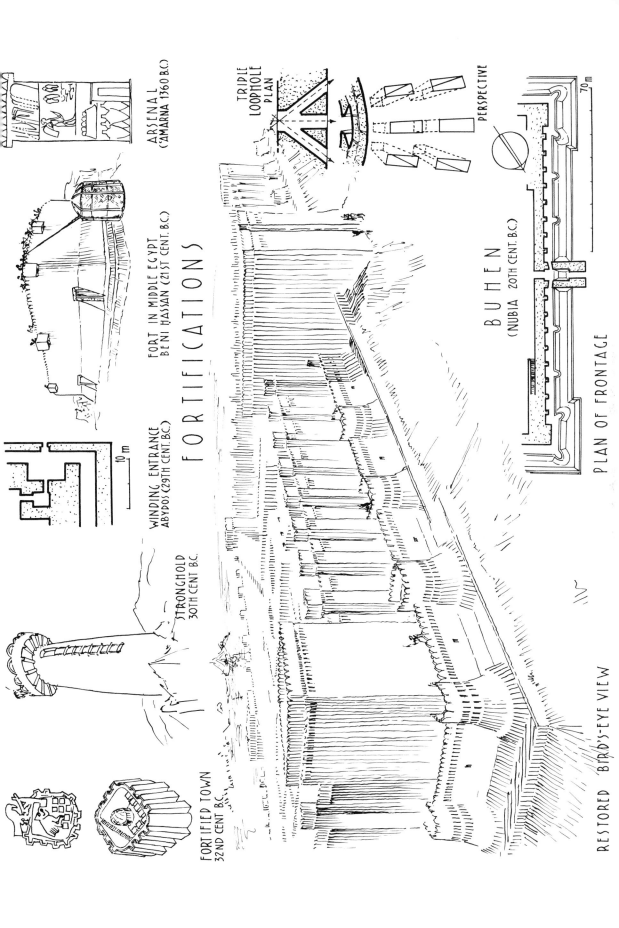

ARSENAL
(AMARNA 1360 B.C.)

TRIPLE
LOOPHOLE
PLAN

PERSPECTIVE

FORTIFICATIONS

FORT IN MIDDLE EGYPT
BENI HASSAN (21ST CENT. B.C.)

WINDING ENTRANCE
ABYDOS (29TH CENT. B.C.)

STRONGHOLD
30TH CENT B.C.

FORTIFIED TOWN
32ND CENT B.C.

BUHEN
(NUBIA 20TH CENT. B.C.)

70 m

PLAN OF FRONTAGE

RESTORED BIRD'S-EYE VIEW

10 m

citizens. Many paintings of military activities from the tombs of the monarchs at Beni Ḥassan (Dynasties XI and XII) represent these small structures, probably built of brick. In the bottom part of the wall, which slants like a glacis, there are one or two doorways of hard stone, and at the top of the wall is a gangway with crenelated and protruding machicolated balconies (Fig. 9, top right).[116] The military dynamism of this period developed into an aggressive policy of conquest in Nubia late in the Eleventh Dynasty and continued through the Twelfth Dynasty. A chain of fortresses built of brick and reinforced with balks was established along the Nile banks and on its islands in Nubia. Where the terrain is rugged rock, the layout follows the irregular contours, with long spur walls extending along the ridges of the island. One main gateway opens between two long side walls at a small end. Internally the axial layout consists of two main arteries intersecting at right angles, a pomerium, and structures grouped according to a zoning plan and later dominated at the focal point by a temple. Barracks and public granaries as well as the essential covered waterway descending to the water bank would eventually allow the citizens to sustain a long siege (Semna, Kumma, Uronarti, Shalfak, Askut).[117] The fortress on flat ground is rectangular in shape and is oriented north–south. With recessed walls, round or rectangular bastions at regular intervals, and one gateway in the middle of every side (Buhen, Ikkur, Kuban), it is surrounded by a moat with scarp and counterscarp, a drawbridge (Buhen), and a landing quay if located near the Nile (ʿAniba).[118] The most elaborate example is perhaps that recently excavated at Buhen (Fig. 9, middle and bottom),[119] which features a massive brick wall (4.8 m. thick and 9 m. high) with square bastions. A surrounding rampart is protected by a loopholed parapet overhanging the scarp of the rock-cut ditch (8.4 m. wide × 6.5 m. deep). Projecting from the scarp are round bastions with double rows of loopholes (Fig. 9, middle right), which allow standing or kneeling archers to shoot arrows. Such a system was more elaborate than that used in the later Elamite Susa[120] or Greek Herakleia or Hellenistic Miletus.[121]

[116] Badawy, *Dessin architectural*, pp. 143–145, Figs. 168–171; *Egyptian Architecture*, Vol. I, Fig. 122.

[117] Smith, *Art*, p. 99, Fig. 43.

[118] Badawy, "Orthogonal and Axial Town Planning," pp. 5–8. S. Clarke, "Ancient Egyptian Fortresses," *Journal of Egyptian Archaeology*, Vol. III, pp. 160 ff. L. Borchardt, *Altägyptische Festungen an der zweiten Nilschnelle* (*Veröffentlichungen der Ernst von Sieglin-Expedition*, Vol. III), (Leipzig, 1923). Badawy, *Dessin architectural*, pp. 145–146.

[119] W. Emery, "A Preliminary Report on the Excavations of the Egypt Exploration Society at Buhen, 1958–59," *Kush*, Vol. VIII (Khartoum, 1960), pp. 7–10.

[120] M. Dieulafoy, *L'acropole de Suse* (Paris, 1893), Figs. 101, 105, 122.

[121] A. von Gerkan, "Die Stadtmauern," in T. Wiegand, *Milet*, Vol. II (Berlin 1935), p. 3, Tables 9, 16, Fig. 6.

With the conquests in Asia during the Empire new types of fortification may have become familiar to the Egyptians, who often showed Syrian and Palestinian fortified towns[122] in the victory scenes on the temples and in private tombs (Ḥesy, Amonmose) at Thebes and even as far south as Abu Simbel. There is no evidence, however, that they ever adopted the compound layout of a citadel within a fortified town, though the mortuary temple of Ramses III may be interpreted as a stylized example of such a scheme (Medinet Habu).[123] Its eastern and western fortified gateways certainly convey the impression of being copied from military architecture though not necessarily foreign. In this instance we may recall that in the Archaic Period we found within the city a palace and temple complex enclosed by a wall, which again could be interpreted as a citadel.

Some idea about strongholds and watchtowers in Egypt can be derived from the representations in the tombs at ʿAmarna (Fig. 9, top right; Dynasty XVIII).[124] From the same period date the remains of Sesebi, a fortified trade outpost in the Sudan. Its rectangular buttressed wall (about 260 × 200 m.), oriented north–south, has on each side one gateway flanked by buttresses with sliding doors and a drain. We have already seen that its internal layout is axial, there is a pomerium, and the area is zoned for houses, magazines, temples, and commandant's quarters (Fig. 2, top right).[125]

Materials and Methods of Construction

Materials.[126] Primitive man in Egypt made abundant use of reeds, palms, and papyrus to build his boats with cabins and later his shelters on the riverbanks. Having discovered how to plaster reeds with mud, he soon replaced the wattle-and-daub technique by construction with massive mud blocks and stone (Maʿadi). An epoch-making invention was that of mud brick, which consists of sun-dried blocks of uniform and handy size made from a mixture of mud, water, and chaff or sand. Brickwork used mortar and plaster of similar composition and was found to withstand the mild climate very well. Elaborate interlocking brick molds were developed for constructing true arches and ribbed vaults (Dynasty V at Giza).[127] Though today relatively little remains of these brick structures, there is no doubt that the vast majority of houses and palaces were built of

122 Badawy, *Dessin architectural*, pp. 148–158.
123 Hölscher, *The Excavation of Medinet Habu.*
124 Badawy, *Dessin architectural*, p. 147.
125 Badawy, "Orthogonal and Axial Town Planning," p. 8, Fig. 8.
126 A. Lucas, *Ancient Egyptian Materials and Industries*, 3rd ed. (London, 1948).
127 Alexander Badawy, "Vaults and Domes in the Giza Necropolis," in A. Abubakr, ed., *Excavations at Giza. 1949–1950* (Cairo, 1953), pp. 129–143.

that material and roofed over with vaults and domes. Actually, in the towns brick dwellings covered much more of the area than did the temples built of stone. Molded glazed faïence of turquoise blue (Djeser, Dynasty III) and later glazed enamels molded in various refined inlays (New Kingdom) added a touch of rich glitter to architectural decoration. Perhaps the availability of good stone for construction was the main deterrent to the evolution toward the manufacture of baked brick. Thick square tiles of terra-cotta were, however, used in paving around drains (fortresses at Askut, Mirgissa) in the Middle Kingdom.

Limestone and even granite from Aswan were quarried from the time of the First Dynasty and transported on the Nile. Alabaster, sandstone, and igneous rocks such as basalt, porphyry, and diorite were consistently used in monumental architecture and sculpture. It is noteworthy that the rather primitive process of quarrying and cutting huge blocks of granite by pounding channels around their outline with dolerite balls never evolved into a more elaborate method. The face of crystalline rocks was leveled off by fire and pounding. Smaller blocks were split out by forcing wooden pegs into grooves cut along the outlines and then moistening these pegs or by hammering metal wedges into the grooves.[128] Artisans used copper adzes and saws with emery to dress the blocks perfectly and chisels to carve the meticulous low-relief scenes that covered them. The Egyptians excelled in a monumental architecture of massive well-dressed stone, which was sometimes polished to a high glitter. In domestic architecture walls and floors subject to dampness were lined with stone slabs (Temple-Palace of Ramses III at Medinet Habu).

Timber had to be imported from Lebanon, and it formed the main trade item with Byblos at least since the Second Dynasty. Costly cedar and pine trunks were essential not only for shipbuilding but also for the lofty flagstaffs of the pylons, the ceilings, columns, and doors in temples and palaces. Even during the decline of the later Ramessids the priests of Amun felt compelled to send Unamun with the divine statue "Amun-of-the-Road" to Byblos, where both messenger and divine protector found no hearty welcome at the prince's court.[129] Local wood such as acacia and especially date-palm trunks was adequate for uprights and cheap supports in the living rooms of artisans' houses (ᶜAmarna) or for reinforcing balks set in massive brickwork. The ceilings of humble houses were of brush-wood and reeds plastered with mud and stucco and whitewashed or painted. In more sophisticated construction the rafters were con-

---

[128] S. Clarke and R. Engelbach, *Ancient Egyptian Masonry* (Oxford, 1930), pp. 24 ff.
[129] A. Erman and A. Blackman, *The Literature of the Ancient Egyptians* (London, 1927), pp. 174 ff.

cealed with a light plastered and painted lathing (palace of Amenḥotep III at Malqata).

Ever since the Neolithic Period metals had been mined, especially copper and later gold in Nubia. Not only were the metals essential for making tools, weapons, and ornaments, but they were directly used in architecture. For example, thin sheets of gold and electrum on a stucco base were used as lining for some of the low relief on walls, ceilings, doors, or obelisks, or as thicker facings on pavement; electrum and copper were used as sheaths for the tips of the obelisks and flagstaffs. Since gold probably symbolized divine life,[130] the lining was supposed to infuse this life into the figures of gods and pharaohs that it covered. Metal dovetails and dowels similar to those made of wood are, however, the only structural metallic elements known.[131]

In the temples at ꜥAmarna a gypsum concrete was poured as a fluid mixture over floors and foundation trenches and was occasionally covered with a layer of earth, which probably had religious symbolism. Mortar and plaster were prepared from gypsum and lime. At ꜥAmarna a public works office examined and tested specimens of gypsum to control their quality. Nevertheless, mortar was not essentially a cohesive medium for the fine joints of stone masonry but was intended as a lubricant and filling. An important material was stucco, which was spread in thin layers over stone and wood alike as a base for painting or carving.

Painting was the finishing process in architecture, sculpture, and carpentry. Walls, columns, ceilings, and rock faces, whether they had a plane or carved surface, had to be painted with scenes and patterns. Even stucco pavements in palaces during the New Kingdom, and probably before that period, were painted. Mineral pigments mixed with a diluted gum or white-of-egg medium were spread over stucco in flat tones or with modeling touches by means of reed brushes.

Techniques. The technique of inlaid pastes was a favorite during the early Fourth Dynasty (tombs at Meydum). The modeled faïence tiles used to decorate walls with scenes during the Third Dynasty (Djeser) and in the Ramesside palaces (temple-palaces at Medinet Habu) add the glitter of variegated colors.

It is questionable whether the Egyptian builders ever knew of construction machines any more elaborate than the sledge hauled by long rows of workmen or beasts up the ramps of sand or brickwork,

---

[130] F. Daumas, "La valeur de l'or dans la pensée égyptienne," *Revue de l'Histoire des Religions*, Vol. CXLIX, Part I (Paris, 1956), pp. 1–17; "Les Mammisis des temples égyptiens," *Annales de l'Université de Lyon*, Troisième Série—Lettres-Fascicule 32 (Paris, 1958), pp. 151–158. P. Lacau, "L'Or dans l'architecture égyptienne," *Annales du Service des Antiquités de l'Égypte*, Vol. LIII (Cairo, 1955), pp. 221–250.
[131] Clarke and Engelbach, *Masonry*, p. 113.

simple windlasses and pulleys (Djeser), crowbars, and ropes. There is no evidence of any machine besides the small wooden models of the so-called "rocker," consisting of a pair of wooden boards in the shape of a crescent held vertically and parallel by connecting transverse bars, which was probably used to adjust a row of stone blocks in a makeshift course during the process of dressing rather than for raising the blocks.[132] As to the tools, we know that stone and wooden hammers, copper saws and drills using moistened sand and emery, adzes, chisels, plumb bobs, wooden triangles, knotted ropes, and simple alidades were in common use.[133] Construction ramps were discovered in the remains next to the pyramid of Snefru at Meydum,[134] Chephren at Giza, Amenemḥat at Lisht, and Pylon I at Karnak.[135] The ramp made of brick caissons filled with sand grew with the monument till it reached the uppermost level, and it was gradually leveled down after the finishing process on the outer faces of the walls or pyramids. Materials and huge monolithic elements were transported sometimes from as far south as Aswan or from the eastern desert quarries to the riverbanks, where they were loaded on river barges. These barges are occasionally represented as laden with columns (causeway of Unas at Saqqara) or twin obelisks (temple of Ḥatshepsut). It is possible that most of the shipping was done during the inundation season. Blocks and large monoliths were hauled on sledges from the quays to the buildings (relief in Ṭura, transport of the colossus of Djeḥutiḥetep from his tomb at Bersha), and even across the rocky tracts of the desert, occasionally gliding on balks that were jagged underneath to provide a firm grip against thrust.[136]

Wooden scaffoldings were erected for carving large statues where a clear view of the whole was essential (tomb of Rekhmireᶜ), and perhaps they were also used in construction, though the courses of brickwork or masonry could have been repeatedly formed into stepped gangways during the building process. It has been assumed, from the evidence of peculiar holes found in the pavement beneath the heavy monoliths, that these blocks could have been set upright by means of windlasses or pulleys (Hölscher's theory).[137] The obelisk

132 *Ibid.*, p. 94.

133 W. Fl. Petrie, *Tools and Weapons* (London, 1917).

134 L. Borchardt, *Einiges zur dritten Bauperiode der grossen Pyramide bei Gise* (Berlin, 1932). Badawy, *Egyptian Architecture*, Vol. I, Fig. 101, p. 153.

135 Clarke and Engelbach, *Masonry*, Figs. 87–88. A. Choisy, *L'Art de bâtir chez les Égyptiens* (Paris, 1904), pp. 86 ff.

136 P. E. Newberry, *El Bersheh*, Part I, "The Tomb of Tehuti-Hetep" (London, 1894), pl. XV, p. 24, n. 2. There is clear evidence from the texts above the watercarriers that the liquid poured in front of the sledge was water, not oil or milk as presumed by Clarke and Engelbach, *Masonry*, p. 85 (oil) and Fakhry, *The Pyramids*, p. 12 (milk). Alexander Badawy, "The Transport of the Colossus of Djehutihetep," *Mitteilungen des Instituts für Orientforschung*, Vol. VIII (Berlin, 1963), pp. 325–332.

137 U. Hölscher, *Das Grabdenkmal des Königs Chephren* (Leipzig, 1912). Clarke and Engelbach, *Masonry*, Fig. 164. Badawy, *Egyptian Architecture*, Vol. I, p. 181, Fig. 123.

could have been slid to the top of an artificial mound of sand so that its bottom would overhang above the prepared base, and then could be tilted gradually down a brickwork shaft filled with sand and set smoothly on the prepared base by letting the sand flow down (Choisy's theory).[138]

Construction proceeded in successive layers, the outline of the structure usually being engraved at each level on the course of masonry beneath it. The final dressing was begun at the top, with the carving of scenes in low relief, and ultimately the surface was covered with thin stucco and painted.

Elaborate foundation ceremonies were performed for official monuments according to a traditional religious ritual enacted by Pharaoh himself. Murals show the various stages of these ceremonies: pegging out the outline of the plan, cutting the foundation trench, pouring sand, and striking the first brick.[139] Foundation deposits consisting of miniature tools, gold or enamel bricks, plaques and vases bearing the name of the building and those of the Pharaoh were laid in special caskets beneath the corners of the building or the gates or even in round holes in the courtyard (Ḥatshepsut at Deir el Baḥari).

The Construction of the Pyramids.[140] This is certainly one of the most fascinating problems of Egyptian architecture, especially the building of such huge structures as the two larger pyramids at Giza, where the techniques of surveying and building attain an astounding degree of accuracy. As we have seen, the construction ramps were the means of access to the structure at successive times during construction. Many special difficulties inherent in the pyramids had to be overcome, such as twist during construction and deflection from exact orientation. The pyramids at Giza were built on the leveled-down bedrock, a process checked with reference to the level of water let into a special channel dug around the area. All pyramids from the Old Kingdom have a prismatic core about which successive layers with a steep slope (74°–77°, 4–5 m. thick) are laid. Construction proceeds, however, in horizontal courses, while the internal apartments are built first. The outer faces are formed from a casing of prismatic blocks set concurrently with the courses and finally dressed from the top downward. It is noteworthy that the various angles of incline were probably laid out empirically and checked consistently during the process by means of triangles that gave the proportions of the height to the horizontal length (abscissa-and-ordinate method).

138 Choisy, *L'Art de bâtir*, pp. 124 ff.
139 Clarke and Engelbach, *Masonry*, pp. 60 ff., Fig. 61.
140 *Ibid.*, pp. 117–129. Edwards, *The Pyramids of Egypt*, pp. 205 ff. Badawy, *Egyptian Architecture*, Vol. I, pp. 152–157.

From the time of the Fifth Dynasty the gables forming a roof for the inner rooms were in two or three layers of inclined blocks (Neuserre^c at Abusir), which were actually superfluous and built with obvious carelessness.

The pyramids of the Middle Kingdom are not set on the bedrock, and their inner structure is different from the earlier ones, since they often show a framework of radiating and transverse retaining walls composed of stone or brick. An initial excavation was dug, into which the huge quartzite burial chamber was slid. This was roofed over with a superimposed series of stone ceiling, stone gable, and brick vault (three rings or more), surrounded by the corridors with their elaborate plugs. The superstructure, which was mostly brick, was then built.

The Style[141]

In the Archaic Period many of the typical stylistic elements had already begun to assume their definitive forms. From the earliest architecture using plant stems such as reeds, palm fronds, and papyrus are derived the following:

1. The torus, a rounded molding beneath the cavetto cornice stretching along the edges of a façade. It is derived from the bundles of stems that formed the framework of a wickerwork wall (Djeser's complex; Fig. 1, upper right).

2. The cavetto cornice,[142] with its sectional outline first seen as a straight slanting edge (Djeser's complex), and later as an elegant curve. It is derived from the top ends fanning out from the vertical plant stems curved into a flat vault (Fig. 1, upper right).

3. The *kheker* frieze, featuring a row of independent vertical elements with an elegant outline, derived from the loose ends of the vertical stems in a wickerwork wall bound together into bundles at regular intervals (cabins of boats in paintings on predynastic pottery; Fig. 1, lower right).

4. The scalloped parapet from the looped upper ends of the uprights (cabins of boats; Fig. 1, lower right).

5. The columns with various capitals were derived originally from a single stem of papyrus (Djeser's complex) or a bundle of reeds bound at the top (concave and convex ribs in Djeser's complex; Fig. 10, top left).[143]

To the structural use of mud must be ascribed the characteristic appearance of the faces of a wall with its rounded top (predynastic

---

[141] Badawy, *Egyptian Architecture*, Vol. I, pp. 190 ff.
[142] *Ibid.*, pp. 79–81, Figs. 58, 59.
[143] *Ibid.*, Fig. 60.

Fig. 10→

BUNDLE OF BUNDLE COLUMN
STEMS (DJESER, 28TH CENT. B.C.)

OPEN PAPYRIFORM
(DJESER, SAQQARA)

PALMIFORM (SAHURE 25TH CENT. B.C.)

PAINTINGS OF LOTIFORM

BUNDLE LOTIFORM
(ABUSIR, 25TH CENT. B.C.)

BUNDLE PAPYRIFORM
(SAHURE 25TH CENT. B.C.)

BUNDLE
LOTIFORM
BENI HASSAN
(18TH CENT. B.C.)

PORTICO OF ANUBIS

TEMPLE OF HATSHEPSUT

(COLUMNS

OPEN
PAPYRIFORM
KARNAK 13TH CENT.
B.C.

COMPOSITE
CAPITAL
(PTOLEMAIC)

TENT-POLE COLUMN
FESTIVAL HALL OF TUTHMOSIS III
(KARNAK, 15TH CENT. B.C.)

14TH CENT. B.C.
PAINTING OF
COMPOSITE
CAPITAL

HATHORIC CAPITAL (HATSHEPSUT. CENT. B.C.)

15TH

model of a house from El ʿAmrah; Fig. 1, bottom right). This feature soon became standard and was kept traditionally throughout the history of Egyptian architecture, though the rounded top was not needed in structures of brick and stone. The role of tradition enforced by the learned priesthood in Egyptian architecture, as well as in other aspects of Egyptian civilization, can never be overstressed. The so-called "recessed paneling" and "palace façade" types of wall articulation resulted from the use of brickwork within a wooden framework with mats hanging over the recesses (Fig. 5, middle right; tombs of the First Dynasty and the *serekh*).[144]

Whereas the earliest extensive building in stone is copied directly from plant structure (Djeser),[145] the huge pyramids and mortuary temples of the Fourth Dynasty[146] represent a completely different stylistic trend. This style expresses frankly and in an impressive way the functional and intrinsic aesthetic value of superior stone, such as large highly polished blocks of granite, alabaster, basalt, and limestone. Plant materials and their forms are no longer copied; now massive quadrangular piers replace the plant columns, and even mural decoration is reduced to the sober use of some ritual scene and inscriptions. This so-called "Giza style" conforms closely to the impressive dignity of royal statuary expressing the concept of the divinity of Pharaoh (Fig. 7, top right).

Contrasting with this style, during the Fifth and Sixth Dynasties[147] the architecture reverts to interpretations derived from plants, but it is highly stylized and extensively employs scenes of ritual or lay character carved in low relief on the walls of the temples and tomb chapels, and always elaborately painted with flat color. This is the period of the elegant monolithic granite columns[148] of the palmiform, bundle lotiform, and bundle papyriform types (Fig. 10, top right and middle left), where the original plant form blends harmoniously with the geometry of the lines as a result of a successful stylization. Rhythm and symmetry evolve more freely in the Sixth Dynasty. The stark structural nakedness of the Fourth Dynasty has long vanished, replaced by a slender grace molded out of hard rocks.

A striking feature of Egyptian culture, and especially its architecture, is its sensitivity to the social and political environment. The troubled First Intermediate Period marks a lull in creative activity, and when it starts again in the Eleventh Dynasty, a rather primitive

[144] *Ibid.*, pp. 60–61, Fig. 45.
[145] *Ibid.*, pp. 190–191.
[146] *Ibid.*, p. 191. H. Junker, "Von der ägyptischen Baukunst des Alten Reiches," *Zeitschrift für Ägyptische Sprache und Altertumskunde*, Vol. 63 (Berlin, 1927,) pp. 1–7.
[147] Badawy, *Egyptian Architecture*, Vol. I, p. 192.
[148] G. Jequier, *Manuel d'Archéologie égyptienne*, Vol. I, *Les Éléments de l'architecture* (Paris, 1924), pp. 196 ff.

approach to realistic aesthetics is conspicuous in the painting, sketchy low relief, or the statuary. The elongated high-waisted figure is perhaps groping for elegance and classicist excellence, to be achieved later in Middle Kingdom art. The term "classicist," which reminds one of the classicism of Greece, is not extraneous, for the so-called "proto-Doric" column (Beni Ḥassan, 5–6 diameters to the height) used in porticoes does resemble the Greek Doric in the rhythm, the slight batter of the shaft (entasis), and the dentils of the architrave. Besides the favored palmiform column carved of wood and common in domestic architecture, the slender lotiform (7 diameters), and the polygonal columns, a new type appears that imitates the handle of the sistrum, the characteristic musical instrument of the goddess Ḥatḥor (Fig. 10, bottom left). Rectangular pillars carved in low relief endow the small peripteral station-chapel of Sesostris I at Karnak with refined classicist simplicity (Fig. 6, upper left). This fine taste in art reflects that in contemporaneous literature.[149]

At a time when the abundant riches of a great empire and the increased influences from Mesopotamia and Crete could have marred Egyptian taste, architecture still exhibits remarkable elegance, rhythm, and a bold concept of spatial treatment in the terraced porticoes of Ḥatshepsut at Deir el Baḥari (Fig. 10, middle). More than ever does colossal but sophisticated statuary become integrated into architecture (Osiride pillars of Ḥatshepsut, alleys of sphinxes, statues of pharaohs in temples). There is a trend toward the colossal in the huge pylons and porticoes, which are sometimes fronted by colonnaded approaches (Amenḥotep III at Luxor and Karnak). Crafts are enriched with new motifs, and fashionable techniques of glazed tile, inlay, wood carving, and stucco are invented for the versatile decoration of palaces. Colors transform common materials with a glittering mantle of bold compositions and lively scenes (palace at Malqata).

Though not entirely an incidental intrusion, the ᶜAmarna interlude certainly strikes a discordant note in the artistic development. Its interpretation of aesthetics can be regarded as a personal achievement of Akhenaten, emphasizing his concept of "truth." The naturalism that often verges on inelegance in sculpture is also responsible for the bulky shapes of columns burdened with pendent bunches of ducks and plants in the rock tombs at ᶜAmarna. There is no doubt that the symbolism of the power of the sun disk Aten as Creator is a basic element in the design. This peculiar style successfully combines efficiency of function, harmony, and economy in the

[149] W. Hayes, "The Middle Kingdom in Egypt," *Cambridge Ancient History*, Vol. I, Chapter XX, §XV, "Art and Architecture," pp. 51 ff. (Cambridge, 1961).

plans of villas, adapting for its purposes new elements such as the so-called "broken lintel" or using new materials and structural techniques such as concrete and plaster casting to meet the depleted finances.

An immediate result of the ʿAmarna Period is an integration of a lively naturalism, often even realism, into later art. The trend toward the colossal in architectural statuary explains the extensive use of the Osiride statues in the courtyards of the Ramesside temples (Medinet Habu) and the colossi of pharaohs seated in front of the pylons and rock-cut temples (Abu Simbel, Gebel Barkal). In this field, as in historical records, Ramses II is the most ubiquitous of all pharaohs, probably using colossal statuary as a means of political propaganda. With an overwhelming demand for hasty execution of colossal monuments, the cheaper techniques introduced by Akhenaten deteriorate into an erratic process (Abu Simbel), while the style loses much of its elegance and life and displays static massiveness or even clumsiness (Osiride pillars, columns). Proportions become unnatural and ugly under Ramses III. Walls and columns in temples are now covered with low relief that is deeply sunken when carved in sunlit areas, but it displays a disconcerting virtuosity in design often verging on confusion. Color also has added its variegated richness to an already dubious subservience to *horror vacui*, an un-Egyptian characteristic.

These are signs of the impending decadence which the patriotic pharaohs of the Saitic Dynasty will try to check for a while by copying rather than interpreting masterpieces from the Old Kingdom heritage.

The obvious uniformity of monumental architecture throughout the ages, which is ascribed to traditionalism and symbolism, could not have been achieved if the design had not conformed from the earliest times, at least from the Third Dynasty, to a harmonic system of proportions. There is evidence that this uniformity was consistently attained by means of a graphic method using the empiric element of an isosceles triangle in the proportion 8:5 and a related square. This system was allied at ʿAmarna, and probably earlier elsewhere (sun temple of Neuserreʿ), with the use of consecutive numbers of a summation called Series of Fibonacci,[150] 3, 5, 8, 13, 21, 34, 55, 89, 144, . . ., for the actual dimensions of monuments in cubits of 0.523 meters of the basic elements in a design (plan or elevation).

Among the various styles of architecture of the ancient Near East

[150] Alexander Badawy, "The Harmonic System of Architectural Design in Ancient Egypt," *Mitteilungen des Instituts für Orientforschung*, Vol. VIII (Berlin, 1961), pp. 1–14; *Ancient Egyptian Architectural Design: A Study of the Harmonic System* (Berkeley: University of California Press, 1965).

that of Egypt is especially noted for its consistent use of the trabeated style and its beautiful columns. The column in Egyptian architecture[151] deserves special notice, for it is more than a structural element with aesthetic effects, because it is always pregnant with religious symbolism, whether it is used in religious or lay structures.

For the purpose of study it is convenient to differentiate the *plant-column* from the *structural column* according to origin. Many of the typical plants of the autochthonous landscape have lent their forms to stylization even before Djeser's complex at Saqqara, where several types of columns, all incorporated with the stone masonry and built in courses appear:

1. The papyrus, whose shaft imitates a single stem, which is triangular in cross section and topped with an open flower as a capital (Fig. 10, top middle). It is symbolic of Lower Egypt and also of "green" or "young," and when set in rows in a temple, it conveys the concept of papyrus thickets, particularly the one where Isis and her infant Horus hid at Chemmis in the Delta (Mammisi chapel design).[152]

2. The lily (?), with a single round stem topped by a flower with two curving sides in the shape of volutes, symbolic of Upper Egypt.

3. The bundle shaft with convex ribs imitating a bundle of reeds bound at the top by a sheath. It is without a capital but is surmounted by an abacus and colored red (Fig. 10, top left).

4. The bundle shaft with concave ribs or flutes, already developed in the First Dynasty (miniature tube for *kohl*).

The plant-column reaches its full development in the very elegant monolithic buildings of hard stone erected during the Fifth Dynasty. The palmiform column, symbolic of the date-palm forests of Lower Egypt, features a capital of palm fronds bound by five rows of rope to a slender, nearly cylindrical shaft on a shallow base (Fig. 10, middle left). The lotiform column imitates a bundle of opening buds of the fragile lotus bound together by a rope in five rows at the top of their round stems (Fig. 10, top right). The bundle papyriform column is similar to the lotiform one except for its stems, which are triangular in section (Fig. 10, middle left).

There is no doubt that these elegant monolithic columns are copied from the slender ones made of stuccoed and painted wood that are used in domestic architecture and represented in contemporaneous scenes (Fig. 10, top middle). Some of the scenes show elaborate columns of an extraordinarily versatile design, consisting basically of

[151] Jequier, *Les Éléments de l'architecture.*
[152] Alexander Badawy, "The Architectural Symbolism of the Mammisi-Chapels in Egypt," *Chronique d'Égypte,* Vol. XXXVIII (Brussels, 1963), pp. 78–90.

three superimposed stages, one with a lotus, one a lily, and one a papyrus flower (Fig. 10, bottom right).

In the early New Kingdom monolithic columns are still aesthetic achievements (Ḥatshepsut, Tuthmosis III), and even the large columns built of drums retain much beauty, though stylized beyond recognition (Amenḥotep III; Fig. 10, lower middle). The open papyriform column already appearing in Djeser's mortuary complex now features a similar capital with a recurving outline, but it is set on a shaft that is circular in section with slight entasis. In the Ramesside monuments the column assumes debased bulky proportions. In the Ptolemaic Period composite capitals are fashionable in monumental architecture of stone, and are derived from the open papyriform capital covered with a rich applied decoration of floral elements such as vines, palmettes, and volutes (Fig. 10, bottom middle).

The structural column is derived from the pillar of quadrangular section chamfered into a polygonal shaft[153] (octagonal at Deir el Baḥari, Dynasty XI; sixteen-sided from Dynasty XII to XVIII). Occasionally slight ridges mark the edges. Whether the fluted shaft developed from the bundle column or from the polygonal pillar is controversial, though the vertical profile would speak in favor of the pillar. Mention should also be made of the tent-pole column with a bell-shaped (campaniform) capital and the shaft with an inverted taper (Festival Hall of Tuthmosis III at Karnak; Fig. 10, bottom right) and of the Ḥathoric pillar or column, which imitates the sistrum handle and is topped with one, two, or four masks of the goddess Ḥathor in high relief just below the façade of her shrine (Middle Kingdom; Fig. 10, bottom left). Both the sistrum and the Ḥathoric column symbolize "joy."

The arrangement of columns in a temple or a tomb conforms to the symbolism implied by the type of column used. In one hall open papyriform columns will be set in the northern part and lily columns in the southern part, emblematic of Lower and Upper Egypt, respectively (tomb of Aḥanekht at Bersha). In the hypostyle hall the taller columns bordering the nave are always of the open papyriform type, while those flanking them in both aisles are of the bundle type, either papyriform or lotiform. It has already been mentioned that the mortuary temples of the Old Kingdom also show symbolism in their column arrangement.

In conclusion, let us appraise briefly the significance of Egyptian architecture. It is undoubtedly the earliest architecture to succeed both in fulfilling functional requirements and in achieving aesthetic refinement, while it very often had to conform also to religious symbolism. Its vitality, upheld by a stark traditionalism, enabled it

[153] Clarke and Engelbach, *Masonry*, pp. 137–138.

to outlast all subsequent architectures. Endowed with originality, the Egyptians invented the basic elements of both trabeated and vaulted systems of construction in stone and brick and devised the stylistic canons and components that were transformed by the Greeks into classical architecture, the basis of architecture till the turn of the century (see Chart 1, pp. 226–227).

PART II

THE ANCIENT NEAR EAST

Mesopotamia

The Physical Environment

Mesopotamia, "the land between the two rivers," was so named by the Greeks because it actually is a narrow alluvial plain between the Tigris and the Euphrates enclosed by a ring of deserts. At the beginning of our geological period the sea penetrated much farther inland, forming a gulf that later filled in gradually with silt deposits from the two rivers. The whole plain was covered annually by water. Unlike the inundation in Egypt, however, this flood was as harmful as it was beneficial, for the salt that impregnated the earth had to be drained from the arable land, and a whole system of canals and dikes was devised in early times, often worked with hand pumps in Herodotus' time.[1] Since the Euphrates proved to be more regular than the Tigris, the earliest settlements grew along its course. Later, however, the bed of the Euphrates rose gradually on account of the silt deposit, causing disastrous floods, while the Tigris, cutting its bed deeper, lost its torrential flow and became navigable, and thus settlers were induced to lay out towns along its banks.

In spite of abundant rains during several weeks in winter, there is a long summer of six months with hot, humid weather that is occasionally relieved by a mild wind from the northeast Zagros Mountains. Whatever unfavorable conditions there might have been, agriculture, which was probably based on a system of rotation, flourished. Mesopotamia is presumably the land where wheat and

[1] Herodotus, *Histories*, Bk. I, par. 193.

75

barley originated. These two staple foods were complemented by the providential date palm and a variety of vegetables as well as the sesame and castor-oil plants. Breeding of cattle, geese, ducks, and chicken provided meat, a welcome addition to the fish diet. Early food gatherers could indulge in hunting wild ducks, cranes, hares, gazelles, boars, onagers, elephants, and even wolves, leopards, bears, and lions,[2] in the tall rushes of the swamps or in the steppes.

These rushes provided materials for the construction of huts, which in due time evolved into houses built of clay. A central courtyard effectively protected the occupants against the sudden scorching winds and the glaring sun. An orientation to the northeast was given to the temples, probably to take advantage of the prevailing mild winds. The structures were set high up on superimposed platforms out of reach of the floods.

At an early stage in the development of Mesopotamian architecture a very ingenious use was made of mud and bitumen, two materials of construction that occurred in rich deposits. A type of plano-convex brick and later also a rectangular one were invented. The latter type, unlike the Egyptian brick, was often baked, set in bitumen, and faced with terra-cotta tiles and rows of pegs for the construction of platforms and walls. Since Mesopotamia, like other alluvial lands, was poor in metals and timber, these formed an essential part of the imports.

Foreign relations maintained by Mesopotamia radiated south to the Indian Ocean, northeast to the mountains of Iran and Armenia, and northwest to the Mediterranean basin.[3] It is noteworthy that the desert of Syria is the land closest to the point where the two rivers flow nearest to each other along the middle Euphrates, so that caravan routes passed through it to reach the Mediterranean coast and thence proceeded south or to the harbors.

The Social Environment

The people who settled toward the end of the fourth millennium B.C. in Sumer in southern Mesopotamia were non-Semitic and called themselves the "black-headed people." The inhabited area of about 20,000 square kilometers expanded from Eridu, Ur, Larsa, Lagash, and Uruk northward to Nippur, Kish, and the Diyala River. Each of these city-states centered around the temenos of the temple of the god who was called the "King of the City," and they were ruled by the high priest,[4] who owned, together with the palace courtiers and

---

[2] H. Schmökel, *Das Land Sumer* (Stuttgart, 1956), p. 44. G. Maspero, *The Dawn of Civilisation, Egypt and Chaldaea* (London, 1922), pp. 556–560.

[3] S. Moscati, *Ancient Semitic Civilizations* (New York, 1960), pp. 48–49.

[4] Schmökel, *Sumer*, p. 81. S. N. Kramer, *The Sumerians* (Chicago, 1963), reviewed in *Archaeology*, Vol. 16 (New York, 1963), p. 137.

priests, about half the city-state, the remainder belonging to the citizens. About the high priest, who carried out the important offices, and his family there were scribes, traders, craftsmen, soldiers, peasants, and slaves. The slave enjoyed certain prerogatives, such as the right to marry a free person and to shift from one master to another.

Pictographic writing appeared here as early as in Egypt, marking the beginning of a period of high civilization and high ethics in family life and public justice, systematized in a code of laws issued by King Lipit-Ishtar of Isin (1875–1865 B.C.). No wonder this Sumerian civilization influenced the Semitic invaders (*ca.* 2350 B.C.) so strongly.

Though the earliest rulers assumed such titles as "King of the Country" (Sumer), "King of Sumer and Akkad," "King of Assur," or even "King of the Four Regions" and "King of the World," it was only much later, in the seventh century B.C., that the Sargonids could pretend to such an extensive dominion, stretching from Lake Van to Upper Egypt and from Cilicia to Media.[5]

The sociological structure appears in clear-cut features, for, as in Egypt, kingship is of divine origin and the king is an intermediary between the gods and the people but with the important difference that in Mesopotamia the king was the servant of the law. There is also an assembly of elders who may delegate their power to one ruler in case of crisis. The king is the commandant of the army and controls a centralized government, also appointing the governors. The state establishes prices and fees and directs public works, cadastre, and farming. According to the Code of Hammurabi (1728–1686 B.C.) of the First Dynasty of Babylon, society consists of three classes: the "man" (citizen), the half-free man, and the slave (who is owned property). The wife enjoys a legally independent status that is restricted under the Assyrians but again fully acknowledged under the Sargonids (7th–6th centuries B.C.).

Religion

Sumerian religion was maintained by the Semites as the framework of the social pattern. In contrast to the cult of the dead in Egypt, it never was given much importance in Mesopotamia, except perhaps under the First and Third Dynasties of Ur. As to the gods, there were universal deities such as Inanna-Dumuzi (later Ishtar-Tammuz), a couple personifying life-death, or Enki, god of the primeval ocean, wisdom, and crafts, or Enlil, state god of destiny. While the main temple of the "Lord of the Town" is the focus of the urban layout,

[5] A. Aymard and J. Auboyer, *L'Orient et la Grèce antique* (Paris, 1959), p. 116.

public chapels appear along the streets, numbering as many as fifty at Lagash (third millennium B.C.).

The temple develops from the earliest shrine into an architectural complex. Often it has a monumental layout and is set on a platform in the best location of the city, with its own workshops, magazines, and library. An autochthonous type of religious building in the shape of a stepped pyramid imitating the cosmic sacred mountain is the ziqurrat. It appears in the Third Dynasty of Ur (2050 B.C.) and is so located in the urban layout as to form the main vista. This ziqurrat and the other religious structures are, as a rule, oriented to the cardinal points by their corners. It is thought that religious factors account for this orientation, though the prevailing wind from the northeast might have been of some influence. On the other hand, it is probably not a mere coincidence that the axis of the temple (Ur) runs northeast–southwest, parallel to the transverse axis of the city, which is oval in shape, extending along the banks of the two rivers, which both flow to the southeast. Flanked by the public monuments, the main street is a processional avenue, along which the people carry their gods to the Feast House in a park outside the city, as prescribed by the ritual of the New Year Festival.

Towns are usually named after the deity to whom they are dedicated. Here, as in Egypt, even walls, gates, streets, and canals are sacred entities bearing religious names of symbolic implication: the gateway of Adad in Babylon is "O-Adad, keep-the-life-of-the-crowds," and a certain street is "Nabu-is-the-judge-of-his-subjects."[6] Boundary stelae of property, as well as the numerous colossi or genii that protect the city, are also dedicated to gods.

The founding of a town can be specifically requested by a god, and we are informed that King Tukulti-Ninurta I (1235–1198 B.C.) is asked by the god Bel to found Kar-Tukulti-Ninurta. Founding ceremonies are celebrated according to an elaborate ritual reminiscent of the one performed in Egypt consecrating the territory and the structure to a god.

History

About the ninth millennium B.C. food gatherers settle in caves (Shanidar) and open sites (Zawi Chemi Shanidar). Later food-producing communities build villages (Jarmo), invent irrigation for agriculture, and breed sheep, donkeys, and oxen.[7] History begins when the Sumerians settle in Lower Mesopotamia, founding city-

[6] P. Dhorme, *La religion assyro-babylonienne* (Paris, 1910), pp. 122–124.

[7] R. J. Braidwood, "Prelude to Civilization," in C. Kraeling and R. M. Adams, eds., *City Invincible* (Chicago, 1960), pp. 297–313, 306–307. R. Adams, "Early Civilizations, Subsistence, and Environment," in *City Invincible*, pp. 269–295.

states that are owned by the god and ruled by priest-kings. Theirs must have been a hectic life indeed, for they regulate irrigation, distribute the means of subsistence, build temples, and write religious and trade documents while feuding with one another. Archaeological finds occur in occupation layers at Uruk (IV–VI, 3000–2800 B.C.) and Djemdet-Nasr (2800–2600 B.C.). When the autocratic royal rule replaces the system of the high priest and the city-state, a functional duality marks the split between the god and the king; thus about 2600 B.C. King Mesilim has his capital at Kish, while Nippur is the religious center.

The kings of the First Dynasty of Ur (2500 B.C.) are accompanied in death by their retainers, who drink voluntarily from poisoned cups, clad in their best garb and performing music in the midst of elaborate furniture. The separation between god and king is often marred by a rivalry that passes through various cycles.

After he conquers Umma, the city of Lugalzaggisi (2350 B.C.), Sargon founds a Semitic dynasty (2350–2150 B.C.), establishing his capital at Akkad, 60 kilometers north of Kish, and strengthening his empire by extending his rule over Elam, Babylonia, Assyria, and even Syria, Cyprus, and Asia Minor. Though he recognizes the god Enlil in Nippur, he destroys the walls of the fortified cities in Sumer. The state becomes a centralized system that is based on the royal power backed by the officials and the soldiers. Official inscriptions are in Akkadian or Sumerian, or perhaps both, but for nonofficial texts Akkadian is used exclusively in the north, while Sumerian predominates in the south. We can thus define Mesopotamian civilization as a synthesis of Sumerian and Akkadian components.[8]

The invasions of the barbarian Guti from the Zagros Mountains (2150 B.C.) are followed by a Sumerian interlude with the peace-loving Gudea of Lagash (2050–2000 B.C.) and the Third Dynasty of Ur (2065–1955 B.C.). Although the Sumerian language enjoys a renaissance, the process of Akkadianization grows in the whole country.

Of the several dynasties founded by the Semitic Amorites at Mari on the middle Euphrates, and Isin and Larsa (1970–1698 B.C.) in southern Mesopotamia, that of the First Dynasty of Babylon attains pre-eminence (1830–1530 B.C.). Its most famous king, Hammurabi (1728–1686 B.C.), unites the whole country with Babylon as capital and brings prosperity through the development of agriculture and irrigation. He also proclaims Marduk the chief god and issues a new code of laws covering both Sumerian and Semitic jurisprudence.

After the First Dynasty of Babylon is brought to an end by a short Hittite rule (1530 B.C.), it is replaced by that of the Kassites, an

[8] Moscati, *Semitic Civilizations*, p. 49.

eastern people with Indo-European elements who had infiltrated Babylonia (1560–1200 B.C.). They try to adopt Sumerian and Babylonian cultures, which they acknowledge as being superior to their own, and the Akkadian language becomes the lingua franca of the whole Near East.

The Assyrian state existed for some centuries. An Akkadian dynasty founded by Ilushuma (19th century B.C.) is followed by the Amorites' rule, under Shamshi Adad I, a contemporary of Hammurabi of Babylon. The period of decline, when the Assyrians are overwhelmed by the Mitanni (1430–1390 B.C.), is followed by independence and growth of power under Tukulti-Ninurta (1235–1198 B.C.), who subdues Babylon. A century later Tiglath-Pileser I (1116–1078 B.C.) founds the New Empire, extending to the Black Sea, the Mediterranean, and Babylonia. Checked by the Aramaeans for a century and a half, the Assyrians resume their conquering march under Tiglath-Pileser III (745–727 B.C.). By nature a warlike people, the Assyrians control the mountain passes to the north, as well as Syria-Palestine to the west with the road to Egypt, but they gain Babylonia through diplomacy. Esarhaddon curbs Egypt for a short period, and Assurbanipal (668–629 B.C.) is the last of the Assyrian conquerors. In its turn Assyria is conquered by the Medes from Iran, who destroy the capital at Nineva (612 B.C.).

Babylonia allies itself with the Medes against Assyria. General Nabopolassar, who helped in the conquest of Nineva, founds the Neo-Babylonian Dynasty (625–538 B.C.), of Aramaean origin. His son Nebuchadnezzar takes Jerusalem (586 B.C.) and raises Babylon to its climax through his wise rule. Its fortifications, however, soon fall to the Persian king Cyrus (539 B.C.).

Towns

While traces of human life appear in the caves of northern Mesopotamia and on open sites at Karim Shahir, no permanent habitations are found before those at Jarmo, a village of 12,000 square meters consisting of solid rectangular buildings dating from between the seventh and the fifth millennia B.C. Besides Jarmo and later Hassuna, thousands of small villages, often surrounded by walls, are established in northern Mesopotamia.[9] Here philology can make its small contribution, for it is noteworthy that there is no word for "city" in either Sumerian or Akkadian, yet a manor or estate, *è* (Akkadian *bitu*), is differentiated from a citylike settlement, *uru* (Akkadian *alu*).[10]

The earliest urban settlements appear in a small district near the

[9] K. Kenyon, *Archaeology in the Holy Land* (London, 1960), p. 59.
[10] I. Gelb, in *City Invincible*, p. 91.

Persian Gulf, perhaps developing from the aggregation of prehistoric settlements. They all feature in their center the temenos of the temple as the nucleus of the layout. The streets radiating from a central plaza are paved with stone and have a public drain (Tepe Gawra);[11] their corners are rounded off for easier circulation. In all periods, subsidiary streets are unpaved, and occasionally dust is controlled by sprinkling water on them. Two types of street layouts can be differentiated: irregular and axial.

The *irregular layout* results from the organic growth of a system of streets, which spreads as one house is built adjacent to the previous one, aggregating in the typical township of the Orient. An oval wall, sometimes very thick (25–30 m. at Ur III) or double (Tepe Gawra VI), surrounds the town. Varying in dimensions, it is 900 by 1,300 meters at Ur (Fig. 11, right top), 2,500 by 3,000 meters at Uruk, 900 to 1,560 by 1,000 meters at Assyrian Assur. At Uruk the wall's remains are still 15 to 18 meters high and 6 meters wide at the top. The oval outline is a natural, intuitive shape given by animals to their shelters and by primitive man to his settlement or house. The orientation of the longer axis of the oval is northwest–southeast, at right angles to its smaller axis, which is itself parallel to that of the main temple. It has already been mentioned that the temple faces northeast whence blows the prevailing wind[12] or for some religious reason, while the town proper expands along the riverbank (northwest–southeast on both Euphrates and Tigris). The internal layout of the town is functionally related to the nucleus formed by the temenos, or sacred enclosure surrounding the temple, and later to a second one around the palace. The temenos is a kind of citadel to provide adequate protection against attack from within the town itself and a last refuge in case of siege. The temenos wall is usually rectangular in outline and oriented by its corners to the four cardinal points. There are recessed panels along its inner and outer faces (Ur III, Tepe Gawra X, Nippur of Dynasty III). Within it are administrative buildings, workshops, and magazines where goods are manufactured with raw materials from the god's estates. The temple proper, set to the rear of a court on a platform (Khafaje, ᶜUbaid) or on the top of a stepped ziqurrat, forms a high landmark in the flat Sumerian plain, a point of contact between heaven and earth, and a constant reminder to the early Sumerian of the omnipresence of his god. The streets are irregular and are connected to one or more arteries running from the gateway to the temenos and to the riverbank. Small public chapels are set at prominent crossings (Ur). Transverse streets, as well as transverse walls, run perpendicular to

[11] E. A. Speiser, *Excavations at Tepe Gawra*, Vol. I (Philadelphia, 1935), pp. 18 ff.
[12] E. Egli, *Geschichte des Städtebaues* (Zurich, 1959), p. 52.

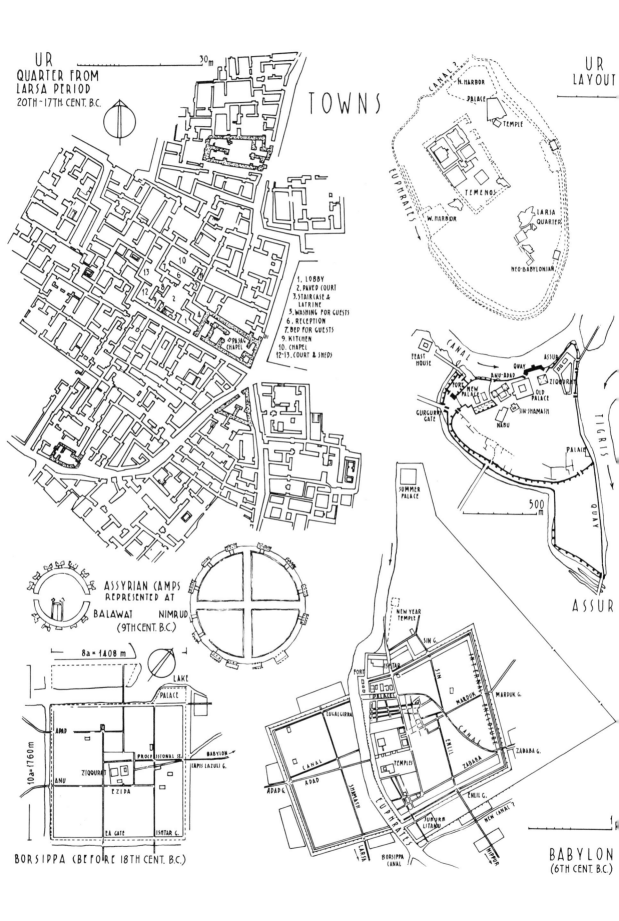

UR
QUARTER FROM
LARSA PERIOD
20TH-17TH. CENT. B.C.

30 m

TOWNS

UR LAYOUT

1. LOBBY
2. PAVED COURT
3. STAIRCASE & LATRINE
5. WASHING FOR GUESTS
6. RECEPTION
7. BED FOR GUESTS
9. KITCHEN
10. CHAPEL
12-13. COURT & SHEDS

PRIVATE CHAPEL

CANAL 2

N. HARBOR
PALACE
TEMPLE

EUPHRATES

W. HARBOR

TEMENOS

LARSA QUARTER

NEO-BABYLONIAN

CANAL

FEAST HOUSE

QUAY ASSUR

ANU-ADAD

FORT
NEW PALACE
ZIQQURAT

OLD PALACE

SIN-SHAMASH

GURGURRI GATE

NABU

PALACE

TIGRIS QUAY

500 m

ASSUR

SUMMER PALACE

ASSYRIAN CAMPS
REPRESENTED AT
BALAWAT NIMRUD
(9TH CENT. B.C.)

8a = 1408 m

LAKE
PALACE

10a = 1760 m

APAD

ANU

PROCESSIONAL ST.
ZIQQURAT
LAPIS LAZULI G.
BABYLON

EZIDA

EA GATE
ISHTAR G.

BORSIPPA (BEFORE 18TH CENT. B.C.)

NEW YEAR TEMPLE

SIN G.
FORT
ISHTAR
SIN
MARDUK
MARDUK G.
PALACES
LUGALGIRRA
ENLIL
ZABABA
ZABABA G.
TEMPLES
CANAL
SHAMASH
ADAD
ADAD G.
ADAD
EUPHRATES
ENLIL G.
NEW CANAL
SUBURB
LITAMU
LARSA
BORSIPPA CANAL
NIPPUR

BABYLON
(6TH CENT. B.C.)

the arteries (Ur; Fig. 11, left top); lanes end in culs-de-sac that form small or large irregular plots, and rounded-off corners on the houses ease circulation of traffic (Ur). Rows of houses stretch with uniform façades along the streets, hiding the internal courtyards and the awnings or small apartments that are erected over the rear area of the terraces as refuges during the hot nights of a long summer. There is no evidence of zoning.

Within this type of layout may be also a system of radiating streets that, although apparently not preplanned, achieves a certain regularity. In the early settlement at Tepe Gawra the streets radiate from a central open area. Much later, at Assur streets run in rings parallel to the enclosure, which is curved as if it were part of a circle drawn from the point of the peninsula upon which the city is built (Fig. 11, middle right).

A more sophisticated *axial layout* is found in the larger cities of later Mesopotamia and occasionally in smaller ones, as in the short-lived city of Kar-Tukulti-Ninurta (1235–1198 B.C., 700 m. to the side). The rectangular outline is oriented by the corners, and its main axis running northwest–southeast is not necessarily straight (880 × 1,408 m., Borsippa; 800 × 1,300 m., Sippar; 2,500 × 5,000 m., Nineva; 1,708 × 1,830 m., Khorsabad; 2,600 × 1,575 m., Babylon). Double walls (Nineva, Babylon) or single walls with bastions (Khorsabad, Babylon) are accessible through two fortified gateways in each of the four sides, and a ditch filled with water surrounds the outer face of the enclosure. As a rule, the axial city is located on a watercourse (Babylon) or a lake (Borsippa; Fig. 11, bottom left). The walls of brick, sometimes combined with bitumen, can reach impressive dimensions (14 m. thick × 19 m. high at Khorsabad). The temenos may be located in the northern area of the layout near the river or in the center of the city. There can be more than one temenos on the hills (Nineva). It may protrude somewhat from the enclosure in the shape of a citadel (Khorsabad) to afford control of the besiegers. At Babylon the temples are grouped within a temenos near the Euphrates bank, while the palaces are near by at the northern end of the city, surrounded by a double wall and covered by a fort extending into the river.

There is clear evidence that the main arteries, some of which are fairly wide (26 m. at Nineva), are laid out in co-ordination with the temenos, since they run at a tangent to it between the opposite gateways of the town. During the New Year Festival the statues of the gods are carried out of the temples in solemn procession to the quay, where they are placed on boats amid the jubilation of the crowds and are rowed against the current to the Feast House, which
←Fig. 11   lies hidden in a palm grove outside the city (Assur, Babylon; Fig. 11,

middle and bottom right). The return itinerary by land is along a processional street leading to one of the gateways of the city. Near the Ishtar Gate at Babylon, both inside and outside the city, the side walls along a considerable stretch of this street are decorated with scenes in colored glazed tiles representing sacred genii and lions. This processional street runs by the entrance of the royal palaces, crosses the temenos of the temples, and winds at right angles along the river-bank to the axis of the bridge crossing the Euphrates to the new city on the opposite bank. Only one of the arteries connects two opposite gateways in the city, possibly a restriction imposed by strategic factors. The others start at one gate and end over against the temenos, which forms an interesting vista in the mannerist style. Only the main streets are paved, and the processional street outside the walls has three tracks of large flagstones forming two runways for chariots (Assur). All public works in urban developments such as streets, gates, and canals are sacred entities bearing theophorous names.

The drab façades along the streets often have a steplike articulation forming a jagged plan in the Neo-Babylonian Period (625–539 B.C.). Behind them the houses are set side by side, each having two stories surrounding one or more courts. There is no zoning, since large plots adjoin smaller ones, and temples are built near small houses in the same block. As soon as one leaves the large paved and drained arteries, one has to follow crooked streets and lanes. The axial system conforms to the general master plan, while the layout of the secondary streets is less systematic.

The typical Assyrian camp, as represented on a low relief (Nimrud, 9th century B.C.; Fig. 11, middle left)[13] with two streets crossing at right angles in the center of a circular enclosed area and connecting opposite gates, is a strictly axial layout with towers protruding from the wall at regular intervals. The scheme calls to mind that represented by the Archaic Egyptian hieroglyph for "town."

The following figures, based on excavation data, give an estimate of the sizes of later cities in Mesopotamia:[14]

City	Hectares (= 10,000 square meters)	Minimum Population
Nineva	647	224,000
Babylon (only royal city inside citadel walls)	202	80,000
Ur, Assur	60–85	18,000

[13] H. Frankfort, *The Art and Architecture of the Ancient Orient* (Pelican History of Art series; Baltimore, 1954), pl. 92B.

[14] H. Frankfort, "Town Planning in Ancient Mesopotamia," *The Town Planning Review*, Vol. XXI (Liverpool, July 1950), pp. 98–115.

The figures given by Greek writers as dimensions of Mesopotamian cities seem, like the Egyptian ones, incredibly large. They should not, however, be too lightly dismissed, especially when they are reported by such a reliable authority as Strabo. The building inscriptions of the kings prove their personal interest in urban works and the existence of public ordinances. It has been recently found that some of the preplanned towns such as Borsippa, Khorsabad, and Babylon are based on schemes conforming to a system of harmonic design.[15]

Houses

The scanty representations of Mesopotamian houses contrast sadly with the numerous paintings showing houses and palaces in the Egyptian tombs. Perhaps the only significant evidence is provided by the typical terra-cotta offering stand from the Third Dynasty of Ur (2065–1955 B.C.) found at Assur in the shape of a model of a house (Fig. 12, middle left),[16] and also shown on seals and reliefs. The original two-storied structure seems to be on a squarish plan with an upper floor covering only the rear of the terrace. Numerous windows open on the façade. The articulation of walls is an imitation of the earliest wattle-and-daub construction using bundles of reeds and mats. The concept of a broad steplike façade is reminiscent of the typical landhouse in Egypt with a terrace or portico facing north. An Assyrian scene represents similar houses both within Susa and in its suburbs.[17] Later representations of huts from Sennacherib's camp at Nineva show a hemispherical roof or high conical dome with a rimmed "eye" or a flat dome surmounted by a semicupola. These are three devices for ventilation similar to the ventilators on the roofs of Egyptian houses or the *mulqaf* of Islamic ones.[18]

Rushes and reeds probably coated with mud were the materials used in the earliest huts, but the prehistoric Sumerians soon invented sun-dried brick for their houses, after an intermediate period during which lumps of mud and plant stems were used (Hassuna I c).[19] This evolution in the use of natural materials of construction was quite similar to what happened in Predynastic and Archaic Egypt. The house plan develops from a single room to a more elaborate scheme

[15] Egli, *Städtebau*, pp. 62–66.
[16] W. Andrae, *Das wiedererstandene Assur* (Leipzig, 1938), p. 76. Alexander Badawy, "Architectural Provision against Heat in the Orient," *Journal of Near Eastern Studies*, Vol. XVII (Chicago, 1958), p. 126, Figs. 2f, 5a.
[17] Frankfort, *Art*, pl. 92B.
[18] Badawy, "Provision," p. 126, Figs. 1, 2a, 2d–e, 5b–c.
[19] S. Lloyd and F. Safar, "Tell Hassuna," *Journal of Near Eastern Studies*, Vol. IV (Chicago, 1945), pp. 255–289, Figs. 31–32, 36, 38. A. L. Perkins, *The Comparative Stratigraphy of Early Mesopotamia* (Studies in Ancient Oriental Civilization, Vol. XXIII), (Chicago, 1949), p. 4.

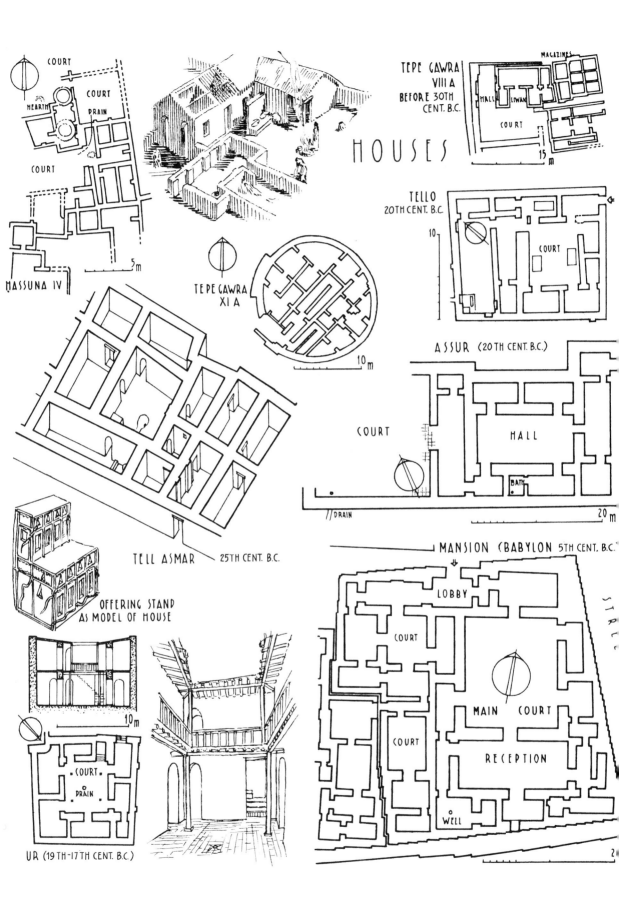

COURT

COURT

HEARTH

COURT

DRAIN

COURT

5 m

HASSUNA IV

HOUSES

TEPE GAWRA
VIII A
BEFORE 30TH
CENT. B.C.

MAGAZINES

HALL   LIWAN

COURT

15 m

TEPE GAWRA
XI A

10 m

TELLO
20TH CENT. B.C.

10

COURT

ASSUR (20TH CENT. B.C.)

COURT

HALL

BATH

DRAIN

20 m

TELL ASMAR   25TH CENT. B.C.

OFFERING STAND
AS MODEL OF HOUSE

MANSION (BABYLON 5TH CENT. B.C.)

LOBBY

COURT

COURT

MAIN   COURT

RECEPTION

WELL

STREET

10 m

COURT

DRAIN

UR (19TH-17TH CENT. B.C.)

with several rooms, bread ovens, jars, floors of rammed earth, and courts (Fig. 12). The central courtyard is perhaps the basic characteristic of Mesopotamian houses. While the courtyard in Egypt stretches in front of the house unit and is usually provided with a columned portico, that in Mesopotamia forms the central open area on which doors and windows open for adequate ventilation and lighting. This difference is related to the difference in the climates, for a central court is the best protection against an exceedingly hot, sunny summer and strong sandstorms from the east and south.

What is striking is the provision, even at such an early stage, for a drain in the court, often the only stone element. Roofs are composed of reeds, and perhaps gabled, on the evidence of contemporaneous models (ʿUbaid, Ḥalaf).[20]

At the beginning of historical times in the Uruk Period (3000–2800 B.C.) the various occupation strata at Tepe Gawra yield data about the development of the house. One example at an early stage (VIII A) is a large structure (15 × 15 m.) with a corner entrance into a courtyard, on one side of which is a hall roofed over with a true vault in brick (Fig. 12, middle top). The main body of the house is symmetrically arranged about a central "liwan," a kind of rectangular exedra flanked by two side chambers beyond which is a large room. Two other rooms may have formed a living area.[21] The attempt at a symmetrical arrangement about a central open space akin to the plan of the contemporaneous temple is further exemplified in later layers (XII, XV). There is a unique circular house (18 m. in diameter; Fig. 12, upper middle) with seventeen rooms on an orthogonal layout. The other houses vary in size between 6.85 by 6.5 meters and 10 by 10 meters, and are oriented by the corners.

A typical house from the Early Dynastic Period (2500 B.C.) at Tell Asmar,[22] the capital of the kingdom of Eshnunna, is rectangular (13 × 18 m.; Fig. 12, middle left). The doorway in its main façade along the street opens into a lobby connected to an anteroom that may be hypaethral. The owners could peep through a small window set high in the wall of the kitchen at persons entering. The largest central room beyond the wooden door is the living room, which contains a mud bench and a hearth. Along the street are two baking ovens. On the three other sides of the living room are a reception room, a suite of two bedrooms, the kitchen, and dependencies. Doorways are arched, and roofs are probably in the shape of sloping gables built of light materials. In the Akkadian Period (2350–2150 B.C.)

20 M. Mallowan and C. Rose, *Excavations at Tell Arpachiyah* (London, 1933).
21 E. A. Speiser, *Excavations at Tepe Gawra*, Vol. I, p. 36, pls. IX–X.
22 H. Frankfort, *Iraq Excavations of the Oriental Institute, 1932–1933*, Oriental Institute Communications, No. 17 (Chicago, 1934), Fig. 5, pp. 13–15. Schmökel, *Sumer*, p. 106.

←*Fig. 12*

this same house was still standing but slightly remodeled. Near a smaller house is a latrine with a bitumen-lined seat.

Beginning with the Third Dynasty the prevailing type of house plan has a squarish court surrounded by one row of rooms. At Tello (Fig. 12, middle right),[23] however, a similar house with a rectangular plan has two rows of shallow rooms at the rear. There are sanitary installations, and drains operate in the central paved area of the court. Baked brick is used as a facing to a core of sun-dried brickwork. Though there is no built-in staircase, it is safe enough to surmise that the terraced roof was made accessible by ladders.

One would be astonished at the huge size of some of the houses, such as one at Assur from the Third Dynasty of Ur,[24] which has a rectangular outline (49 × 20 m., making 980 sq. m.; Fig. 12, middle right) and a square court (300 sq. m.) surrounded by gypsum plastered walls and paved with brick tiles or a gypsum layer. From the court a wide doorway (3.5 m.) leads into a broad, shallow hall, an arrangement similar to that of contemporaneous palaces. Beyond is the usual inner apartment, perhaps a court or a hall surrounded by a row of shallow rooms and a bathroom. Drains from this bathroom and the outer courtyard run south to the street. From the great thickness of the wall (2 m.) around the inner court one would infer that the latter is a hall with high walls and clerestory windows.

At Ur of the Isin-Larsa Period (1970–1698 B.C.) the centered plan (10 × 10 m.; Fig. 12, bottom left) is definitely used in two-storied houses.[25] A staircase ascends to a wooden balcony built on uprights around the square courtyard and connecting the upper rooms. A house chapel is situated in the rearmost room. Such a house can have as many as fifteen rooms (No. III on Straight Street in Ur; Fig. 11, top left)[26] arranged within a square plan (17 × 17 m.) and entered from a small lobby leading to the square court. On its south side is a latrine combined with the staircase. On its southeast side is a servant's room; on the southwest are a kitchen and bread oven, a small court, and a series of three open sheds. Along the north side is a reception suite complete with an alcove for washing and a bedroom for guests. Beyond is the house chapel, which is rather large and elaborately arranged. Along its rear wall a brick altar is plastered in a pattern resembling recessed paneling and is surmounted by a flue. It is significant that in most private chapels there is, in front of the altar, a clay jar containing the bones of an infant, presumably the relics of

[23] A. Parrot, *Tello, Vingt campagnes de fouilles (1877–1933)* (Paris, 1948), pp. 276–278, Fig. 57.

[24] Andrae, *Assur*, p. 82.

[25] Frankfort, *Art*, p. 55, Fig. 21.

[26] C. Leonard Woolley, "Excavations at Ur 1930–1931," *The Antiquaries Journal*, Vol. XI (London, 1931), pp. 361–363, pl. XLVII.

a cherished child who died at an untimely age and who was kept in the house.

During later periods in large cities such as Babylon and Ur the house plots are irregular quadrangles, as a result of the mixed system of layout, with large houses set adjacent to smaller ones along irregular streets. Perhaps this irregularity in the street system accounts for the peculiar jagged treatment of the external faces of walls during the Neo-Babylonian Period in an attempt to recall through this steplike façade the general orientation of the inner layout of the house (Fig. 12, bottom right). The plan of the house of the Neo-Babylonian Period borrows from the layout of the palace a formal symmetry and a subtle division of the elements into a reception area and private quarters, with a broad, shallow reception hall beyond the square courtyard, and subsidiary courts surrounded by the units of the complex. This is well exemplified in a large house at Babylon (37 × 42 m.; Fig. 12, bottom right).[27] From the entrance lobby one group to the east, which has a main court, a reception unit with a main hall, and their dependencies, is completely separated from the second group to the west, which has smaller rooms around two small courts.

In the mansions that spread over whole insulae in Babylon and in Ur,[28] there is a definite orientation: the entrance doorway is on the north side, and the reception unit is beyond the south side of the main court so that it faces north. This arrangement is similar to the one current in Egypt at least since the Middle Kingdom. Basements provided since the earliest period (Tello), were perhaps shady, cool refuges from the excessive heat, not unlike the serdab in modern houses in Iraq[29] and Iran.

It may be noticed that there is no evidence of gardens (Tell Asmar),[30] though this does not rule out their existence. The importance of trees in urban development is duly acknowledged, for King Sennacherib mentions specifically that he "set out trees" in the streets of Nineva.

Palaces

It has been mentioned that the temenos forms a focus toward the northern end in the oval layout of the earliest towns. Its setting is either a natural hill or an artificial platform. The northern location is

---

[27] R. Koldewey, *Das wiedererstandene Babylon* (Leipzig, 1925), pp. 279–283, Figs. 235–236.

[28] C. Leonard Woolley, "Ur," *The Antiquaries Journal*, Vol. XIV (London, 1934), pp. 375–377, pl. L.

[29] Badawy, "Provision," p. 127, Fig. 6e.

[30] Frankfort, *Iraq Excavations*, p. 4.

chosen because of the prevailing cool winds from the north, much the same as in Egypt. During the Uruk Period (3000–2800 B.C.) the temple is the only building within the temenos of the city-state not allied to any palace, since the high priest is at the same time the ruler, called *ensi*. He resides in or near the house of his god, which is built of small narrow bricks and lavishly faced with stone mosaics.[31]

During the reign of King Mesilim (2600 B.C.), when the theocracy is challenged, there appears near the temple a royal palace that rivals it both as to its size and as to the excellence of its materials (plano-convex baked brick). A wall encloses each building as if to define its entity.[32] Kish has become the metropolis, and here Mesilim builds a large palace, the earliest and best-preserved Sumerian palace known (Fig. 13, top left). Its layout consists of two rectangular structures, the residence and an annex, oriented by their sides to the cardinal points. The residence stands within an enclosure (41 × 70 m.) in a citadel-like layout with a passageway (2.3 m. wide) around its four sides. Its square courtyard (14.5 × 15 m.) is surrounded on three sides by one row of shallow rooms and a block of rooms on its east. Columns in one row supporting the roof of a hypostyle or forming a portico, as well as the stairways, stuccoed walls, and friezes of slate inlaid with limestone figures, are evidence of a surprisingly sophisticated architecture.[33] Two similar palaces were found at Eridu with double massive walls of plano-convex brick.[34]

In the new capital of Ur, Urnammu, the first king of the Third Dynasty of Ur (2065–2046 B.C.), builds a ziqurrat to Nannar, the moon god, to the north of a rectangular temenos and a palace, E-Khursag, to its south (Fig. 13, bottom right).[35] All the structures are oriented by their corners to the cardinal points. The palace, on a square plan with buttressed faces, features the characteristic use of units, each consisting of a court surrounded by shallow rooms. The temenos is located in the northern half of the oval-shaped layout of the town.

The available evidence suggests that it had become a constant rule to set the temenos and the palace in the northernmost part of the town, exposed to the fresh air from the northeast (Kish, Tell Asmar, Assur, Dur-Kurigalzu, Khorsabad, Babylon, Ur).

At Tell Asmar, or ancient Eshnunna, the earlier palace built during Ur III on Akkadian ruins stands close to the north end of the

[31] Schmökel, *Sumer*, p. 53.

[32] *Ibid.*, p. 57.

[33] E. Mackay, *A Sumerian Palace and the "A" Cemetery at Kish, Mesopotamia*, II, in Department of Anthropology Memoirs, Vol. I, Nos. 1, 2 (Chicago, Field Museum of Natural History, 1929), pp. 84–111. Schmökel, *Sumer*, p. 36. A. Parrot, *Sumer* (London, 1960), p. 100, Fig. 128.

[34] Schmökel, *Sumer*, p. 27.

[35] *Ibid.*, p. 74.

Fig. 13→

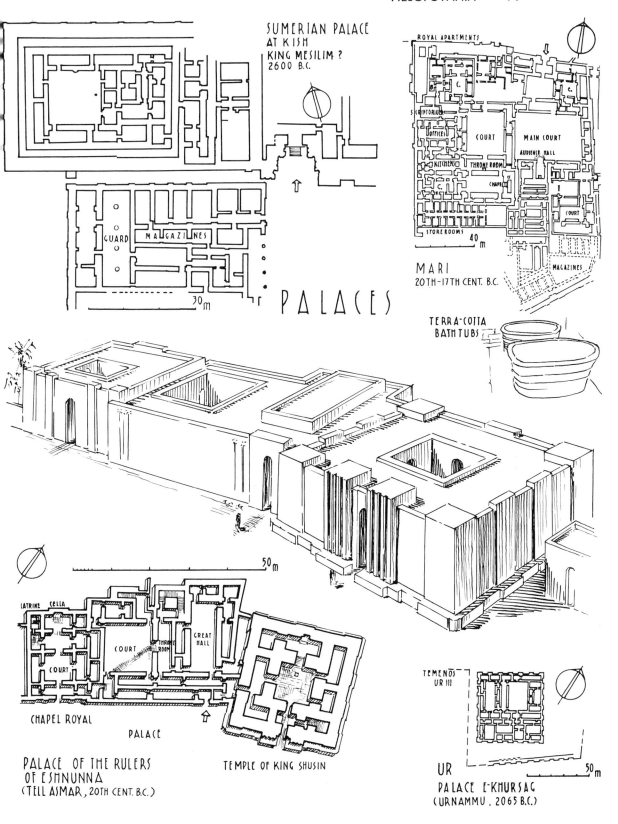

SUMERIAN PALACE
AT KISH
KING MESILIM ?
2600 B.C.

GUARD   MAGAZINES

30 m

PALACES

ROYAL APARTMENTS

SCRIPTORIUM

OFFICES   COURT   MAIN COURT

AUDIENCE HALL

KITCHENS   THRONE ROOM

CHAPEL

COURT

STOREROOMS   40 m

MAGAZINES

MARI
20TH-17TH CENT. B.C.

TERRA-COTTA
BATH TUBS

50 m

LATRINE CELLA

GREAT
HALL

COURT   THRONE
ROOM

COURT

CHAPEL ROYAL

PALACE

PALACE OF THE RULERS
OF ESHNUNNA
(TELL ASMAR, 20TH CENT. B.C.)

TEMPLE OF KING SHUSIN

TEMENOS
UR III

UR
PALACE E-KHURSAG
(URNAMMU, 2065 B.C.)

50 m

city. It is a long rectangular complex (north–south) subdivided into three groups, each centering about a courtyard. The master's apartments are to the north and south of the main court, but the living quarters and the *harim* are independently arranged. The elaborate sanitary system, which consists of latrines and lavatory drains discharging into a main collector (1-m.-high vault in baked brick) and running along the eastern wall, is a masterpiece. For Tell Asmar, a small provincial capital subservient to Ur, two palaces were indeed many. Yet a second small palace was built contiguous to the temple of Shusin, king of Ur (1989–1980 B.C.).[36] The access to the palace is through a long passage, also leading to the chapel royal. A paved pathway runs diagonally through the main court to the throne room, which faces southwest. Beyond this there are a great hall (6 m. broad) and various reception rooms (Fig. 13, bottom left). The residential quarters might have been located on the upper floor, to which a staircase rises from the throne room. A suite and a second staircase can be entered from the court. The palace has been described as a structure of the Assyrian type but with a Babylonian façade (Fig. 13, middle).[37]

At Mari, on the outskirts of western Mesopotamia and in a Semitic environment influenced by Sumer, the palace existing from the end of the third millennium B.C. was destroyed by Hammurabi as a reprisal against the last king, Zimrilim. This colossal complex (200 × 120 m.; Fig. 13, top right),[38] oriented by its sides to the cardinal points, with an area of one hectare and containing more than 260 rooms, abuts on the south wall of the city. Accessible only through one north entrance, the palace has two large courtyards, with the audience hall to the south of the main court and the throne room, along the south side of the inner court, which also services the residence at the northwest corner, two subsidiary units (office with scriptorium, kitchens), and numerous magazines to the rear (south). There is even a school for the children of the officials. Curiously enough, the royal residence is connected directly to the throne room, indirectly to all the quarters, and through a ramp to the top of the city wall. The bathroom in the royal suite has two terra-cotta bathtubs, one for hot water and the other for cold water, which had to be

---

[36] Frankfort, *Iraq Excavations*, pp. 23–33. H. Frankfort, S. Lloyd, and T. Jacobsen, *The Gimilsin Temple and the Palace of the Rulers at Tell Asmar* (Chicago, 1940), pp. 27–37.

[37] Frankfort, Lloyd, and Jacobsen, *The Gimilsin Temple*, pp. 27–35, pls. I, IX. Frankfort, *Art*, pp. 52–53, Fig. 19.

[38] A. Parrot, "Les Fouilles de Mari," *Syria*, Vol. 17 (Paris, 1936), pp. 14–22; Vol. 18 (1937), pp. 65–74; Vol. 19 (1938), pp. 8–13; Vol. 20 (1938), pp. 14 ff. A. Parrot, *Mission archéologique de Mari: II, Le Palais*; Vol. I, *Architecture*; Vol. II, *Peintures Murales*; Vol. III, *Documents et Monuments* (with the collaboration of Mme. Barrelet and MM. Dossin, Ducos, and Bouchud) (Paris, 1958–1959). H. Schmökel, *Hammurabi von Babylon* (Munich, 1958), p. 15.

emptied by scooping the water out; it also contains a brazier with a chimney and a slab latrine. Baked brick set in bitumen lines the bottom part of the walls and the floors. Courts are paved. Disposal of rainwater is provided by terra-cotta gargoyles emptying into underground drains ten meters below the foundations. This huge complex was at the same time the royal residence and the center of administration and religion.

The two units for official reception, the main court with its audience hall and the court of the throne room, as well as the rear chapel court, laid out axially, are decorated with mural paintings in vivid colors. Some represent narrative series of mythological, military, and religious scenes, and others have ornamental patterns protected by awnings along the sides of the courtyard. The walls of the royal suite are also painted with ornamental patterns and scenes, perhaps even inlaid with rosettes. Whether this prominent use of mural painting was characteristic of Mari only or whether it was a favorite in Mesopotamian palaces in general is not substantiated, though the early occurrence of painting on walls at Tepe Gawra, in the Proto-literate temple at ʿUqair, and later at Nuzi and Kar-Tukulti-Ninurta supports the second presumption.[39]

Not only does Mari afford unique evidence about mural painting, but it also embodies two elements that are characteristic of later Babylonian palaces: the square outline and the basic planning unit, consisting of a court and a shallow transverse hall of the same width (here a throne room unit) to the south. Similar characteristics can be detected in the scanty remains of the so-called "Old Palace,"[40] dating perhaps to Shamshi-Adad (early 18th century B.C.) at Assur. At Dur-Kurigalzu[41] the palace from the Kassite Period (1560–1200 B.C.) has six units grouped around a central one in the shape of a square court. The court is oriented by its corners to the cardinal points and has a doorway in the middle of each side leading to a central transverse hall surrounded by rooms. This concept of a basic planning unit is similar to, though more elaborate than, the typical Babylonian one. Wall paintings showing processions of figures and decorative patterns, as well as a pillared portico, characterize the northern unit. In each unit ramps in several flights rise to the upper floor. At Kar-Tukulti-Ninurta the palace is located near the Tigris toward the center of the citadel.[42]

The palace of Sargon II at Khorsabad (713–707 B.C.)[43] does not

39 Frankfort, *Art*, p. 61. Schmökel, *Hammurabi*, p. 88. Taha Baqir, "Iraq Excavations at Aqar Quf," *Iraq*, Supplement 1943–1944, p. 80.

40 Andrae, *Assur*. pp. 94–96, Fig. 43.

41 Baqir, "Aqar Quf," pp. 74–81.

42 Andrae, *Assur*, Fig. 52.

43 Gordon Loud and Charles Altman, *Khorsabad*, Vol. I (Chicago, 1936), pp. 20–128. Frankfort, *Art*, pp. 78–81.

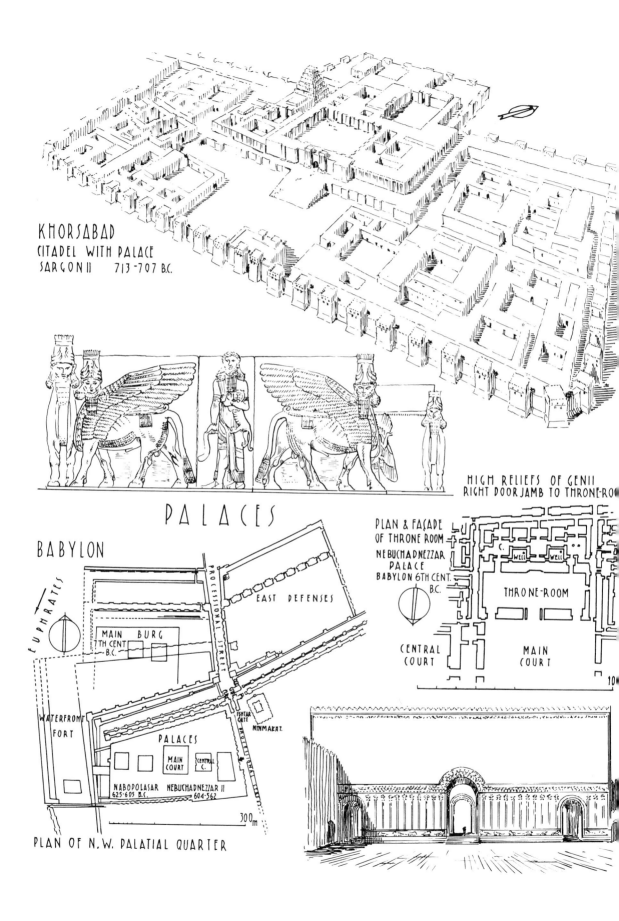

KHORSABAD
CITADEL WITH PALACE
SARGON II   713-707 B.C.

HIGH RELIEFS OF GENII
RIGHT DOOR JAMB TO THRONE-RO[O]

PALACES

BABYLON

EUPHRATES

PROCESSIONAL STREET

EAST DEFENSES

MAIN BURG
7TH CENT.
B.C.

WATERFRONT
FORT

ISHTAR
GATE
NINMAKAT

PALACES
MAIN
COURT   CENTRAL
C.
NABOPOLASAR   NEBUCHADNEZZAR II
625-605 B.C.   604-562

300 m

PLAN OF N.W. PALATIAL QUARTER

PLAN & FAÇADE
OF THRONE ROOM
NEBUCHADNEZZAR
PALACE
BABYLON 6TH CENT.
B.C.

WELL   WELL

THRONE-ROOM

CENTRAL
COURT

MAIN
COURT

10[0]

comply with the rule of the planning unit except, partly, for the unit of the ambassadors' courtyard with its short transverse room. The throne is set not axially but along the small end. Neither the outline nor the layout is regular; instead, there is an agglomeration of courts, each surrounded by rooms shaped according to their function: entrance, reception, residence, and services (Fig. 14, top). This palace is also closely connected to the temple of Nabu by a bridge that affords direct access to the king. It could be said that in this complex the palace clearly supersedes the temple and forms the rearmost refuge in a citadel surrounded by double walls and built on a platform. One more characteristic that is not found in southern palaces is the extensive use of stone slabs as plain facing or carved orthostats. These slabs were set first, then backed with a filling of rubble, behind which sun-dried brick walls were built. Stone orthostats cover the lower part of the walls in the bathroom and the ambassadors' court, where they form a large-scale composition featuring colossal man-headed bulls, or Lamassu, flanking the doorways (Fig. 14, middle). Glazed brick with molded figures are used in the pedestals on both sides of the gateways. Inside, painted murals glowing with brilliant flat colors on plaster show the same stylized solemnity as the reliefs.

The smaller palace bordering the south wall of the city is similar, with a throne room suite and an open western wing fronted by a columned portico.

The two palaces that were built by Nabopolassar (625 B.C.) and Nebuchadnezzar II (604–562 B.C.) along the north walls of Babylon, set on a terrace twelve meters high stretching between a fort on the Euphrates and the Ishtar gate on the processional street, are different from Sargon's. The general trapezoidal outline is more regular (300 × 120–200 m.; Fig. 14, bottom left), with a series of contiguous strips running north–south, each having a central square courtyard flanked to the south by a transverse hall as throne room and reception quarters, and to the north by residential quarters. The residential quarters consist of small suites, each with a court and two or three rooms side by side in one or two rows along passages (north–south). The eastern half of this impressive architectural complex may have been built by Nebuchadnezzar on the remains of an earlier palace (Nabopolassar's?; Fig. 15, bottom). The reception unit resembles the typical Babylonian unit found in the "Old Palace" at Assur, Mari, and in the mansions at Ur and Babylon. There are some basic differences in planning, construction, and style between these late palaces at Babylon and the Assyrian ones at Khorsabad. In two of the units the main transverse hall on the south side of the court is a throne room in which the throne is set against a niche in the middle of

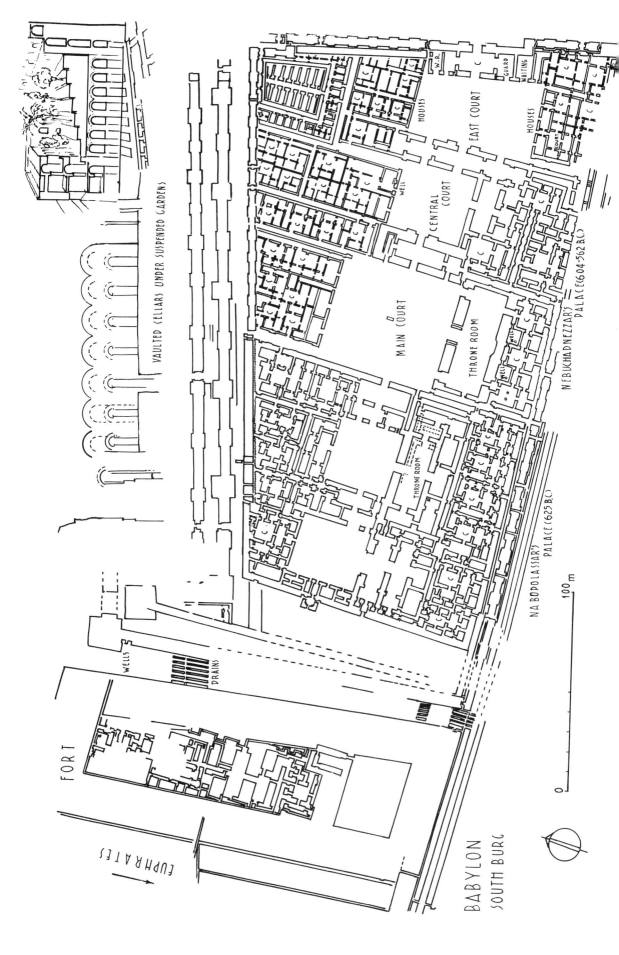

VAULTED CELLARS UNDER SUSPENDED GARDENS)

FORT

WELLS

DRAINS

EUPHRATES

BABYLON
SOUTH BURG

0   100 m

NABOPOLASSAR'S
PALACE (625 B.C.)

NEBUCHADNEZZAR'S
PALACE (604-562 B.C.)

HOUSES

EAST COURT

CENTRAL
COURT

GUARD

WAITING

W.R.

COURT

HOUSES

WELL

MAIN COURT

THRONE ROOM

THRONE
ROOM

WELL

the rear long wall, axially with the doorway, and not at one small end as in Khorsabad. The technique of using earth to fill retaining walls of baked brick is very common. The decoration is also different, since glazed brick is used instead of stone. The façade of the throne room represents a pattern of slender columns with capitals imitating the volute of the sacred tree. Above this is a frieze of looped flowers in white and yellow against a deep blue background. A dado depicting lions is the only reminder of the power of the king, quite a meek treatment when compared to the impressive stone colossi at Khorsabad.[44] At the northeast corner is a series of seven massive vaults on either side of a corridor running north–south surrounded by a passage and an outer row of rooms. It has been suggested that these vaulted cellars may be the substructure of the hanging gardens described by Josephus (XII), Diodorus (II, 10), and Strabo as one of the seven wonders of the ancient world. The palaces are completely independent of the sacred temenos of the temples, which are located farther south in the middle of the city.

At Ur the last of the Babylonian kings, Nabonidus (555–539 B.C.), built a large palace, perhaps for his daughter, in the northern corner of the city.[45] It is on a trapezoidal plan and oriented north–south (90 × 47–90 m.); the residence proper contains no less than eighty rooms, surrounded by a passage and subsidiary rooms. The main group of rooms at the rear follow the pattern of the typical Babylonian planning unit.

It is in the shallow rooms opening transversely onto the court of the Babylonian palace that the idea of the Parthian and Sassanian liwan had its origin.[46]

Temples

The writing of the title of the Sumerian priest, *sangu*, with an archaic ideogram for "offering" implies that he was the man who transmitted the offerings to the deity.[47] But there is a great difference between the simplest food offering, the "repast with god" of the early hunter, and the elaborate ritual performed in the large temples from the period of Uruk IV.[48] Though the smaller shrines may have been serviced by only one priest, there was usually a staff of several priests who had been trained in seminaries. At a very early stage the priest-king, *ensi*, must have delegated the high priest to perform the ritual in his stead, as did the pharaoh in Egypt. We are informed about the

[44] Koldewey, *Babylon*, pp. 32–49.
[45] Frankfort, *Art*, p. 108.
[46] C. Leonard Woolley, "Ur," *The Antiquaries Journal*, Vol. XI (London, 1931), pp. 376–381.
[47] Koldewey, *Babylon*, p. 110.
[48] Dhorme, *Religion*, p. 284.

←—*Fig. 15*

religious institutions and rites from Sumerian texts dating mostly after the Sumerian Period. Besides performing the regular cult ritual, the priests often had to interpret oracles by "reading" the liver of sacrificial animals or floating oil on water and to cure patients by incantations.[49] People gathered at the temple for the two monthly feasts, on the first of the month, at the new moon, and on the fifteenth at the full moon, as well as on numerous other occasions.[50]

The Predynastic Period. The pre-Sumerian sanctuary at either Eridu or Tepe Gawra, sometimes as small as a cella 4 by 4 meters, develops later into a well-planned structure of sophisticated style. The typical symmetrical plan, which is long and rectangular, is oriented by the corners to the cardinal points. An inner T-shaped courtyard is surrounded by rooms serving as lodgings of priests, offices, and magazines; the courtyard contains an offering table, a statue of the god set in a niche at the small end, and sometimes also a platform where the symbolic divine wedding was performed. There are doorways in the long side and behind the sanctuary.

A second type of temple is set on a platform and has a rectangular courtyard flanked on its two long sides by rooms. It is accessible from a lateral doorway near one small end. The altar, podium, and hearth are at the opposite end. This type, with the lateral entrance implying Semitic influence, evolves with a gradually higher platform into the high chapel on the top of a stepped pyramid, or ziqurrat.[51]

Sun-dried brick, already known in the Neolithic Period (Uruk XVI), is used to build the retaining walls of the terrace and the structure itself, which is often ribbed with convex shafts fitted together to imitate walls of reeds or recessed paneling. Terra-cotta conical pegs that have colored heads are inserted in the thick plaster with the heads showing in a mosaic resembling textile patterns (Uruk VI). This technique is developed further by arranging pegs with rosette heads, animals, or figures to form ornamental friezes (Uruk III). Stone is used occasionally in the masonry and once in the foundations. Ceilings in the rooms were made from reed bundles and mats. Floors are still of mere clay, probably for symbolic reasons. Stairways, podiums, drains, and white plaster are elements used in this monumental architecture.[52]

At Eridu (Abu Shahrein),[53] even as early as the ꜥUbaid Period, the temple (levels VII–VI), set on a platform, has a so-called tripartite

---

[49] Schmökel, *Sumer*, p. 135.

[50] Dhorme, *Religion*, pp. 284 ff.

[51] Schmökel, *Sumer*, p. 142.

[52] *Ibid.*, p. 137. W. Andrae in W. G. A. Otto, ed., *Handbuch der Archäologie* (Munich, 1939), pp. 656–659.

[53] S. Lloyd and F. Safar, "Eridu," *Sumer*, Vol. III (Baghdad, 1947), Figs. 2–3. Perkins, *Stratigraphy*, pp. 87–88.

plan. The symmetrical structure with corner rooms projecting like bastions, is approached from a stairway on one long side.

From the next period of Uruk (Warka) date numerous large temples of a monumental style. At Uruk the temple of Anu (Fig. 16, top right)[54] is built upon an extensive terrace that is irregular in plan and has battered recessed walls of brick topped with bands of pegs. The temple itself (17.5 × 22.3 m.) is symmetrical (as those at Eridu) and oriented by the corners to the cardinal points. Set on a brick platform, it has a staircase room (north), a long central cella with recessed walls, a central slab combining the offering table and the hearth, and at its northern end an altar in the shape of a brick pedestal for the statue, which is accessible from a stairway. Doorways open in the center of the long side (west) and at both ends. The ascent to the terrace is along a ramp and a stairway. The walls are of brick that is plastered and whitewashed—hence its modern name of "White Temple." This complex was remodeled at three subsequent levels, and ultimately the temple was filled in with mud brick.

A similar complex on a terrace occurs at ʿUqair (Fig. 16, middle)[55] in the "Painted Temple," so called because its cella walls are painted with a red dado (1 m. high) and topped with a band of geometric ornament, as well as animal and human figures in red line on a white ground. Here the terrace has recessed retaining walls parallel to the temple and oriented by the corners. A lower platform with one side rounded stretches farther and is accessible through two symmetrical stairways (northwest and southeast). Here also rows of pegs top the walls.

The technique of inserting cones into plaster to form decorative facings is used extensively on the internal and external walls and pillars of the so-called "Mosaic Temple" at Uruk.[56]

At Tepe Gawra (Fig. 16, bottom right)[57] the temple is at ground level and is strictly symmetrical. Accessible from one entrance at a small end, it has recessed paneling on its outer façades (level VIII c). The other type of temple at ground level is exemplified in the temple of Sin at Khafaje (I–IV; Fig. 16, top left),[58] built on a nearly symmetrical plan, with a double entrance on one long side. An axial cella containing an altar at its farther end is flanked by a staircase on one side and a sacristy on the other.

[54] Perkins, *Stratigraphy*, pp. 110–113. E. Heinrich in A. Nöldeke, A. v. Haller, H. Lenzen, and E. Heinrich, *Uruk-Warka* (Berlin, 1937), Figs. 3, 5.

[55] S. Lloyd, F. Safar, and H. Frankfort, "Tell Uqair," *Journal of Near Eastern Studies*, Vol. II (Chicago, 1943), pp. 131–158.

[56] Perkins, *Stratigraphy*, p. 119.

[57] Speiser, *Tepe Gawra*, Vol. I. p. 24. A. J. Tobler, *ibid.*, Vol. II, pls. XI, XXII. Andrae in *Handbuch*, p. 665, Fig. 49. Parrot, *Sumer*, p. 316, Fig. 391B.

[58] P. Delougaz and S. Lloyd, *Pre-Sargonid Temples in the Diyala Region* (Chicago, 1942), p. 305, Figs. 5, 10. Perkins, *Stratigraphy*, p. 132.

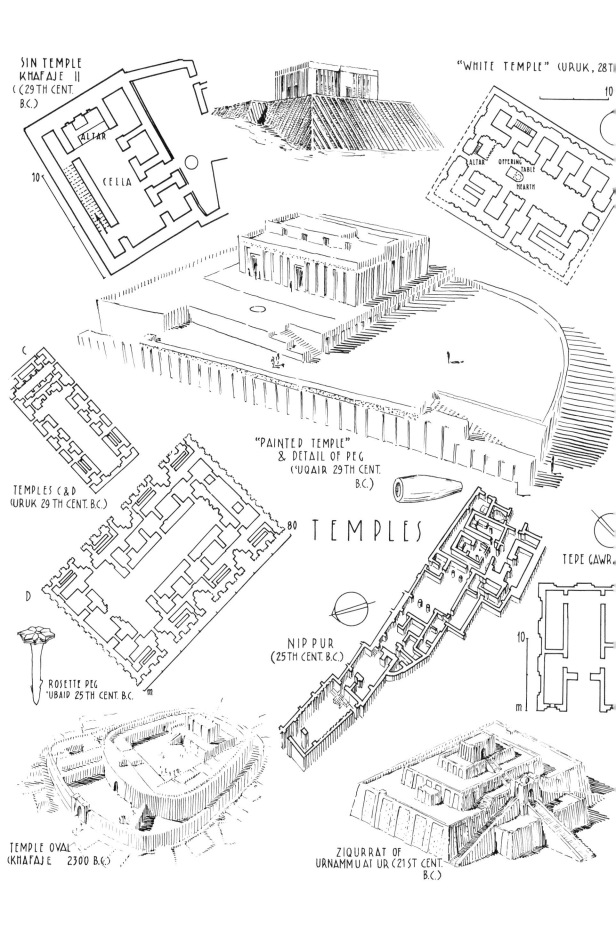

SIN TEMPLE
KHAFAJE II
((29TH CENT.
B.C.)

ALTAR

CELLA

10

"WHITE TEMPLE" (URUK, 28T

10

ALTAR   OFFERING
         TABLE
         HEARTH

C

TEMPLES C&D
(URUK 29 TH CENT. B.C.)

D

ROSETTE PEG
'UBAID 25 TH CENT. B.C.

"PAINTED TEMPLE"
& DETAIL OF PEG
('UQAIR 29 TH CENT.
B.C.)

80

T E M P L E S

NIPPUR
(25TH CENT. B.C.)

TEPE GAWR.

10

m

TEMPLE OVAL
(KHAFAJE   2300 B.C.)

ZIQURRAT OF
URNAMMU AT UR (21ST CENT.
B.C.)

Let us also mention a small shrine set in the thickness of the town wall at Khoshi[59] at the turning point in a winding entrance to the town. It remains there in the Early Dynastic Period, but it is no longer on an axial plan.

The Early Dynastic Period. The type of temple with a winding entrance on the long side persists; it is sometimes referred to as "Hurrian" by scholars who imply some borrowing from the type of living room used by these tribes, who lived east of the Tigris.[60] When built at ground level, it is allied to the complex of a courtyard containing a well, a place for ablution, a granary, an oven, and often two shrines[61] (Shara temple at Tell Aqrab, Sin at Khafaje VI–X, Abu at Tell Asmar, Assur, Ishtar at Mari).

In the temple set on a platform[62] the terrace is a regular feature, and the temple is erected upon a socle that delimits the sacred area. An oval enclosure forms a temenos at the rear of which is the terrace (Temple Oval at Khafaje, ʿUbaid; Fig. 16, bottom left). The Temple Oval is located about thirty meters from one of the gates near the west edge of the southern part of the town. Two walls form the temenos (80 × 60 m.), with one western doorway in each and a house for the priests at the back of the court between them. The inner court is at a high level, surrounded by rooms (workshops, storerooms), and has two wells, an altar, and to the rear the rectangular terrace oriented by the corners. A stairway rises from the western side to the top of the terrace in the axis of the doorway. The temple itself is a simple long cella accessible from a side doorway, with the altar at the farther end. It is noteworthy that the whole structure is built within an excavation on a filling of "pure" sand for symbolical reasons similar to those noted in the construction of Egyptian temples.

The temple at ʿUbaid,[63] dating from the First Dynasty of Ur (2500 B.C.), has a similar oval enclosure (80 × 65 m.) with an inner wall around a quadrangular terrace (33 × 26 m.) that is oriented by its corners. It is approached from its southeast side by a stairway, fronted by a low altar. The sides of the stairway are paneled with wooden planks, and the steps are of stone. They lead to a porch that has two slender columns made of wood and lined with copper sheets to which correspond two engaged columns incrusted with mosaic slabs and flanking the doorway. Here also the cella is a

[59] S. Lloyd, "Iraq Government Soundings at Sinjar," *Iraq*, Vol. 7, Fig. 7.

[60] Andrae in *Handbuch*, p. 675, n.2.

[61] Delougaz and Lloyd, *Pre-Sargonid Temples*, pp. 302–304, Figs. 133, 166, pl. 23.

[62] P. Delougaz, *The Temple Oval at Khafajah* (Chicago, 1940).

[63] H. J. Lenzen, *Die Entwicklung der Zikurrat* (Leipzig, 1941), pp. 29–31. H. R. Hall and C. L. Woolley, *Ur Excavations*, Vol. I, *Al ʿUbaid* (London, 1927), pp. 61–76. P. Delougaz, "A Short Investigation of the Temple of al-ʿUbaid," *Iraq*, Vol. V, pp. 1 ff, 1938.

←*Fig. 16*

simple room. A similar porch and doorway front the small east face. On the external façades are two lower friezes of copper bulls (one in the round and the other in high relief) and three upper friezes of inlaid animals. Pegs with rosette heads in three colors probably formed a frieze at the top (Fig. 16, lower left) of the terrace. At Nippur (Fig. 16, lower right),[64] the main religious center, an Early Dynastic temple grew by accretion along a curved axis, with at least three courts and vestibules in front of two cellae, as did the cult temples in Egypt.

Akkad and Gudea of Lagash. The Semitic Akkadians (2350–2150 B.C.) restored buildings already in existence. We know about the building activity of Gudea of Lagash from several texts and from the famous statue representing him with an architect's plan and ruler on his lap.[65]

Dynasty III of Ur. With this dynasty, the so-called Neo-Sumerian Period (2065–1955 B.C.), there begins outstanding activity in temple construction. Both the high temple and the one at ground level become standardized. The high temple is set at the top of a stepped pyramid, called the "ziqurrat," etymologically the "pointed one" or the "high one."[66] The spirit of the god alighted on it, and its cosmic power as a connecting link between heaven and earth is often defined clearly by its names, such as the "house-of-the-link-between-heaven-and-earth" at Larsa or the "house-of-the-foundation-of-heaven-and-earth" in Babylon.[67] Monumental stairways rise in the axis of one face (at Nippur) and also abut on it as two subsidiary approaches (at Ur). Recessed paneling articulates the battered faces. All these characteristics recur in the later ziqurrats (Uruk, Babylon), but the prototype may have been the small Anu terrace at Uruk.[68] The upper chapel was the "wedding hall" for the sacred wedding, a basic rite in the Sumerian religion.

In the temple at ground level the plan featuring a court and a shallow broad room, already met in the Early Dynastic Period house at Fara (Ur I),[69] is used instead of the deep hall of the Sumerian type. It was thought that the god actually lived in this palace, which was approached through a fortified gateway.

---

[64] V. E. Crawford, "Nippur, The Holy City," *Archaeology*, Vol. 12 (New York, 1959), pp. 74–83.

[65] Andrae in *Handbuch*, pp. 679, 681–682.

[66] A. Ungnad, *Grammatik des Akkadischen* (Munich, 1949), p. 207.

[67] W. Andrae, *Das Gotteshaus und die Urformen des Bauens im alten Orient* (Berlin, 1930), pp. 12, 17 ff. A. Parrot, *Ziggurats et Tour de Babel* (Paris, 1949), pp. 207 ff.

[68] Andrae in *Handbuch*, p. 685. Schmökel, *Sumer*, p. 102.

[69] Andrae in *Handbuch*, p. 685, n. 3; p. 674.

Urnammu, the first king of Dynasty III of Ur (2065–2046 B.C.), built ziqurrats in the capital at Ur and in Nippur, perhaps also at Uruk.[70] The one at Ur (Fig. 16, bottom right) is a well-preserved rectangular monument (62.5 × 43 m.), with slightly convex sides at the rear of its own court (107 × 78 m.), beyond that of the moon god Nannar. It is approached from an independent stairway rising from the middle of the northeast face, flanked by two massifs and two lateral stairways on this same face. The three stairways meet at an intermediate landing, whence the central stairway proceeds to the top platform. Erected in an excavation, the core of crude brick is faced with recessed battered walls of baked brick and asphalt (2.5 m. thick), and there are drains at regular intervals (every 1.2 m. in height).[71] The ziqurrat at Ur is similar, with a front temple added by Sargon II (720 B.C.). The ziqurrat at Nippur may have been remodeled from an earlier structure built by Naramsin.[72] At Kish an undated ziqurrat on a squarish plan (56.32 × 60.35 m.) is of the northern type.[73] In the irregular temple complex at Mari the ziqurrat embodies the "lions' temple" (Fig. 17, bottom left).

While the temple of Ishtar and that of Assur (by Shamshi Adad, 18th century B.C.) at Assur have a typical deep cella with a lateral entrance,[74] the so-called "Hurrian" type, characterized by a shallow broad cella to the rear of the square court, is exemplified in the temple of the goddess Inanna, "Lady of Heaven," at Nippur,[75] which was dedicated by Shulgi, son of Urnammu, and the two temples in the palace complex of the rulers of Eshnunna at Tell Asmar (Fig. 13, bottom left).[76] Here the temple dedicated to Shusin, king of Ur (1989–1980 B.C.), by his vassal at Eshnunna is a massive structure on a perfect square plan that is nearly symmetrical, with rooms about a central court, beyond which is a small shallow cella. The entrance is flanked by two massive towers with recessed paneling. It has been pointed out that the Shusin temple does not face northeast, as the Babylonian ones do, but faces southeast, perhaps toward the residence of Shusin, 300 kilometers distant, at Ur. At the opposite end of the palace is a chapel royal with a forecourt, square court, antecella, and shallow cella on one axis, flanked by two rows of rooms.[77] The chapel faces southeast in Assyrian fashion.

70 *Ibid.*
71 Lenzen, *Entwicklung der Zikurrat*, pp. 40–46.
72 Andrae in *Handbuch*, p. 689. Parrot, *Ziggurats*, pp. 148–155, Figs. 96–97.
73 S. Langdon, *Excavations at Kish*, Vol. I, 1923–24 (Paris, 1924), pp. 65–67, pl. XLIV. Parrot, *Ziggurats*, pp. 90–91.
74 Andrae in *Handbuch*, p. 691, Fig. 58.
75 Crawford, "Nippur," pp. 74–83.
76 G. Martigny, *The Orientation of the Gimilsin Temple and the Palace Chapel* (Chicago, n.d.), pp. 92–96.
77 Frankfort, Lloyd, and Jacobsen, *The Gimilsin Temple*, pp. 9–27, 37, frontispiece, pl. I.

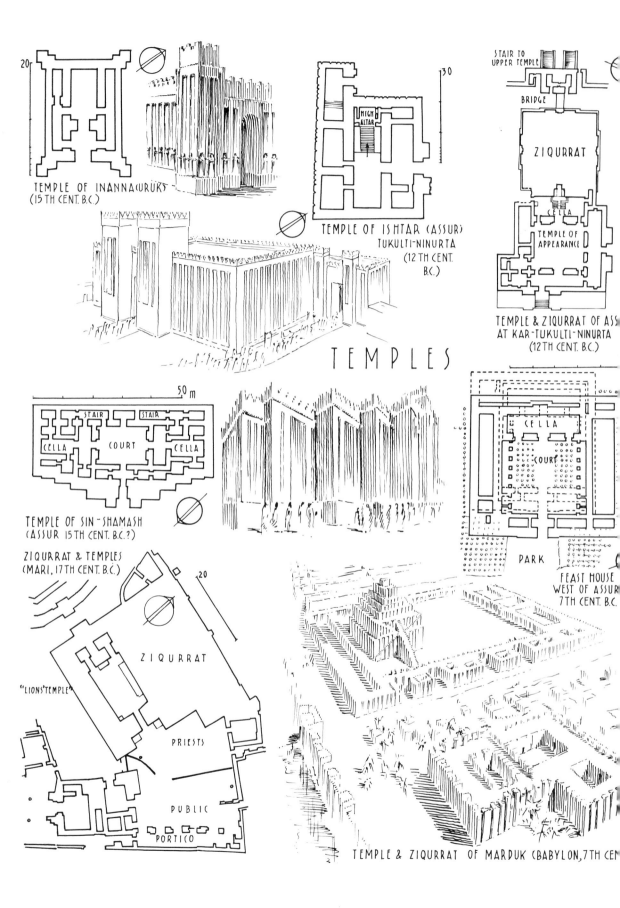

TEMPLE OF INANNA(URUK)
(15TH CENT. B.C.)

TEMPLE OF ISHTAR (ASSUR)
TUKULTI-NINURTA
(12TH CENT. B.C.)

STAIR TO
UPPER TEMPLE

BRIDGE

ZIQURRAT

CELLA

TEMPLE OF
APPEARANCE

TEMPLE & ZIQURRAT OF ASS
AT KAR-TUKULTI-NINURTA
(12TH CENT. B.C.)

HIGH
ALTAR

T E M P L E S

5.0 m

STAIR   STAIR

CELLA   COURT   CELLA

TEMPLE OF SIN-SHAMASH
(ASSUR 15TH CENT. B.C.?)

CELLA

COURT

PARK

FEAST HOUSE
WEST OF ASSUR
7TH CENT. B.C.

ZIQURRAT & TEMPLES
(MARI, 17TH CENT. B.C.)

ZIQURRAT

"LIONS"TEMPLE

PRIESTS

PUBLIC

PORTICO

TEMPLE & ZIQURRAT OF MARDUK (BABYLON, 7TH CEN

Isin-Larsa (1970–1698 B.C.). It is in the Isin-Larsa Period that monumental planning attains a consistent accuracy, with right angles and harmonic proportions. The most conspicuous example is the temple of the goddess Ningal, consort of the moon-god Nannar in the sacred temenos at Ur (Temple of Ishtar at Ishlali). Here the norms of Babylonian architecture have reached their final development.[78] It is noteworthy that small chapels are built at prominent corners of streets, according to the layout of the city, and are accessible from a few steps, probably in order to offer a vista (Ur).

Babylon and the Kassites. The First Dynasty of Babylon and its great monarch Hammurabi restored and built temples that were remodeled by the Kassites (1560–1200 B.C.), Indo-European tribes who came from the east. It has been recently suggested that they attempted to restore Sumerian civilization, and this theory probably finds its most convincing confirmation in the fact that in their temples they reverted to the deep cella of the Sumerians. Their earliest activity is the restoration of the temples at Ur.[79] The Hurrian cella occurs in the two sanctuaries facing southwest and northeast in the Sin-Shamash "Moon and Sun" temple of the Old Assyrian Period (15th century B.C.) at Assur (Fig. 17, middle left)[80] and later in the twin sanctuaries and ziqurrats of Anu-Adad "Heaven and Storm" at Assur (Tiglath-Pileser I, 1116–1078 B.C.).[81]

Most characteristic is the small temple built by King Karaindash to the mother goddess Inanna at Uruk (Fig. 17, top left). This is on a symmetrical plan and heavily bastioned at the corners, with one deep axial cella and antecella flanked by two rooms. The façades are articulated with recesses (Sumerian or Babylonian), and at the bottom of these niches built of molded brick are slender figures of fertility deities, alternating gods and goddesses holding a flowing vessel. This innovation in technique is characteristic of the Kassites and will recur one thousand years later in Neo-Babylonian temples with glazed brick murals.[82]

The Assyrians. Besides inheriting from the Old Assyrians the Hurrian cella, the Middle Assyrians borrowed from the Kassites many basic elements such as the deep cella with an axial entrance and the dual arrangement of a ziqurrat and a lower temple.[83] Narrow

[78] Andrae in *Handbuch,* p. 692.
[79] *Ibid.,* p. 699.
[80] Andrae, *Assur,* pp. 98–101, Figs. 44–45.
[81] *Ibid.,* pp. 130–133, Figs. 54–55.
[82] J. Jordan, *Erster Vorläufiger Bericht über die von der Notgemeinschaft der Deutschen Wissenschaft in Uruk-Warka unternommenen Ausgrabungen* (Leipzig, 1930), pp. 30–33, pls. 15–17.
[83] Andrae in *Handbuch,* p. 699.

←*Fig. 17*

vaults are built with radiating voussoirs of stone. The complex of
Assur built by Tukulti-Ninurta (1235–1198 B.C.) at Kar-Tukulti-
Ninurta (Fig. 17, top right) is fronted by a "temple of appearance"
with a court and a shallow cella abutting on the ziqurrat. It is from
this cella that the god came out at the foot of the artificial mountain
and appeared in a flat niche in the central recess of the mass of the
ziqurrat itself. At the back is the stairway rising on a bridge to the
upper temple.[84] This dual arrangement is found later for Nabu at
Borsippa and Shamash, "the Sun," at Sippar. The temple of the
goddess Ishtar (the same as the earlier "Lady of Heaven," or
Inanna), also built by Tukulti-Ninurta in Assur (Fig. 17, top), has
no forecourt, and its Hurrian-type cella has a rear alcove at the top
of some steps, a typical Assyrian arrangement.[85] Middle Assyrian
temples therefore used one of three types of cellae: the Hurrian,
with the lateral entrance; the deep Kassite, with the axial entrance;
and the shallow one (Babylonian).

Middle Assyrian tradition lives on in the Late Assyrian temples,
especially in the plan and the murals representing the sacred volute
tree and symbolic animals. There are, however, more Egyptian
elements, such as the lotus and figures of deities, perhaps borrowed
from Phoenicia.[86] The deep cella with a rear alcove at a higher level
(Nabu, Ishtar at Assur) or with this alcove developing in the shape
of a small sanctuary (Khorsabad) are current, though the shallow
cella occurs occasionally (Eanna temple of Sargon II at Uruk).[87] It
is noteworthy that the rear wall of the cult niche at Khorsabad is
ribbed with engaged shafts imitating reeds behind the statue of the
god,[88] probably symbolic of the passageway to heaven. Moreover,
the row of pegs inserted just below floor level in the temple or palace
platform is considered so important that the early texts (Shamshi
Adad) recommend replacing it when destroyed. Silver plaques or
embossed bronze lines the doors, rows of pegs in the form of rosettes
and figures are inserted in walls, and shafts of columns flank the
entrance to the temples, with alabaster statues holding a vase of
flowing water.

The ziqurrat behind the six temples outside the palace at Khorsabad was perhaps of a new type with a continuous ramp and vertical
faces with recessed paneling.

Two more features pertaining to religious architecture should be
mentioned. Two rows of stelae[89] between the fortifications of the

[84] Andrae, *Assur*, pp. 123–125, Figs. 47–49; *Handbuch*, p. 714, Fig. 69.
[85] Andrae, *Assur*, pp. 109–113; *Handbuch*, p. 712, Fig. 68.
[86] Andrae in *Handbuch*, pp. 719–721.
[87] *Ibid.*, p. 723.
[88] G. Loud and C. Altman, *Khorsabad*, Part II, "The Citadel and the Town," Oriental
Institute Publications, Vol. XL (Chicago, 1938), pp. 42, 62.
[89] Andrae, *Assur*, pp. 105–107.

New City and the southwest front of the inner city at Assur were erected by kings and officials over a period of seven centuries to represent them in the presence of the god. It has already been mentioned that the New Year Festival was marked by a procession of the gods in boats, rowed against the current (symbolic of the death of the year) from the quay to the Feast House outside the city. At Assur this was a structure built by Sennacherib (704–681 B.C.), with a shallow cella just behind a formal park (Fig. 17, middle right).[90] The procession returned on chariots along the paved processional road (symbolic of the new year) through the Gurgurri Gate. This practice was actually borrowed from the cult of Marduk, the Babylonian god corresponding to the state god Assur, in his Esagila temple at Babylon. The processional road ran from the Feast House southward to Babylon, passed through the Ishtar Gate, proceeded by the royal palaces, and crossed the court of the temples to the bank of the Euphrates (Fig. 11, bottom right).

The Neo-Babylonians. With the Late Babylonians the dual temples of Sumerian origin come to an end. The ziqurrat of Marduk at Babylon,[91] "house-of-the-foundation-stone-of-heaven-and-earth," which is probably a very ancient structure, was later covered with vertical walls of baked brick by Nabopolassar and Nebuchadnezzar (Fig. 17, bottom right). Three stairways lead to its south side. Its double peribolos along the Euphrates north of the Esagila temple features an elaborate row of shallow cells faced internally and externally with recessed paneling. The Esagila[92] has a conspicuous square plan and a central court directly accessible through a vestibule to its east. In the axis are an antecella and west cella, which are both shallow and broad. This basic type of Babylonian lower temple is also exemplified by that of Ishtar in Babylon. The flat niche of step-like cross section in the western rear wall forms the "false-door" through which the god appeared. A life-size statue representing him either standing or seated was inlaid with semiprecious stones and metals.[93] At Borsippa,[94] the Ezida temple of the setting sun Nabu, first-born of Marduk, which was built by Hammurabi (1728–1686 B.C.), stood in the axis of its ziqurrat (southwest). The same layout

90 *Ibid.*, pp. 19–22; *Handbuch*, pp. 721–722, Fig. 72.
91 Koldewey, *Babylon*, pp. 189 ff.
92 *Ibid.*, p. 200. F. Wetzel, *Das Hauptheiligtum des Marduk in Babylon, Esagila und Etemanki (Wissenschaftlische Veröffentlichungen der deutschen Orient-Gesellschaft*, Vol. 59), (Leipzig, 1938), pp. 4–13, pl. 2.
93 Andrae in *Handbuch*, p. 726.
94 *Ibid.*, p. 733. R. Koldewey, *Die Tempel von Babylon und Borsippa (Wissenschaftliche Veröffentlichungen der deutschen Orient-Gesellschaft*, Vol. 15), (Leipzig, 1911), pp. 64–68, pl. XII. Parrot, *Ziggurats*, pp. 59–68, Figs. 36–39.

recurs at Sippar[95] and Kish.[96] This Babylonian type of temple lasted throughout the Greek and Seleucid Periods.[97]

Tombs

Funerary architecture never achieved monumentality in Mesopotamia as it did in Egypt, except at Ur III. It is not, however, that the destiny of an afterlife was ignored nor that the dangers of the roving spirits, *ekimmu*,[98] of the unburied dead were minimized.

The cult of the dead is an important concept in Sumerian culture. Funerary furniture, cups and vessels filled with food, and weapons are placed with the body, which is partly or completely cremated after the fleshy parts had been removed (Surghul, El Hibba). An earthenware vessel is set above the remains. After these are incinerated, they are placed in an urn. Partly burned bodies are buried in an oblong jar (Djemdet-Nasr Period).[99] Contemporaneous graves in Ur have crouching bodies with the hands holding a pot near the face. Occasionally also rectangular coffins of wickerwork are used, though it is more common to dig a grave and line its walls with mats.

In the prehistoric period bodies are buried under the houses (Hassuna) or packed within walls of brick or pisé (Samarra).[100] Odd circular buildings of stone, sometimes with a transverse anteroom and a long forecourt or hall, recall the Mycenaean "tholoi." Those at Arpachiya are built in layers (5.6–4 m. diameter; Fig. 18, top left)[101] and are similar to the funerary chapels (4.25 m. inner diameter) of beehive or conical shape built above the graves at Tepe Gawra (XVIII).[102] The domical outline may have a cosmic implication as a representation of the world.[103] An earlier funerary chapel at Tepe Gawra (X) is a small rectangular room with buttresses at the corners and a doorway and two symmetrical niches in the rear wall. Brick flooring that is one meter thick is supposed to prevent the desecration of the holy soil above the grave (Fig. 18, top right).[104] The tombs themselves are mostly of brick, sometimes lined or roofed over with stone; they have an oblong or rectangular plan with one corner to the

[95] W. Andrae and J. Jordan, "Abu Habbah-Sippar," *Iraq*, Vol. I (Baghdad, 1934), pp. 51–55, Fig. 1.

[96] Ch. Watelin, *Excavations at Kish*, Vol. III (Paris, 1930), pl. II, pp. 1–15. Andrae in *Handbuch*, p. 733.

[97] Andrae in *Handbuch*, pp. 737–738.

[98] Maspero, *Dawn*, p. 689, n. 3.

[99] H. Schmökel, *Ur, Assur und Babylon* (Zurich, 1955), pp. 151–152.

[100] Perkins, *Stratigraphy*, p. 5.

[101] *Ibid.*, p. 37, Fig. 3.

[102] Tobler, *Tepe Gawra*, Vol. II, p. 43, pl. XVIII.

[103] Maspero, *Dawn*, p. 543 and its figure.

[104] Tobler, *Tepe Gawra*, Vol. II, p. 11.

Fig. 18→

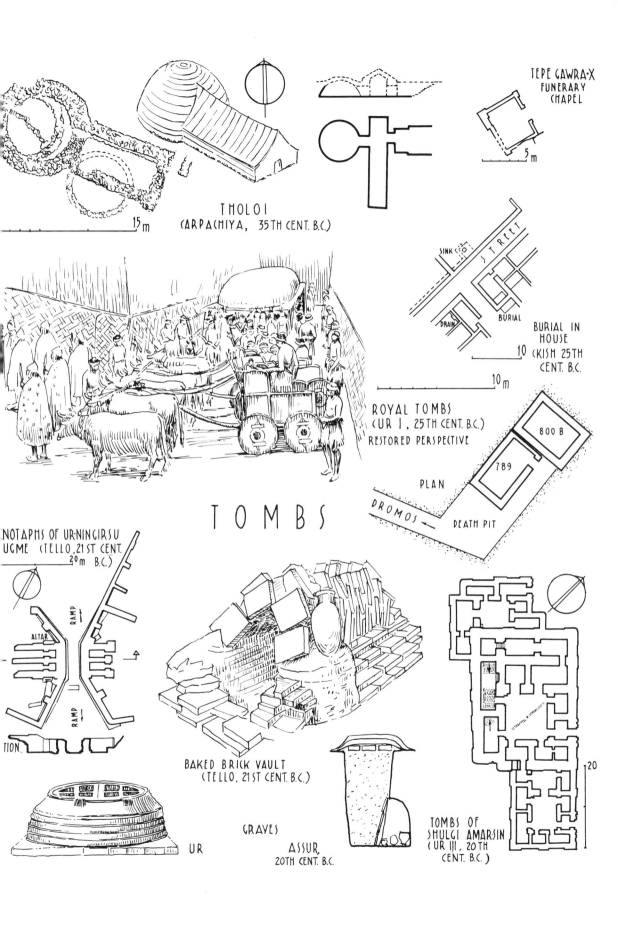

TEPE GAWRA·X
FUNERARY
CHAPEL

5 m

THOLOI
(ARPACHIYA, 35TH CENT. B.C.)

15 m

STREET

SINK

DRAIN   BURIAL

BURIAL IN
HOUSE
(KISH 25TH
CENT. B.C.
10

10 m

ROYAL TOMBS
(UR I, 25TH CENT. B.C.)
RESTORED PERSPECTIVE

800 B

789

PLAN

DROMOS

DEATH PIT

TOMBS

NOTAPHS OF UR-NINGIRSU
UGME (TELLO, 21ST CENT.
20 m   B.C.)

RAMP

ALTAR

RAMP

TION.

BAKED BRICK VAULT
(TELLO, 21ST CENT. B.C.)

20

UR

GRAVES

ASSUR,
20TH CENT. B.C.

TOMBS OF
SHULGI AMARSIN
(UR III, 20TH
CENT. B.C.)

north along a northwest–southeast axis (like the temple; 3.25 × 2.65
m. to 0.75 × 0.50 m.).[105] Some rare cists have rock walls roofed
over with stone slabs.

Toward the middle of the third millennium B.C. the cult of the dead
king develops, probably stimulated by the myth of Inanna-Dumuzi,
who symbolize "Death and Renewal," the prototypes of Ishtar-
Tammuz. At Kish corbeled brick tombs, which are the size of the
body or larger (2.4 × 1.8 m.), are built in a corner of a room in the
house with a special brick or pottery floor, or directly on the floor of
the room (Fig. 18, upper right).[106] As many as 154 bodies are buried
in the chambers of the Sumerian palace and on the enclosure walls
at Kish.[107] It is there also that the earliest burials of servants with a
span and chariot occur in three royal tombs (2600 B.C.). This custom
is well illustrated in the royal tombs found intact at Ur I (2500–2360
B.C.)[108] to the south of the temple of the moon-god Nannar (Fig.
18, middle right). The royal wooden coffin is set in a deep underground chamber of limestone roofed with a corbel or pseudoradiating
dome. A ramp or dromos whose side walls are lined with mats leads
down to one or more burial chambers. The whole death pit is an
imitation of a typical reed enclosure and mat hut (Fig. 18, middle
left).[109] Groups of servants from the king's retinue, in one case even
as many as eighty, accompanied their master, dressed in their best
attire and carrying harps, lutes, weapons, jewelry, and models of
funerary boats or even leading spans of oxen and chariots. They had
probably drunk from poisoned cups to rejoin their royal master. The
funerary rites were performed at the beginning of the funeral, again
when the excavation was half filled up, and ultimately when it was
leveled up. The queen was buried later through a gap opened in the
roof near her partner, deified as Dumuzi. The higher classes sought
to be buried near the kings. Among the 1,800 earlier tombs at Ur,
16 date from Ur I. The architectural value of these tombs is less
significant than the aesthetic achievement represented by furniture.

The Neo-Sumerian Period is the only era when monumental tombs
are found in Mesopotamia. Perhaps dating from the time of the two
ensis, Ur-Ningirsu and his son Ugme at Tello,[110] is an enigmatic
complex of two cenotaphs (?). These are laid out symmetrically east
and west of a central passageway that runs into two ramps, and are
built with thick walls of baked brick (Fig. 18, lower left). The shape
of each element resembles the outlines of the side view of a boat,

[105] *Ibid.*, pp. 70–76.
[106] Watelin, *Kish*, Vol. IV, pp. 17–19, Fig. 2. Schmökel, *Sumer*, p. 36.
[107] Mackay, *Sumerian Palace*, p. 105.
[108] Woolley, *Ur*, Vol. II, *Royal Cemetery*. Schmökel, *Sumer*, pp. 33, 61.
[109] Andrae in *Handbuch*, p. 669.
[110] A. Parrot, *Tello* (Paris, 1948), pp. 211–219; *Sumer* (London, 1960), p. 203, Fig. 250.

probably with some symbolic implication. Bodies of private individuals were buried in ribbed terra-cotta tubs (Fig. 18, bottom left), in bell-shaped double jars set rim to rim, or in baked brick vaults of a coarse type (Fig. 18, lower middle).[111] The tomb was occasionally reopened for other members of the family.

The simple tomb at Kish and Ur I developed into a monumental structure in Ur III,[112] rivaling the early mastabas of the Egyptian pharaohs. To the southeast of the temenos at Ur, King Shulgi (2045–2000 B.C.) and King Amar–Sin (1999–1990 B.C.) built two large tombs beneath a superstructure for the funerary cult. The plan was like that of a Babylonian house, with large corbeled rooms (7.7 × 4.15 m.; 10.7 × 4 m. and 5.5 m. high) and a substructure accessible from internal stairs (Fig. 18, bottom right). Its design is based on the square as a planning unit and conforms to a harmonic system.

During this period tombs are usually not beneath the houses but in cemeteries, as in earlier Eridu, Kish, and Ur. At Assur one tomb and several graves for families at the bottom of pits contain the bodies and some copper artifacts. A brick hearth for the funeral fire covers the pit (Fig. 18, bottom middle).[113] When the grave is beneath the house, there is a small chapel above it.[114] This custom seems to have been revived during the First Dynasty of Babylon (1830–1530 B.C.).[115] It is in the Middle Assyrian Period (1356–1078 B.C.), however, that the true radiating arch is invented and that vaults cover the tombs.[116]

When King Assurnazirpal II (883–959 B.C.) renovates the Old Palace at Assur, he builds in it a large vaulted tomb of brick (6–8 m. and 3 m. high) with a basalt door and, inside, his basalt sarcophagus.[117] His successors imitate him.

Private graves at Assur dating from the reign of Sargon II (721–705 B.C.) are still roofed over with corbel rings.[118] Perhaps the royal tomb (Nabopolassar's?) in the north wall of the south citadel at Babylon is analogous to those in the palace at Assur. Some of the gold lining on the walls was found *in situ*.[119]

Fortifications

The earliest trace of fortifications is the temenos wall that surrounds the temple and the residence of its high priest who also acts as the

[111] Parrot, *Sumer*, pp. 278–282, Fig. 58.
[112] C. L. Woolley, *Antiquaries Journal*, Vol. IX, pl. 45. Andrae in *Handbuch*, p. 686, Fig. 56. Schmökel, *Sumer*, pp. 152–153, Fig. 4.
[113] Andrae, *Assur*, pp. 79–80; *Handbuch*, p. 691.
[114] Schmökel, *Sumer*, p. 154.
[115] Andrae in *Handbuch*, p. 696.
[116] *Ibid.*, p. 711.
[117] *Ibid.*, pp. 716–717.
[118] Andrae, *Assur*, p. 169.
[119] Andrae in *Handbuch*, pp. 730–731.

ruler. When the palace is built as an independent structure and starts to rival the temple as an urban focus, the king surrounds it with a wall transforming it into a citadel. This is probably the normal type of fortification in the Mesilim Period (2600–2500 B.C.).[120]

The early town, whether irregular or preplanned, is surrounded by a large enclosure, which is sometimes double (2.5 × 3 km. at Uruk). As in Egypt, the temple is set within a temenos and the palace within its citadel, a large rectangular enclosure that is partly buttressed and accessible through a gateway flanked by towers. Here again a parallel could be drawn between this and the type of citadel in Archaic Egypt (Abydos, Hierakonpolis). Two such structures have been found at Eridu (one is 65 × 45 m.) and one at Kish. The concept of the city as a "fortress" of a god or a king is clearly implied, at least since the First Dynasty of Babylon, in such names as Kar-Ilu-Shamash ("Fortress-of-Shamash"), Kar-Tukulti-Ninurta ("Fortress-of-Tukulti-Ninurta"), Dur-Ili ("Wall-of-the-God"), or Dur-Sharrukin ("Wall-of-Sargon").[121]

This tradition was carried on when the country was unified under the Akkadian rulers (2350–2150 B.C.). At Tell Brak, King Naramsin (2200 B.C.) built an enclosure ten meters thick with only one gateway. It has already been mentioned that the citadel is usually laid out at the northernmost end of the town because of the favorable exposure to the north wind (Ur, Tell Asmar, Khorsabad, Babylon, Assur). These fortifications are built of sun-dried brick or have a filling of earth between two retaining walls that are battered or buttressed. Baked brick is used later by the Babylonians. Very often the fortifications stretch along the bank of the river or the canals (Ur, Assur, Babylon).

Numerous fortified structures were erected by the kings of the First Dynasty of Babylon (Mound B at Khafaje), a sign of the political instability of the times.[122] Texts from the later years of Hammurabi inform us about a besieged Babylonian fortress manned by a garrison of one thousand soldiers,[123] but no actual remains are known.

In the short-lived city of Kar-Tukulti-Ninurta (1235–1198 B.C.) one south gate flanked by two towers forms the access to the top of the buttressed brick enclosure. An inner buttressed wall running parallel to the Tigris isolates the area of the temples and the palace, which is set as a citadel along the river apart from the rest of the city.[124] One gate with a double doorway opens in the south side of the enclosure.

120 Schmökel, *Sumer*, p. 104.
121 Dhorme, *Religion*, p. 123.
122 Andrae in *Handbuch*, p. 685.
123 Schmökel, *Hammurabi*, p. 42.
124 Andrae, *Assur*, pp. 121–122, Fig. 52.

More information is available about Middle Assyrian (1356–1078 B.C.) military architecture, especially from the remains at Assur. In its semicircular walls are several gateways with either a double or a triple doorway (Gurgurri Gate; Fig. 19, top) enclosing a shallow transverse room from which two lateral staircases rise inside the masonry to the top of the walls.[125] Two towers (8–10 m. front, 4 m. deep, and 15 m. high) flank the entrance; and farther along, a postern (Gurgurri) appears as an inconspicuous entrance. The walls are seven meters thick and eleven to twelve meters high. The Gurgurri Gate is set askew to the alignment of the walls in the direction of the processional street. From it slant outer walls running at a lower level as a quay along the Tigris. They are built of limestone and lined with baked brick set in bitumen. A canal flows outside the walls, so that the city is virtually surrounded by watercourses. The names of thirteen gates and the history of the walls are recorded in the foundation inscriptions to perpetuate the entity of those architectural features that were considered as gods. It was Shalmaneser III (858–824 B.C.) who doubled the fortifications on the west (Fig. 19, middle right) and topped them with the traditional crest of enameled blue brick with a yellow outline. It is significant that the besiegers who took Assur in 614 B.C. attacked the extension of the outer walls south of the new city with pitch and arrows but ignored the gates.

Orthostat slabs of alabaster carved with scenes of war in high relief line the lower part of the gates in New Assyrian cities (909–612 B.C.).[126] Colossal man-headed bulls, probably the Lamassu ("god-protector-of-the-city"), or statues of the king are erected at the city gate. Gateways as well as walls and canals bear names of deities to whom they are dedicated.[127]

At Khorsabad,[128] twelve kilometers northeast of Nineva, King Sargon II founded a new capital, Dur Sharrukin ("Wall-of-Sargon"), which was never completed (722–705 B.C.). The city walls of brick on stone foundations form a huge quadrangular outline, oriented by the corners, with two gates in each side except the northwest one where the citadel protrudes outside the wall. This citadel (ca. 250,000 sq. m.) has two enclosures, with the inner one surrounding the terrace. The palace buildings are entered from a ramp and a monumental gateway with triple doorway flanked by man-headed bulls (Fig. 19, middle left). Between the two citadel enclosures are the temple of Nabu (southwest), the residence of the vizier (southeast), and a few other buildings. Bastions protrude from the outer face of the city wall at regular intervals (about 37.5 m. axis to axis). A smaller palace

---

[125] *Ibid.*, pp. 59–68, 140–143. Andrae in *Handbuch*, pp. 717 ff., Fig. 70.
[126] Andrae in *Handbuch*, p. 715.
[127] Dhorme, *Religion*, p. 124.
[128] Loud and Altman, *Khorsabad*, Part II. pp. 8 ff.

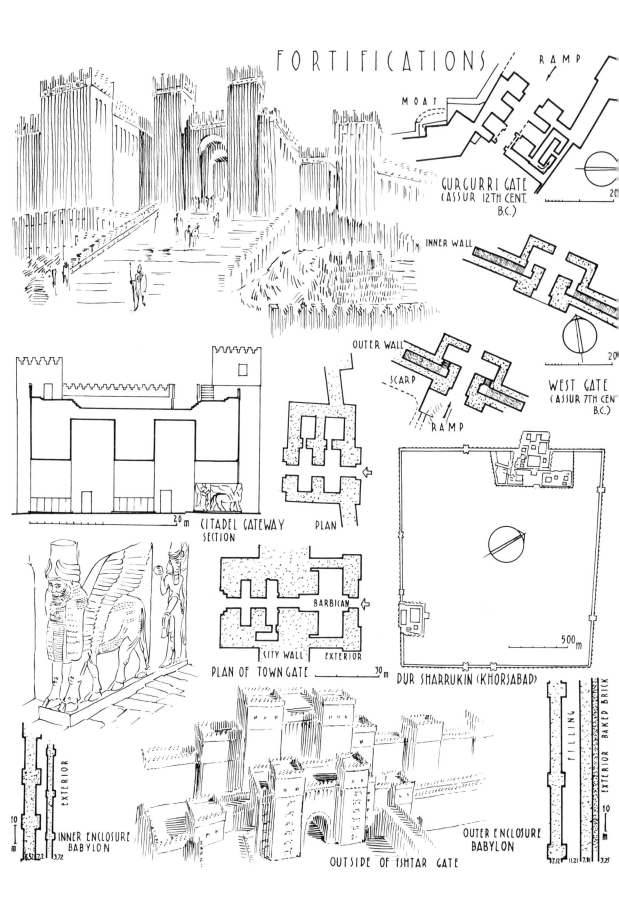

FORTIFICATIONS

RAMP

MOAT

GURGURRI GATE
(ASSUR 12TH CENT.
B.C.)

20

INNER WALL

20

WEST GATE
(ASSUR 7TH CENT.
B.C.)

OUTER WALL

SCARP

RAMP

CITADEL GATEWAY
SECTION

PLAN

20 m

BARBICAN

CITY WALL   EXTERIOR

PLAN OF TOWN GATE   30 m

DUR SHARRUKIN (KHORSABAD)

500 m

EXTERIOR

INNER ENCLOSURE
BABYLON

10
m

OUTSIDE OF ISHTAR GATE

OUTER ENCLOSURE
BABYLON

FILLING

EXTERIOR   BAKED BRICK

10

m

is located along the south side of the enclosure as a "cavalier"
element to control riots from within and attacks from outside the
city. The gateways are of a uniform type, with a long passageway
(about 52 m.) that crosses two transverse vestibules in a tower
protruding inside the city wall; in front of the passage is a barbican
with an outer gate (52 × 28 m.; Fig. 19, middle).

The royal citadel in Babylon (Babili, or "Gate-of-the-Gods")
occupies a similar location, controlling the northern access to the
city, adjacent to a fort on the west, which juts out into the Euphrates,
and to the Ishtar Gate on the east, which spans the processional
avenue.[129] The city walls are double (Fig. 19, bottom left) in the
inner enclosure and triple in the outer one (Fig. 19, bottom right).
The inner walls are 7.2 m. apart, with small cavalier towers on the
eastern side (3.2 m. thick) and alternating small and large bastions
on the waterfront (2.5 m. thick). There are vertical drains in the
courtines (east) and the small bastions (west). In the larger city on the
western bank the outer enclosure follows the alignment of the inner
walls of the eastern layout. The outer enclosure stretches far to the
north around a suburban district and then curves southwest to follow
the Euphrates bank. It consists of an inner wall (7.12 m. thick) with
alternating large and small cavalier towers (every 100 cubits, or about
52.5 m.). The inner wall is 11.2 meters from an outer wall (7.81 m.
thick), which is faced with a baked brick lining (3.25 m.). The inter-
vening space is filled in with earth, and at the top runs a paved street
wide enough (29.4 m.) for a four-span chariot. Because this part of
the report by Strabo[130] is so exactly corroborated, there is no reason
to doubt the accuracy of the figure he gives for the total length of the
enclosure as being 69 kilometers, provided it receives a proper
interpretation.[131] The citadel has its own double walls with cavalier
towers. The Ishtar Gate forms the north entrance to the city at about
mid-length in the processional avenue (Fig. 19, bottom middle).
This monumental structure has an outer shallow vestibule fronted
by two towers and an inner deep hall also fronted by two towers to
its north. It was heightened for the last time by Nebuchadnezzar as
an adjustment to the gradual rise in the level of the processional
street as it filled with detritus. The faces of the gate are of blue glazed
brick with representations of wild bulls and dragons (perhaps a
total of 575) in alternate rows, the upper ones being in low relief.
They symbolize the union of nature and divinity, as did the lions on
the walls of the processional street. There were eight other gateways
in the city walls, each dedicated to a god. It has been discovered that

[129] Koldewey, *Babylon*, pp. 32–49.
[130] Strabo, *Geography*, Bk. XVI. Chap. I, par. 5; H. C. Hamilton and W. Falconer,
eds. (London, 1906), III, p. 144.
[131] See section on "Towns."

←Fig. 19

the location of these gates along the walls conforms to a modular system that is based on harmonic ratios for the spacing between the gates and the corners of the enclosure.[132]

The Style

No architectural style has ever proved to be so much the result of the physical environment as the Mesopotamian one. There was no choice for the architects but to adapt their designs and construction to the harsh climatic conditions, and it is to their credit that their achievement is of significant aesthetic value.

The problem of the annual floods in the plain of the two rivers was solved by erecting all monuments on artificial brick terraces. Though the concept of the ziqurrat is probably purely religious, there is no doubt that the early use of the artificial terrace on a wide scale could have stimulated the invention of a stepped pyramid to carry the high temple.

People had to evade the scorching sun and dust storms even more than in Egypt, and as a result houses were built of one or more units, each with an internal court surrounded by rooms and blind walls along narrow shady alleys. The prevailing mild wind blows from the northeast, and this factor played a role in determining the orientation of the temples to this direction, at right angles to the longer axis of the town growing along the Euphrates and the Tigris, both of which flow northwest to southeast. Unlike Egypt, Mesopotamia has a rainy season but no sandy soil to absorb rain waters. Thus early houses had to be roofed over with gables and courts, which were paved entirely with baked brick set in bitumen, or at least pathways had to be provided to allow for circulation even when the earth had become a hopeless morass. A drainage system was developed at an early stage, and waste waters were collected in the center of the court-yard and led to the street drain.

Materials of construction were only reeds, palm fronds, mud, and bitumen. These scanty resources, exploited to their limits, allowed for the development of a bold and highly original style. The bundles of reed and wattlework that formed the walls and vaults of early structures were imitated in brick with engaged columns and rounded pillars (temple of level IVa at Uruk, temple at ʿUbaid), in the "false-door" at the rear of the sanctuary with stepped recesses (Sin temple at Khafaje) or ribbed cross section (Khorsabad), and in the recessed paneling that covered the external and internal façades of most structures, temples, palaces, podiums, and even houses from the earliest times till the end of Babylon. Occasionally also walls

[132] Egli, *Städtebau*, p. 66.

were left plain (temple of level IVa at Uruk, houses at Hassuna, Arpachiya, Tepe Gawra, Sin temple at Khafaje, Early Dynastic Sumerian palace at Kish).

Versatility is the characteristic of this recessed paneling. It may be simple, with only a few pilasters or buttresses framing wide areas of plain wall, or it may be elaborate, with a regular alternation of projecting pilasters and recesses, often steplike or extremely intricate, with secondary recesses of rectangular or triangular cross section. The rhythm in the contiguous stretches of walls of the same structure may vary according to the sequence of the dimensions of the grooves in brick lengths: 2.5:2:2.5:...(southwest wall in the Neo-Babylonian temple at Kish) or 1.5:2:1.5:... or 2.5:3:2.5:... (southeast).[133] The alignment of a monumental façade, especially that of the main entrance, is often stepped or askew so as to assume a convex outline (Sin-Shamash at Assur), probably a device to create an optical illusion (southeast wall of citadel at Khorsabad, ziqurrat of Urnammu at Ur, front and rear of temple of Gudea at Lagash). Another device for achieving an optical illusion has been noticed as a variation in size in the mural reliefs in the large court east of the throne room at Khorsabad.

That these recesses had a religious implication as in Egypt is proved by the occurrence of statues of gods and goddesses holding the flowing vessel on the external façade of the Kassite temple of Inanna at Uruk.[134] These deities were supposed to emerge from the mountain clefts,[135] as did the god himself, through the rear false-door in the temple or the niche in the side of the Assyrian ziqurrat (Assur at Kar-Tukulti-Ninurta).[136]

The elaborate style of recessed paneling was not the only result of the almost exclusive use of mud brick. Arches, vaults, and domes in the shape of corbels and later as true radiating systems (Old Assyrian)[137] rendered watertight with bitumen were built extensively as roofs. With the abundant reeds dried for use as cheap fuel, brick could be baked to make it impervious, allowing at the same time for more aesthetic possibilities. Bricks could be modeled with high relief scenes (Uruk) or, when painted and glazed, would form glittering compositions of weatherproof murals in vivid colors (Khorsabad, Assur, Calah, Nineva, Babylon). Later, glazed brick with small patterns was used in facing or crenelations (Assur, Calah, Nineva). Brick casing was applied as a protective layer in restoration work. Areas liable to dampness (bathrooms, courtyards, quays) were also

---

[133] Watelin, *Kish*, Vol. III, p. 10.
[134] Jordan, *Uruk-Warka*.
[135] Frankfort, *Art*, pp. 63–64.
[136] Andrae, *Assur*, p. 123.
[137] Andrae in *Handbuch*, p. 711.

paved with baked brick or tile. The technique reached a high point, even utilizing weep holes in terraces, drainage channels, and expansion joints in massive walls (citadel of Babylon).[138]

It is noteworthy that all the walls, except those of terraces and ziqurrats, had vertical faces, which were emphasized by pilasters, buttresses, and recessed paneling, towers flanking gateways of towns, or portals of temples and palaces, and bastions in the enclosures of towns. No entablature checked this surging movement, which was carried upward to the top frieze of circles and the steplike crenelation, itself a symbol of the sacred mountain.

In the earliest monuments conical pegs of clay (*sikkati*), and later of terra-cotta, were inserted into the thick plaster in horizontal rows just beneath the top of the terraces. Though their heads appearing on the face of the wall were treated in a decorative pattern with recessed colored circles ("Painted Temple" at ʿUqair) or rosettes (ʿUbaid), this aesthetic use could not have been their initial purpose. On the analogy of the occurrence of similar pegs set in one or more rows at the top of the façade of the tomb chapel from the Eighteenth Dynasty in Egypt, it is fairly safe to state that they were reminiscent of the butt ends of reeds that formed the ceilings of primitive structures.[139]

In addition to mud brick, various building materials were used. Bitumen proved to be extremely valuable as a waterproof mortar and plaster or modeled into the cores of statues (ʿUbaid, Tello). Wood was practically nonexistent, and Nebuchadnezzar had to import cedar for the roofs of his palace at Babylon. In Assyrian palaces and temples stone came to be used with brick but never replaced it. Besides such structural uses as stairs or as slabs lining the walls of bathrooms, there were nonstructural uses of stone, such as symbolic stelae and pillars (Assur), colossal man-headed bulls protecting the entrances (Calah, Khorsabad, Babylon), carved thresholds, and sacred furniture (Khorsabad). Perhaps the palaces at Khorsabad are the ones where stone occurs most.

It should be mentioned that during an early period small triangular pieces of stone allied with shell were arranged in geometric patterns to form an incrustation facing (Mosaic Temple in level IV a at Uruk, ʿUbaid). Another decorative use of stone occurred in orthostats lining the lower part of walls in palaces (Assur, Khorsabad); these were carved with impressive scenes of warfare and the hunt, probably under the influence of the Hurrians.[140]

Mural painting seems to have been used only occasionally, though

[138] Koldewey, *Babylon*, p. 71.
[139] Andrae, in *Handbuch*, p. 671, mentions that they imitated actual pegs used to nail mats or rugs to the wall.
[140] *Ibid.*, p. 716.

it occurred as early as the Archaic Period (Painted Temple at ʿUqair, 29th century B.C.), with figures in flat variegated colors within a black outline on a white ground (ʿUqair, Mari).

Metals, namely copper and silver, were used in the embossed plating of statues and doors (bronze at Khorsabad, copper in Babylon) as well as in solid copper statues set in friezes (ʿUbaid) or around doorways (Babylon),[141] and in pivots with iron caps (Khorsabad).

The design of monumental structures initiated by the Sumerians was marked by many influences from later settlers. We have described the various stages of development in the temple. Perfect symmetry is successfully achieved from the earliest times (temples at Uruk) and still favored later by the Kassites (Inanna at Uruk) and the Assyrians (Sin-Shamash at Assur). It does not, however, play the same basic role that it did in Egyptian architectural design. Symmetry is actually often impaired where the central element in a plan, itself symmetrical, is flanked by dissimilar units (White Temple). This dissimilarity can even lead to balance in design when the entrance opens at right angles to the main axis (Sin temple at Khafaje, Ishtar temple at Assur). In general, the Mesopotamian architect makes an ingenious and versatile use of the axis. To secure privacy the axis of an entrance is often offset with respect to the main one (temple of Assur at Kar-Tukulti-Ninurta, house at Ur, mansion at Babylon), or both cross at right angles (house at Tell Asmar, Tello). Houses are set at right angles to the alignment of the street even in irregular town layouts (Ur). It is a peculiarity of Mesopotamian domestic architecture that the container does not correspond to the contained: a right-angled house plan may be set within a circular outer wall (Tepe Gawra XI A), or outer façades may often be offset in a stepped outline reminiscent of the inner orthogonal plan (Neo-Babylonian houses). Such a concept reflects the early and universal prevalence of brickwork. In monumental planning the orthogonal system supersedes the symmetrical one, best exemplified in Egyptian monumental design where the axis of symmetry always predominates, even when it is slightly curved. One can speak of Mesopotamian rigidity in design, compared with Egyptian flexibility, a contrast apparent in other aspects of these cultures as well.

There is evidence of the occasional use of a harmonic design in preplanned cities both in the layout of streets (Borsippa) and in the spacing of gates in the enclosure wall (Khorsabad, Babylon).[142] Monumental plans are also designed harmonically (Temple D, White Temple at Uruk, tomb of Shulgi and Amar-Sin at Ur III, temple and ziqurrat of Assur at Kar-Tukulti-Ninurta).

[141] Koldewey, *Babylon*, p. 44.
[142] Egli, *Städtebau*, pp. 62–65.

Asia Minor and North Syria

The Physical Environment

Between Asia and Europe the peninsula of Anatolia forms a link that has often been overrun by migrating peoples.[1] It is pan-shaped, with a central plateau (800–1,300 m. high) surrounded by mountain ranges: to the north is Pontus, with peaks as high as 3,000 meters, decreasing toward the west; to the south are the Taurus Mountains, to the east another range of mountains, and along the Aegean coast a series of valleys running east–west.

The climate of this encircled high plateau is continental except on the Mediterranean coast, which has mild weather. Forests must have been more extensive in antiquity, since timber from coniferous trees was used freely as reinforcement against frequent earthquakes. The wooden beams were set in the stone or sun-dried brick structures, which had stone foundations and ceilings as well as corbel vaults of stone or true vaults of brick. The frequency of earthquakes in both Asia Minor and North Syria also accounts for social upheavals in antiquity.

To the east of the Anti-Taurus Mountains, North Syria, which spread along a deep bay of the Mediterranean and was separated from Mesopotamia by the Amanus Mountains, was bound to receive many influences from both Mesopotamia and Anatolia. Commonly used building materials in this area included chalky stone, breccia, even diorite and basalt, as well as sun-dried square brick or rammed

[1] R. Naumann, *Architektur Kleinasiens* (Tübingen, 1955), pp. 1 ff. E. Egli, *Geschichte des Städtebaues* (Zurich, 1959), pp. 92 ff.

earth. In the zone of Mesopotamian influence bitumen was used as mortar in brickwork or baked brick paving. Reinforcing balks and clamps of wood were embodied in brick construction.

The Social Environment

There had been food-gathering communities on this plateau since the seventh millennium B.C. (Haçilar),[2] but food-producing tribes did not appear in the south and on the plateau before the fourth millennium B.C.[3] The earliest historical records go back to the expedition of Sargon of Akkad (2350–2295 B.C.) and toward the end of the third millennium, when numerous trading posts (*karum*) importing textiles and lead and exporting metals had been established by the Assyrians near the autochthonous towns. Evidence about early relations with Egypt is found in the gift of a wooden throne inscribed with the name of Pharaoh Saḥureᶜ (25th century B.C.), made to a king in northwest Anatolia.[4] The trade activities shifted over about 1800 B.C. to the Hittites in central Anatolia, Indo-Germanic people who had infiltrated the plateau and curbed the native population, establishing their capital at Boğazköy. The coastal area of Asia Minor had been in contact with Crete and Greece since the sixteenth century B.C.

The history of the Hittites is as short as it is impressive. During a period of seven centuries (1900–1200 B.C.) the kings at Boğazköy ruled over city-states and led expeditions eastward against Aleppo and Babylon, bringing the dynasty of Hammurabi to an end. After they had destroyed the Mitanni, their empire spread to Syria and Lebanon, as indicated in their treaty with Egypt after the indecisive battle of Qadesh (1286 B.C.). Friendly relations with Egypt account for the gesture of Pharaoh Merneptaḥ, who sent food "to keep alive that land of the Kheta [Hittites]" (1219 B.C.).[5] This empire was brought to its downfall (1190 B.C.) by a coalition of peoples from Europe that was ultimately stopped by Pharaoh Ramses III.

The Hittites, like the Assyrians, achieved the paradox of combining warfare with extensive building of numerous fortified towns that conform closely to the rugged landscape. Their culture was not impervious to foreign influences: Though they had their own hieroglyphs, their archives were written in cuneiform, the lingua franca

[2] J. Mellaart, "Two Thousand Years of Haçilar," *The Illustrated London News*, April 8, 1961, pp. 588–591.

[3] S. Lloyd, *Early Anatolia* (Harmondsworth, 1956), pp. 10 ff.

[4] J. Mellaart, "The Royal Treasure of Dorak," *The Illustrated London News*, November 28, 1959, pp. 754 ff.

[5] G. A. Wainwright, "Meneptah's Aid to the Hittites," *Journal of Egyptian Archaeology*, Vol. 46 (Oxford, 1960), pp. 24–25.

of the ancient Near East; and many Hurrian elements were integrated into their religion.

At a late date the Phrygians, who came from Thrace, established their political rule (8th–7th centuries B.C.), but their farmers' culture did not supersede the local one, which was still that of the Hittites and Hurrians, who had remained in southern Anatolia and North Syria, permeated by Assyrian and Aramaean influences.

The Lydians, who succeeded the Phrygians for a century (650–546 B.C.), were brilliant craftsmen in textiles and metals and enjoyed a civilized life. They were made famous by their last king, Croesus, who was conquered by the Persians (547 B.C.).

Towns

More favorable conditions and defensive possibilities were among the factors that induced communal groups to settle on the plateau, though no community flourished on the coast except at Troy. There are remains of the earliest settlements in the south (Haçilar, Mersin, Sakçagözü) in the form of mounds, some as high as 35 meters. An early preplanned cantonment flourished about 3600 B.C. at Mersin. However, a recent excavation of a settlement in twenty layers at Haçilar, dating back to the seventh millennium B.C. gives some evidence of the possibility that groups settled in villages and towns much earlier than it was previously believed. Troy I and Thermi are contemporaneous with the Early Helladic Period (3000–2600 B.C.), while Alishar O, Gülücek, and Dunbartepe date from the end of this period. In the Copper Age the settlements are informal villages (citadel of Troy II, 2600 B.C.; Troy III–IV, Alishar I–III).

In the first quarter of the second millennium Assyrian traders built numerous cantonments near the native towns. That of Karum Kanesh (Kültepe) is contemporaneous with Boğazköy IV and Troy VI.

As to North Syria, the Hittite culture survived in such towns as Samʾal (Zinçirli), Carchemish, and Karatepe (8th century B.C.).

A wide variety of town plans was a direct result of the diversity in the environment. In general, the native Hittite town is oval in shape, and the Syrian one is round; but farther east three other varieties show strong Mesopotamian influences. All towns feature, however, the characteristic citadel as a last refuge for a population bent on the pursuit of war in a mountainous country.

1. The typical Hittite town is surrounded by a strongly fortified wall that is oval in plan, with towers and usually three gateways. The palace of the ruler, set on the top of a hill, is surrounded by a wall forming a citadel (Arslan Tash, Alishar, Troy, Hattusha). Both

enclosures conform in their alignment to the contour lines of the terrain.

2. The circular outline with double walls, three gateways, and a central citadel occurs in North Syria (Sam'al), in eastern Anatolia (Kültepe), and in South Syria (Qadesh). This geometric type is probably derived from the circular Assyrian camp.

3. A semicircular outline occurs once at Tell Barsib (Tell Ahmar) on the Euphrates, with the palace located in its center.

4. The traditional Mesopotamian plan is copied in the quadrangular outline of Tell Halaf.

5. Both oval and quadrangular outlines occur in the inner and outer enclosures, respectively, at Carchemish on the Euphrates.

Unlike the cities of the flood plains (Egypt and Mesopotamia), those in Asia Minor have preserved their enclosures, and these remains are mines of information about ancient town planning. A comparative estimate of their area shows that Boğazköy was by far the largest, with 168 hectares, while an average large city would have ranged about 50 hectares (Tell Halaf, Roman Troy, Qadesh, Sam'al) (Fig. 20, top).[6] The citadel is only one tenth the total area or even less in the larger cities.

Haçilar.[7] This is, to date, the earliest site known in Anatolia and possibly in the world. It is in the shape of a mound with as many as twenty layers of occupation. Each building stage marks the leveling off of the earlier remains and the shifting of the new structure over the courtyard of the previous one. Curiously enough, even the earliest settlements dating back to a Neolithic culture unfamiliar with pottery feature well-built houses of mud brick on stone foundations with red burnished floors and walls or painted floors, bins, ovens, and hearths set in the courtyard. Level VI settlement (*ca.* 6000 B.C.) already shows a sense of urban development in the quadrangular houses arranged around a rectangular open space twenty meters wide. Each house has one large room with inner partitions, smaller open rooms in front (Fig. 21, top left), and a stairway leading to an upper floor. The use of plaster on walls of plano-convex brick and of plastered cupboards, timber posts, fire-boxes, and stone slabs with incised eyes dedicated to the genius of the house shows astonishing standards of domestic architecture.

Troy.[8] Only the citadel has been excavated, though the enclosure of the Roman city has been traced to the south. The claim that the

6 Naumann, *Architektur*, p. 206.
7 Mellaart, "Haçilar."
8 Lloyd, *Anatolia*, pp. 6, 64, 101. Egli, *Städtebau*, pp. 95–98. Carl W. Blegen *et al.*, *Troy*, Vol. I (Princeton, 1950).

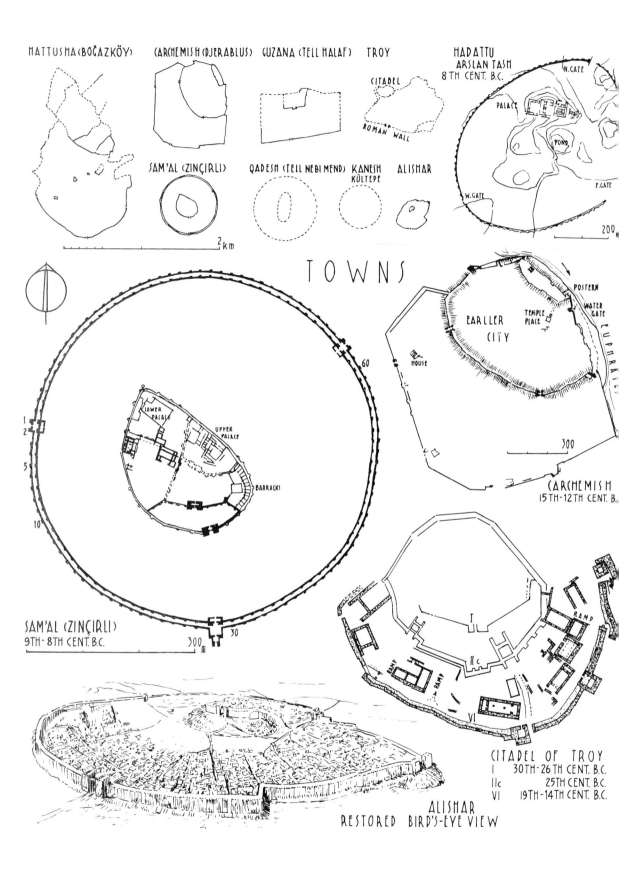

HATTUSHA (BOĞAZKÖY)   (ARCHEMISH (DJERABLUS)   GUZANA (TELL HALAF)   TROY   HADATTU
ARSLAN TASH
8TH CENT. B.C.

CITADEL

ROMAN WALL

N. GATE

PALACE

POND

SAM'AL (ZINÇIRLI)   QADESH (TELL NEBI MEND)   KANESH KÜLTEPE   ALISHAR

W. GATE   E. GATE

200

2 km

T O W N S

POSTERN
WATER
GATE

EARLIER
CITY

TEMPLE
PLACE

HOUSE

E U P H R A T ES

60

LOWER PALACE

UPPER PALACE

BARRACKS

300

CARCHEMISH
15TH-12TH CENT. B.

1
2

5

10

30

SAM'AL (ZINÇIRLI)
9TH-8TH CENT. B.C.   300 m

RAMP

II c

RAMP

RAMP

VI

CITADEL OF TROY
I   30TH-26TH CENT. B.C.
IIc   25TH CENT. B.C.
VI   19TH-14TH CENT. B.C.

ALISHAR
RESTORED BIRD'S-EYE VIEW

successive nine layers of the citadel date from the end of the fourth
millennium is based on a comparison with Aegean cultures, to which
Troy belongs as much as it does to Anatolia. The successive settlements have enclosure walls of an oval polygonal shape increasing in
size and spreading gradually southward (Fig. 20, bottom right).
While the earlier settlements have sun-dried brick walls on stone
foundations with projecting towers (Troy I) or two gateways (Troy
II), Troy VI (1725–1275 B.C.) is surrounded by a stone enclosure
about 200 meters across with jagged stretches and a tower projecting
at each entrance. Streets (3 m. wide) radiate from the center. The
structures are two-storied *megaron* units (long narrow rectangular
rooms with an entrance at one small end) arranged lengthwise in a
ring parallel to the enclosure wall. The Roman town, with its quadrangular enclosure (1060 × 700 m.), is the only excavated evidence
of the city proper.

Boğazköy.[9] The Hittite capital called Hattusha is located on strategic routes in north central Anatolia. Built on the northern slope of a
steep hill, it consists of an earlier lower city to the north (probably
the capital of Hattusili I), guarded by a citadel, and a later much
larger city to the south on a higher terrace (Fig. 20, top left). Each
district is surrounded by its enclosure, with towers probably of
brick on a stone foundation. Five gateways open in the later enclosure, each with two parabolic arched portals. Four temples are
located perpendicularly to a main street that runs to the Royal
Gate (east). The lower district is subdivided into three areas by
transverse walls, and in the central one is the largest temple. The
citadel (modern Büyükkale) between both towns contains the royal
buildings.

The paved streets (3–4 m. wide) have no straight alignment and
run northwest to southeast. They are bordered by contiguous houses
that are built as complete entities with independent walls (Fig. 21,
lower right). Earthenware pipes[10] carry potable water to Temple I,
and drainage channels show the possible existence of public utilities.
Boğazköy is a typical Hittite urbanistic answer to the need for a
large, strongly fortified capital on a mountainous terrain.

Alishar.[11] Located about eighty kilometers southeast of Boğazköy,
this town dates back to the end of the fourth millennium B.C. It is

[9] J. Garstang and O. R. Gurney, *The Geography of the Hittite Empire* (London, 1959),
p. 3. Lloyd, *Anatolia*, pp. 130 ff. Egli, *Städtebau*, pp. 100–102. K. Bittel and H. G.
Güterbock, *Boghazköy* (Berlin, 1935). K. Bittel, *Boğazköy-Ḫattuša*, 2 vols. (Stuttgart,
1952–1958).
[10] Naumann, *Architektur*, pp. 182–184, Figs. 214–215.
[11] *Ibid.*, p. 212, Fig. 254. Remzi O. Arik, *Les Fouilles d'Alaça Hüyük* (1937).

←*Fig. 20*

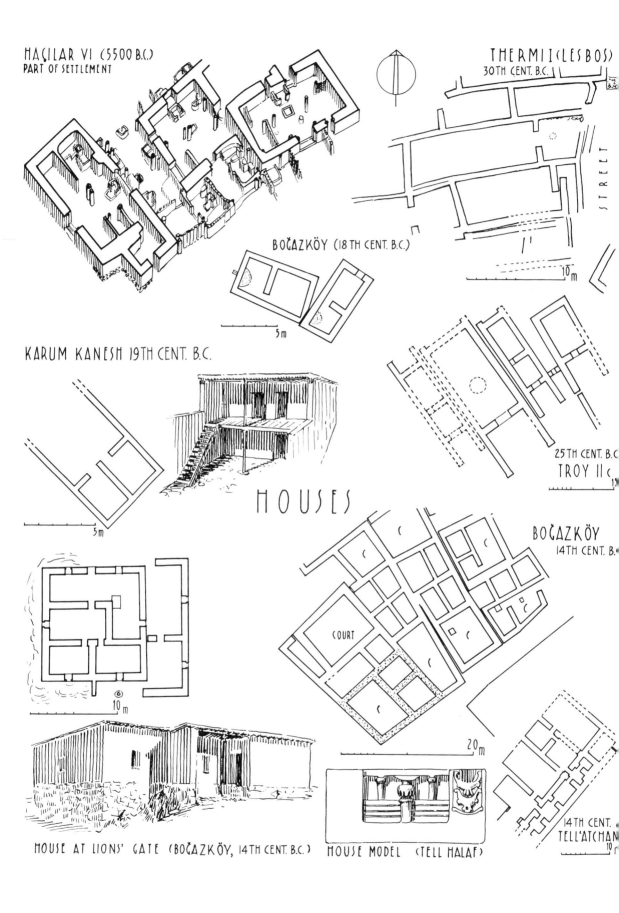

HAÇILAR VI (5500 B.C.)
PART OF SETTLEMENT

THERMI I (LESBOS)
30TH CENT. B.C.

STREET

BOĞAZKÖY (18TH CENT. B.C.)

5 m

KARUM KANESH 19TH CENT. B.C.

25TH CENT. B.C
TROY II c

5 m

HOUSES

BOĞAZKÖY
14TH CENT. B.

COURT

10 m

20 m

HOUSE AT LIONS' GATE (BOĞAZKÖY, 14TH CENT. B.C.)

HOUSE MODEL (TELL HALAF)

14TH CENT.
TELL 'ATCHAN

surrounded by a jagged oval enclosure (northeast–southwest 480 × 320 m.) and contains the earliest postern known (northeast), as well as a citadel to the northwest and residential quarters on the terraced slopes (east and south; Fig. 20, bottom left). The inner layout consists of radial streets leading to the citadel and crossing ring streets and a pomerium.

Kültepe ("Mound-of-Ashes"). The Hittite settlement of Kanesh in the center of eastern Anatolia some distance south of the Halys River is slightly oval in shape (north–south 550 × 450 m.; Fig. 20, top). It is important because of the cantonment Karum Kanesh of Assyrian traders that abuts on its east side (19th century B.C.). The *karum* was a chamber of commerce, tribunal, and post office of the Assyrian merchants who monopolized caravan trade, importing lead and textiles from Assyria along the Euphrates and crossing to Sam²al. Several other Assyrian trade outposts are known only by name.[12] The Assyrian colonists seem to have adapted themselves to the local environment and married Hittites. Streets in Karum Kanesh were in dog-legged stretches, bordered by houses having a courtyard in the center and two contiguous rooms to the south.[13]

Sam²al (modern Zinçirli). At the junction of Anatolia and North Syria on the caravan route from Assyria, perhaps dating back to the Bronze Age, this town was surrounded in about 900 B.C. by a perfectly circular wall, duplicated in the Assyrian Period (Fig. 20, middle left).[14] Its diameter is 720 meters, and there are 100 towers and three equidistant gateways, the south one forming the approach to the citadel set high on a central hill. The city is subdivided by internal transverse walls into four areas at different levels. Remains of barracks are extant to the east, and at least two palaces fronted by the shallow columned entrance portico, or *hilani*, as well as dual apartments for winter and summer seasons, lie to the north. There is some evidence that this settlement contained the earliest known water system.

As to the city itself, nothing has yet been uncovered. The geometric circular outline for a town had been known since the third millennium in Archaic Egypt, and it recurs later at Ecbatana, in the Assyrian camps (9th century B.C.), in Syria, in Sassanian Gur, and in Islamic Baghdad (A.D. 762).[15]

[12] Garstang and Gurney, *Geography*, p. 4. Lloyd, *Anatolia*, pp. 112 ff.

[13] Naumann, *Architektur*, pp. 329–332, Figs. 409–413.

[14] *Ibid.*, p. 215, Fig. 259B. Landsberger, *Sama²al* (Ankara, 1948). F. von Luschan, *Ausgrabungen in Senschirli* (*Königliches Museum in Berlin, Mittheilungen aus den orientalischen Sammlungen*, Vols. XII–XIV) (Berlin, 1893–1911).

[15] K. A. C. Creswell, *A Short Account of Early Muslim Architecture* (Harmondsworth, 1956), pp. 163 ff.

←*Fig. 21*

Carchemish. Near Djerablus on the Euphrates is a unique layout combining an earlier oval citadel, an oval city (13th century B.C.), and to its west a quadrangular city added still later (first millennium B.C.; Fig. 20, middle right). Both the shape of the latter enclosure and the use of mud brick indicate Assyrian influence. The total area (95 ha.) is the largest known next to that of Boğazköy. The earlier town was connected to the citadel by a stairway starting from an open area in front of the main temple.[16]

Hadattu (Arslan Tash, "Lions' Rock").[17] Located east of the Euphrates on the route from Assyria to Syria, it was surrounded in the eighth century B.C. by an oval enclosure (northeast–southwest 728 × 560 m., about 31 ha.). This wall had bastions at regular intervals and three gateways (Fig. 20, top right), reminiscent of Sam'al, Kültepe, or Alishar.

Houses

The harsh climate and the abundance of timber and stone were instrumental in the evolution of the peculiar style of Anatolian houses. There was no need for a central courtyard as in Mesopotamia, nor for a regular orientation of the façade and the front portico toward the north breeze as in Egypt.

The earliest houses, recently discovered at Haçilar near Burdur in central eastern Anatolia, show an unexpectedly high standard in both style and construction, much higher indeed than in other countries at that time. Even in the small room (4 m. long) of mud brick on a stone foundation at the Aceramic level (seventh millennium B.C.), some of the walls and floors are colored red and burnished, or even painted with patterns.[18] In the sixth millennium B.C. each house is a two-storied structure with one large room (8–10.5 × 5–5.5 m.) entered through one doorway in the middle of the long side. Built with stout timber posts in one longitudinal row, the house has a stairway to the upper story and smaller open rooms in front of the façade (workshops, kitchens; Fig. 21, top left). Inner partitions, rectangular windows, plastered wall cupboards, peepholes, grain bins, fireboxes, and the use of plano-convex brick, as in Mesopotamia, are the elements of a remarkably advanced

16 Naumann, *Architektur*, p. 220, Figs. 263, 484. D. G. Hogarth, *Carchemish*, Vol. I; C. L. Woolley, *Carchemish*, Vol. II; C. L. Woolley and R. D. Barnett, *Carchemish*, Vol. III (London, 1952). W. Helck, *Die Beziehungen Ägyptens zu Vorderasien im 3. und 2. Jahrtausend v. Chr.* (Wiesbaden, 1962), p. 300.

17 Naumann, *Architektur*, p. 220, Fig. 261. F. Thureau-Dangin *et al.*, *Arslan Tash* (Paris, 1931).

18 Mellaart, *Haçilar*, pp. 588–591.

architecture. It is significant that by level II in the Early Chalcolithic Period (5219 B.C.) the houses are poorer, consisting of a main room and a so-called "protomegaron" anteroom.

This is actually the type of primitive house that replaced the megalithic buildings at Mersin,[19] which had small rooms built of loose rubble (proto-Chalcolithic Period), and later clay or brick walls set on a stone foundation in the shape of socles with plastered inner partitions (Chalcolithic). The unit in the preplanned cantonment (third millennium B.C.), as exemplified at Thermi in Lesbos,[20] has a forecourt and a room (3 × 3 m.; Fig. 21, top right). Whether this early type evolved into the monumental megaron common in the citadel of Troy (3500–2600 B.C.) is a matter of speculation. Here the megaron assumes its typical shape,[21] as a long narrow rectangular room of undressed stone fronted on one small end (south) by a porch with one doorway and backed by a shallow recess (Fig. 21, middle right). A circular hollow is sunk in the center of the room for the hearth. The layout of the units, all oriented toward the southeast (Troy II c) or in a ring parallel to the enclosure (Troy VI), shows preplanning.

The megaron type found on the western coast of Anatolia is but rarely evidenced inland (Kültepe). The Old Hittite houses (Boğazköy, Alishar)[22] follow the plan found at Mersin, each house as an independent rectangular unit consisting of two rooms (2–4 m. long) built of mud brick and set on a stone socle. Larger houses are compounded of two such units, usually without any court, or occasionally with one in front (Fig. 21, upper middle). At Karum Kanesh (1900–1800 B.C.)[23] the basic plan features at the rear of a court (Fig. 21, middle left) two rooms side by side fronted by an awning and connected to the first floor by a stairway. Such an arrangement is reminiscent of the simple peasant house in Egypt as represented in the numerous models, the so-called "soul houses" of the Middle Kingdom (Fig. 4, top middle). Curiously enough, there seems to be a prevailing orientation toward the northwest. This two-roomed type is maintained during the Empire (lower city at Boğazköy) and sometimes duplicated within the square outline (Boğazköy, house at Lions' Gate; Fig. 21, bottom left). Timber posts on stone blocks carry a ceiling of balks, and walls evolve from thin brick partitions into thicker ones to allow for larger spans. Nowhere is there any emphasis on the entrance or the layout, which lacks any vestibule or court. Even in crowded

---

[19] J. Garstang, *Prehistoric Mersin* (Oxford, 1952)

[20] Naumann, *Architektur*, pp. 311–315, Figs. 389–392. W. Lamb, *The Excavations of Thermi in Lesbos* (Cambridge, England, 1936).

[21] Naumann, *Architektur*, pp. 316–318, Figs. 393 ff.

[22] *Ibid.*, p. 327, Figs. 404–405.

[23] *Ibid.*, Fig. 410. Lloyd, *Anatolia*. pp. 120–121.

houses a court never assumes the character of a central open area surrounded by rooms as in Mesopotamia.

In North Syria early houses from the fifteenth century B.C. to the fourteenth century B.C. are known in Tell Atchana;[24] they have an elaborate layout of two adjacent rows of well-differentiated rooms featuring a main room and one to three secondary rooms with drains (Fig. 21, bottom right). Basalt orthostats or mural paintings form the decorative elements as do sophisticated façades with columned porticoes, windows, and awnings represented in models (Fig. 21, bottom). There is, however, no evidence of a central court, though occasionally private and public apartments are arranged in two complexes on both sides of a yard (Tell Atchana). The type is still strongly reminiscent of Anatolian houses.[25]

Palaces

It often happened in Hittite Anatolia that the ruler was also, as in Sumer, the high priest who resided in the temple. Some of the palaces seem to have had a definitely official character, perhaps of a religious nature, as did the ceremonial palace at the Scorpion Gate at Tell Halaf (Fig. 22, bottom left).[26] Other residences are characterized by rolling hearths, or metal containers on four wheels rolling on two rails in the main hall in the winter aisle (Sam'al, Arslan Tash, Tell Halaf). Palaces are located on the highest terrace of the citadel or royal stronghold, and they are similar in their style and large scale to the temples. The palace grounds are surrounded by a wall (Troy, Boğazköy). The main entrance is in the shape of a hilani portico with pillars (Sam'al, Tell Tayinat) or statues on the backs of lions (ceremonial palace at Tell Halaf), an element much favored by the Assyrians in their own palaces (Khorsabad).

In western Anatolia the only palaces known are those in the various layers at Troy, always with separate megara of indefinite use oriented to the southeast (Troy II c;[27] Fig. 22, top left). A megaron from the Late Bronze Age has, however, been found at Kültepe.[28] In inner Anatolia the palace is also built on the highest spot (Boğazköy) or on an artificial platform (Kültepe). At Boğazköy the whole citadel is seemingly occupied by the palace complex, consisting of independent structures, the peripheral ones being smaller administrative rooms (Fig. 22, top right).[29]

[24] Naumann, *Architektur*, pp. 338–340, Fig. 421.
[25] *Ibid.*, p. 342.
[26] *Ibid.*, p. 345.
[27] *Ibid.*, p. 346, Fig. 268.
[28] Lloyd, *Anatolia*, p. 86 n.
[29] Naumann, *Architektur*, p. 350, Figs. 431–433.

Fig. 22→

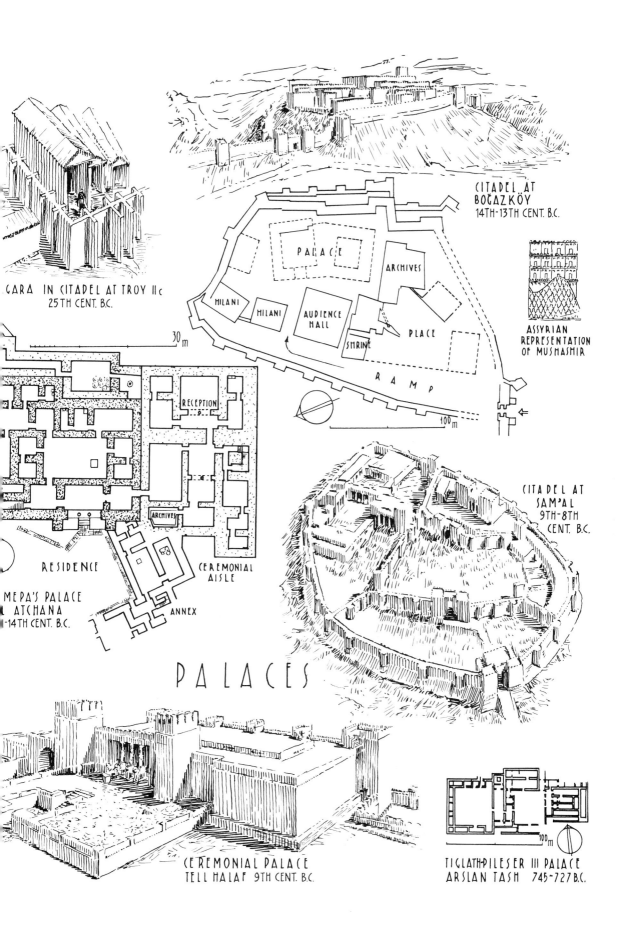

GARA IN CITADEL AT TROY IIc
25TH CENT. B.C.

CITADEL AT
BOĞAZKÖY
14TH-13TH CENT. B.C.

PALACE

ARCHIVES

HILANI

HILANI

AUDIENCE
HALL

SHRINE

PLACE

RAMP

30 m

100 m

ASSYRIAN
REPRESENTATION
OF MUSHASHIR

RECEPTION

ARCHIVES

RESIDENCE

CEREMONIAL
AISLE

MEPA'S PALACE
ATCHANA
-14TH CENT. B.C.

ANNEX

CITADEL AT
SAM'AL
9TH-8TH
CENT. B.C.

PALACES

CEREMONIAL PALACE
TELL HALAF 9TH CENT. B.C.

TIGLATHPILESER III PALACE
ARSLAN TASH 745-727 B.C.

100 m

The Mesopotamian integrated plan is recalled by the palace at Kültepe, with shallow halls around a square courtyard (26 × 26 m.), being exactly oriented, like that at Alaça Hüyük, around a smaller court (12 × 13 m.). The use of square pillars in the halls, the materials of construction, and the flat ceilings tend, however, to give to the Hittite palace a style of its own, differing from both the Mesopotamian and the Syrian ones.

Curiously enough, Syrian palaces of the second millennium B.C. are more elaborate than Hittite ones. The palace of Yarimlim (17th century B.C.) at Tell Atchana, though built about two centuries later than the one at Eshnunna (Tell Asmar) on the Tigris, resembles it in more than one aspect. The same narrow rectangular layout running north–south (30 × 95 m.) is divided into three principal areas, each with its own light court and a corridor along the eastern side. To the north of the central court are the ceremonial apartments with a reception suite and a staircase to the upper floor. To the south are the residential apartments with another staircase and at the rear the dependencies. On the first floor along the south side of the central court a large pillared hall with painted walls is reminiscent of a Cretan ceremonial hall.[30] Besides the latter trend in decoration, the Syrian palace is characterized by its small rooms, the separated units around a light court, some in several stories, the bathrooms, the lack of large courts or wide halls, and the use of timber columns. From the evidence of the representations of Syrian towns on Egyptian or Assyrian reliefs and the occurrence of staircases in the ruins of the palaces there seems little doubt that these structures were many-storied, perhaps in the style of the Urartu or Arabian façades.[31]

The same points are recognizable three centuries later in the palace of Niqmepa at Tell Atchana (15th–14th centuries B.C.). Its general layout has three main parts: ceremonial, residential, and dependencies in self-contained units several stories high (Fig. 22, middle left). Here again the entrance is on the south façade through a two-columned hilani, the oldest yet known and possibly an indication that Syria was its land of origin.[32] The main entrance of the hilani, flanked by two towers, leads to a vestibule and staircase connected to the residence (north) and to the ceremonial aisle (east), with its double reception halls and a special archives room with a bench used as a shelf for the tablets. Later a series of rooms was built as dependencies abutting on the southern façade.

After a period of stagnation palatial architecture in North Syria produces the prestigious complexes at Tell Halaf and Sam'al. The

[30] *Ibid.*, p. 356, Fig. 437.
[31] *Ibid.*, pp. 370–372, Figs. 449–455.
[32] *Ibid.*, p. 427.

ceremonial palace of Kaparu at Tell Halaf (9th century B.C.)[33] shows, in the monumental approach through the Scorpion Gate, the stairway to the terrace, the glazed tile altar, and the attempt at a symmetrical front, some evolution toward a more formal, effective style, reminiscent of the concept of Mesopotamian monumental architecture (Fig. 22, bottom left). The hilani is decorated by three caryatid statues on the backs of lions, with an orthostat on either side. Two griffins flank the doorway between the front and the main halls, where a movable hearth on rails dispensed heat during the chilly Anatolian winter. The bastions at the back lend a fortified aspect to this structure, which has a shallow plan. At Sam'al (Zinçirli) the same tripartite plan is exemplified in the northernmost palace of the citadel (Fig. 22, lower right). In all the structures a prominent feature is the hilani entrance with one (IV) or two columns (I, II, III) in the façade fronting two shallow broad halls set transversely, one behind the other. When the palace has a separate aisle around a court to provide for summer (northeast) and winter (northwest) quarters, a movable hearth on rails is set in the winter aisle (upper palace at Sam'al). Independent hilani structures (730–680 B.C.) are little more than the hilani entrances complemented by one row of small rooms at the rear, perhaps for ceremonial purposes or a residential suite with latrine and bathroom (II, III).

A similar North Syrian palace is found at Sakçagözü and at Tell Tayinat, the latter perhaps being a copy from the northernmost palace at Sam'al.[34]

Quite different with regard to layout are the palace built by Tiglath-Pileser III (745–727 B.C.)[35] at Arslan Tash and the one at Tell Halaf (9th century B.C.).[36] Here a large square court surrounded on its four sides by shallow rooms set transversely is a dramatic imitation of the typical Assyrian palace. This Assyrian influence was integrated into local trends, such as the dual aisles in Tiglath-Pileser's palace for summer (west: Fig. 22, bottom right) and winter (south) with the rolling hearth, or the lack of ceremonial apartments in the main palace at Tell Halaf since these had been separated into an independent structure erected near the Scorpion Gate.

Temples

An outcome of the harsh climatic conditions is the predominance of weather gods represented as anthropomorphic figures holding a

[33] M. Fr. von Oppenheim, *Tell Halaf II: Die Bauwerke*, von F. Langenegger, K. Müller und R. Naumann (Berlin, 1950), pp. 36–50. Naumann, *Architektur*, pp. 360–363, Figs. 439–443.

[34] Naumann, *Architektur*, p. 366, Fig. 446. Compare Sindjerli, Fig. 444.

[35] F. Thureau-Dangin, A. Barrois and M. Dunand, *Arslan Tash* (Paris, 1931), plan. Naumann, *Architektur*, Fig. 461.

[36] Oppenheim, *Tell Halaf II*, Fig. 115. Naumann, *Architektur*, Fig. 464, p. 378.

weapon in the right hand or a cosmic symbol in the left and standing on a sacred animal.[37] Besides a sun-god or sun-goddess, both Hurrian deities (Hebat and Teshub) and Mesopotamian (Anu, Enlil, Ea) were introduced by the Hurrians. Later the Nubian Bes, affected in Egypt and Phoenicia, is found, perhaps introduced by Phoenician traders.[38] The tablets from Boğazköy provide ample evidence of a state religion strongly influenced by local cults.

The earlier temples are nature shrines in the vicinity of a spring (Eflatun Punar, Yazilikaya). At Eflatun Punar[39] an artificial lake (30 × 35 m.) was formed behind a rock barrier and a dam with three channels (Fig. 23, top left). At the north end of the lake near the pool from which flowed the water, a well-dressed stone platform formed what was probably part of an altar carved on its south face (7 m. long) with a scene in low relief representing the sun-god and sun-goddess seated on thrones. Above them was a winged sun-disk topped with a huge sun symbol (Fig. 23, top left). At Yazilikaya (Turkish "Inscribed-Rock")[40] near Boğazköy a cleft in the limestone cliffs about 200 meters above the valley was converted into an open-air shrine (Fig. 23, top right) by blocking the front of this roofless grotto with a complex of buildings on a terrace. This was remodeled at least four times during the three centuries of continuous use. Sixty-three figures carved in high relief in one register on the vertical faces of the rock represent a procession of gods and goddesses whose main group is led by the weather god Teshub and the sun-goddess of Arinna, named Hebat. Benches are set beneath the reliefs. A secondary room, accessible from the main one and from the exterior through a portal, is probably the sanctuary where rock faces were carved with figures of deities and of King Tudhaliyas IV (1250–1220 B.C.). A hieroglyphic inscription on an otherwise plain wall suggests that it could have been fronted by a statue. The buildings in front of the rock shrine include an independent propylon on a square plan with an inner stairway, a large structure with a central court, and a lateral portico leading to the rock chamber and, behind a separate vestibule, to the rock chamber. The style of these structures, with their numerous windows, axial vestibule, and court surrounded by pillared porticoes, resembles that of the five temples in Boğazköy, a style which has been described as palatial since the palace was the prototype of the temple.[41]

[37] O. R. Gurney, *The Hittites* (Harmondsworth, 1954), pp. 133 ff.

[38] M. Riemschneider, *Die Welt der Hethiter* (Stuttgart, 1954), pls. 86, 89, p. 247.

[39] Naumann, *Architektur*, pp. 188, 382, Figs. 221, 222, 466–468. Lloyd, *Anatolia*, p. 146.

[40] Naumann, *Architektur*, pp. 382 ff, Figs. 469–470, 472, 474. Lloyd, *Anatolia*, pp. 138–143. Riemschneider, *Hethiter*, pls. 3, 34–37.

[41] Naumann, *Architektur*, p. 389.

Fig. 23→

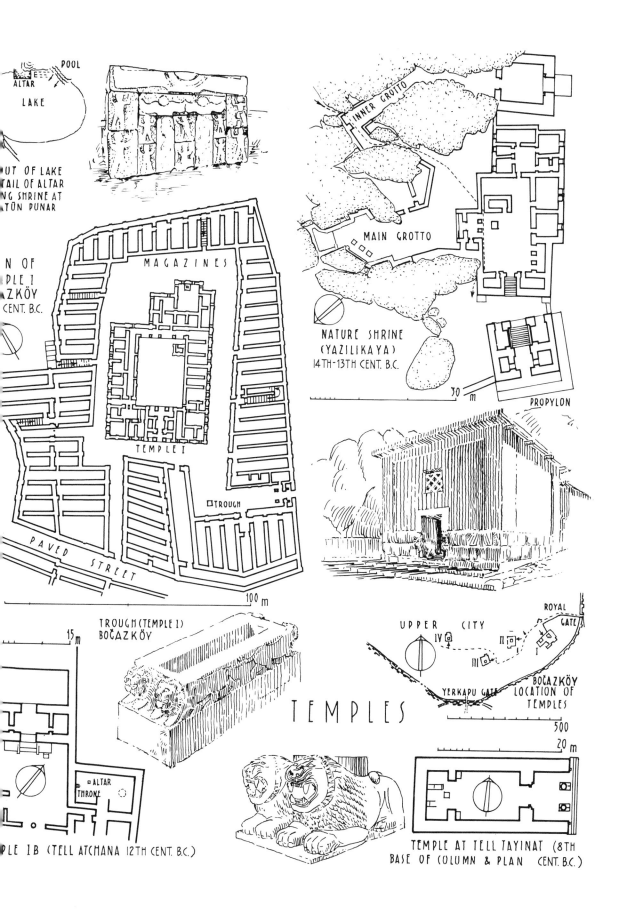

POOL

ALTAR

LAKE

...UT OF LAKE
...TAIL OF ALTAR
...NG SHRINE AT
...TÜN PUNAR

...N OF
...PLE I
...ZKÖY
... CENT. B.C.

MAGAZINES

TEMPLE I

TROUGH

PAVED STREET

100 m

INNER GROTTO

MAIN GROTTO

NATURE SHRINE
(YAZILIKAYA)
14TH–13TH CENT. B.C.

30 m

PROPYLON

TROUGH (TEMPLE I)
BOĞAZKÖY

15 m

UPPER CITY

IV

II I

III

ROYAL GATE

YERKAPU GATE

BOĞAZKÖY
LOCATION OF
TEMPLES

500

T E M P L E S

20 m

...PLE IB (TELL ATCHANA 12TH CENT. B.C.)

ALTAR
THRONE

TEMPLE AT TELL TAYINAT (8TH
BASE OF COLUMN & PLAN   CENT. B.C.)

The entrance façade of the Hittite temple (Alaça Hüyük, Boğazköy) stretches along the main street leading to the city gateway in its vicinity. There is no evidence of a cosmic orientation. Four of the five temples at Boğazköy are located in the upper city on the street to the royal gate. Temple I, which is the largest, stands in the lower city on the street to the north gate (Fig. 20, top left). This temple is set within a court surrounded by a continuous row of long narrow contiguous rooms that have an irregular outline; they are accessible from two doorways and are used as magazines (Fig. 23, middle left). The arrangement of the storerooms around the temple is reminiscent of that of Egyptian temples during the Empire, which is similar but has a rectangular outline. The temple proper, built of limestone also on an irregular plan, is of a standard type that has one entrance portal or portico with two or more doorways, one behind the other, and a rectangular court along the rear side of which stretches a pillared portico (*hilammar*). Behind this the sanctuary, which protrudes from the outline, is reached through a bent-up approach and leads to the most private cells where the statue is washed. Several windows supply profuse light and sunshine for the statue, which represents a weather god. The location on the main street to the city gate, the generous lighting through long windows reaching down almost to the floor, the consistent asymmetry, and the paved court surrounded by rooms are all characteristics that, except for the latter one, are thoroughly autochthonous. It seems possible, at least for the temples of the upper city, that the statue could be seen from the court through its front windows. Huge blocks of limestone and occasionally of granite for the sanctuary (Temple I) were set into the megalithic masonry and dressed back after construction,[42] a process also employed by the Egyptians. Timber, besides being used as reinforcement, could also form a whole floor (V).[43]

On the western coast small rectangular cellae seem to have been dedicated to the Mother Goddess (Cybele at Larissa).[44] The purpose of the reliefs carved on the rock faces overlooking rivers (Seyhan) or mountain passes (Karabel, Gezbel) is still undecided. Some archaeologists interpret them as monuments symbolizing royal power,[45] while others consider them religious.[46] The latter interpretation is in all probability the right one for the figure of a mother goddess ten meters high carved in a niche on Mount Sipylos above Manisa[47] and for the relief at Fraktin.

[42] Lloyd, *Anatolia*, p. 136, Fig. 9.
[43] Naumann, *Architektur*, p. 146, Fig. 163.
[44] *Ibid.*, p. 380, Fig. 465.
[45] *Ibid.*, p. 381.
[46] Lloyd, *Anatolia*, pp. 143–148.
[47] *Ibid.*, p. 145. Riemschneider, *Hethiter*, pl. 6, p. 237. H. Bossert, *Alt-Anatolien* (Tübingen, 1942), Nos. 560–562.

In North Syria the temple is also located in the city on the main street leading to the city gate and to the citadel ("piazza" at Carchemish). It is of an autochthonous type featuring the hilani entrance. At Tell Atchana[48] the same small sanctuary underwent five phases of remodeling between 1370 and 1190 B.C., from an asymmetrical plan with a raised statue cella fronted by an altar in a small court (Fig. 23, bottom left) to the symmetrical layout with a square court, hilani front, shallow transverse vestibule, and shallow broad cella (levels III–IV). Statues of lions, orthostats, and wood paneling compensated for the small scale of the structure. The two shrines from the late Hittite period at Carchemish[49] still have a symmetrical layout, though they have a square outline and only one cella with massive walls fronted by a hilani. The shrine at Tell Tayinat (Fig. 23, bottom right) is still symmetrical but long and narrow (12 × 25.5 m.), reminiscent of a megaron, though it could only have been influenced by the deep temple of Assyria.[50] The two columns of its portico were set on the backs of paired lions in the Assyrian style (8th century B.C.; Fig. 23, bottom).

A remarkable group of Phrygian monuments has a gabled façade cut from the rock and carved with geometrical ornament in an imitation of a house façade with doors and windows partly opened, a heraldic or religious motif. The inner chambers call to mind the arrangement of a house, and though they have been labeled as tombs, they are now thought to be shrines, perhaps having evolved from the Hittite rock nature shrines.[51]

Tombs

The study of the tombs of Asia Minor presents but little of architectural interest in spite of the numerous cemeteries. Some are located outside the earliest settlements at Yortan and Troy;[52] more are found in Polatli from the Copper Age (shaft graves, urn burials, and a cist tomb)[53] and at Alaça (4 × 8 × 0.75 m.; deep graves roofed over with timber beams, a row of stones, and heads and hoofs of sacrificed animals).[54] At Karum Kanesh (19th–18th centuries B.C.) bodies were buried beneath the floor of the house, and at Kültepe they were in terra-cotta coffins or in a cist lined with stone.[55] It is noteworthy that graves were located in a rocky setting, probably for

[48] Naumann, *Architektur*, pp. 400–404, Figs. 482–483.
[49] *Ibid.*, p. 404, Figs. 484–485.
[50] *Ibid.*, p. 405, Figs. 137, 486.
[51] Lloyd, *Anatolia*, pp. 200–203, pl. 32.
[52] Naumann, *Architektur*, p. 406.
[53] Lloyd, *Anatolia*, pp. 95–96.
[54] *Ibid.*, pp. 96–97.
[55] *Ibid.*, p. 122.

some religious reason. Intramural interments were also made at Alishar, Hüyük, and Boğazköy in the third and second millennia B.C.[56] A Hittite cemetery (17th century B.C.) at Boğazköy near an overhanging rock showed fifty graves with cremated remains out of a total of seventy-two.

Archaeologists have endeavored to interpret the corbeled stone chamber built in an artificial terrace at Gavur Kalesi,[57] on the axis and above a religious carving, as a "stone house." This was described in the funerary rituals as the place where the cremated bones of the deceased were anointed with oil and received offerings. Another structure that may be a "stone house" is a central chamber reached by a trap door in a quadrangular complex in the citadel of Boğaz-köy.[58] Still another underground room in late Hittite Sam'al is identified as a stone house. Cist graves also occur at Carchemish (10th century B.C.). At Tell Halaf Aramaean influences can be recognized in elaborate tombs that have several chambers vaulted in the Assyrian manner and have, in addition to the burial chamber, a chapel containing the funerary statue or a washroom with drains.[59]

Phrygian tombs contain cist graves for interments or urns (8th–6th centuries B.C.) or wooden chambers reminiscent of the Alaça graves. These are always covered with a tumulus whose center is marked by two crossing rows of stones.[60] This tumulus is the forerunner of the Lydian conical mausoleum exemplified in the so-called Tomb of Tantalus at Sardis.

Fortifications

It was in military architecture that the warlike Hittites displayed the full measure of their building ability in the ingenious forts that conform to the rugged country. In addition to the strategic factor essential in the choice of a location for a fort, the vital problem of water provision, which was solved in Egypt and Mesopotamia by building settlements and forts along rivers or canals, required in Anatolia the vicinity of a watercourse or springs. Mersin, the earliest fortified settlement known, is located on the left bank of a stream near its mouth and seems to have marked the site of a ford.[61] The capital, Boğazköy (Hattusha), is a fortified city in the mountains with rich springs on a road running north–south through a pass between two deep valleys.[62] A hilly area at the fork of a river allows

[56] Naumann, *Architektur*, p. 406.
[57] *Ibid.*, p. 408, Fig. 487.
[58] *Ibid.*, pp. 408–409, Fig. 420.
[59] Oppenheim, *Tell Halaf II*, pp. 100, 159, 357, 395.
[60] Lloyd, *Anatolia*, pp. 198–200.
[61] *Ibid.*, p. 75.
[62] Naumann, *Architektur*, p. 301.

sometimes for the possibility of using these as natural water ditches in the defensive system of a town (Alishar; Fig. 20, bottom left). Such a location may even form an isolated knoll reached only through a tongue of land (Qadesh; Fig. 24, top left).

The Hittite architects always show great ability in adapting their defensive layout to the physiographical environment of individual sites and providing individual solutions to each problem.[63] As a rule, a hill affords the best possibilities, care being taken to provide a hilltop for the citadel and palace of the ruler. One such example is the impregnable knoll and high plateau of Büyükkale at Boğazköy.[64]

The enclosure walls are built to take full advantage of the contour of the terrain, and inner partition walls subdivide the town into several independent quarters that could sustain a desperate defense. At Boğazköy the earlier lower city is subdivided by two transverse walls (Fig. 20, top left).[65] The citadel is always surrounded by its own enclosure, of a type different from that of the city, since it is set along the edge of the cliff and acts concurrently as a retaining wall. In small forts the houses are often built next to the walls so that the defenders could use their terraced roofs (Mersin, Thermi II, Nişantepe; Fig. 24, middle left). Walls are laid out in a jagged outline with some straight stretches to allow for lateral control of fire (Troy VI, Alishar, Carchemish; Fig. 24, bottom left).

In North Syria the defensive system is far less ingenious. The use of certain elements sometimes even seems irrelevant, such as the unaccountable irregular stretches in the high stone wall along the river edge at Carchemish[66] or the duplicated inner enclosure at Sam'al.[67] It must be said that the trend toward the geometrical outline, circular as at Sam'al (Fig. 20, middle left) or rectangular as at Tell Halaf (Fig. 20, top), conforming to the Oriental town-planning tradition of the plains, was not favorable to an efficient design of fortified elements. The fortification system of the mountain town of Karatepe on the frontier between Syria and Anatolia is regarded as an exceptional imitation of Boğazköy, with its bastions and towers at the angles of the polygonal wall, which takes advantage of the physiography of the river.[68] The Syrian citadels are, however, as strongly fortified as those in Anatolia, even having inner partition walls (Sam'al).

The skyline of Anatolian and Syrian fortified towns must have been quite impressive, indeed, judging from their representations on

[63] *Ibid.*, p. 308.
[64] *Ibid.*, pp. 301, 307, Figs. 387–388.
[65] *Ibid.*, p. 303, Fig. 382.
[66] *Ibid.*, p. 308, Fig. 263.
[67] *Ibid.*, p. 309, Fig. 259.
[68] *Ibid.*, p. 310.

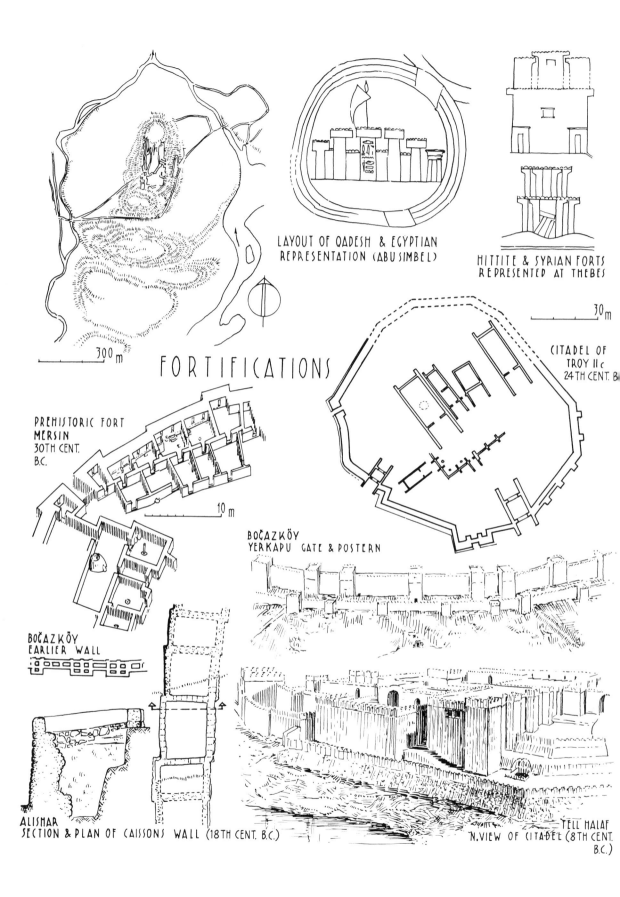

LAYOUT OF QADESH & EGYPTIAN
REPRESENTATION (ABU SIMBEL)

HITTITE & SYRIAN FORTS
REPRESENTED AT THEBES

300 m

30 m

FORTIFICATIONS

CITADEL OF
TROY IIc
24TH CENT. B.

PREHISTORIC FORT
MERSIN
30TH CENT.
B.C.

10 m

BOĞAZKÖY
YERKAPU GATE & POSTERN

BOĞAZKÖY
EARLIER WALL

ALISHAR
SECTION & PLAN OF CAISSONS WALL (18TH CENT. B.C.)

TELL HALAF
N. VIEW OF CITADEL (8TH CENT.
B.C.)

contemporaneous Egyptian[69] and Assyrian[70] monuments. Though both groups follow slightly different traditions in drafting, one can still recognize, especially in Egyptian scenes, the tall towers looming above the citadel crenelations, the machicolated bastions projecting from, or towers rising above, both the citadel and the town walls, and even the windows and the gates. Some environmental characteristics have been painstakingly represented, such as the hilly setting (Syrian Geder at Karnak; Fig. 24 top right)[71] or the watercourses encircling Qadesh (Fig. 24, top middle).[72] The conspicuous horizontal joints in massive stone masonry, most unusual to an Egyptian, are often shown.

Most of these walls were actually of stone, except in the earliest works (Mersin, Troy) and in Syrian Carchemish. The external face was battered in courses slanting outward; the slant was more pronounced in the lower part, which formed a glacis, but it was gradually reduced when stone superseded brick (from 1:3 to 1:4 at Troy VI).[73] At regular intervals (about 20–30 m.) buttresses projected, sometimes into bastions (more than 1.2 m. deep), which could prove effective for firing along the *courtines*. Some bastions were square in plan and of impressive dimensions (4 × 7 m. at Karatepe; 6–7 m. × 2–3 m. projection at Arslan Tash), and probably were carried up as towers (7–9 × 4–5 m. projection at Tell Halaf). As a result of a judicious choice of the site, the wall was planned so that it followed the upper edge of a natural deep declivity. Occasionally the latter was created artificially (Boğazköy, Sam'al, Carchemish, 13th century B.C.), and the earth from the excavation formed a rampart that was plastered into a convex profile quite recognizable in some of the Egyptian representations. The only other dry ditch besides that at Boğazköy occurred at Tell Halaf (9th century B.C.); this ditch around the city was usually wide but narrowed along the east side of the citadel, where it was strengthened by a terrace built upon the scarp (Fig. 24, bottom right).[74]

Walls varied in thickness according to the materials used, tending to increase in the later larger fortresses (1.5 m. brick at Mersin; 1.5 m. stone and brick at Alishar; 2 m. stone and brick at Thermi; 2.8–4 m. brick at Troy II b; 4–5 m. at Troy VI; 1–1.1 m. at Boğazköy; 3.1 and 3.5 m. stone at Sam'al; 5 m. brick at Carchemish). During the second millennium B.C. the caisson type of wall was perfected,

[69] Alexandre Badawy, *Le Dessin architectural chez les Anciens Égyptiens* (Cairo, 1948), pp. 150 ff., Figs. 175 ff. Naumann, *Architektur*, pp. 290–295, Figs. 365–366, 372–374, 376–377.

[70] Naumann, *Architektur*, pp. 296–298, Figs. 378–381.

[71] Badawy, *Dessin architectural*, Figs. 183, 184, 187, 188.

[72] *Ibid.*, Fig. 180. Naumann, *Architektur*, Figs. 256–258.

[73] Naumann, *Architektur*, p. 228, Fig. 269.

[74] *Ibid.*, p. 286, Figs. 255–256.

←*Fig. 24*

and it evolved rapidly from a row of contiguous square walled-in compartments (5–6 m. Alishar; Fig. 24, bottom left)[75] to a system of two thick parallel walls bound with transverse partitions and having towers that projected at regular intervals (Boğazköy; Fig. 24, lower left; Hüyük, Sozuksutepe).[76] In Syria,[77] however, caisson walls were never used, but occasionally a timber grid of transverse balks was inserted above the stone foundations (Samʾal, 13th century B.C.),[78] or brick skin-walls were added next to the external and internal faces of an earlier enclosure (Tell Halaf).[79]

It is probably from the early arrangement of small rooms along the wall (Mersin, Thermi; Fig. 24, middle left) and from the caisson type of construction that the casemated wall derived. Its rooms were usually too small to have been used for living, except at Samʾal, but were used rather for storage or as blockhouses for firing (Boğaz-köy, Carchemish).[80]

The gates evolved from a simple passageway through a bastion (Troy I, 2 m. broad; Troy II a, 8–15 m. long; Fig. 25, top left) to an axial gate chamber (Troy II b) in the shape of a megaron abutting on the inside of the gate (Troy II c), and later a bent-up approach was added (Troy VI, Fig. 25, top middle; Alishar). At Boğazköy the latter type becomes standardized as a symmetrical gate chamber with outer and inner flap doors flanked by two deep towers and approached obliquely from a ramp abutting on the outer face of the enclosure (Fig. 25, top right).[81] The bay in both inner and outer doorways curves into an elegant parabola, and the massive doorjamb is occasionally carved in high relief with a royal figure (Royal Gate at Boğazköy east)[82] or the forepart of a lion (Lions' Gate at Boğazköy, Fig. 25, upper right).[83] Trabeated doorways are used concurrently with arched ones, sometimes with monolithic doorjambs each in the shape of a winged female sphinx of Egyptianizing style (Hüyük near Alaça, Yerkapu at Boğazköy, Fig. 25, middle left).[84]

Influences from Syria can be detected in the development of the Hittite gateway in the second millennium B.C., but the process was reversed at the end of the same millennium and replaced with Assyrian influences beginning with the first millennium B.C.[85] The pre-Hittite gate in Syria had three doorways that determined the position of two

[75] *Ibid.*, p. 232, Figs. 273–275.
[76] *Ibid.*, p. 234, Figs. 277–279.
[77] *Ibid.*, p. 238.
[78] *Ibid.*, p. 243, Fig. 285.
[79] *Ibid.*, pp. 246 ff., Figs. 287–288.
[80] *Ibid.*, pp. 288–289, Figs. 357–360, 445.
[81] *Ibid.*, Figs. 309–317.
[82] *Ibid.*, Fig. 310.
[83] *Ibid*, p. 263, Fig. 311.
[84] *Ibid*, p. 263, Figs. 57–59, 322–324.
[85] *Ibid.*, p. 265.

Fig. 25→

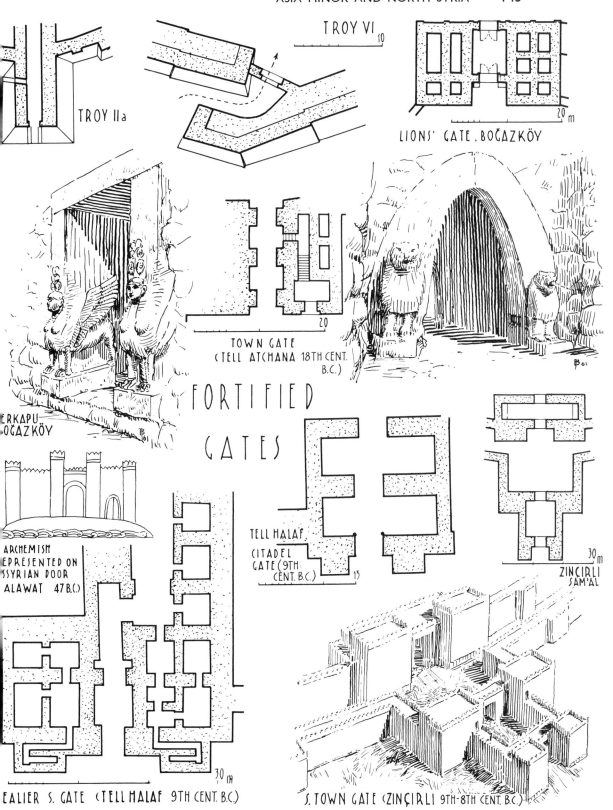

TROY IIa

TROY VI

LIONS' GATE . BOĞAZKÖY

20 m

TOWN GATE
(TELL ATCHANA 18TH CENT.
B.C.)

ERKAPU
BOĞAZKÖY

FORTIFIED

GATES

TELL HALAF

ZINÇIRLI
SAM'AL

ARCHEMISH
REPRESENTED ON
ASSYRIAN DOOR
BALAWAT 47 B.C.)

CITADEL
GATE (9TH
CENT. B.C.)   15

30 m

EARLIER S. GATE (TELL HALAF 9TH CENT. B.C.)

S. TOWN GATE (ZINÇIRLI 9TH-8TH CENT. B.C.)

gate chambers on a longitudinal axis flanked by two massive towers (Tell Atchana,[86] Fig. 25, upper middle; Qatna, Gezer; Carchemish, Fig. 25, lower left). The Hittite type with deep towers on both sides of a forecourt influenced the Syrian gateway fronting a shallow broad gate chamber of Assyrian type (Samʾal, Fig. 25, lower right), [87] which eventually stretched along the whole breadth of both towers. Another difference is the fact that the towers never projected enough to block the surrounding counterscarp. There were two shallow gate chambers, one behind the other (Carchemish, Tell Halaf, Fig. 25, lower middle),[88] shut only by the outer doorway, which was probably arched. Ultimately the towers were dissociated from, and became narrower than, the gate structure to assume the role of applied bastions in the Assyrian fashion (citadel Gate at Tell Halaf, Fig. 25, lower middle).[89] A peculiarly ingenious device consists of a deep passageway blocked by a portcullis and bending twice at ninety degrees between an outer and an inner gate chamber (Tell Halaf citadel, Fig. 25, bottom left).[90] This was surrounded by rooms and staircases between the two flanking towers. The latest gates had only one shallow gate chamber fronted by a very deep forecourt, flanked by two towers, and approached obliquely from the left (Karatepe, 730 B.C.)[91] by a ramp or a stairway.

Posterns[92] had their use in peace and war. Consisting of a corridor about fifty meters long, five meters high, and roofed over with a corbeling vault, they opened in the side of the hill or rampart, protected by nearby towers and slanting up toward the city (one at Alishar, Hüyük, Ras Shamra; seven at Boğazköy).

The Style

The recent discovery of plastered and painted houses dating from the sixth millennium B.C. at Haçilar,[93] evidently the earliest instance of such refinement in the ancient world, considerably enhances the significance of the architecture of Asia Minor. Ever since the earliest times it showed an autochthonous character, and while the primitive house in the Near East or in Mediterranean lands appeared first with an oval plan, that in Anatolia was always rectangular.

Architectural style on the western coast is different in more than one aspect from that on the inner plateau. The typical megaron and

[86] *Ibid.*, pp. 265–267, Figs. 325–327.
[87] *Ibid.*, Figs. 329–331.
[88] *Ibid.*, Figs. 335–342.
[89] *Ibid.*, p. 276, Fig. 341.
[90] *Ibid.*, p. 276, Figs. 343–344.
[91] *Ibid.*, p. 278, Figs. 348–349.
[92] *Ibid.*, pp. 281–283, Figs. 105–107, 174, 352–354.
[93] Mellaart, *Haçilar*.

the small stone construction were not used in Anatolia, where the many-roomed type of plan, which differs from the Mesopotamian centered plan or the Mediterranean unit plan, and the cyclopean masonry and carving are consistently found. There are, however, some similarities in military architecture in the jagged outlines of walls without towers (Troy, Alishar).[94] From the texts describing the temple as the "House-of-God" it could be inferred that religious architecture derived from that of houses in protohistoric times. The Hittite monumental plan featuring a two-halled structure with a doorway in the middle of its long side (Boğazköy IV b) is utterly different from the megaron. Even with the conquest of North Syria by the Hittites, no outside influence appears in Hittite architecture, although the Assyrian trade outposts, or *karum*, borrow Hittite characteristics. The origin of the monumental style of the Empire (1460–1190 B.C.) has been ascribed to the Indo-Germanic elements of the Hittites and the Luians.[95]

Among the technical characteristics of Hittite architectural style are the cyclopean masonry, the corbel vault, and the stone socle, with decorative carved orthostats that developed independently from the orthostats facing brickwork in Syrian monuments. Other important features of this style are a mixed construction of brick and stone piers, fortified caisson walls on a jagged or buttressed outline, the exclusive use of quadrangular pillars, and the flat roof without parapet. As to elements of architectural design let us mention the parabolic arch, the numerous windows opening almost at floor level in temples, staircases in one or two parallel flights, asymmetrical planning except for gateways, layout in ring zones (temple, citadel),[96] and the vestibule fronted by two pillars (hilammar). While the latter element is akin to the Syrian hilani and perhaps had the same Mitannian origin, there is no instance of any Hittite contribution to the architecture of neighboring countries. That there are foreign influences from North Syria and Crete in the Hittite style is shown in the low reliefs flanking the gateways (Boğazköy).[97] Egyptian influences, probably through Phoenicia, are obvious in the female winged sphinxes flanking a trabeated doorway (Boğazköy, Alaça Hüyük), though the motif itself has been regarded as a Hittite invention (14th century B.C.) and used regularly in monumental architecture in Mesopotamia.[98]

North Syrian architecture shows little in common with the Anatolian style, though mixed construction of stone with wood

[94] Naumann, *Architektur*, pp. 421 ff.
[95] *Ibid.*, p. 424.
[96] *Ibid.*, p. 429, citing V. K. Müller.
[97] *Ibid.*, p. 263.
[98] S. Lloyd, *The Art of the Ancient Near East* (London, 1961), p. 194.

reinforcement may be related to the similar Hittite one or may also have been devised as a protection against frequent earthquakes. Characteristic elements of Syrian style include the geometric town plan, the hilani, which is an extremely common feature in the palace since the first millennium B.C., the column usually set on the back of an animal, the courtyard used only as a light shaft, the symmetrical Assyrian type, and the stairway winding around a gateway of quadrangular newel. In addition, certain trends and techniques in decoration (fresco, faïence) as well as in design are clearly borrowed from Crete (subdivision of a hall by means of a columned party wall at Tell Atchana).[99] The use of colossal statues, either freestanding or as portico piers (Carchemish, Malatya), is the result of Mesopotamian influence.

In the earlier Hittite sculpture there are various styles conforming to materials, but later styles (9th–8th centuries B.C.) affect historical scenes rather than religious ones, with an increasing Assyrian influence on the technique.[100] The column set on an animal base appears to have had a strong influence on the Aeolian-Ionic style.

In Anatolia the Phrygians carved their temples in rock cliffs and topped them with gablelike skylines above a frieze of painted reliefs. The façade of their so-called "Tomb of Midas" was covered with geometric ornament. The Phrygians' use of the gable and the frieze foreshadowed the Greek style.[101]

[99] Naumann, *Architektur*, pp. 356–357, 428–429.
[100] Lloyd, *Anatolia*, pp. 174–175. Naumann, *Architektur*, p. 431.
[101] Lloyd, *Anatolia*, p. 197.

The Levant

The Setting

The land stretching immediately beyond the eastern coast of the Mediterranean, otherwise known as Syria, Phoenicia, and Palestine, was to play a unique role as the cradle of the great monotheist religions initiated by the Semites. The location between the two earliest cultural centers of Egypt and Mesopotamia and at the crossroads of communication predestined this area to be overrun by nomadic tribes who were at the mercy of their powerful neighbors.

The limestone in the soil determines such physiographic characteristics as the deeply eroded system of mountains with numerous ravines, caverns, and valleys which are poorly watered by small rivers.[1] To the east stretch desert steppes with reddish sandstone in their southern area; they are connected at the northern end to the Anti-Lebanon Mountains. Between this hilly range and the Lebanon Mountains the Leontes (Litani) River flows through a luxuriant plateau (*beqᶜa*) that slopes down to the Phoenician coast near Tyre and connects the flourishing harbors to Damascus.

The rest of the land is divided by a coastal range of mountains and the Jordan River, which flows north–south in three stretches. The coastal area is quite narrow, but it has flourishing vineyards spreading from the Lebanon range and is intensively cultivated to the south. It was settled by active Phoenician sea traders who established their harbors at regular intervals: Byblos, Berytos, Sidon, Tyre, and ᶜAkka. West of the Jordan Valley, which reaches its lowest level

[1] C. Watzinger, *Denkmäler Palästinas* (Leipzig, 1933), pp. 1–6.

around the Dead Sea (394 m. below sea level), nature is more favorable in Galilee, Samaria, and Judea, the districts that make up Palestine, named after the tribe of the Philistines. After the rainy season in early spring the hillsides and fields are covered with light green grass, interspersed with the silvery gray of olive groves. This is the most heavily populated land, and even its less luxuriant southern districts form a strange contrast with the barren upland southwest of the Jordan River or the high plateau to the east. It is along this coastal area as well as in the corridor parallel to it from the Gulf of ᶜAqaba, Wadi ᶜAraba, Beqᶜa, and the Orontes that the likelihood of earthquakes increases as one goes northward.[2]

An idea about the size of the land is dramatically conveyed by the fact that the Dead Sea is only 75 kilometers from the coast, a distance that could be covered on horseback in one day. Actually, this frontier land could not achieve a political destiny of its own, and its original genius was curbed by the inevitable strong influences from Egypt and Mesopotamia, and to a lesser degree from Asia Minor. The Levant had been linked, mostly as a tributary, to both countries ever since Neolithic times, since it formed the middle part of the Fertile Crescent, stretching south along the Nile Valley and northeast along the Tigris-Euphrates plain.[3] From the fourth millennium B.C. the natural environment in the plains of the great rivers was favorable to the birth of great cultures and national unity, while the Levant was sparsely populated by nomads who ultimately settled in city-states falling under the sway of various invaders. Egyptian hegemony was periodically reinstated by military expeditions,[4] checked only during the Hyksos interlude (1670–1570 B.C.). The archives of ᶜAmarna in Egypt and Ugarit in North Syria yield rich evidence of the political effervescence during the fourteenth and thirteenth centuries when the Syro-Palestinian states asserted their independence as soon as they were left on their own by Egypt.

About 1200 B.C. these Canaanites were attacked by the "people of the sea" who destroyed the Hittite empire. A group of these invaders, whose ethnic characteristics were so successfully rendered in Egyptian murals, settled here and became known as the Philistines; they were briefly followed in the south by Semitic tribes of Hebrews, Midianites, Edomites, Moabites, and Amorites and in the north by the Aramaeans.[5] A Hebrew monarchy was formed in the tenth century B.C., but it survived for only about three quarters of a century.

[2] C. Schaeffer, *Stratigraphie comparée et chronologie de l'Asie occidentale* (Oxford, 1948), p. 4.
[3] K. Kenyon, *Archaeology in the Holy Land* (London, 1960), p. 23.
[4] S. Moscati, *Ancient Semitic Civilizations* (New York, 1960), p. 109.
[5] W. Helck, *Die Beziehungen Ägyptens zu Vorderasien im 3. und 2. Jahrtausend v. Chr.* (Wiesbaden, 1962). Moscati, *Semitic Civilizations*, pp. 109–110.

The Phoenicians, however, remained independent, carrying on their trade under the supremacy of Sidon and later Tyre, and founding colonies since the tenth century B.C. along the Mediterranean coast (Aegean islands, Cilicia, Malta, Sicily, Sardinia, Cyprus, North Africa, Spain).

When the interest of the great powers regarding the Levant revived, the Hebrew monarchy split into the northern kingdom of Israel and the more primitive Judah (9th century B.C.) and smaller independent states. Beginning with the eighth century the Levant was gradually annexed by the Assyrians and the Babylonians (6th century B.C.), ultimately becoming a Persian province (538 B.C.).

Despite influences from Egypt and Mesopotamia the religion of the Canaanites remained basically that of the nomadic Semites, which had cruel rites and a crude emphasis on sexual elements[6] but lacked any defined pantheon or fully organized clergy. There was a "god" par excellence called El, but each city also had its own deity. Ba'al was the god of storm and lightning, who was associated with two fertility goddesses, Anat and Astarte. In Byblos there was a vegetation god, Adonis, who was the equivalent of the Babylonian Tammuz.

The Phoenicians first settled along the coast, with Byblos as their center. But after the fall of the Egyptian and Hittite empires toward the end of the thirteenth century B.C., they founded independent cities, rivaling and feuding with one another (Tyre against Sidon).[7] Each city was ruled by a hereditary king who was helped by a council of elders and magistrates from the richer families. Crafts flourished: purple dyeing of woolen textiles, ceramics, luxury items of glass, jewelry, perfume, and furniture. Their fleet, built with Lebanese timber, transported their own products or those brought by inland caravans. From the twelfth to the eighth centuries B.C. they traded around the Mediterranean, adding a traffic in slaves to their freights. To the Egyptians they were the "woodcutters" (*fenkhou*) who built and sailed the only seafaring vessels; this explains why the Egyptians called such boats *kebenwe*, meaning "Gublos' (Byblos) ships."[8] Their policy of colonization resulted from the installation of trading outposts and led them to be friendly with Greek settlers but never to form an organized thalassocracy. Phoenician art, being essentially eclectic, borrowed elements from the Mycenaeans (tombs), Egyptians (ornament, sphinx, funerary customs),[9] and Greeks (craftsmanship, ivories), among others. Their most original contribution to

6 Moscati, *Semitic Civilizations*, p. 113.
7 A. Aymard and J. Auboyer, *L'Orient et la Grèce Antique* (Paris, 1957), pp. 233 ff. Helck, *Beziehungen*, pp. 515–535.
8 Helck, *Beziehungen*, p. 22. A. Gardiner, *Egypt of the Pharaohs* (Oxford, 1961), p. 36.
9 W. F. Albright, *From the Stone Age to Christianity* (New York, 1957), p. 163. H. Frankfort, *The Art and Architecture of the Ancient Orient* (Baltimore, 1954), pp. 136 ff.

culture was the use of an alphabet, found in the texts from Ugarit in the fifteenth century B.C. It consisted of thirty cuneiform signs that later evolved into twenty-two original signs (Ahiram's sarcophagus, 13th? century B.C.).

Though the Aramaeans emulated the Phoenicians in inland trade, their cultural importance was less significant. Nevertheless, their language, written with alphabetical signs derived from the Phoenician ones, spread throughout the Orient. Aramaean scribes worked in Assyrian offices, and the Aramaean language was adopted by the Persian administration.

Towns

The earliest communal groups lived and buried their dead in caves (Mount Carmel). During the Mesolithic Period (Natufian), while still experimenting with agriculture and the domestication of animals, man settled in the open, choosing the site of the spring at Jericho on which to build the earliest round houses in plano-convex brick. This settlement was ultimately surrounded with a massive oval wall (2.4 m. thick) that extended north–south and was protected by a stone tower (10 m. high),[10] possibly dating from about 7000 B.C. The Neolithic village of Seyl Aqlat near Petra dates from 6500 to 5500 B.C.[11] Though these are the earliest settlements known, one cannot speak of urban development, since their internal layouts do not imply preplanning or even primary planning factors such as alignment or orientation of streets. As a matter of fact, it is relatively late that Palestinian settlements assume the shape of towns with some evidence of planning. This rather slow start is perhaps the result of the nomadic character of people subjected to perennial political disturbances. In the Early Bronze Age, about 3000 B.C., a large Canaanite town, triangular in shape and about 25 acres in area, was surrounded by a stone wall 2.3 meters thick with round bastions.[12] The most sophisticated layout features a ring street servicing a band of houses twenty meters wide next to the enclosure, and an inner arrangement of one or two main streets running north–south (Tell Beit Mirsim; Fig. 26, middle right). A similar layout appears in the Late Bronze Age (Tell el Ajjul, 2–4 m. wide)[13] and during the monarchy (10th

10 Kenyon, *Holy Land*, pp. 43–44.
11 D. Kirkbride, "Ten Thousand Years of Man's Activity around Petra: Unknown or Little Known Sites Excavated or Explored," *The Illustrated London News*, Sept. 16, 1961, pp. 448–453.
12 Y. Aharoni and R. Amiran, "Arad, a Biblical City in Southern Palestine," *Archaeology*, Vol. 17, pp. 43–53, Fig. p. 44.
13 W. Fl. Petrie, *Ancient Gaza*, Vol. I (London, 1932–1933), pp. 5 ff., pl. IV, pp. 1 ff. A.-G. Barrois, *Manuel d'archéologie biblique* (Paris, 1939–53), Vol. I, pp. 288–289.

century B.C., Megiddo,[14] Tell Beit Mirsim,[15] Beth Shemesh II[16]). A central covered drain or pipes run below the main street (Tell el Ajjul, Jericho, Tell el Farᶜah). There is no provision for a pomerium except occasionally along the inner part of the wall (Solomonic Megiddo), which is a long or rounded oval vaguely oriented north–south, with an inner area averaging 4 hectares[17] (Jericho, 2.3; Tell Beit Mirsim, 2–3; Tell el Nasbeh, 4; Megiddo, 5) or occasionally more (Gezer, 9; Tell el Ajjul, 12). The Biblical description of Palestinian towns as rectangular in shape and oriented by their corners (Num. 35:4–5) has not yet been evidenced by finds, though it could have existed in Phoenicia. There is usually no paving except an occasional stone or pebble layer (stables at Megiddo); thus the street and town level grows as layers of rubble pile up. Such a town must have looked much like the typical irregular contemporaneous town in the Orient, with craft shops zoned into special quarters (Jer. 37:21; Neh. 3:11).[18] During the rule of Israel and Judah (9th century B.C.) there seem to have been two types of towns, one dominated by an official quarter and the other consisting of private buildings.[19]

Inland towns sought the vicinity of a water supply, a river or spring, and trade routes. Towns along the coast became the centers for sea trade and crafts. Most of the Phoenician towns had two harbors, one for trade and the other for military activities. Their layout was closely adapted to their site, a characteristic suggesting that Phoenician town planning could have been a forerunner of the Greek method.[20] On the other hand, some of the larger towns seem to have had an orthogonal layout oriented by the corners (Sidon?).

Perhaps the most significant achievement of Canaanite urban development is the provision for a public water supply *intra muros*. Only a few villages benefited from the vicinity of a watercourse or could erect a dam across a valley to form a lake to be filled with rain water (*berikah*). Therefore the usual water supply was from a spring often located outside the enclosure. Deep underground tunnels (*sinnor*) were dug from the highest central area of the settlement and were made accessible through a vertical shaft (Megiddo, Jerusalem) or a slanting corridor with steps (El Gib, Gezer, ᶜAin Umm el Darag). Most of these systems date back to the Iron Age (Megiddo, 12th century B.C.) or even to the Middle Bronze Age (Gezer, 1900 B.C.). The total length of the gigantic S-shaped tunnel at Jerusalem that feeds the pool of Siloe is no less than 512.5 meters. These ambitious

[14] Kenyon, *Holy Land*, p. 250.

[15] *Ibid.*, p. 254.

[16] *Ibid.*, p. 252.

[17] W. F. Albright, *The Archaeology of Palestine* (Harmondsworth, 1956), p. 18.

[18] Barrois, *Manuel*, Vol. I, pp. 301–302.

[19] Kenyon, *Holy Land*, p. 277.

[20] E. Egli, *Geschichte des Städtebaues* (Zurich, 1959), p. 77.

works to ensure a constant water supply during long sieges[21] were supplemented by underground cisterns (*bor*) for storing rain water (Tell Ta^cnnah, Beth Gebrin, Beth Sur).

Jericho (Fig. 26, top left). Pre-Pottery Jericho had two stone walls enclosing the city (about 8000 and 6000 B.C.). Its Early Bronze Age enclosure follows the outline of the earlier ones, though it is shortened to the north and south. It is built of mud brick (1 m. wide) on stone foundations and reinforced with timber;[22] it also has a semicircular tower (west) and a ditch. Since there were no town-planning or urban ordinances, the rubbish was allowed to accumulate in layers. After a spell when the newcomers who had burned down the enclosure did not rebuild it,[23] the town slowly developed again in the Middle Bronze Age, and was rebuilt several times and destroyed (Middle Bronze Age II). It is surrounded by an enclosure 2 meters thick, with a gate at its south end and a rampart faced with stone (19th century B.C.).[24] At the end of the Middle Bronze Age (16th century B.C.) two streets (2.2 m. wide) ran up the slope, with wide cobbled steps beneath which are drains.[25] This late enclosure was destroyed, and nothing remains from the later occupation (1400 B.C.).

Gezer (Fig. 26, top right). This large town (9 ha.), located to the southeast near the coast, is in the shape of a long trapezium running east–west. The site had been occupied since the Neolithic times by settlers in grottoes and tents who surrounded the mound with a coarse rampart. In the Bronze Age the settlement develops, and bodies are buried in the grottoes. About the twentieth century B.C. (Middle Bronze Age) the internal enclosure is built with a triple gate. The town reaches its climax in the Late Bronze Age as an active trade center with Aegean influences and Egyptian relations. It is given a new enclosure with towers at 30-meter intervals, and a tunnel is extended to a spring (29 m. long). After a period of stagnation during the reign of Solomon, it declines rapidly in the post-Exilic period.[26]

Megiddo (Tell el Mutesellim). This town guarded the pass between the coastal and the central mountains on the route from Syria to Egypt.[27] Its occupation (twenty strata) dates from the thirty-third

[21] Barrois, *Manuel*, Vol. I, pp. 212–243, Figs. 76–90.
[22] Kenyon, *Holy Land*, p. 105.
[23] *Ibid.*, p. 135.
[24] *Ibid.*, pp. 174–178.
[25] *Ibid.*, p. 187, pls. 35, 36A.
[26] Barrois, *Manuel*, Vol. I, pp. 43–44, Fig. 6. R. A. S. Macalister, *The Excavation of Gezer*, 3 vols. (London, 1912).
[27] G. Schumacher and C. Watzinger, *Tell el-Mutesellim*, 2 vols. (Leipzig, 1908–1929). R. S. Lamon and G. Loud, *Megiddo*, Parts I–II (Chicago, 1939–1948). Helck, *Beziehungen*, index, p. 632.

Fig. 26→

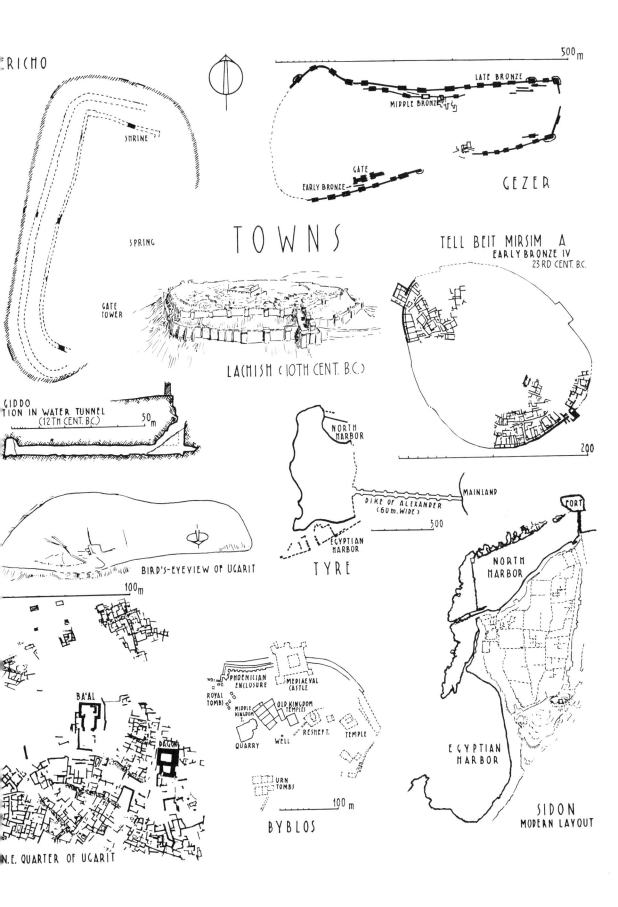

JERICHO

500 m

LATE BRONZE

MIDDLE BRONZE

GEZER

GATE

EARLY BRONZE

TOWNS

TELL BEIT MIRSIM A
EARLY BRONZE IV
23 RD CENT. B.C.

SPRING

GATE
TOWER

LACHISH (10TH CENT. B.C.)

200

MEGIDDO
...TION IN WATER TUNNEL
(12TH CENT. B.C.)   50 m

NORTH
HARBOR

MAINLAND

DIKE OF ALEXANDER
(60 m. WIDE)   500

FORT

NORTH
HARBOR

BIRD'S-EYEVIEW OF UGARIT

EGYPTIAN
HARBOR

TYRE

100 m

BA'AL

DAGON

PHOENICIAN
ENCLOSURE
ROYAL
TOMBS
MIDDLE
KINGDOM
T.

MEDIAEVAL
CASTLE

OLD KINGDOM
TEMPLES

QUARRY   WELL   RESHEF.   TEMPLE

EGYPTIAN
HARBOR

URN
TOMBS

100 m

N.E. QUARTER OF UGARIT

BYBLOS

SIDON
MODERN LAYOUT

century B.C. Though burned down several times and rebuilt, the city flourished under the Canaanites (1550–1150 B.C.) and the Israelites (*ca.* 1000 B.C.). It was ultimately destroyed by Tiglath-Pileser III (733 B.C.) and abandoned about 350 B.C. The strong oval enclosure (northeast to southwest, 300 × 240 m.) surrounds an area of five hectares with a layout characterized by irregular streets and the contrast in the sizes of its houses with central courtyards.[28] As early as the thirty-second century B.C. it contains a shrine. It was under the monarchy that its layout assumed the typical aspect of a peripheral band of radiating houses (20 m. wide) serviced by a street circling an inner area with houses oriented north–south (layer V).[29] It is well equipped with an elaborate defensive system of gates and towers and an underground water-supply system (12th century B.C.; Fig. 26, middle left). It is provided with rich palaces, two monumental stalls (layer IV) for 450 horses, and a temple. Megiddo is a typical example of a Palestinian town where the official quarter dominates the urban settlement. The latest stage (layer II) in the post-Exilic Period features large insulae on an un-Palestinian layout inspired by Assyria.[30]

Byblos (Gebeil, ancient Gubla or Gublos; Fig. 26, bottom middle). This is probably the Phoenician town that had the closest and most durable trade relations with Egypt as well as connections with Mesopotamia. Mesopotamian seal impressions from the Jemdet-Nasr Period (3100–2900 B.C.) were found in the lowest urban stratum.[31] Ever since early dynastic times it provided costly cedar wood for Pharaoh's navy and constructions, and Pharaoh Nebka sent votive offerings to Byblos during the Second Dynasty.[32] This town became virtually an Egyptian colony under the Fifth and Sixth Dynasties.[33] Culture and crafts were vividly influenced by Egypt since the time of the Old Kingdom and particularly at the end of the Middle Kingdom (19th–18th century B.C.).[34] Vases of Cretan import of Middle Minoan I (2100–1900 B.C.) prove that Byblos was the earliest center to have had trade relations with Crete.[35] A pseudohieroglyphic syllabic script derived from Egyptian hieroglyphs was used between the eighteenth and fifteenth centuries B.C.[36] Unamun was sent at the low ebb of Egyptian power early in the eleventh century B.C. from

[28] Egli, *Städtebau*, p. 76.
[29] Kenyon, *Holy Land*. p. 250.
[30] *Ibid.*, p. 286.
[31] Albright, *Palestine*, p. 71.
[32] Albright, *Stone Age*. p. 158. Helck, *Beziehungen*, pp. 21–22, index. p. 630.
[33] Albright, *Stone Age*, p. 160. Helck, *Beziehungen*, pp. 310–311.
[34] Albright, *Palestine*, p. 95. Byblos is the only site where Egyptian monuments from the Old Kingdom were found. Helck, *Beziehungen*, p. 69.
[35] Schaeffer, *Stratigraphie*, p. 66.
[36] Albright, *Palestine*, p. 186.

Thebes accompanied by the god "Amun-of-the-Road," to acquire cedar for the bark of Amun, and the prince of Byblos had to acknowledge that Amun was still supreme.[37]

The site features a hillock (30 m. above sea level) whose western slopes form the coastal fringe; it was separated to the east and south from the Lebanese Mountains by a curved depression.[38] Though the prevailing winds blow and the sea currents surge from the southwest, the medieval inhabitants had in the southern bay a harbor open to the southwest. Along the north edge of a sandy plateau about six hectares in area an enclosure wall with internal bastions was built by the Phoenicians, and to its south stretched various colonnades and temples from the Egyptian Old Kingdom, Middle Kingdom, and later periods (Fig. 26, bottom middle). The earliest urban settlement (level 24 m.) has a street curving from an irregular central area (Early to Middle Bronze Age) to the northwest toward the enclosure. It is along the edges of this important piazza, which was paved at various epochs, that the temples from the Old Kingdom, the later temple (south), and a well are located.[39] There does not seem to be any regular street orientation, though some of the secondary streets run north–south or east–west. In the second stage (Dynasty XII) the tortuous street is replaced by another one running east–west and separating two different groups of structures. The medieval town stretched north of the Phoenician enclosure, within its own wall.

Sidon (modern Saida; Fig. 26, bottom right). On the coast to the south of Byblos this town has two harbors: the one to the north is trapezoidal and is bordered by quays between islands communicating with the larger irregular one to the south, the so-called "Egyptian harbor," which later became filled with sand. Little is known about the layout, which possibly had an orthogonal system that was oriented north–south. A line of fortifications runs along the ridge between both harbors forming an enclosed residential area (north), while an industrial area lies outside (south).[40] Sidon gained the supremacy over Byblos, and its Baʿal replaced El; but it later lost to Tyre. Alexander the Great connected the town to the coast by a dike 60 meters wide.

Tyre (modern Sur; Fig. 26, middle). This city, founded by colonists from Sidon, lay on an offshore island. Originally there were two

---

[37] Albright, *Stone Age*, p. 217. On Unamun, see Helck, *Beziehungen*, index, p. 642.

[38] M. Dunand, *Fouilles de Byblos*, Vol. I (Paris, 1939), p. 11, pl. CCI.

[39] *Ibid.*, pp. 288–289, 363–364, pl. CCVIII.

[40] Egli, *Städtebau*, p. 80, Fig. 54. About Sidon and Egypt, see Helck, *Beziehungen*, index, p. 633, which mentions a visit of Tuthmosis IV as the last visit of a pharaoh to Syria; *ibid.*, p. 311.

islands, but they were connected by King Hiram (969 B.C.). Tyre had two harbors: a trade port to the north (the modern one) and a military or Egyptian port[41] consisting of two basins flanking a central channel. As evidence of close cultural ties as well as trade relations, an Egyptian scribe from Tyre wrote letters in Akkadian to the Egyptian Court at ʿAmarna (1365 B.C.)[42] and translated two Egyptian poems in Akkadian. In the Bible a prince of Tyre says (Ezek. 28:2), "I am a god; I sit on the throne of god in the midst of the seas,"[43] a graphic reference to the unusual topographic location of the city. The local Baʿal assumed the title of Melqart, "King-of-the-City."[44] Toward 1200 B.C. Tyre gained supremacy over other Phoenician towns.

Ugarit (Ras Shamra; Fig. 26, bottom left). Though it was located in Syria and was the northernmost city of the Levant, Ugarit is nonetheless relevant here because, ever since the second millennium B.C., it was the trade center of the Levant and the gateway to Cyprus and Crete. Its mythical poetry was written by Phoenicians in the north Canaanite alphabetic script (Ugaritic),[45] and it was a colony of Tyre (Late Bronze Age).[46] It lies near the harbor now called Mina el Beida within a fork of the river Nahr el Fidd. The city was laid out on an irregular outline conforming to the terrain. Its enclosure was rebuilt (550 × 660 m.) after the Hyksos invasion (1800 B.C.). Only the northeast district has been excavated, and it reveals an irregular system of curved lanes, unoriented houses of stone around central courts, and two temples facing south.[47] The five occupation strata indicate Mesopotamian influences (pre-Pottery, Pottery Periods), the arrival of the Phoenicians (third level), and Egyptian and later Minoan influences (second level)[48] on a very flourishing trade outpost. Following the *pax aegyptiaca* (1440–1380 B.C.), the city enjoyed a period of prosperity. Along curving, vaguely parallel streets there are several extensive residential areas. The houses have many rooms and are equipped with adequate sanitary facilities that discharge waste into cesspools. A well and a basin lie beneath an awning in every court, and a disposal system for collecting rain water runs

---

[41] A. Poidebard, *Un grand port disparu, Tyr* (Paris, 1939), considers it of Roman date; but see Helck, *Beziehungen*, index, pp. 634, 312.

[42] Albright, *Stone Age*. pp. 210–211.

[43] *Ibid.*, p. 216.

[44] *Ibid.*, p. 307. Aymard and Auboyer, *L'Orient*, p. 237.

[45] Albright, *Stone Age*, pp. 36, 39, 230.

[46] Watzinger, *Denkmäler Palästinas*, p. 49. Helck, *Beziehungen*, index, p. 634.

[47] C. Schaeffer, *Ugaritica* (Paris, 1939). Egli, *Städtebau*, pp. 82–83, Fig. 56. W. G. A. Otto, ed., *Handbuch der Archäologie* (Munich, 1939), pp. 802 ff.

[48] G. Contenau, *Manuel d'archéologie Orientale*, Vol. IV (Paris, 1947), pp. 1744–1745. Perhaps under Egyptian domination since Tuthmosis IV, cf. Helck, *Beziehungen*, pp. 303–304, index, p. 634.

into the street.[49] The city was destroyed twice, probably by fires resulting from earthquakes (2400–2300 and 2100–2000 B.C.).[50]

Houses and Palaces

The earliest houses in Palestine are found in Mesolithic Jericho (7000 B.C.; Fig. 27, top left). They are round in shape and have battered walls probably with a dome. In front there is a porch, with stone steps leading down to the sunken floor. Curiously enough, the houses are built of plano-convex bricks as in Haçilar (6000 B.C.) and probably show a direct derivation from primitive shelters made of light materials.[51] A similar type of house plan is found in prehistoric Greece (Orchomenos) and Cyprus (Erimi). Later, in the Neolithic Period, houses are larger and have large and small rectangular rooms around a central court, built of handmade bricks and paved with plaster.[52] As the result of an obscure retrogression, these relatively well-developed houses are later replaced by underground pit dwellings scooped out by the newcomers in the remains of the earlier settlements, with sides lined with pisé or stone,[53] similar to those in Chalcolithic Beersheba (Abu Matar; Fig. 27, top middle).[54] They are also reminiscent of protodynastic houses at Maʿadi, though the latter were deeply sunk in the gravel below ground level. Contemporaneous freestanding houses, either round or rectangular, built with plano-convex bricks on stone foundations, are also found at Jericho.[55]

From the Chalcolithic Period date well-built houses of brick, some on stone foundations roofed over with timber; a few are decorated with polychrome mural paintings (4.5 m. wide), of geometric designs or scenes with figures and masks (Ghassul, before 3400 B.C.).[56] A stylized type of house roofed over with a gable (Khodeirah; Fig. 27, upper left)[57] is represented by painted caskets of clay used as urns. In the rectangular houses of that period at Byblos there is a striking contrast between their burnished plaster floors, similar to those of Neolithic Jericho,[58] and their light superstructures of brushwood or skins. Toward the end of the fourth millennium B.C.

49 Schaeffer, *Ugaritica*, Vol. I, p. 30, Fig. 9.
50 Schaeffer, *Stratigraphie*, p. 63.
51 Kenyon, *Holy Land*, p. 43.
52 *Ibid.*, p. 48.
53 *Ibid.*, p. 60.
54 *Ibid.*, pp. 77–79, Fig. 101.
55 *Ibid.*, p. 65.
56 Albright, *Palestine*, pp. 66–68, Fig. 10. Barrois, *Manuel*, Vol. I, pp. 488–491.
57 Albright, *Palestine*, p. 68, Fig. 11.
58 Kenyon, *Holy Land*, p. 66.

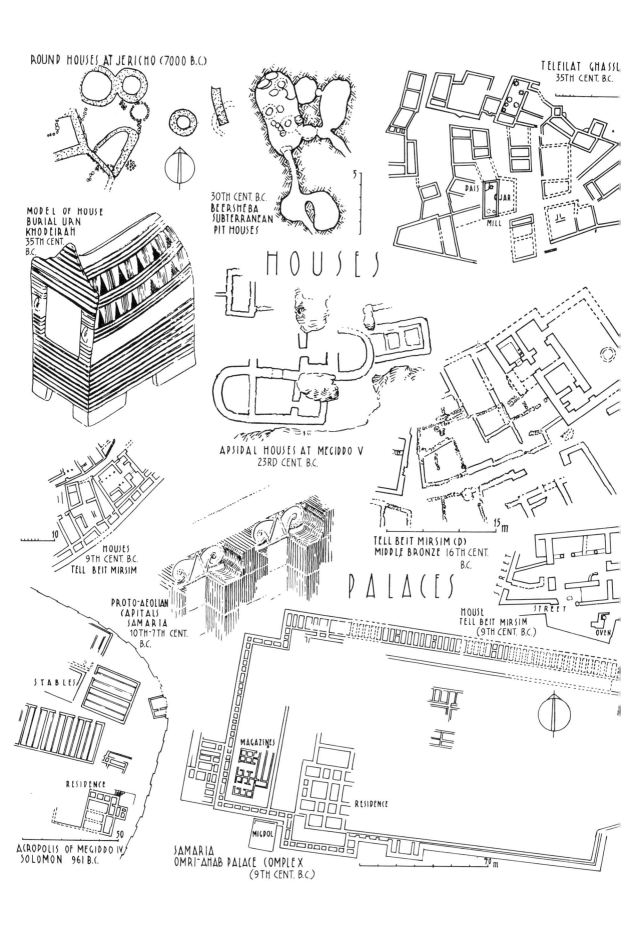

ROUND HOUSES AT JERICHO (7000 B.C.)

TELEILAT GHASSL
35TH CENT. B.C.

30TH CENT. B.C.
BEERSHEBA
SUBTERRANEAN
PIT HOUSES

MODEL OF HOUSE
BURIAL URN
KHODEIRAH
35TH CENT.
B.C.

DAIS
JAR
MILL

H O U S E S

APSIDAL HOUSES AT MEGIDDO V
23RD CENT. B.C.

HOUSES
9TH CENT. B.C.
TELL BEIT MIRSIM

TELL BEIT MIRSIM (D)
MIDDLE BRONZE 16TH CENT.
B.C.

15 m

PROTO-AEOLIAN
CAPITALS
SAMARIA
10TH-7TH CENT.
B.C.

P A L A C E S

HOUSE
TELL BEIT MIRSIM
(9TH CENT. B.C.)

STREET
STREET
OVEN

STABLES

MAGAZINES

RESIDENCE

RESIDENCE

MIGDOL

ACROPOLIS OF MEGIDDO IV
SOLOMON 961 B.C.

SAMARIA
OMRI-AHAB PALACE COMPLEX
(9TH CENT. B.C.)

70 m

(3200 B.C.) houses are only slight structures (Megiddo, Tell el Farʿah, Jericho).⁵⁹

It is then (Bronze Age I) that peculiar types of brick houses (plano-convex, later rectangular) featuring rectangular rooms with one rounded, or "apsidal," end appear (Fig. 27, upper middle, Beth Shan XVI, later at Jericho VI–VII, Megiddo V),⁶⁰ to which the houses with one rounded corner at Tell el Farʿah could be related. The apsidal house seems to be of foreign origin, imported for a short period. The truly Mediterranean apsidal type can be recalled in this connection, as it occurs in Greece in prehistoric times (Olympia, Orchomenos, Thessaly), perhaps marking the origin of the classical megaron.

It is during this Early Bronze Age that the typical Palestinian house develops, with quadrangular rooms of brick or pisé erected on rough rubble.⁶¹ A clay model is roofed with a flat terrace, and its walls are painted with red stripes, one horizontal at mid-height and others vertical, perhaps indicating wood reinforcements (Arad, Fig. 36, middle right).⁶² The typical house is rectangular and has one door hinged on the left opening in the middle of the long side; steps descend to the single room, which has benches around its walls and a central stone table. It is also the period when well-built towns appear (Early Bronze Age II, 2800 B.C.; Beth Shan XIII, Beth Yereh III, Megiddo XVIII–XVI, Jericho IV),⁶³ perhaps inspired from a northern type. The earliest town at Byblos dates from 3100 B.C.⁶⁴ Just before the Middle Bronze Age small irregular rooms were built of green brick (one brick thick) on the slopes of the mound at Jericho.⁶⁵ At Ghassul the rectangular houses open on an irregular court and very often stand independently, separated by tortuous lanes or small piazzas from neighboring houses (Fig. 27, top right).⁶⁶ As a rule, a house has one large room furnished with a hand mill in its southwest corner, a hearth at the northeast end, a mortar, three basins sunk in the floor, and a dais (2 × 1.4 m.), while the water jar is set against the middle of the east wall (Ghassul No. 23). In some houses a small room may be added. It is a characteristic of the Palestinian house that its rooms aggregate around the court without any planning.

The prosperity prevailing during the Middle Bronze Age, which corresponds to the late Twelfth Dynasty and the troubled period of

⁵⁹ *Ibid.*, p. 98.
⁶⁰ Albright, *Palestine*, p. 70. Barrois, *Manuel*, Vol. I, pp. 247–251, Figs. 92–94.
⁶¹ Barrois, *Manuel*, Vol. I, p. 251.
⁶² Y. Aharoni and R. Amiran, "Arad, a Biblical City in Southern Palestine," *Archaeology*, Vol. 17 (New York, 1964), pp. 46–47.
⁶³ Albright, *Palestine*, p. 74.
⁶⁴ Kenyon, *Holy Land*, p. 121.
⁶⁵ *Ibid.*, p. 153.
⁶⁶ Barrois, *Manuel*, Vol. I, pp. 253–254, Fig. 96.

←Fig. 27

the Hyksos in Egypt, does not indicate public security; thus towns and palaces are fortified. The middle-class house now consists of more rooms, which are arranged around a court, perhaps denoting Mesopotamian influence. A few houses have latrines that are connected to a tank or a pottery container (Tell el Ajjul).[67] At Tell Beit Mersim (layer D, 1600 B.C.; Fig. 27, middle right) many palaces and patrician houses feature a court and one or more rows of squarish rooms along it, one room being large enough to require a middle row of three wooden posts. The living quarters are on the upper floor.[68] Influence from Asia Minor has been presumed by some scholars.[69] Similar large houses are found at Megiddo, Bethel, Jericho, and in the largest palace at Tell el Ajjul. At Jericho shops unconnected to the houses behind them line the streets.[70] In the Late Bronze Age three houses near the gate of Megiddo VIII are remodeled into a large palace,[71] and at Bethel a well-built system of stone-lined drains discharges rain and waste waters outside the city wall.[72]

Architecture shares in the general decline of civilization that marks the Israelite Period (Iron Age I, 13th century B.C.). Ruins of earlier Canaanite houses are again occupied or coarsely built over, and the ground floor is used for habitation (Bethel, Tell Beit Mirsim).[73] Occasionally houses are built on the tripartite plan (court flanked by rooms) and set in a regular pattern, back to back along parallel streets (Tell el Far'ah).[74] It is only when Phoenician craftsmen from Tyre are engaged by the kings of the united monarchy that architecture flourishes again in official buildings, while no progress is marked in private houses.[75] At Megiddo IV, Solomon (961 B.C.) builds a residence for the governor and huge stables for more than 450 horses (Fig. 27, bottom left), consisting of contiguous units, with a central passage (3 m. wide) flanked by a row of eleven stone pillars, mangers for thirty horses, and an aisle (3 m. wide). Floors are cobbled and courts plastered,[76] while walls are probably of brick on stone foundations. They seem to have remained in use for about two centuries. Similar installations existed at Tell el Hesy (V), Hazor, and Ta'nnah. Solomon's masonry shows the beautiful Phoenician craftsmanship, characterized by well-dressed quoins alternating with

[67] *Ibid.*, Vol. I, pp. 261 ff., Fig. 99.
[68] Albright, *Palestine*, pp. 92–93, Figs. 16–17. Barrois, *Manuel*, Vol. I, pp. 261–264.
[69] Otto, ed., *Handbuch*, p. 800.
[70] Kenyon, *Holy Land*, p. 187, Fig. 45.
[71] *Ibid.*, p. 197, Fig. 46.
[72] Albright, *Palestine*, p. 101.
[73] *Ibid.*, p. 119.
[74] Kenyon, *Holy Land*, p. 254, Fig. 60.
[75] Barrois, *Manuel*, Vol. I, p. 265.
[76] Albright, *Palestine*, pp. 124–125. Barrois, *Manuel*, Vol. I, pp. 266–268, Fig. 102, pp. 284–285. P. L. O. Guy, Oriental Institute Communications, No. 9 (Chicago, 1931). Watzinger, *Denkmäler Palästinas*, pp. 87–88, Figs. 80–81.

rubble, or entirely dressed alternating courses of headers and stretchers. The proto-Aeolian type of capitals of pilasters (Megiddo IV, Samaria, Hazor, Ramat Rahel) was borrowed from Phoenicia by the Greeks of Cyprus and Ionia (8th century B.C.).[77] The origin of the paired volutes could be sought in the so-called iris capital of Egypt or the sacred volute tree of Assyria. Though not relevant to domestic architecture, the refineries at the copper mines should be mentioned, those at Ezion Geber (Gulf of Aqaba) showing particularly elaborate plans (also at Jemmeh).[78]

Of the palaces of David and Solomon at Jerusalem (I Kings 7:1–12) nothing remains, and no satisfactory restoration can be derived from their description in texts.[79] Excavations have revealed the extensive palace of Omri (876 B.C.) and Ahab at Samaria (Fig. 27, bottom right), the new strategically located capital that replaced Tirzah (Tell el Far'ah). This palace was laid out on a monumental scale, with the royal quarter on a plateau (compare Solomon's at Jerusalem). Its rectangular area running east–west (2 ha.) was surrounded by an earlier wall (compare the palace of Sargon II at Khorsabad). Near it outside the enclosure is a fort (*migdol*). To its west are magazines consisting of a central corridor flanked by rooms where wine jars, oil, and grain that had been collected as taxes were stored. Phoenician craftsmanship is evidenced in the beautifully dressed masonry and in the rich ivory inlays of Egyptianizing style.[80] Some similarity to Assyria could be recognized in the centered plan about a court.

The typical private house as exemplified at Tell Beit Mirsim consists of a central court along one side of which runs a pillared portico and on the other one or two rooms, while an outer stairway rises to the upper floor (Fig. 27, middle right).[81]

During the Babylonian and Persian Periods (Iron Age III, 6th–5th centuries B.C.) Greek influences permeated Palestine through the trading posts established on the coast. From that period dates a large palace at Lachish (400 B.C.), which shows strong analogies with Parthian buildings. It features a central square courtyard oriented to the cardinal points and surrounded on three sides by small rooms and on the fourth, at a higher level, by a double liwan and residential

[77] Albright, *Palestine*, p. 126, Fig. 35.

[78] *Ibid.*, pp. 127–128.

[79] Barrois, *Manuel*, Vol. I, p. 278, Vol. II, p. 446. Watzinger, *Denkmäler Palästinas*, pp. 95–97.

[80] J. W. Crowfoot, K. M. Kenyon, and E. L. Sukenik, *Samaria-Sebaste*, 3 vols. (Palestine Exploration Fund, London, 1938–1957). Barrois, *Manuel*, Vol. I, pp. 278–282. Watzinger, *Denkmäler Palästinas*, pp. 87–98, pl. 37.

[81] W. F. Albright, *Tell Beit Mirsim*, Vol. III (New Haven, Conn., 1943); *The Iron Age*, Annual of the American School of Oriental Research, Vols. XXI–XXII. Albright, *Palestine*, p. 140, Fig. 46.

apartments, probably vaulted over.[82] Such integral borrowing of foreign types of plans had already occurred much earlier in several mansions, such as the fortified house of an officer from the reign of Amenḥotep III near the migdol at Beth Shan and the residence of an Egyptian governor (Dynasty XIX) at Tell el Farᶜah, curiously similar to Villa T. 36. 11 at ᶜAmarna.[83]

Caverns of troglodytes are found in the coastal plain of Phoenicia near ᶜAdlun between Tyre and Sidon.[84] Later, in Aeneolithic Byblos the rectangular houses have plastered and burnished floors like those in Neolithic Jerusalem and probably a superstructure of light materials.[85] After a period of abandonment a Mediterranean race builds mostly circular houses. Contemporaneously with Djemdet-Nasr (beginning of third millennium B.C.) the subterranean spring on the promontory of Byblos is excavated and remains in use till the Hellenistic Period. Houses consist then of two or three rooms. Still later (2700 B.C.), this type develops into a larger rectangular plan with a central corridor flanked by rooms. After the Amorite invasion (2100 B.C.) large houses consist of a vaulted room and are grouped rather like the arrangement of a nomad camp. In the Iron Age the formerly deserted necropolis is again covered with dwellings.[86]

In Ugarit (Middle Kingdom) a structure housing the library and scriptorium near the temples consists of rooms arranged around a central court according to the ancient Mesopotamian type of plan. The palace at Ugarit features, besides the scriptorium, a stable and the residence of the military governor. In one hall were found two bases of copper columns plated with silver. The system of a central courtyard is also followed in stone houses built along narrow streets (14 × 10; 15 × 15 m.). In their court are a well, a water basin, and a lateral stairway rising to the upper floor, and sometimes also a bathroom. The tomb beneath the ground floor is accessible from a dromos with steps. There are two periods of occupation: fifteenth to fourteenth centuries B.C. and fourteenth to thirteenth centuries B.C.[87] The inhabitants in the larger mansions are Mycenaean immigrants who settle here during the Egypto-Hittite wars.

At Hama, on the Orontes southeast of Ugarit, rectangular houses (north–south) with stone foundations and basalt hearths appear in

[82] Albright, *Palestine*, p. 125, Fig. 47. Barrois, *Manuel*, Vol. I, pp. 275–276, Fig. 106.

[83] Barrois, *Manuel*, Vol. I, pp. 270–273, Figs. 104–105.

[84] Watzinger, *Denkmäler Palästinas*, Vol. I, p. 18.

[85] Kenyon, *Holy Land*, pp. 66–67.

[86] M. Dunand and F. Furlani in *Enciclopedia dell'Arte Antica*, Vol. II, C (Rome, 1959), pp. 99–101.

[87] Watzinger in Otto, ed., *Handbuch*, pp. 802–803. Schaeffer, *Ugaritica*, Vol. I, p. 25, Figs. 13–15.

the first half of the third millennium B.C.[88] Later (1750 B.C.), houses on a similar plan have brick walls that are plastered and articulated with niches and pilasters and contain a circular oven (?) and oval hearths of stone plastered with clay.[89] Still later (1200–950 B.C.), there is evidence of brick pillars and a drain made of two rows of stones (7.5 m. long).[90] It is at level E (720 B.C.), which ended with the destruction of Hama by Sargon, that architecture is at its best in several monumental buildings on the citadel. Brick masonry with much timber reinforcement and the use of stone orthostats carved with lions in low relief with only their heads protruding in high relief characterize Hama as the southernmost bastion of North Syrian style with Hittite influence.[91] Near the monumental gateway to the citadel there is a large structure, possibly an official palace, with a rectangular plan (northeast and southwest, 74 × 40 m.). Here a columned vestibule leads to three groups of shallow transverse rooms without a corridor, probably the servants' quarters, magazines, and stables (east). The upper story, which is accessible from a staircase, contains the living quarters.[92] Several lesser structures feature a shrine (III), a house (IV), and a palace (V). Shallow rooms of the same width, the one opening into the next, characterize the planning.

Temples

Very little is known about pre-Canaanite religion. From the poems found at Ugarit one can gather some ideas about the Canaanite cosmic gods El and his wife Atherat, Ba'al and Anat, Reshef, or local gods such as Ba'al Ugarit, Mekal "Lord-of-Beth-Shan," Eshmun at Sidon, Hadad at Damascus, and Melqart at Tyre.[93] Besides regular sacrifices implying the slaughter of animals and a communal repast, other rites were performed. These included carrying the images of the gods in a public procession at the New Year festival in autumn, the cult of Ba'al, and pilgrimage rites in such centers as Byblos (fertility god Adonis), marked by funerary ceremonies and sacred prostitution. The temple personnel comprised priests (kohanim), who were presided over by a hereditary high priest (at Carthage), prostitutes of both sexes (qedeshim), eunuchs (kumrum), and lesser officials (sacrifice offerers, barbers).[94]

To identify pre-Semitic structures as shrines is still a hazardous process. At the northern end of Neolithic Jericho a small area

[88] H. Ingholt, *Rapport préliminaire sur sept campagnes de fouilles à Hama en Syrie (1932–1935)* (Copenhagen, 1940), pp. 12, 28.

[89] *Ibid.*, pp. 29, 65.

[90] *Ibid.*, pp. 67, 84.

[91] R. Naumann, *Architektur Kleinasiens* (Tübingen, 1955), p. 30.

[92] Ingholt, *Hama*, pp. 87–89, Fig. 3.

[93] Barrois, *Manuel*, Vol. II, pp. 324 ff. Albright, *Stone Age*, pp. 230 ff.

[94] Barrois, *Manuel*, Vol. II, pp. 333–342. Albright, *Stone Age*, p. 231.

surrounded by an enclosure contains two blocks with holes that are presumably for totem poles.[95] Also at Jericho there is a shrine with a portico on six wooden posts, an antechamber, an inner sanctuary, and near it models of cattle and male organs.[96] In Neolithic Jericho a volcanic rock pillar of oval section (0.45 m. high) set in a niche in a private house could have been a private shrine.[97] Still another shrine features a rectangular basin in the center of a large room (6.7 × 4 m.). At Megiddo XIX (3000 B.C.), more specific cult elements occur in the form of a rectangular brick altar (5 m. high), which is plastered; at the front are steps set opposite the doorway of a large hall (12 × 4 m.). Flat stones in the floor could have formed bases for posts.[98] A similar structure at ʿAi (26th century B.C.)[99] has been occasionally labeled as a palace.[100]

The cult in high places, which flourished in Canaanite times and was carried forth by the Israelites, centered around a sacred high spot, sometimes featuring a tree or grove, a spring (Tell el Qadi), or a high upright stone (*massebah*).[101] The latter type seems to have been popular during the Early Bronze Age IV, as exemplified in alignments of stones at Lejjun and Ader[102] or in the menhirs near the graves at Bab edh-Dhraʿ. The peculiar conical stone altar (8 m. diameter, 1.4 m. high) located on the upper terrace at Jericho, accessible from a stairway, may possibly be such a high place dating from the Early Bronze Age (Fig. 28, top left).[103] Quite remarkable is the installation at Beth Yereh (Khirbet Kerak), where eight stone-work circles (8 m. diameter), each having four inner radiating partitions, leaving a central cavity, are set within an enclosure (30 sq. m.).[104] The most significant shrine from the Early Bronze Age occurs at ʿAi (Fig. 28, top middle), where the basic elements of the typical Israelite temple of Solomon's time can be recognized as an outer enclosure, a hall (*hekal*) with inner and outer benches, and a Holy of Holies (*debir*) set at an angle with a low altar carrying stone vases from Egypt (Dynasties II–III).[105] Also at ʿAi is a controversial structure interpreted as either a palace or a temple of the type featuring a broad hall with a central row of four pillars.

During the Middle Bronze Age in Palestine the temple assumes the shape of a massive structure symmetrical along the longitudinal axis,

[95] Kenyon, *Holy Land*, p. 41.
[96] Albright, *Palestine*, pp. 62–63.
[97] Kenyon, *Holy Land*, p. 51.
[98] *Ibid.*, pp. 98–99. Albright, *Palestine*, p. 76.
[99] Albright, *Palestine*, p. 76.
[100] Barrois, *Manuel*, Vol. I, pp. 256–259, Figs. 97–98; Vol. II. pp. 356 ff.
[101] Barrois, *Manuel*, Vol. II, pp. 345–346.
[102] Albright, *Palestine*, pp. 77–78.
[103] Kenyon, *Holy Land*, p. 112, pl. 23.
[104] *Ibid.*, pp. 114–115.
[105] *Ibid.*, pp. 116 ff. Barrois, *Manuel*, Vol. II, pp. 356–358, Fig. 309.

Fig. 28→

AR AT JERICHO (EARLY BRONZE AGE III, 26TH CENT. B.C.)

'AI
(EARLY BRONZE)
10 m

GATE (MIDDLE BRONZE, 18TH CENT. B.C.)
TEMPLE (LATE BRONZE, 14TH CENT. B.C.)
AT SECHEM   25 m

ALTAR

LACHISH (2nd STAGE)
(14TH CENT. B.C.)   15

ALTAR

BETH-SHAN N°2
(13TH CENT. B.C.)   10 m

BASIN & 3 MONOLITHS
HIGH PLACE AT GEZER   (EARLY TO LATE BRONZE)

PHOENICIAN ENCLOSURE   50 m

TEMPLES

TOMBS

OLD KINGDOM

MIDDLE
KINGDOM

BLOS

BA'AL

STREET

STREET

DAGON

UGARIT
2000 B.C.

50 m

with one deep cella preceded by an antecella that is open on the outside. It is flanked by towers and accessible through a ramp (Sechem)[106] or a monumental approach with stairs (Megiddo).[107] There is no consistent orientation, and the thickness of the walls and the inner columns imply a many-storied structure.

When the Israelites begin to settle in the Late Bronze Age, temples become more numerous. At Lachish a small temple shows three superimposed stages (1500–1230 B.C.), having one squarish cella with a ceiling on posts; it is entered from an angle doorway screened behind a walled-in court. Along the rear wall of the cella is a bench (0.32 m. high), and opposite it are three blocks (altars?; Fig. 28, middle left). In later stages small rooms are added behind the cella.[108] In the temple at Megiddo (1500–1150 B.C.) a niche for a cult object is cut in the rear wall, while the entrance lobby or portico is flanked by two small rooms, perhaps carried up as towers.[109] At Beth Shan two temples (14th–13th centuries B.C.) show more Egyptianizing influences, though the irregular layout of the earlier ones is Canaanite, with a series of hypaethral courts and a conic massebah symbolizing the city god Mekal. The later temple facing south is, however, of a new type: a forecourt with a two-columned portico fronts a raised shallow sanctuary containing a stela of "Ashtarte-with-Two-Horns" (Fig. 28, middle).[110] The type is strikingly similar to the small chapels at ʿAmarna. In fact, a direct copy would not have been impossible in the context of Egyptianization both in cult representations and in style of artifacts, some of which were even imported. The three later temples at Beth Shan date from the Iron Age (12th–11th centuries B.C.), the earlier of which is very similar to that of the Late Bronze Age though more symmetrical, and the papyriform capitals and bases in its portico denote further evidence from Egypt.[111] In its two later stages the temple is oriented east and has a hypostyle hall lit by clerestory windows and an altar accessible from some steps at the rear.[112] A similar arrangement is featured in the sanctuary at Arad, with three steps, two altars facing east, and the Holy of Holies facing west.[113]

[106] E. Sellin, "Die Ausgrabung von Sichem," *Zeitschrift des Deutschen Palästinavereins* (1926), pp. 309–311; (1927), pp. 206–207. Barrois, *Manuel*, Vol. II, pp. 364–365; Vol. I, Fig. 63. Albright, *Palestine*, Fig. 15, pl. 104.

[107] Kenyon, *Holy Land*, p. 156, Figs. 34–35.

[108] *Ibid.*, p. 204, Fig. 49. Albright, *Palestine*, p. 103. Barrois, *Manuel*, Vol. II, pp. 365–370, Figs. 315–317.

[109] Kenyon, *Holy Land*, p. 203. Albright, *Palestine*, p. 103.

[110] A. Rowe, *The Topography and History of Beth-Shan: The Four Canaanite Temples of Beth-Shan*, Vol. I, *The Temples and Cult Objects* (Philadelphia, 1940). Kenyon, *Holy Land*, pp. 218–219. Barrois, *Manuel*, Vol. II, pp. 370–374, Figs. 318, 320. Otto, ed., *Handbuch*, p. 813.

[111] Barrois, *Manuel*, Vol. II, pp. 374–375, Fig. 320.

[112] *Ibid.*, Vol. II, p. 375, Figs. 321–322. Kenyon, *Holy Land*, p. 251.

[113] Aharoni and Amiran, "Arad, a Biblical City," pp. 52–53.

There is no archaeological evidence of Solomon's temple, known to have been built near his palace in Jerusalem, but its description in texts (I Kings; II Chron.) provides valuable information. The rectangular structure (50 × 100 cubits), which was symmetrical and faced east, comprised a vestibule or forecourt (*elam*) flanked by two freestanding bronze columns, a "house" (*hekal*) lit by clerestory windows and surrounded by a three-storied ambulatory divided into cells, and a rear Holy of Holies (*debir*), which was a cubical room (20 cubits) without any other opening besides the doorway and contained the Ark. This plan recalls vividly the basic tripartite plan of the cult temple in Egypt during the New Kingdom. The elements, including interior wood paneling, a front porch flanked by towers (hilani), and the cherubs, seem to have been of an Egyptianizing style similar to that of Phoenician ivories.[114]

Sacred high places were already known in the Early Bronze Age and still used in the Iron Age, but the character of the cult performed has not yet been defined. At Gezer (Early–Late Bronze) a row of eight monolithic round-topped stones (1.65–3.28 m. high) runs north–south, possibly connected to a massive monolithic basin (1.85 × 1.52 × 0.76 m.; Fig. 28, middle right).[115]

In Phoenicia two types of temples can be differentiated: the Egyptianized one first exemplified at Byblos (Egyptian Dynasty II) and the Phoenician one (Fig. 28, bottom left). The two Egyptianizing temples at Byblos (Old Kingdom and Middle Kingdom) are an adaptation of the tripartite plan typical of the cult temple in Egypt. In front of the west entrance façade are an altar and five colossi imitating in a coarse style the statues of seated deities and standing pharaohs.[116] At Ugarit the two identical massive temples on the second level, one dedicated to Baʿal and the other, fifty meters southeast, to his father Dagon (Middle Kingdom), are also on a similar plan facing south. Beyond a court (*hesr*) in which stands an altar (2 × 2.2 m.), there are an antecella and a broader cella (*bet*) with a lateral stand used as an offering table (Fig. 28, bottom right).[117] These are surrounded by an outer wall, leaving a passageway for guards. Lists of sacrificed animals are inscribed on stelae.[118] A peculiar offering to the spirits of vegetation in concomitance with the dead was made within

114 Barrois, *Manuel*, Vol. II, pp. 436–446, Figs. 348–350. Kenyon, *Holy Land*, pp. 245–247, Fig. 58. Watzinger, *Denkmäler Palästinas*, pp. 89–95. Otto, ed., *Handbuch*, pp. 813–814, Fig. 83.

115 Macalister, *Gezer*, Vol. II, pp. 381–406. Barrois, *Manuel*, Vol. II, pp. 358–360. Albright, *Palestine*, p. 104.

116 Contenau, *Manuel d'archéologie Orientale*, Vol. IV, pp. 2281–2285, Figs. 1295–1297. Dunand and Furlani, in *Enciclopedia*, Vol. C, p. 100.

117 Contenau, *Manuel d'archéologie Orientale*, Vol. IV, pp. 2288–2289. C. Schaeffer, "Les Fouilles de Ras Shamra–Ugarit, Sixième campagne," *Syria*, Vol. XVI (1935), pp. 154–156, pl. XXXVI. Schaeffer, *Ugaritica*, Vol. I, pp. 15 ff.

118 Barrois, *Manuel*, Vol. II, p. 335.

enclosures at small libation altars set on concrete platforms and connected to jars sunken in the subsoil near the tombs.[119]

The Phoenician type of temple is exemplified by that of Reshef at Byblos (Dynasty XII). This typical temple, with a court, an antecella, and a raised cella, is surrounded on three sides by about twenty "obelisks" (0.8–3.5 m. high).[120] Two naoi, two offering tables, and three ablution basins are set in the court. It was remodeled five times, the last time during the reign of Ramses II.

The shrine represented on the coins of Macrinus is probably that of Aphrodite of Byblos; it features a high enclosure surrounding an altar and a pillar of Adonis. The shrine, which consists of a large court cut from the bedrock at Marathus (ᶜAmrit), north of Sidon, with a central Egyptianized naos, probably surrounded by a portico on wooden pillars, is related to the hypaethral Semitic type.[121] Of a similar style are the small chapels topped with the cavetto, torus, and uraeus frieze at ᶜAin el Hayyat.

Tombs

Prehistoric hunters who lived in caves buried their dead beneath the occupied area in communal pits and later in single graves. One skeleton in a group was adorned with a fan-shaped shell ornament on the sides of its head and with necklaces (Mugharet el Wad at Mount Carmel). The site is marked by basins hollowed out of the rock, stone circles on a pavement (ᶜAin Mullaha), or a plain pavement (ᶜErq el Ahmar).[122] Skulls plastered to represent the features, with inlaid shells for the eyes and paint for the hair, are later placed in a room, though the bodies are buried beneath the floor of the house.[123] The megalithic dolmens that occur in large numbers in Jordan (Fig. 29, top middle) have been identified as funerary monuments associated with cist graves dating probably from the Aeneolithic Period. Several cists are covered by one circular mound marked along its periphery by vertical stones (tumulus at El ᶜAdeimah; Fig. 29, top left).[124] In the Chalcolithic Period bones from earlier burials or from bodies from which the flesh has been scraped are placed in terra-cotta

[119] Contenau, *Manuel d'Archéologie Orientale*, Vol. IV, p. 2293. Watzinger in Otto, ed., *Handbuch*, p. 803.

[120] Barrois, *Manuel*, Vol. II, pp. 361–362.

[121] E. Renan, *Mission de Phénicie*, pp. 63, 68, pls. 8–10. Watzinger, *Denkmäler Palästinas*, Vol. I, pp. 66–67.

[122] Kenyon, *Holy Land*, pp. 37–38, pl. 2; pp. 51–53, pl. 13. Barrois, *Manuel*, Vol. II, pp. 274–275.

[123] Kenyon, *Holy Land*, pp. 52–53.

[124] M. Stekelis, "Les monuments mégalithiques de Palestine," *Archives de l'Institut de Paléontologie Humaine*, Mémoire 15. Barrois, *Manuel*, Vol. II, pp. 276–278, Figs. 272–273.

Fig. 29→

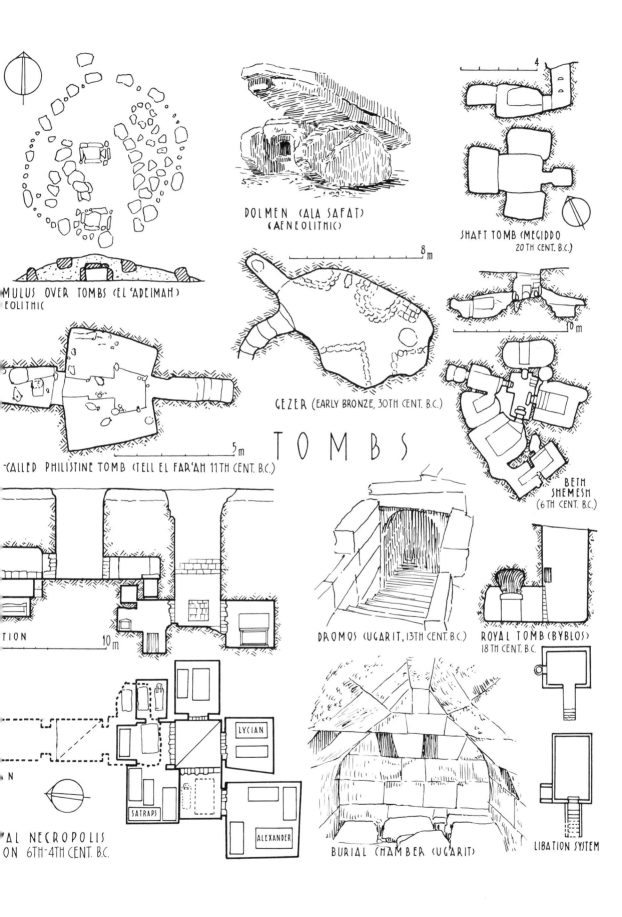

DOLMEN (ALA SAFAT)
(AENEOLITHIC)

SHAFT TOMB (MEGIDDO
20TH CENT. B.C.)

...MULUS OVER TOMBS (EL 'ADEIMAH)
...EOLITHIC

GEZER (EARLY BRONZE, 30TH CENT. B.C.)

-CALLED PHILISTINE TOMB (TELL EL FAR'AH 11TH CENT. B.C.)

BETH
SHEMESH
(6TH CENT. B.C.)

T O M B S

...TION   10 m

DROMOS (UGARIT, 13TH CENT. B.C.)

ROYAL TOMB (BYBLOS)
18TH CENT. B.C.

LYCIAN

SATRAPS

ALEXANDER

...AL NECROPOLIS
...ON 6TH-4TH CENT. B.C.

BURIAL CHAMBER (UGARIT)

LIBATION SYSTEM

ossuaries (0.5 × 0.3 × [0.27–0.54] m. high) representing houses (Khodeira).[125]

Just before the Bronze Age shafts are cut in the rock, or caves are used, for mass burials of three to four hundred bodies.[126] There is some evidence of cremation (Jericho, 23rd century B.C.),[127] and of piling aside earlier bones, a practice still followed in the Early Bronze Age.[128] Toward the end of this period nomad invaders have individual tombs, some with large square or round shafts and chambers (Jericho,[129] Tell el Ajjul, Megiddo, Lachish). Shaft tombs (Early or Middle Bronze), which never assume the preplanned monumentality of the Egyptian mastaba tombs of the Old Kingdom, feature a square vertical shaft (2 m. deep) with foot holes leading down to a central chamber, which is connected on three sides to three smaller rooms with higher floors, similar to loculi. The bottom doorway of the shaft was blocked, as in Egyptian ones, with stones and the shaft itself filled in after each burial (Megiddo; Fig. 29, top right).[130] In one type the burial chamber is accessible from a slanting corridor, and the whole excavation is irregular in shape (Jericho, Tell el Farʿah).[131]

The practice of burying single bodies beneath houses is allied to that of communal burials in the Middle Bronze Age. Actual tomb structures are used for successive burials (Tell Duweir, Tell el Farʿah, Jericho).[132] In the so-called Philistine tombs at Tell el Farʿah (Fig. 29, upper left),[133] reached by a rough stairway, wide ledges are left along the sides to receive the bodies or anthropomorphic sarcophagi made from terra-cotta, which were found in the vicinity of Beth Shan, ʿAmran, and in Egypt at Tell el Yahudiya, Tell Nebesheh, Saft el Hennah.[134] Perhaps such evidence indicates some connection with the "people of the sea" before their invasion under Ramses III. The shaft type of tomb deteriorates in the Iron Age, superseded by graves lined and covered with stone (Tell el Farʿah), or underground rock-cut tombs with a bench along three of their sides (Beth Shemesh), which develop into multiple rooms in post-Exilic times (Beth Shemesh; Fig. 29, upper right), under Neo-Babylonian and Persian

[125] Barrois, *Manuel*, Vol. II, pp. 279–280. E. L. Sukenik, "A Chalcolithic Necropolis at Hederah," *Journal of the Palestinian Oriental Society*, Vol. XVII (1937), pp. 15–30. Kenyon, *Holy Land*, p. 77.

[126] Kenyon, *Holy Land*, p. 86.

[127] *Ibid.*, p. 98.

[128] *Ibid.*, pp. 122–123.

[129] *Ibid.*, pp. 139 ff.

[130] *Ibid.*, p. 150. Barrois, *Manuel*, Vol. II, pp. 283–284.

[131] Barrois, *Manuel*, Vol. II, pp. 285–286, Figs. 280 ff.

[132] Kenyon, *Holy Land*, pp. 188 ff.

[133] W. Fl. Petrie, *Beth-Pelet*, Vol. I—*Tell Fara* (London, 1930), pls. LI, LXIV. Barrois, *Manuel*, Vol. I, p. 291, Fig. 284. Kenyon, *Holy Land*, p. 227.

[134] Barrois, *Manuel*, Vol. II, pp. 293–295, Figs. 285–286.

occupations.[135] There is evidence that the bench in the burial chamber occurs also in Phoenicia at the turn of the second millennium B.C. and in Idalion in Cyprus, whence it may have been derived. Single graves are also common in the Solomonic Age (Tell el Farᶜah).

In Chalcolithic Phoenicia the dead are buried in graves covered with stone slabs. At Byblos the shaft tombs of the rulers of Tyre, contemporaneous with the Middle Kingdom and the New Kingdom, have yielded gifts from Egyptian pharaohs (Ramses II) and rich furniture of Egyptianized style.[136] Two of these tombs are interconnected by an underground gallery so that the son could visit his father.[137] The unique sarcophagus of Ahiram is marked by influences from Egypt (lotus, sarcophagus shape, royal figures) and North Syria in the indigenous style (offering bearers, mourning women, three-legged altar, throne).[138]

At Ugarit (second level, Middle Kingdom) the tombs are similar, with a libation table near the entrance. In the Hyksos Period tombs consisting of a shallow antechamber and a burial chamber are arranged beneath the houses. This type later develops a stairway or dromos of Mycenaean style leading down to a rectangular chamber that is built of well-dressed masonry and roofed with a pointed corbel adjacent to an ossuary (Fig. 29, bottom middle). A device for offering consists of a jar set in a niche in the burial chamber or a channel or window connecting the outer offering place to the interior of the tomb (Fig. 29, bottom right).[139] This was used by families over centuries. Certain aspects, such as the rectangular chamber, the axial dromos, and the corbel vault (instead of the earlier slabs), point to Crete for the possible prototype (tomb of Isopata).

Shaft tombs with lateral burial chambers assume a larger scale in the Persian Period as family tombs featuring several rooms with rectangular graves under the floor slabs. The most famous example is the royal necropolis at Sidon (6th–4th centuries B.C.; Fig. 29, bottom left), where a few Egyptian sarcophagi were reused by indigenous princes, while anthropoid or classical sarcophagi were made by local Greek craftsmen (470–460 B.C.) in a style adapted to Phoenician taste.[140] From one of these tombs come the so-called "Lycian sarcophagus" and "Alexander's sarcophagus" (in Greek style).

135 *Ibid.*, Vol. II, pp. 295–297, Figs. 287–288. Watzinger, *Denkmäler Palästinas*, pp. 104, Fig. 29.

136 Dunand and Furlani in *Enciclopedia*, Vol. C, pp. 99–100. P. Montet, *Byblos et l'Égypte* (Paris, 1928), pp. 239–240.

137 Montet, *Byblos*, pp. 143 ff.

138 Watzinger, in Otto, ed., *Handbuch*, pp. 801–802, pl. 189.

139 Contenau, *Manuel d'archéologie Orientale*, Vol. IV, pp. 2293–2295, Figs. 1302–1303. Schaeffer, *Ugaritica*, Vol. I, pp. 68 ff. Frankfort, *Art*, p. 162.

140 Watzinger in Otto, ed., *Handbuch*, pp. 818–819, Fig. 84.

Fortifications

Early settlements in Canaan must have been quite adequately fortified, since Jericho was surrounded in the seventh millennium B.C. by a stone wall 2.2 meters wide guarded by a round tower more than ten meters high.[141] However, a comprehensive study of the art of fortification can start only with the Middle Bronze Age, when brick, stone, or even earth is used in the enclosures surrounding the towns, depending upon the possibilities of the sites and the trends of the settlers. Rammed earthworks appear in sites located in flat country, where chariots were used by Indo-Aryan and Horite invaders from the north after the eighteenth century B.C. (Middle Bronze),[142] at Lachish, Hazor, Tell Beit Mersim, Sechem, and Tell el Ajjul. The vertical wall is sometimes reinforced at the bottom by an earth glacis faced with stonework (Tell Gerishah, Gezer; Fig. 30, top middle). As a rule, the site is so chosen as to take utmost advantage of the natural defenses in the shape of two ravines flanking a mound (east and west at Tell el Hesy;[143] north and south at Tell el Far'ah; Fig. 30, top left;[144] to the north at Tell Gemmah; on all sides at Tell Zakariya;[145] to the north and west at Tell Beit Mirsim;[146] on three sides at Lachish)[147] or a swampy district (southwest of Tell el Ajjul).[148] Inland sites are usually chosen with regard to their strategic value for defending a pass or a trade route (Tell Gemmah, Tell el Far'ah, and Tell el Ajjul defending southern entrance; Beth Shemesh at crossroads to upland; Tell Beit Mirsim on the north–south route; Lachish, Megiddo on pass of Wadi 'Ara; Ta'nnah; Beth Shan blocking valley of Jordan). This strategic factor sometimes requires the choice of an open site without natural defenses (Gezer, Beth Shemesh), where artificial fortifications have to be provided on the whole periphery.

Glacis may be made of dry rubble (Lachish, Jericho; Fig. 30, top middle), often supplemented by scarp and counterscarp separated by a ditch (Tell el Far'ah;[149] Tell el Ajjul;[150] Tell Beit Mirsim[151]), or a convex glacis may be faced with rubble and topped with bundles of brushwood (Gezer). Occasionally, no glacis is built (Beth Shemesh), but a batter is given to the whole wall (Sechem, Jericho) of cyclopean

141 Kenyon, *Holy Land*, p. 44, pls. 7–8.
142 Albright, *Palestine*, p. 86. Barrois, *Manuel*, Vol. I, p. 206.
143 Barrois, *Manuel*, Vol. I, p. 137.
144 *Ibid.*, pp. 132–133, Fig. 37.
145 *Ibid.*, p. 139, Fig. 23.
146 *Ibid.*, p. 156.
147 *Ibid.*, p. 158.
148 *Ibid.*, pp. 130, 135.
149 *Ibid.*, pp. 132–133, Fig. 37.
150 *Ibid.*, p. 135.
151 *Ibid.*, p. 157. Albright, *Palestine*, p. 89.

Fig. 30→

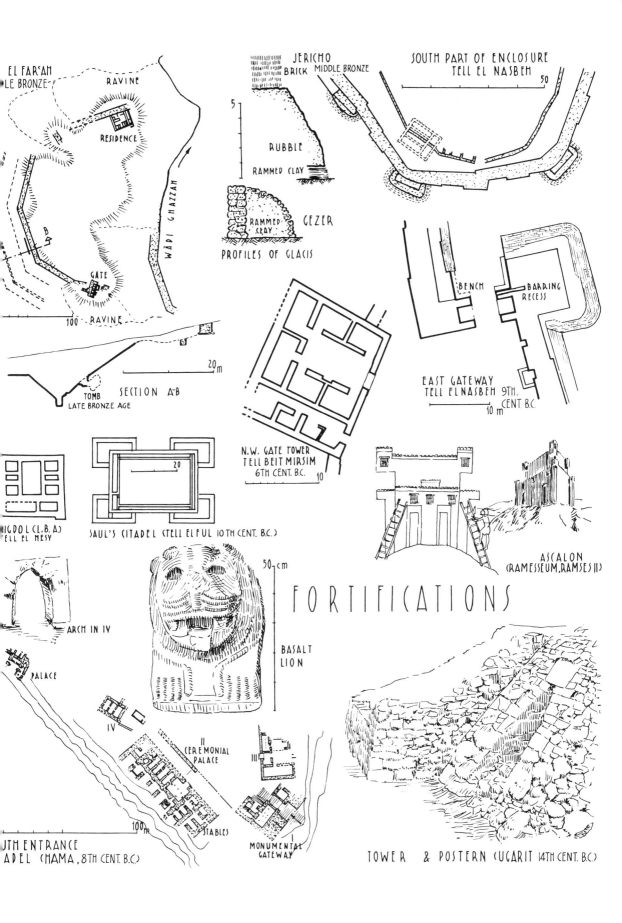

EL FAR'AH
LE BRONZE

RAVINE

RESIDENCE

WADI GHAZZAH

GATE

100 RAVINE

SECTION A-B

TOMB
LATE BRONZE AGE

20 m

JERICHO
BRICK   MIDDLE BRONZE

SOUTH PART OF ENCLOSURE
TELL EL NASBEH

50

5

RUBBLE

RAMMED CLAY

RAMMED CLAY   GEZER

PROFILES OF GLACIS

BENCH   BARRING RECESS

EAST GATEWAY
TELL EL NASBEH 9TH. CENT. B.C.

10 m

N.W. GATE TOWER
TELL BEIT MIRSIM
6TH CENT. B.C.

10

IGDOL (L.B.A.)
ELL EL MESY

SAUL'S CITADEL (TELL EL FUL 10TH CENT. B.C.)

20

ASCALON
(RAMESSEUM, RAMSES II)

ARCH IN IV

PALACE

IV

BASALT
LION

50 cm

FORTIFICATIONS

II
CEREMONIAL
PALACE

III

STABLES

JTH ENTRANCE
ADEL (HAMA, 8TH CENT. B.C.)

100 m

MONUMENTAL
GATEWAY

TOWER & POSTERN (UGARIT 14TH CENT. B.C.)

masonry topped with brickwork.[152] It has been suggested that both the glacis and the battered wall came from Asia Minor.[153]

A double or triple enclosure on terraces (Lachish under Israelite monarchy; Jericho, ᶜAi, Megiddo) is another type of fortification that seems to be more autochthonous than the broad glacis of the Hyksos. Casemated enclosures with earth filling are known (citadel of Saul at Tell el Ful, Sechem, Tell Beit Mirsim, Beth Shemesh, Samaria, ᶜAi)[154] and seem to have been common in the Iron Age. The plan of the wall is often jagged, according to the system affected in Troy and Asia Minor (Lachish, Beth Shemesh), or it may consist of stretches projecting alternately inward and outward (wide buttresses, Megiddo).

Bastions are not a regular feature in enclosure walls, though they occur at the corners (Tell el Hesy, ᶜAi) or along straight stretches (Tell el Hesy, Lachish, Tell el Nasbeh) and are built of massive or casemated masonry. Towers are erected on each side of a gateway or along the enclosure, sometimes alternating with bastions (Beth Shemesh, Tell Beit Mirsim, Beth Sur, Tell el Nasbeh). At Tell el Nasbeh angle towers (10 m. wide × 2 m. projection) alternate with bastions or are set in pairs to protect a gateway (east). They are also built next to the enclosure on a glacis (4–5 m. high).[155] Gezer was reinforced with towers (second enclosure) according to a process that spread during the Late Bronze Age and resulted in a rational military architecture initiated by the Canaanites and imitated by the Israelites.[156] The appearance of these fortifications can be ascertained from Egyptian and Assyrian contemporaneous representations (Fig. 30, middle right).[157] It is noteworthy that at the top of the towers there always are cantilevered machicolations, sometimes of timber (Assyrian representation of Lachish).[158]

Gateways are of the axial type, occasionally with a double doorway (Tell el Nasbeh), but more often with a triple doorway, which may be roofed over (Beth Shemesh, Megiddo, Gezer, Tell el Farᶜah, Sechem) and flanked by two towers protruding externally from the enclosure. The type of gateway with a triple doorway was known earlier in Mesopotamia, from which it probably spread to Mari, North Syria, and Palestine in the second millennium B.C. A second type of gateway, with bent-up entrance, is adopted later under the Israelite

---

[152] Albright, *Palestine*, p. 88.
[153] *Ibid.*, p. 89. Barrois, *Manuel*, Vol. I, p. 206.
[154] Albright, *Palestine*, pp. 121, 122, 137.
[155] Barrois, *Manuel*, Vol. I, p. 193, Fig. 69.
[156] *Ibid.*, pp. 208–209.
[157] Alexandre Badawy, *Le dessin architectural chez les Anciens Égyptiens* (Cairo, 1948), pp. 148–158. Naumann, *Architektur*, pp. 290 ff, Figs. 361–378. Helck, *Beziehungen*. pp. 338–341.
[158] Barrois, *Manuel*, Vol. I, p. 209, n. 1.

monarchy[159] (Lachish, Tell Beit Mirsim, 6th century B.C.; Fig. 30, middle). An intermediate type in both design and date is seen in the east gate at Tell el Nasbeh (9th century B.C.; Fig. 30, upper right) and in the early east gate at Tell Beit Mirsim, which has a double doorway set tangent to the enclosure. It is interesting to note that a guesthouse is installed in the structure of the northwest gateway at Tell Beit Mirsim VI and that benches are arranged along the sides of the porch of the gate at Tell el Nasbeh where the elders could sit during their meetings, according to the custom in the Levant.[160] Since there is no published evidence about posterns, the two long irregular tunnels approaching Tell el ᶜAjjul could well be sapping approaches excavated by the enemy, like the one at Lachish.[161]

The early type of independent dungeon or migdol (Beth Shan) evolved during the Iron Age into a large citadel on the acropolis of the town (Tell el Hesy; Fig. 30, middle left; Taᶜnnah, Tell Zakaryia, Beth Shan, Tell el Ful XI),[162] surrounded by its own enclosure at the top of the hill as in Hittite and Greek towns. At Tell el Ful, three miles north of Jerusalem, Saul (1020–1000 B.C.) built a citadel on a rectangular plan (east–west) with four angular bastions in well-dressed casemated walls (Fig. 30, middle left).[163] At Arad the fortress from the time of Solomon was surrounded in the ninth century B.C. by a strong ashlar wall four meters thick. This was remodeled five times, up to the end of the seventh century B.C., the last two versions having a rectangular plan with casemated walls and projecting towers.[164]

There is sporadic evidence about the contribution of foreigners to fortified layouts in Palestine. At Abu Hawan the cyclopean enclosure dates from the time of the Mycenaean founders of the harbor.[165] There is no doubt that the numerous occupations of the country by the Egyptians and ultimately by the Assyrians left deep impressions. The brick enclosure with slightly projecting panels at regular intervals built at Tell el Safy after the Assyrian destruction is reminiscent of that of Sennacherib at Assur.[166] A house at Tell Gemmah (7th century B.C.) has been compared to the forts of Psammetik at Naukratis and Daphnae or to an Assyrian mansion.[167]

At Byblos the settlement on the promontory was fortified against attacks from the mainland (about 2700 B.C.) by a wall about four

[159] *Ibid.*, p. 212. Albright, *Palestine*, p. 138, Fig. 44.
[160] Albright, *Palestine*, pp. 139 ff.
[161] *Ibid.*, pp. 136–137, Fig. 4.
[162] Barrois, *Manuel*, Vol. I, p. 210, Figs. 39–40.
[163] Albright, *Palestine*, pp. 120–121, Fig. 30.
[164] Aharoni and Amiran, "Arad, a Biblical City," pp. 44–51.
[165] Barrois, *Manuel*, Vol. I, p. 128.
[166] Watzinger, *Denkmäler Palästinas*, Vol. II. p. 3.
[167] *Ibid.*

meters wide with internal bastions and reinforced after the Amorite invasion (2100 B.C.; Fig. 26, bottom middle). The acropolis was abandoned by the settlers after another invasion in 1750 B.C., and it became the domain of the dead kings. The bastions were often repaired, and an esplanade was added in the Persian Period.[168]

Ugarit is the only North Syrian town[169] that adopted an elaborate system of fortification in the Hittite style with a battered postern five meters high (first half of the 14th century B.C.; Fig. 30, bottom right) in which a corbeled pointed arch protected by a tower (14 m. wide) rose above a flight of low steps.

At Hama the entrance to the citadel (8th century B.C.) is designed as a gateway of impressive style, approached by a wide stairway with low steps rising to a porch with two columns flanked by two massive brick towers. Beyond the deep passage a second wide stairway branches off, which may have been used as a stepped tribune during processions.[170] Stone orthostats line the walls, ornamented at the corners of the outer and inner passages by two pairs of lions carved in low relief but with heads in the round. One double door shuts the inner doorway (Fig. 30, bottom left). A similar inclined approach through only one doorway occurs at the spring gate at Tell Halaf.

Construction and Style

Though excellent stone abounds in Palestine, it was never used extensively except under the united monarchy (10th century B.C.) when Phoenician master builders were in charge of large construction projects that required huge well-dressed stone blocks. Stone was indeed used at a very early age but only as coarse rubble in small (pre-Pottery Neolithic tower at Jericho, seventh millennium B.C.) or large blocks. As in Sumer, plano-convex brick was often used (Beth Shan, Jericho), but later it was replaced by handmade oblong blocks (Teleilat Ghassul) and still later cast in molds. Brickwork never achieved regularity and was often reinforced with wood to an extent comparable with that in Asia Minor.

Only false vaults or corbels are used to roof over small rooms, though the slight slant in some of the courses would point to some Mesopotamian influence.[171] Mycenaean influence appears later in the corbeled tomb (No. 3 at Megiddo). A common style is the flat roof, supported by a central row of wooden pillars (hall at ʿAi, "House of Lebanon Wood" in Solomon's palace) or masonry piers

168 Dunand and Furlani in *Enciclopedia*, pp. 100–101.
169 Naumann, *Architektur*, pp. 222, 281–283.
170 *Ibid.*, pp. 171, 279, Fig. 347. Ingholt, *Hama*, pp. 85–87, Fig. 1.
171 Barrois, *Manuel*, Vol. I, p. 120.

(stables at Megiddo, manufactory at Tell Beit Mirsim), for covering large spans. Timber is imported from Lebanon into Palestine to be used as supports and lining. There is no archaeological evidence of columns, though they may have existed (two in the temple at Beth Shan, two in front of Solomon's temple), but pilasters with the earliest proto-Aeolian capitals are attested (Samaria; Fig. 27, lower middle; Megiddo, Hazor, Ramat Rahel, 10th–7th centuries B.C.), perhaps even being prototypes of the ones in Cyprus.[172] The motif of the volute on either side of a triangular leaf in the proto-Aeolian capital originates from Egypt and is allied to palmettes in the Phoenician "tree of life." As elsewhere in the Orient and in contrast to Hittite façades, those in Palestine-Phoenicia have a few small windows, often with tracery in the Egyptian fashion.[173] Occasionally clerestory windows are used (Egyptian mansion at Tell el Farᶜah, Temple of Solomon). It could not be expected that Palestine would be favorable to the growth of a refined style, since this hilly land was populated by seminomads who were often raided by other nomads, so that they never achieved political unity.[174] Little of intrinsic value there is autochthonous, and whatever attracts aesthetically originates from Mesopotamia, Egypt, Asia Minor, or the Aegean. This is the earliest eclectic trend in art followed by a whole country. This is also true of the Phoenicians, those able sea traders and craftsmen who copied extensively from Egypt and less from Assyria with admirable good taste for symmetrical and geometric composition,[175] but their eclecticism was not centrally directed by a ruler or a government. They were at their best during the period when architecture flourished between the twelfth and the seventh centuries B.C., and much of the Archaic style in Greece (8th century B.C.) was initiated through the Phoenician style. Later, in the fifth and fourth centuries B.C., Greek artistic elements were introduced into Phoenicia itself by Greek craftsmen.[176]

No outstanding achievement can be found in urban development in Palestine, and probably not in Phoenicia either, for towns grew organically there, as is typical of unplanned settlements in the Orient.

After the early round or apsidal houses, possibly of foreign import, the Palestinian house borrows the typical Mesopotamian plan, with rooms in more than one story arranged around a central court. Even palaces are patterned after this plan, though they are decorated with proto-Aeolian pillars and ivory inlays. Occasionally Egyptian houses (Tell el Farᶜah) or Parthian ones (Lachish) are copied.

[172] Watzinger in Otto, ed., *Handbuch*, p. 816.
[173] Barrois, *Manuel*, Vol. I, p. 123.
[174] Moscati, *Semitic Civilizations*, p. 121.
[175] Watzinger in Otto, ed., *Handbuch*, p. 824.
[176] *Ibid.*, p. 823.

As to temples, the autochthonous ones are connected with the sacred high places and the upright stones, and they can hardly have offered much architectural interest. It is only with the later closed type derived from Egypt (Beth Shan, Solomon's temple), or even copied therefrom (Megiddo), that aesthetic achievement is marked by an Egyptianized style (hypostyle hall, tripartite plan, cherubs). The Egyptian style is conspicuous in the very early temples from the period of the Old Kingdom at Byblos (tripartite plan, colossi fronting façade), though more essential indigenous contributions are evolved in other temples (rows of stelae).

The typical shaft tomb of Palestine does not show any stylistic achievement. However, late Phoenician ones (Sidon) borrow extensively from Egypt even to the reuse of Egyptian sarcophagi.

Perhaps more significant, as to efficacy rather than to style, is the achievement in the art of fortification in Palestine (often two or three enclosures with towers, citadel, jagged outline). Here foreign contributions are also conspicuous (triple doorway, alternating panels projecting in brick enclosures).

Elam and Persia

The Environment[1]

The natural setting of Elam and Persia is the plateau of Iran, a triangular highland surrounded by mountains and stretching between Mesopotamia, the Persian Gulf, and the Caspian Sea. The Zagros Mountains along the western edge of the plateau, once forested and cultivated, are now pastureland, while the naturally arid central depression becomes fertile when water is provided. Though an agricultural country, it also has mineral riches (stone, carnelian, turquoise, lapis lazuli, iron, copper, tin, and lead). Earlier the plateau had woods, which were exploited by the Sumerians and later by the Assyrians. Special mention should be made of underground oil in Susiana that was used in lamps and hearths. Probably because there is no large river, the early settlements were dispersed and showed local characteristics.[2]

Toward the fifth millennium B.C. food gatherers who had been living on the mountain slopes ever since the postpluvial period (15,000–10,000 B.C.) gradually descended as the central lake shrank and uncovered new tracts of arable land. The various phases of settled life are marked by the huts built of light materials (Period I), the oval mud brick, painted pottery, hammered copper, and

---

[1] R. Ghirshman, *Iran* (Harmondsworth, 1954). A. V. Pope and P. Ackerman, *A Survey of Persian Art from Prehistoric Times to the Present*, 6 vols. (Oxford, 1938). E. Herzfeld, *Iran in the Ancient East* (Oxford, 1941). L. V. Berghe, *Archéologie de l'Iran ancien*, preface by R. Ghirshman (Leiden, 1959). R. Ghirshman, *Iran, Parthians and Sassanians* (Harmondsworth, 1962).

[2] Ghirshman, *Iran*, p. 114.

domesticated animals (Period II), the rectangular molded brick and cast metals (Period III) at Siyalk, Qumm, Savah, Rayy, and Damghan.

Toward 3000 B.C. civilization features proto-Elamite writing and is probably influenced by the Djemdet-Nasr culture of Mesopotamia. The plain of Susa (southwest) becomes a center of urban life, contrasting with the northern districts, which are infiltrated from central Asia. The Elamites, fated to be dominated by their powerful neighbors in Mesopotamia, add the Sumerian script to their own and are virtually vassals of the various dynasties. Only for a brief time, when the Indo-Europeans invade northern Mesopotamia, does a national Elamite dynasty hold Babylonia under its sway, only to be defeated by Hammurabi (1728–1686 B.C.). It reappears later, again for a short period, and wrests the Diyala region from the Kassites, but Elam is finally taken by Nebuchadnezzar I (1000 B.C.).

At the beginning of the first millennium B.C. new groups of Indo-Europeans, the Iranian horsemen, settle in the Zagros valleys, adapting their culture to the autochthonous ways and serving as mercenaries to the local princes. In due time they supplant the native people, building fortified towns inhabited by well-defined classes: prince and nobles, free landowners, free men, and slaves. Iron is exploited extensively, and Assyria becomes a regular customer for it. The Persians learn more from the Urartians to whom they are vassals (8th century B.C.), and they later develop into a political power, though still under the suzerainty of the Medes (7th century B.C.). When Media is taken by Assurbanipal, the Persian ruler Cyrus I recognizes the suzerainty of Assyria.

Shortly afterward, however, Cyrus the Great defeats the Medes and founds the Achaemenian dynasty of Persia (7th–4th centuries B.C.). Though active in warfare, its kings are also great builders in Susa and Persepolis, drawing heavily upon the architecture of Mesopotamia, Syria, and Egypt. The various attempts to bring Greece under Persian sway fail, though Egypt is invaded. Decline sets in rapidly, and the dynasty comes to an end with the victories of Alexander the Great at Granicus, Issus, and Arbela (331 B.C.).

Towns

Elamite towns are represented on Assyrian monuments, but few sites have been excavated. It appears, however, that a town under Mesopotamian influence like Tshoga-Zambil (Fig. 31, top left; 13th century B.C.) had an oval outline (1,440 × 1,000 m.) and an

Fig. 31→

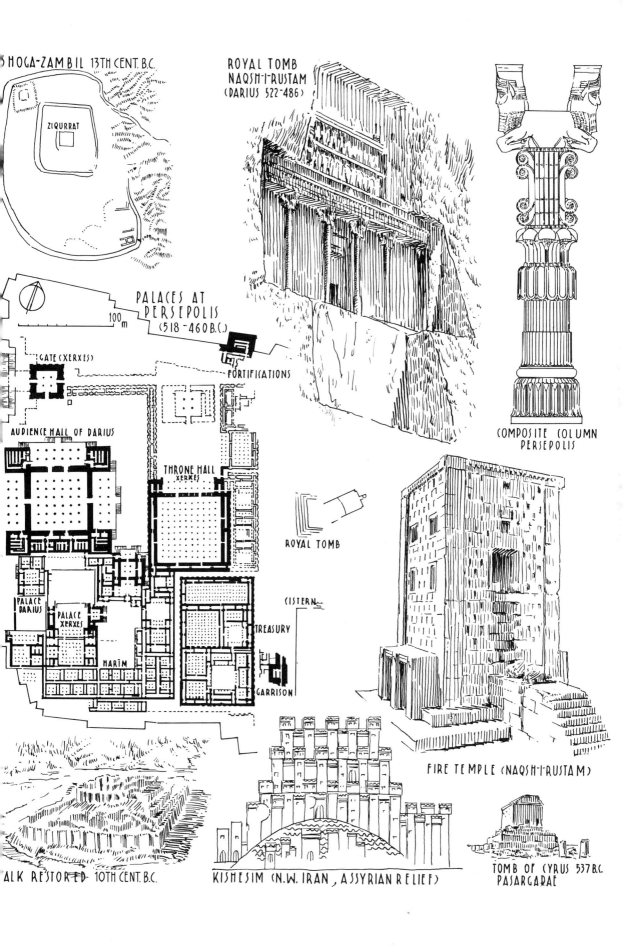

SHOGA-ZAMBIL 13TH CENT. B.C.

ZIQURRAT

ROYAL TOMB
NAQSH-I-RUSTAM
(DARIUS 522-486)

PALACES AT
PERSEPOLIS
(518-460 B.C.)

100 m

GATE (XERXES)

FORTIFICATIONS

AUDIENCE HALL OF DARIUS

THRONE HALL
XERXES

ROYAL TOMB

CISTERN

PALACE
DARIUS

PALACE
XERXES

TREASURY

HARIM

GARRISON

COMPOSITE COLUMN
PERSEPOLIS

FIRE TEMPLE (NAQSH-I-RUSTAM)

ALK RESTORED 10TH CENT. B.C.

KISHESIM (N.W. IRAN, ASSYRIAN RELIEF)

TOMB OF CYRUS 537 B.C.
PASARGADAE

orthogonal system of streets, with a sacred temenos located in its northwestern half.[3]

As to Persian towns, our conjectural information is derived mainly from descriptions by classical writers (Herodotus, Strabo), though archaeological evidence about royal palaces is available. Ecbatana is the only layout described as being surrounded by seven enclosures,[4] a type otherwise known from Assyrian low-relief murals that represent Elamite towns as surrounded by several enclosures with machicolated towers and arched gateways.[5] At Pasargadae, Susa, and Persepolis the citadels including the royal palaces on terraces have been uncovered, and it is presumed that urban settlements extended around them. However, neither the enclosure of a town, if any, nor its street system has been excavated.[6]

Houses and Palaces

Prehistoric hunters lived in mountain caves and holes roofed over with branches. Their successors who settled in the plain built shelters with plant stems and later from pisé,[7] a material eventually replaced in the fourth millennium B.C. by handmade oval brick. Even at such a primitive stage an impulsive need for decoration leads them to paint the interior walls red.[8] Bodies are buried beneath the floors. Rectangular molded brick is used at Siyalk (Period III) to build houses with external buttresses, low doorways, and windows along narrow rambling lanes.[9] At that time pottery is modeled on the wheel. Later houses are more elaborate, with an oven at the entrance, a water jar, and wall niches (Siyalk, Susa).[10]

The Bronze Age does not seem to have been marked by important changes in urban development (2000 B.C.),[11] but the invasion of the Iranians introduces new trends in housing and burial customs. A residence is now located at the top of a mound, while the town around it is fortified by a double or triple enclosure with towers (Siyalk),[12] a type of town represented on Assyrian murals (Kisheshim).[13] Graves are arranged in a cemetery outside the town.

[3] E. Egli, *Geschichte des Städtebaues* (Zurich, 1959), pp. 70–71. E. F. Schmidt, *Flights over Ancient Cities of Iran* (Chicago, 1940). For the earliest villages, see F. Hole and K. V. Flannery, "Excavations at Ali Kosh, Iran, 1961," *Iranica Antica*, Vol. II, Fasc. 2 (Leiden, 1963).

[4] Herodotus, *Histories*, Bk. I, par. 101.

[5] Ghirshman, *Iran*, p. 85, Fig. 34.

[6] Egli, *Städtebau*, pp. 90, 92.

[7] Ghirshman, *Iran*, pp. 27, 29.

[8] *Ibid.*, p. 32.

[9] *Ibid.*, pp. 35–36.

[10] *Ibid.*, p. 47.

[11] *Ibid.*, p. 71.

[12] *Ibid.*, p. 77, Fig. 28.

[13] *Ibid.*, p. 84, Fig. 34.

It is only from the Achaemenian Period onward that more substantial information can be derived from the excavations of royal palaces, which were, as a rule, set on terraces at the foot of a cliff and approached by monumental stairways in the permanent residence of Cyrus the Great (559–529 B.C.) at Pasargadae,[14] on the road from Ecbatana to the Persian Gulf. The palace, once surrounded by a park, stands within a quadrangular enclosure oriented by its corners to the cardinal points. Only the monumental gateway (southwest–northeast) still remains. The audience hall across a creek exemplifies the typical plan, which is characterized by a central rectangular hypostyle hall lit by clerestory windows, bordered on each of its four sides by a much lower columned portico. The residence (76 × 42 m.) to the north has also a central hypostyle hall with thirty columns flanked on its sides by rooms and on its front and rear by a columned portico. The slender wooden columns are stuccoed and painted and carry impost blocks in the shape of the foreparts of two crouching animals antithetically set back to back, perhaps reminiscent of the top pole ornaments of Luristan. Mud brick and dark limestone are used for the walls, which are lined with low reliefs. Colossal winged bulls once guarded either side of the entrances, a characteristic design borrowed directly from Mesopotamia, as was the orientation of the structures by their corners.

At Susa, Darius builds his citadel with a palace set on an artificial platform (521 B.C.),[15] using materials and commissioning craftsmen from various countries (Lebanon, Egypt, Ethiopia, Media, Sardis, and Babylonia). The layout is oriented by its sides to the cardinal points and fronted with three courts from east to west, containing various structures. The throne room is in the northwest part of the complex.

At Persepolis (518–460 B.C.; Fig. 31, middle left)[16] the remains of a ceremonial complex of palaces are far more informative. Built on a terrace (530 × 330 m.) next to a cliff are the ceremonial halls and residences of Darius I (Audience Hall, residence) and Xerxes (Throne Hall, residence, and *harim*) plus a treasury. A monumental gateway preceded by a double stairway of the scissors type forms the approach. It is noteworthy that the typical plan of a Persepolis palace consists always of a square columned hall, or "apadana," flanked on one side (as in the Throne Hall with 100 columns, residences) or on three sides (as in the Audience Hall) by a portico with two rows of columns. Even the smallest unit in the *harim* suites consists of a square hall

[14] A. T. Olmstead, *History of the Persian Empire* (Chicago, 1959), pp. 61 ff.

[15] R. de Mecquenem, *Contribution à l'Étude du Palais achémenide de Suse* (Paris, 1947).

[16] E. Schmidt, *Persepolis*, Vol. I (Chicago, 1953), pp. 64 ff. A. U. Pope, "Persepolis as a Ritual City," *Archaeology*, Vol. 10 (New York, 1957), pp. 123–130.

with four columns set in two rows along corridors so that it can be completely isolated for better control of the inmates. Also for security purposes, a similar corridor surrounds the Throne Hall, the palaces of Xerxes, and the treasury. The complex is certainly preplanned as a whole, all structures being oriented northwest and southeast, with their main axes slightly offset with respect to one another. Each structure is totally or partly axial, but the general layout is intentionally not axial. Impressive man-headed bulls guard the doorways, and decorative low reliefs representing a restricted repertory of tribute bearers and guardsmen line the stairways, doorjambs, and halls. Columns of two types show a tasteful eclecticism in the composition and the choice of elements (bull imposts from Assyria, double volutes from Egypt or Greece, palmiform capital from Egypt). The Egyptian cavetto cornice consistently tops doorways and windows, and as in Egypt, a strict internal symmetry with niches set to balance the arrangement of windows is observed. Architectural symbolism, both in the layout and in the elements, forms a basic feature of the design.

Temples

The earliest religious centers lay along the natural lines of communication around the central salt desert (Siyalk, Qumm, Rayy, Damghan). At an early period a fertility goddess and later an Indo-European mountain god and a goddess of the sun or earth were worshiped.[17] At the climax of Elamite history, temples were built all over the kingdom.[18] Not only was the statue of Marduk of Babylon sent off to Susa, but various Mesopotamian characteristics were copied, the most important being a ziqurrat very similar to the Mesopotamian one, which had at Tshoga-Zambil (12th century B.C.) a stairway against three of its sides, each ending at a gate house that gave access to the upper stages.[19]

The Persians must have been influenced by the culture, and in particular by the religion, of the Urartu people of whom they were the vassals. Graphical evidence of a Persian temple is found in an Assyrian low relief representing the town and temple of Musasir in northwestern Iran.[20] Cyrus showed a liberal attitude when he conquered Babylon, restoring temples and touching the hand of the god Bel to legalize his new line of Babylonian kings.[21] He also decreed that the Jews could return to Jerusalem and rebuild their temple.

[17] Ghirshman, *Iran*, p. 62.
[18] *Ibid.*, p. 66.
[19] H. Frankfort, *The Art and Architecture of the Ancient Orient* (Harmondsworth, 1954), p. 204.
[20] Ghirshman, *Iran*, p. 93, Fig. 35.
[21] *Ibid.*, p. 132.

The religion of these Achaemenids[22] was monotheistic Zoroastrian-ism, the ritual of which was performed in open-air shrines with fire altars, perhaps by the king himself, as represented on a low relief at Naqsh-i-Rustam. The god Ahuramazda was shown in official scenes as a bust within a winged sun-disk fluttering above the king. It is probably because of this open-air ritual that Herodotus specifies that the Persians had no temples.[23]

Some structures, however, can be identified as temples. It has been suggested that the terraced complex at Masjid-i-Suleiman, possibly an earlier Persian palace, contained such a fire temple fed by natural gas (8th century B.C.).[24] A similar complex nearby could have had a second temple (Bard-i-Nishandi). A later temple at Pasargadae north of the palace of Darius has been identified; this rectangular tower of dressed stone is set on a platform of three steps with a narrow stairway rising to a door high up in the façade, which opens into a single room (Fig. 31, lower right). Two stepped fire altars, each with its stairway, stand in the vicinity. This fire temple was copied by Darius in front of his tomb at Naqsh-i-Rustam.[25]

Near Susa a complex has been conjecturally identified as a temple. It consists of a long corridor opening into a forecourt at the rear of which a broad stairway rises to a porch with two columns and a columned room.[26]

Northwest of Persepolis there is a temple to Ahuramazda and other Iranian deities that are parallel to certain Greek ones. To the south a similar structure built by Darius features a columned portico leading to an open court in front of a hall flanked by three columned porticoes (east, north, and west) and rooms at the corners and the back of the shrine.[27]

Artaxerxes introduced the cult of Anahita, whose statues were worshiped at Susa, Persepolis, and Ecbatana.[28] Achaemenian religion passed into Cappadocia, where it initiated the cult of Mithra, pre-dominant in the Roman army.

Tombs

In an attempt to keep the ancestors in the home and let them partake of family life, the dead were buried under the floor of the

[22] Olmstead, *History*, pp. 195 ff.
[23] Herodotus, *Histories*, Bk. I, par. 131.
[24] Ghirshman, *Iran*, p. 123. H. H. von d. Osten and R. Naumann, *Takht-i-Suleiman, Vorläufiger Bericht über die Ausgrabungen* (Berlin, 1961).
[25] Ghirshman, *Iran*, p. 135, Fig. 53. Olmstead, *History*, pp. 64–65, 196.
[26] M. Dieulafoy, *L'Acropole de Suse* (Paris, 1893), pp. 390, 410 ff. Olmstead, *History*, p. 196.
[27] E. Herzfeld, *Iran in the Ancient East* (Oxford, 1941), p. 231. Olmstead, *History*, p. 196.
[28] Ghirshman, *Iran*, pp. 160, 204.

house ever since prehistoric times.[29] This remained the custom in settled communities (Siyalk III),[30] even into the third millennium B.C.,[31] when pottery and jewelry were placed with the dead, who were buried individually in a contracted position. An influence from the first Iranian tribes who reached the western part of the country about 1000 B.C. was the establishment of cemeteries at some distance from towns (Cemetery B at Siyalk).[32] The individual grave was topped by a mound covered with stone slabs or brickwork imitating a gabled house, a custom known in Nordic Europe. The tombs show a differentiation according to classes, some of the poorer graves having no roofing slabs.[33]

The rock-cut tomb of the Achaemenian rulers probably still represented a princely mansion, though the idea of cutting it into the cliff could have been derived from the rock-cut tombs of the Medes in western Zagros and in Kurdistan.[34] A Persian prototype of the royal tombs at Naqsh-i-Rustam could be the rock-cut tomb at Da-u-Dukhtar in Fars, which has a pseudopalatial façade featuring a pair of engaged columns on each side of the central doorway and an entablature and a cresting at the top.[35] An exception was the tomb of Cyrus at Pasargadae (Fig. 31, bottom right), a monumental imitation of a plain gabled house with a cyma cornice. Set on a high pyramidal platform on six steps in well-dressed masonry,[36] it resembled the traditional graves of the earliest Iranians.[37] Since the reign of Darius, however, the royal tombs had been cut in the vertical cliff at Naqsh-i-Rustam and at Persepolis. They are all of the same type, that of Darius (Fig. 31, top middle) having a cruciform façade (20 m. wide × 26 m. high) with a horizontal arm imitating in high relief a palace portico with two engaged columns topped by antithetical bull capitals on either side of a central doorway. An entablature with dentils runs along the whole width. Above it in the vertical branch of the cross are three registers of scenes in low relief representing Darius standing on his throne-couch, upheld by thirty delegates of the empire.[38] Four niches in the burial chamber contained three sarcophagi each.

---

[29] *Ibid.*, pp. 30–31, pl. 1c.
[30] *Ibid.*, p. 36.
[31] *Ibid.*, pp. 48, 58.
[32] *Ibid.*, pp. 71, 77–80.
[33] *Ibid.*, p. 84.
[34] *Ibid.*, Figs. 46–47.
[35] *Ibid.*, p. 124, Fig. 50.
[36] Olmstead, *History*, pp. 66–67, pl. X. W. G. A. Otto, ed., *Handbuch der Archäologie* (Munich, 1939), p. 736, pl. 180.
[37] Ghirshman, *Iran*, p. 133.
[38] Olmstead, *History*, pp. 228 ff., pl. XXX. Frankfort, *Art*, pl. 187. F. Sarre and E. Herzfeld, *Iranische Felsreliefs* (Berlin, 1910).

Fortifications

The earliest prehistoric settlements at Siyalk do not show any attempt at fortification; in fact, this seems to have been the case all through the various stages of urban evolution up to the period of brick houses and villages. Perhaps this was a result of the physiography of the land, which "favoured the development of small centres which were remote from one another, and were therefore saved from disputes likely to lead to war."[39] Even the stela of Naramsin does not represent any fortified settlement (23rd century B.C.). With the establishment of Babylonian governors in Iran, some fortification must have been introduced, at least in the plains of Elam within the area of Mesopotamian influence.

The Elamite town of Tshoga-Zambil (13th century B.C.) is surrounded by an oval enclosure abutting on the mountain along its northwest side.[40] With the gradual unification by the Iranians, a type of fortified settlement is introduced by their rulers. Siyalk (10th century B.C., Fig. 31, bottom left) is surrounded by an enclosure with towers, and the residence is also fortified as a citadel.[41] These fortified cities, as represented on Assyrian low-relief murals (Fig. 31, bottom middle), have double or triple enclosures staged at different levels on a mound with machicolated towers topped with crenelations, and they are surrounded by a moat or a diverted watercourse.[42] When the Assyrians take over in Iran, they endow the towns they rebuild (Giyan)[43] with fortified systems (citadels, palaces).

The Achaemenian kings surround the terraces of their palaces with double walls. At Susa, Darius I builds a strong citadel and encloses the whole city with a strong brick wall with towers and a moat filled from the Khabur River.[44] At Persepolis, he starts a complex of palaces and fortifies its terraces with a wall of dressed masonry capped with brickwork (north, 20 m. high). Along the eastern foot of the mountain are a brick wall, a moat, and a line of fortifications with towers and casemated barracks (20 m. sq.) in rubble core faced with brick.[45]

Construction and Style

In Persia architecture is the art that conforms most closely to the universalist doctrine claimed by the Achaemenian kings as expressed

[39] Ghirshman, *Iran*, p. 44.
[40] Egli, *Städtebau*, p. 70.
[41] Ghirshman, *Iran*, p. 77, Fig. 28.
[42] *Ibid.*, p. 84, Fig. 34.
[43] *Ibid.*, p. 94.
[44] *Ibid.*, p. 165. Olmstead, *History*, pp. 167 ff.
[45] Olmstead, *History*, pp. 173–174.

in their title "king of the world quarters, king of lands,"[46] translated into Egyptian as "great chief of every foreign land."[47] Like the
Hittites, another group of warlike mountain dwellers, the Persians
laid out their temples (Pasargadae) and palaces (Persepolis) at the
foot of a mountain, into which they cut their tombs (Naqsh-i-
Rustam) adorned with scenes in low relief. The trend of using isolated units (Pasargadae) has been regarded as a remnant of their
original nomadic life.[48] This does not, however, imply a lack of
planning (as it has been inferred by Frankfort and Lloyd),[49] for there
is a consistent northwest–southeast orientation (Pasargadae, Persepolis) and at Persepolis structures are grouped along slightly offset
axes in a layout preplanned as a whole, as is proved by its drainage
system.[50] Moreover, each building is subsidiary to a secondary axis
in relation to the rectangular or square unit that forms the nucleus
of its plan. While the nucleus of a typical Mesopotamian plan is a
square courtyard, that of a Persian plan is a square columned hall
(apadana) fronted or surrounded by porticoes on three sides. Symmetry governs the internal arrangement in each unit, even to the
niches balancing actual doorways (as in ʿAmarna villas). The external
effect, which assumes much more importance than elsewhere in the
Orient, is enhanced by a monumental approach with a stairway and
a gateway to a terraced system (open-air temples). This is actually an
architectural display of power paralleled by the propagandist texts in
which kings claimed to rule the world (compare rock-cut temples of
the Empire in Egypt). It is noteworthy that the main façade of the
columned apadana has only two doorways, one on either side of the
central axis.

The universalist trend in architecture resulted in an eclectic style
for which different materials were used and craftsmen from foreign
countries were commissioned. After enumerating various lands from
which materials were brought for his palace at Susa, Darius proceeds:
"The goldsmiths who wrought the gold were Medes and Egyptians.
Those who worked the inlays were Sardians and Egyptians. Those
who worked the baked brick [with figures] were Babylonians. The
men who adorned the wall were Medes and Egyptians."[51] Such an
eclecticism directed by the ruler contrasts with the one dictated by
commercial demand, as in the Levant (Phoenicia, Palestine, and
Cyprus). The universalist doctrine is again responsible for the choice
of stylistic elements representative of various arts: composite

[46] Ibid., p. 51.
[47] A. Gardiner, Egypt of the Pharaohs (Oxford, 1961), p. 366.
[48] Frankfort, Art, p. 216.
[49] Ibid., p. 218. S. Lloyd, The Art of the Ancient Near East (London, 1961), p. 277.
[50] Pope, "Persepolis as a Ritual City," p. 125.
[51] Olmstead, History, p. 168.

columns consisting of an Ionian shaft, a palmiform capital with drooping leaves and the Levantine double volute of Egyptian origin, the foreparts of two man-headed bulls or lions from Mesopotamian architecture used as imposts antithetically topping the capitals (as the Ḥathoric capitals in Egypt; Fig. 31, top right), and the cavetto and torus cornice from Egypt.

Methods of construction were equally varied. Trabeated architecture (columns and ceilings) using timber contrasts with the vaults of Mesopotamia. Stone construction and glazed colored modeled brickwork are reminiscent of Assyria, as to both technique and style.[52] Variegated stone, painted stucco applied to wooden shafts, and gilding are used for effect. One can define the method of construction as a carving technique rather than a structural one, for not only are the lintel and the upper part of both uprights cut from one block, but the steps and balustrade are also carved from monolithic blocks.[53]

Confident of his inherited ability for decorative metalwork (Luristan bronzes), the Achaemenian artist creates a wide scope for modeling and carving, intimately relating sculpture in low relief to architecture. Plant elements and figures in a monotonous iteration of clear expressive silhouettes carved in stone with a rounded modeling as if of metal[54] emphasize the outline of the façades and monumental stairways. As in the Egyptian and Babylonian scenes, the king is represented on a heroic scale, a characteristic that had been relinquished by the Assyrians. Persian scenes, however, are never of a historical narrative character, and statues in the round made of metal are only in small sizes.

Monumental layouts and their elements (doorways, windows at Persepolis) conform to harmonic design as in Egyptian architecture, even following the same canons of proportions. Refinement in the details (animal heads of imposts of columns slightly bent toward the spectator)[55] is introduced to relieve a monotonous repetition planned to impress with power.

Architectural symbolism in Persian monuments interprets the metaphysical world of forces as it had done before in the Orient. Some examples are the use of crenelation as the symbol of a sacred mountain, the entrance pavilion at Persepolis as the "Gate of All Nations," the apadana as a grove of sacred trees, the column base as an inverted lotus for life-giving power, and protome capitals for the vitality of the palm.[56]

52 Lloyd, *Art of the Ancient Near East*, p. 246, Figs. 205–206.
53 Frankfort, *Art*, p. 221.
54 Lloyd, *Art of the Ancient Near East*, pp. 244–246.
55 Olmstead, *History*, p. 286.
56 Pope, "Persepolis as a Ritual City," pp. 126 ff.

Cyprus

The Environment

The unique location of this island near Asia and at the turning point of the sea route between the Orient and the Aegean made Cyprus a stepping-stone to the civilizations of the Levant (Map 1, frontispiece). This accounts for its inclusion in the study of the architecture of the ancient Orient. Cyprus has two plains between two ranges of mountains running east–west, the northern range along the coast with a steep, forbidding side against Anatolia (Map 2). In the other direction, the open east and south coasts provide natural harbors that at an early date helped to establish easy connections with commercial and cultural centers located less than two hundred kilometers to the east at Ugarit and Byblos. An incentive to early trade relations was the richness of the island in copper, from which its name "Kypros" is derived.

Styles of Neolithic pottery imply racial affinities with western Asia Minor (red polished and partly incised) and the Levant (painted with linear or naturalistic ornament).[1] Toward the end of the Chalcolithic and Bronze Periods cultural relations with Phoenicia become even more prominent. Only after the decline of Minoan sea supremacy (14th century B.C.) does Cyprus import Mycenaean wares, mostly pottery (Enkomi), which are soon imitated locally. Colonization is achieved by proto-Doric groups and later by the Achaeans.

---

[1] E. Watzinger in W. G. A. Otto, ed., *Handbuch der Archäologie* (Munich, 1939), pp. 826 ff. *Encyclopédie photographique de l'art, photographies inédites par A. Vigneau*, Vol. II (Le Musée du Louvre, Paris, 1936), pp. 142 ff.

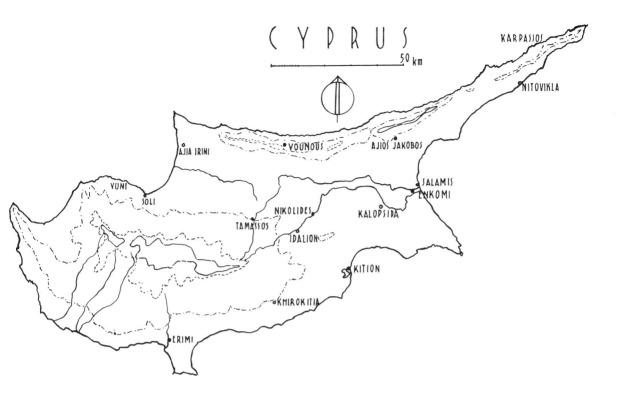

Map 2.   Cyprus and its archaeological sites

Trade relations are carried on with the Aegean areas, Syria, and Egypt. Late Mycenaean influences are asserted in the development of the dromos tomb (13th century B.C.) and in the domed tomb.

After the twelfth century B.C. relations cease with the west and decrease with the east. About this time a local style develops from the autochthonous art and the imitation of Mycenaean products (Cypriote Geometric, 10th century B.C.). Curiously enough, this trend is not influenced by the strong Phoenician infiltration from the south, spreading over more than half the island (8th century B.C.) with the founding of new towns (Kart-hadasht founded by Sidon).[2] A stela records the voyage of seven kings of Cyprus who went to present gifts to Sargon II at Babylon (713 B.C.).[3] As evidenced in the statuary and stelae (to the north and northwest in terra-cotta; to the south and east in limestone), both the Hittite and the Levantine cultural zones slowly absorb the Greek style during the sixth century B.C. Egyptianizing styles emerge sporadically, stimulated perhaps by a brief subjection of some of the towns to King Amasis of Egypt (570–526 B.C.).

[2] Watzinger in Otto, ed., *Handbuch*, p. 831. A. Aymard and J. Auboyer, *L'Orient et la Grèce Antique* (Paris, 1957), p. 236.
[3] H. Frankfort, *The Art and Architecture of the Ancient Orient* (Harmondsworth, 1954), p. 195.

"Phoenician periods" are actuated by political reactions, as during the Persian supremacy after the peace of Callias. Classical Greek trends are, however, very slow to flourish, though Attic style is encouraged locally by such rulers as Evagoras of Salamis (early 4th century B.C.). In the Hellenistic Period, Cyprus, now a Ptolemaic colony, follows the art of Alexandria.[4]

Towns

Though settlements are marked by houses, graves, and temples, very little information about the process of urban development can be derived from published material. In the largest town, Enkomi-Alasia, only partly excavated, three levels are revealed (1200–1050, 1550–1225, 1900–1600 B.C.).[5] The earliest layout in an Oriental style is different from that of the two later ones, with parts of an enclosure wall running east–west in stretches nearly parallel on the north and south borders of the city.[6] The south wall (13th century B.C.) is built with fill enclosed between two facings, the outer one of huge blocks without mortar, while the inner one is of rubble and clay. Square massive towers project (2–3 m.) at regular intervals (5–9 m.). In the western area of the town workshops and bronze foundries that produced the characteristic copper ingots in the second millennium B.C. are still extant. A street uncovered for more than two hundred meters runs east–west, straight from the entrance of the residence in the direction of the sea, parallel to a second one at thirty-three meters (Street of the Sanctuary).

Houses and Palaces

Cypriote houses are of a Mediterranean type built of stone. The Neolithic round (Fig. 32, top left)[7] and oval houses (Khirokitia), sometimes with central stone pillars (Erimi), are similar to those found elsewhere in the Near East (Tepe Gawra in Mesopotamia, Jericho in Palestine) or in Neolithic Italy (Lucera).

In the Chalcolithic Period houses contain rectangular rooms along one side of a courtyard (Alambra near Idalion; Fig. 32, top left)[8] or are set irregularly around three sides of a central vestibule (Kalopsida; Fig. 32, middle left).[9] The latter structure is a large rectangular

---

4 Watzinger in Otto, ed., *Handbuch*, p. 838.

5 C. Schaeffer, *Enkomi-Alasia* (Paris, 1952).

6 *Ibid.*, pp. 25 ff, 411 ff., pl. LXXX.

7 Watzinger in Otto, ed., *Handbuch*, p. 826. H. Bossert, *Alt-Syrien* (Tübingen, 1951), Figs. 1, 3.

8 Bossert, *Alt-Syrien*, Fig. 7.

9 *Ibid.*, Fig. 8. Watzinger in Otto, ed., *Handbuch*, p. 827.

Fig. 32→

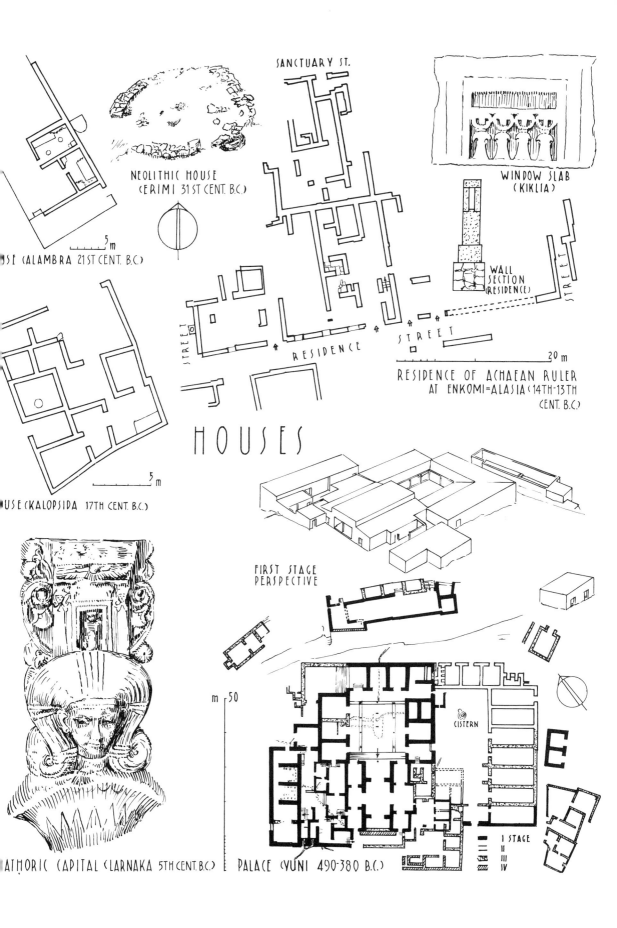

NEOLITHIC HOUSE
(ERIMI 31ST CENT. B.C.)

SANCTUARY ST.

WINDOW SLAB
(KIKLIA)

WALL
SECTION
(RESIDENCE)

STREET

STREET

RESIDENCE

5 m

...SE (ALAMBRA 21ST CENT. B.C.)

STREET

RESIDENCE OF ACHAEAN RULER
AT ENKOMI=ALASIA (14TH-13TH
CENT. B.C.)

20 m

5 m

...USE (KALOPSIDA 17TH CENT. B.C.)

HOUSES

FIRST STAGE
PERSPECTIVE

m 50

CISTERN

I STAGE
II
III
IV

...ATHORIC CAPITAL (LARNAKA 5TH CENT. B.C.)

PALACE (VUNI 490-380 B.C.)

mansion open to the north, consisting of living and work rooms (eleven). The so-called "House of the Bronzes" at Enkomi (Mycenaean, 7th century B.C.), like the houses uncovered in later excavations, has rubble walls at right angles forming rectangular rooms with numerous circular shafts, which are probably used for funerary purposes.[10] Contiguous houses have common partition walls with doorways indicated by monolithic sills. A large structure (Fig. 32, top right)[11] in huge dressed blocks, identified as the residence of a Mycenaean or Achaean ruler (14th–13th centuries B.C.), stretches over a whole block delimited by the main street (40 m. along Street of the Residence), two crossing secondary roads (north–south), and a parallel rear street (Street of the Sanctuary). On its façade (south) each of the four square windows and four doorways has a stone sill adjacent to an interior wooden sill. In its central area a rectangular compound of small rooms, one containing a well, are arranged along a corridor and a lateral staircase. A remarkable feature in the construction is the use of a course of double slabs, internal and external, of the orthostat type that are separated by a void (for insulation or as a device against the frequent earthquakes?; Fig. 32, upper right). Floors are of rammed white earth and show five levels of occupation (1350–1200 B.C.), brought to an end by a fire. Beneath the residence was the family shaft tomb, which yielded some extremely rich equipment (weapons, jewelry), mostly of Mycenaean origin, and tall skeletons whose crania had been artificially deformed into an elongated shape similar to that of Akhenaten's family in Egypt. The architectural style of this period is not the result of an autochthonous evolution but probably was borrowed from Mycenae.[12]

For the later period, when Cyprus became impervious to foreign influence, no evidence concerning houses is available. The palace at Vuni (Fig. 32, bottom right)[13] dates from the Persian Period (early fifth century B.C.) and was occupied for a century. The original entrance to the southwest in the Persian style was blocked and replaced by a northern one (450–440 B.C.). The central part of the original structure is strictly symmetrical (northeast–southwest), featuring an entrance suite with an anteroom (southwest), a rear columned portico flanked by a magazine, kitchen, lavatories, and a broad stairway leading down to a peristyle court surrounded on three sides by rooms. This Persian apartment was used as a magazine when the entrance was blocked. Its various elements show eclecticism:

[10] C. Schaeffer, *Missions en Chypre, 1932–1935* (Paris, 1936), p. 84, Fig. 46; *Enkomi-Alasia*, pls. XI, LXXXVI.
[11] Schaeffer, *Enkomi-Alasia*, pp. 239 ff, pls. LXXXVII–LXXXVIII, Fig. 90.
[12] *Ibid.*, pp. 336, 343.
[13] Watzinger in Otto, ed., *Handbuch*, pp. 841–844, Fig. 87. Bossert, *Alt-Syrien*, Figs. 31–33.

the entrance is reminiscent of the Hittite gateway with its double doorway, the porch with one column similar to the hilani from Asia Minor or Crete, the Egyptianized Ḥathoric capital (Fig. 32, bottom left) possibly imitated from those in the temple in Phoenician Kition, and the general layout in the Persian style, similar to the Persian residence at Lachish. At a later stage (Periods II–III) a row of deep rooms along a large court with a cistern were added to the east.

In contemporaneous tombs the burial chamber imitates the interior of a house, with rounded rafters forming a gabled roof, a door valve with a wooden lock, an upper window with an openwork panel of Phoenician ornament (Fig. 32, top right).[14]

Temples

Idols representing nude female deities occur in prehistoric settlements and tombs, but no structure from the Neolithic Period has been identified as a temple. A clay model from the Early Bronze Age (3000–2100 B.C.) represents a rounded sacred temenos[15] that contains a large sitting figure and a woman holding a child, probably the deities surrounded by priests and worshipers, and two bulls in their enclosures flanking the doorway. This chthonian (?) sanctuary is obviously hypaethral (Fig. 33, top left). Also hypaethral is the actual sanctuary at Ajios Jacovos (Late Bronze; Fig. 33, top right),[16] consisting of a polygonal stone floor (9–10 m.) with two circular altars (north edge) and a clay libation basin about which the offering vessels are set. In the Geometric Period (10th century B.C.) a sanctuary entered from the small side was built; later it was altered by the addition of a transverse partition (7th century B.C.).

A temple on the west citadel at Idalion, consisting of an anteroom and a sanctuary containing an altar, was rebuilt in the Geometric Period as a court with an altar and a cult niche dedicated to Athena.[17] At Ajia Irini (Fig. 33, middle left) a larger cult installation near the enclosure of the citadel features a court, a cella entered from the long side and containing an altar slab, a bench, hearth, and a lateral room, and separate structures (storerooms and dwellings). At the end of the Geometric Period (7th century B.C.) the earlier site was filled in with earth, and within an earth enclosure were arranged a stone offering slab and a sunken offering area, to which a stone altar was added later, surrounded by a stone enclosure and a gate. Among the peculiarities of this later shrine were two sacred trees enclosed within a low stone wall, an egg-shaped black stone, probably a cult

14 Watzinger in Otto, ed., *Handbuch*, pp. 846–947. Bossert, *Alt-Syrien*, Figs. 15, 20.
15 Watzinger in Otto, ed., *Handbuch*, pp. 827 ff. Bossert, *Alt-Syrien*, Figs. 97–99.
16 Watzinger in Otto, ed., *Handbuch*, pp. 829, 832. Bossert, *Alt-Syrien*, Figs. 11 ff.
17 Watzinger in Otto, ed., *Handbuch*, p. 832.

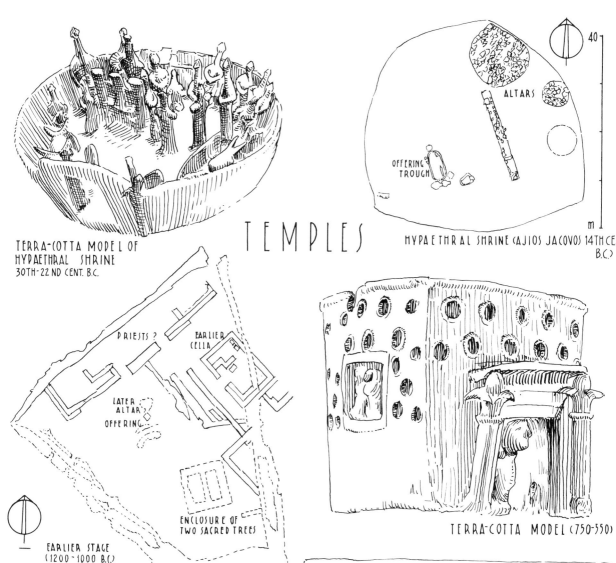

TERRA-COTTA MODEL OF
HYPAETHRAL SHRINE
30TH-22ND CENT. B.C.

TEMPLES

40

ALTARS

OFFERING
TROUGH

m

HYPAETHRAL SHRINE (AJIOS JACOVOS 14TH CE)
B.C.

PRIESTS ?

EARLIER
CELLA

LATER
ALTAR

OFFERING

ENCLOSURE OF
TWO SACRED TREES

EARLIER STAGE
(1200-1000 B.C.)
LATER (650 B.C.)
15 m

TEMENOS (AJIA IRINI)

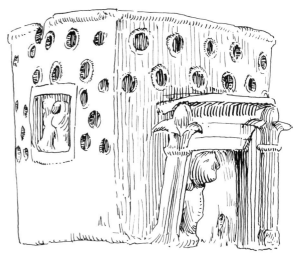

TERRA-COTTA MODEL (750-550)

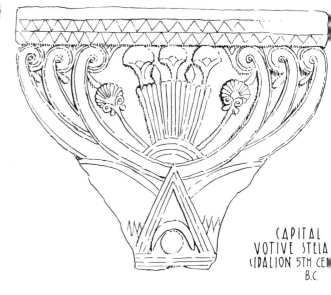

CAPITAL
VOTIVE STELA
(IDALION 5TH CE)
B.C.

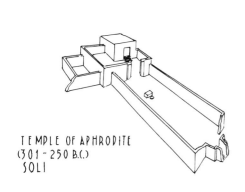

TEMPLE OF APHRODITE
(301-250 B.C.)
SOLI

object, and numerous vessels and figurines (2,000) deposited near the altar.

A votive terra-cotta from Idalion (Fig. 33, middle right; 750–550 B.C.)[18] represents a structure fronted on its long side by a porch on two palmette columns and having a niche or window on the small side and circular holes in offset rows in the upper part of the wall. Whether the original structure was a temple cannot be ascertained. In the temple of Astarte-Aphrodite at Idalion freestanding pillars topped with proto-Aeolian capitals (Fig. 33, bottom right), which developed from the Palestinian-Phoenician type (Megiddo, Beth Shan), were erected as votive stelae dedicated to the goddess (5th century B.C.)[19] (compare obelisks at Byblos, stelae at Assur). These stelae were in common use in the fifth century during the Phoenician supremacy, from Kition to Idalion. The temple near the palace at Vuni has a rectangular sanctuary with an inner podium surrounded by a court within a temenos, to which a second court was added. Similar layouts seem to have occurred at Idalion and Kythera. The temple of Athena at Vuni (end of 5th century B.C.) has two courts and a cella with a nave and narrower aisles separated by wooden partitions. The temple of Aphrodite-Oreia at Soli in its earlier stage (250 B.C.) is still a simple house on a podium within its precincts, fronted by a deep court (Fig. 33, bottom left).[20]

Tombs

In Neolithic times bodies were buried in individual graves adjacent to the houses.[21] In the Chalcolithic Period several underground chambers roughly cut at a shallow depth were accessible from a common dromos (Vounous, 30th–21st centuries B.C.; Fig. 34, top left)[22] or a short shaft blocked by a stone slab, a type similar to the contemporaneous one in Phoenicia. In the Middle Bronze Age the dromos became a regular feature and was cut into several steps. A larger number of bodies were buried in one room, and toward the Late Bronze Age mass burial was common, without a tumulus to mark the shaft or the dromos, except in the northeast of the island (Karpassos, 18th–17th centuries B.C.).[23]

Mycenaean influence is conspicuous in the development of a rough cupola to roof over the circular burial chamber (2–3 m. diameter) of

18 Bossert, *Alt-Syrien*, Fig. 16.
19 Watzinger in Otto, ed., *Handbuch*, pp. 843–844. Bossert, *Alt-Syrien*, Fig. 23.
20 Watzinger in Otto, ed., *Handbuch*, p. 844. Bossert, *Alt-Syrien*, Fig. 35. A. Westholm, *The Temples of Soli* (Stockholm, 1936).
21 Bossert, *Alt-Syrien*, Fig. 3.
22 *Ibid.*, Fig. 5. Watzinger in Otto, ed., *Handbuch*, p. 826. Schaeffer, *Enkomi-Alasia*, pp. 105 ff, Fig. 40.
23 Watzinger in Otto, ed., *Handbuch*, p. 827. Schaeffer, *Missions*, p. 59.

←Fig. 33

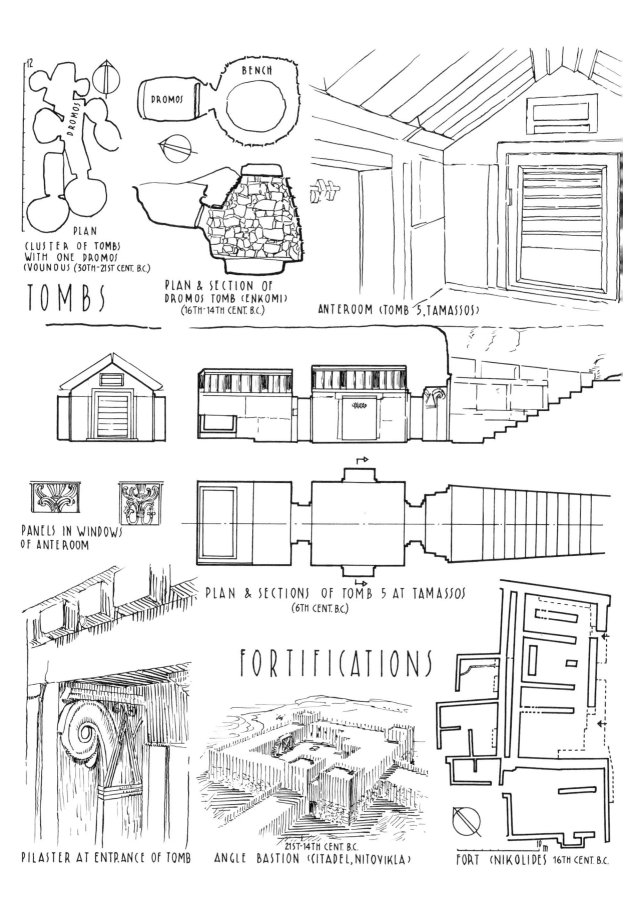

TOMBS

PLAN
CLUSTER OF TOMBS
WITH ONE DROMOS
(VOUNOUS (30TH-21ST CENT. B.C.)

BENCH
DROMOS
PLAN & SECTION OF
DROMOS TOMB (ENKOMI)
(16TH-14TH CENT. B.C.)

ANTEROOM (TOMB 5, TAMASSOS)

PANELS IN WINDOWS
OF ANTEROOM

PLAN & SECTIONS OF TOMB 5 AT TAMASSOS
(6TH CENT. B.C.)

FORTIFICATIONS

PILASTER AT ENTRANCE OF TOMB

ANGLE BASTION (CITADEL, NITOVIKLA)
21ST-14TH CENT. B.C.

FORT (NIKOLIDES 16TH CENT. B.C.
10 m

rubble sunken at a much lower level than its dromos, from which it is blocked by a stone slab (Enkomi, 1600 B.C.).[24] On a bench cut from the bedrock along the walls are placed the bodies (Fig. 34, top middle), and a square hole in the central free area contains the funerary equipment, mostly pottery (Enkomi-Alasia, No. 2). The simpler tombs without masonry, sometimes very small and paired on either side of a dromos, are still used for family burials (Enkomi-Alasia, No. 11; 1450–1350 B.C.).[25] It is noteworthy that a large proportion of the crania from graves at Enkomi (15th century B.C.–Iron I) had been artificially deformed into an oblong shape,[26] similar to that of Akhenaten and his family in contemporaneous Egypt (1370–1362 B.C.). This characteristic was also found in the skulls buried beneath the residence of the Achaean ruler at Enkomi (burial No. 18).[27] This tomb consists of a vertical shaft leading down to a squarish chamber with a bench on three sides and an ossuary in the northwest corner.

In the course of the thirteenth century B.C. there appears the Mycenaean type of dromos tomb roofed with a pointed vault formed by walls slanting toward the axis (Kurion, Lapithos).[28] The types of dromos tombs remain unchanged during the Geometric Period. Toward the beginning of the Archaic Period foreign influences lead to the arrangement of low niches on the sides of the burial chamber for bodies or sarcophagi, and also to the construction in dressed masonry of geometrically shaped rooms roofed with gables imitating the contemporaneous house.[29] Simple graves without any structure are still used, but they assume regular shapes. A well-built tomb at Trachonas (8th–7th century B.C.) has a dromos 6.5 meters long with fourteen steps leading down to a small doorway (1 m. high) that opens into the burial chamber (3.3 × 2.3 m.) and is roofed with a pointed corbel. Above the entrance are represented two male dancers performing in an obscene dance.[30] Similar tombs, either built of stone or carved underground, were discovered recently in the vast necropolis of the capital Salamis. Two horses were sacrificed and laid symmetrically on the sloping floor of the dromos in each tomb. The tombs were reopened for subsequent burials. The body was cremated, and its remains were placed in a two-handled painted vase. A large tumulus (60 m. diameter by 9 m. height) contains a

---

24 Watzinger in Otto, ed., *Handbuch*, p. 829. Bossert, *Alt-Syrien*, Fig. 6. Schaeffer, *Enkomi-Alasia*, pp. 115–116, Figs. 47–48, pl. XII.
25 Schaeffer, *Enkomi-Alasia*, pp. 135 ff., pl. XXVII.
26 *Ibid.*, p. 229, pl. XXXIV.
27 *Ibid.*, p. 319, Fig. 94.
28 Watzinger in Otto, ed., *Handbuch*, p. 829.
29 *Ibid.*, pp. 845–846.
30 Schaeffer, *Missions*, p. 65, pl. XXIX, Fig. 1.

←*Fig. 34*

similar dromos tomb, perhaps that of a king.[31] The walls and floor were sometimes plastered with concrete. At Tamassos (Fig. 34, top right)[32] two tombs of warriors provide adequate examples of the most elaborate type, which imitates a house (6th century B.C.). A stairway of trapezoid plan descends, fanning out to the entrance doorway, carved in low relief on either doorjamb with Aeolian pilasters. The door opens into a square antechamber that has on either lateral wall a false-door with an imitation of a wooden lock. A second axial doorway opens into the burial chamber, containing a huge sarcophagus. Above both doorways are windows with panels of Phoenician ornament. The roof is a gable made of slanting blocks carved on their underside to imitate wooden rafters.

In the Hellenistic period the loculus type of tomb was borrowed from Alexandria, as it was elsewhere in the Mediterranean basin.

Fortifications

The earliest fortified installation known is a citadel of refuge on a hill overlooking a bay at Nitovikla in Karpassos, consisting of an enclosure of cyclopean masonry on a rectangular plan (400 × 100–200 m.) with fortified bastions at the corners.[33] The one to the southeast is a massive square structure (40 m., 21st–14th centuries B.C.) accessible through a gateway with a winding entrance flanked by two towers. Beyond this is a central court surrounded by rooms (Fig. 34, bottom middle). This citadel has been compared to types in the Near East.

The fort at Nikolides (16th–14th centuries B.C.) is a rectangular structure accessible from its long eastern side (18 × 9 m.), with three rooms, two staircases, and a court (Fig. 34, bottom right).[34] It has been mentioned that Enkomi-Alasia was probably surrounded by a stone enclosure fortified, at least on its south side, by square towers erected at irregular intervals. The fortified settlement at Idalion (1200–1100 B.C.) was surrounded by a brick wall set on a stone foundation. It followed the contour lines of the hill and was accessible from two main gateways and a secondary one, which was often restored and remained in use till the end of the Geometric Period (7th century B.C.).[35]

[31] B. V. Karageorghis, "The Necropolis of Salamis: Recent Excavation of the Ancient Capital of Cyprus," Part I, *The Illustrated London News*, Aug. 29, 1964, pp. 294–296; Sept. 5, 1964, pp. 332–334.

[32] Watzinger in Otto, ed., *Handbuch*, pp. 845–847, Fig. 88. Bossert, *Alt-Syrien*, Figs. 19–22.

[33] Schaeffer, *Missions*, p. 62. Watzinger in Otto, ed., *Handbuch*, p. 829. Bossert, *Alt-Syrien*, Fig. 10.

[34] Watzinger in Otto, ed., *Handbuch*, p. 829, Fig. 12.

[35] *Ibid.*, pp. 831–832.

Construction and Style

Among the arts of Cyprus, architecture is the one that benefited least from the variety of styles and elements introduced into that island through trade or invasion. It is difficult to recognize eclecticism in the process of borrowing from the two outstanding foreign sources, Phoenicia to the east and Crete-Mycenae to the west.

Stone is the most common of materials, though occasionally brick on a stone foundation is also used. Cyclopean stonework, rubble, and well-dressed masonry with dry joints occur according to periods and influences. As in other countries of the East, the circular plan precedes the invention of brick, but it is still found in the third millennium B.C., long after the orthogonal house plan was known in Asia Minor and Palestine. In the Middle Bronze Age (2100–1600 B.C.) new elements are acquired from trade contacts with Phoenicia and North Syria, such as dromos tombs, rectangular rooms surrounding a court, and megaron units. During the Late Bronze Age (1600–1000 B.C.) the island enters, through trade relations, into the orbit of the eastern and southern Mediterranean.[36] With the Achaean invasion (14th century B.C.)[37] the style is affected by Mycenaean influences. In the capital, Enkomi-Alasia, a residence exhibits a monumental style with ashlar stone masonry, square windows, and double orthostat courses. Tombs are built to imitate the dromos and vaults of Mycenaean ones, hypaethral shrines are laid out (Ajios Jacovos), citadels (Nitovikla) and enclosure walls (Enkomi) are fortified with square towers. Toward the end of the thirteenth century B.C. the residence at Enkomi is occupied for a short period by other Achaeans from Rhodes or the Dodecanese islands, ending with the destructive invasion by the "people of the sea" (Philistines, 1200–1150 B.C.). Although autochthonous products imitate former Mycenaean imports, relations are still maintained with Phoenicia. The residence at Enkomi is transformed into a settlement of bronze smelters, where the levels of streets and houses rise as a result of torrential rains and earthquakes (1150–1100 B.C.). This leads to the construction of temples on hills (Idalion, Ajia Irini).

The Geometric Period (1000–650 B.C.) marks the isolation of the island, which is unaffected by the Phoenician colonization of the southern coast or the Assyrian rule (8th century B.C.).[38] In the following centuries two zones of influence can be differentiated: to the north and northwest from Asia Minor and North Syria, and to the south and east from Phoenicia and Egypt. At Vuni (north) the palace is definitely on a Persian plan, though the Ḥathoric columns point to

---

[36] *Ibid.*, p. 828.
[37] Schaeffer, *Enkomi-Alasia*, pp. 350 ff.
[38] Watzinger in Otto, ed., *Handbuch*, p. 831.

a southern influence from Kition, and its temple with nave and aisles are from Asia Minor. On the other hand, the tombs at Tamassos (central valley) are clearly borrowed from Phoenicia or Egypt (rectangular room, windows with ornament, proto-Aeolian capitals, dentils, false-doors, sarcophagi), the Ḥathoric capitals from Kition and elsewhere (south coast, 6th century B.C.), and proto-Aeolian stelae from Idalion. To this latter sphere of influence could be ascribed the type of sanctuary set on a podium (Idalion, Kythera in the central valley; later also north at Soli, 3rd century B.C.).

PART III

ARCHITECTURE IN
THE ANCIENT WORLD

The Ancient Orient and
the Aegean

Because of its geographical location the Levant became a link between the ancient Near East and the countries of the Aegean, especially so since the sea routes followed the coastline from the numerous Aegean islands to the south coast of Asia Minor, Cyprus, and the Levant.[1] It was the only connection between the north and Egypt and Mesopotamia, skirting the forbidding stretches of the Syrian desert. Ugarit was the head of this bridge to the Mesopotamian hinterland on the east and to the Aegean on the west, and trade relations occur there as early as the fourth millennium B.C.[2] Farther south along the Levantine coast Byblos was in close relations, commercially and politically, with Egypt during the Old Kingdom and under its influence even built temples in the Egyptian style. Gifts from Pharaoh Saḥureᶜ (Dynasty V) have recently been found in northwest Anatolia.

Curiously enough, the sites that exemplify the earliest architectural achievement are neither in Mesopotamia nor in Egypt but at Jericho in Palestine, where a stone enclosure with a tower dates back to the seventh millennium B.C., and at Haçilar in Anatolia, where an urban settlement with quadrangular houses in plano-convex plastered brick dates back to the sixth millennium B.C. The fact that these premises of urban civilization did not lead to more spectacular developments while the two cultural poles in the ancient Orient developed two architectural styles, related to each other in their earliest phases but soon diverging at the beginning of the third

[1] C. Schaeffer, *Ugaritica*, Vol. I (Paris, 1939), p. 10.
[2] *Ibid.*, p. 11.

millennium B.C., can only be explained by the unfavorable environment in Asia Minor and the Levant.

More than other arts, architecture requires stability and peace, two factors secured only within a settled community undisturbed by natural or political upheavals. The importance of natural factors in the evolution of ancient cultures has only recently been appraised through the study of comparative stratigraphy. At various points in the eastern Mediterranean a hiatus in the sequence of history is evidenced at the same date, a fact that can result only from the sweeping action of some natural perturbation. At least three earthquakes ravage the eastern Mediterranean with fires and destruction about 2300 B.C., 2100–2000 B.C., and again in 1365 B.C., while a hiatus occurs about 1600 B.C. in all countries.[3] Besides the violent destruction an earthquake has secondary disastrous effects, such as climatic disturbances and epidemics. These, however, can occur independently in the drying up of a district through a climatic cycle (Sahara) or deforestation (Negev, Lebanon, Anatolia). Epidemics can be imported by groups of foreigners, such as the pest introduced into Anatolia by the Gasga prisoners in the reign of Mursilis,[4] or propagated by natural factors, such as malaria in the swamps of Etruria.

The ultimate effect of these natural calamities is occasionally the migration of population but consistently retardation in architectural development. While the eastern Mediterranean is plagued with recurring earthquakes, the alluvial plains of Mesopotamia and Egypt are practically free from them. This fact together with the constant water supply from the rivers would account to a large extent for the continuous evolution of an original architecture in both countries, contrasting with the reduced process of stylistic eclecticism in the Levant (Syria, Palestine, Cyprus).

These natural factors are paralleled by cultural ones, among which the religious discipline predominant in Egypt, to a lesser degree in Mesopotamia, and still less in Asia Minor and the Levant is the main incentive in the formation of a more or less rigid tradition in architectural style and technique.

Eclecticism in architecture, though basically a result of a natural environment unfavorable to original creation, is enhanced by human factors, mainly political and trade relations. Migration of people, such as the invasion of the eastern Mediterranean by the "people of the sea" about 1200 B.C. stopped by Ramses III, could be caused by natural calamities, famine, or political pushes.

---

[3] C. Schaeffer, *Stratigraphie comparée et chronologie de l'Asie Occidentale* (London, 1948), pp. 2 ff., Table IX.
[4] E. Cavaignac, *Subbililiuma et son temps* (Paris, 1932), p. 72.

There is a basic difference between the two approaches to eclecticism, one stimulated by political factors and the other resulting from trade relations. A political upheaval leading to the establishment of a centralized authority can at the same time create an eclectic movement directed by this authority. In a newborn state with a deficient autochthonous culture, such as Persia and later the Islamic Caliphates, it is the privilege of an enlightened ruler to adapt to his artistic policy the cultural legacy, local resources, and craftsmen recruited from among the countries he conquers. The result was a brilliant though hybrid Persian architecture embodying Egyptian, Mesopotamian, and Greek elements. It also happens that petty rulers are attracted into the sphere of influence of a powerful civilization so as to become virtually its vassals. In the early third millennium B.C., Byblos becomes subservient to the pharaohs of the Old Kingdom, and later Palestine and Syria are also controlled by the ambassadors of the pharaohs of the New Kingdom. As a result of political subservience, eclecticism in monumental architecture is achieved mainly through imitation and borrowing. Temples and tombs in Byblos are obvious attempts at copying the tripartite plan and the elements of Egyptian prototypes (colossi fronting the façade). At Ugarit (Middle Ugarit, 1900–1750 B.C.), which was an ally or vassal of the Twelfth Egyptian Dynasty, offerings of statues by Khnumit Neferhuy and of sphinxes by Amenemhat II were presented to the Temple of Ba‘al.

The second type of eclecticism, resulting from trade relations, can flourish concurrently with the first one, as at Byblos and Ugarit. It is a nonconformist process characterized by a wider freedom in the choice and adaptation of alien elements. The main factor responsible for a strong influence from Egypt and Libya at the dawn of history in the Aegean as well as for its relations with the Cyclades is the location of Crete as a stepping-stone between the two areas. Seals and statuettes of Middle Minoan II imitating Egyptian ones evidence a foreign stimulus, especially in the techniques (invention of faïence, color conventions of brown for the male figure and white for the female).[5] Trade of the Levant with Middle Minoan Crete as well as with Egypt flourished, probably enhanced by Minoan migration along the coast of North Syria (Tell Atchana) in the eighteenth century B.C.[6] One of the immediate results in architecture is the appearance of the dromos type of tomb in Ugarit, with a rather short dromos and corbel vault derived from the Minoan one,[7] and its

[5] R. Dussaud, *Les civilisations préhelléniques dans le bassin de la Mer Égée* (Paris, 1914).

[6] Schaeffer, *Ugaritica*, Vol. I, pp. 25, 99.

[7] *Ibid.*, pp. 68, 76.

later evolution (14th–13th centuries B.C.), with the addition of autoch-thonous inventions (windows, rectangular plan and central arched doorway, T-shaped voussoirs, niches).[8] The use of wood as reinforce-ment within masonry and the erection of a central row of pillars in a hall could be ascribed either to Mitannian or to Minoan-Mycenaean influences. By that time Mycenae had established colonies in Ugarit and Cyprus.[9]

In Egypt the evidence from Middle Minoan pottery found at El Lahun, Abydos, Haraga, and Tell el Yahudiya (Dynasty XIII–Hyksos dynasties)[10] and from its coarser local copies allows for the presumption that Syrian or Cretan artisans were established in the royal building plants as they were at Ugarit. Curiously enough, the Hyksos rule did not curtail Egyptian trade with Crete or Mesopo-tamia.[11] Mycenaean infiltration into Ugarit seems to have increased with the decline of its political subservience to the Amenhotep pharaohs of the Eighteenth Dynasty,[12] but ultimately ended when it was allied with the Hittite Mutawalli (14th century B.C.). Egyptian murals painted in Theban tombs represent contemporaneous people from the Aegean and Syria bringing in choice specimens of pottery and metal crafts (tombs of Senmut, Rekhmireᶜ). Cretan goldsmiths seem to have been established in Memphis, which would account for the Aegean features of contemporary jewelry in Egypt.[13] It is mainly in mural paintings from the New Kingdom but also in its crafts (introduction of griffin, two antithetic goats flanking a tree of life, man-headed rams, or Lamassu, a unique statuette of Amenhotep III with crossed hands) that Minoan and Syrian influences in Egyptian art are apparent.[14] Some influence in the feminine idealistic sculpture of Ḥatshepsut has also been attributed to the Minoan world.[15] Reciprocally, characteristic Egyptian elements (scroll, monkey, predatory cat in papyrus thicket) are found in Cretan frescoes or in sculpture (sphinx). As to architecture, the inverted tapering shaft used at Knossos and later in Mycenae is reminiscent of those in the Festival Hall of Tuthmosis III at Karnak and of their prototype, the wooden tent pole of Protodynastic times. Influences from North Syria on Crete have also been presumed.[16] But few Minoan motifs can be considered as parallel to Egyptian ones, and though Minoan

[8] *Ibid.*, p. 92.

[9] *Ibid.*, p. 100.

[10] *Ibid.*, pp. 66 ff., 68–69. W. Helck, *Die Beziehungen Ägyptens zu Vorderasien im 3. und 2. Jahrtausend v. Chr.* (Wiesbaden, 1962), pp. 73–75.

[11] W. S. Smith, *The Art and Architecture of Ancient Egypt* (Baltimore, 1958), p. 124.

[12] Schaeffer, *Ugaritica*, p. 104.

[13] S. Lloyd, *The Art of the Ancient Near East* (London, 1961), pp. 164–165.

[14] Smith, *The Art*, pp. 140–141, 146. Helck, *Beziehungen*, pp. 542–543.

[15] Lloyd, *Art of the Ancient Near East*, pp. 165–166, Fig. 127.

[16] Schaeffer, *Stratigraphie*, p. 105.

art might have borrowed technical processes, it evolved its own interpretation of nature.[17]

Cypriote pottery found in Egypt at El Lahun, Abydos, and
Deshasha (Dynasty XVI or XVIII?) testifies to trade relations,
perhaps through Syria. Here alien influences in architecture pile
up in various styles and periods: Mycenaean and Achaean (palace,
dromos tomb), Egyptian (Ḥathoric capital), Palestinian-Phoenician
(proto-Aeolian capital, votive stelae, tombs), and Persian (palace).
Eclecticism is arbitrary and akin to that affected by Phoenician
architecture.

Though Hellenic architecture derives basically from the Minoan-
Mycenaean legacy, its indebtedness to direct borrowings from the
Orient cannot be denied. The Greeks of Ionia and the islands imitated
the Phoenicians in art as well as in piracy, and they borrowed the
Phoenician alphabet.[18] Sculpture from the Geometric Period is
undoubtedly closer to Oriental styles than to the Minoan one. This
debt is recognized by the Greeks themselves, who boast about the
Egyptian and Mesopotamian origins of their culture. Greeks had
actually traveled through the Orient as traders and scholars seeking
instruction in Egyptian temples or had even settled there as craftsmen
or mercenaries (Egypt, Babylonia) from the seventh century B.C.
There were also Greek ports in the Levant and in Egypt (Naukratis,
Daphnae). Greek craftsmen worked for the Phoenicians and the
Persians (Darius). There is scarcely a doubt that many of the most
enlightened among those early Greeks, curious by nature, had been
impressed by the aesthetic value and the symbolic significance of the
monuments on the Nile and the Euphrates-Tigris. It is safe enough to
presume that the creation of some of the most characteristic elements
in Greek architecture had been concomitant with Oriental ones. I
shall mention only the cavetto cornice, dentils, Doric column, Ionic
and Corinthian capitals, peripteral temple, stoa, lion gargoyle or
spout from Egypt, and the peristyle court and tholos from Mesopotamia. In the general discipline, both orthogonal and axial systems of
urban developments may have been derived from Egypt, as well as
the symmetrical plan in monumental architecture. While a few of
these elements obviously bear the imprint of Phoenicia as an intermediate stage, most of those originating from Troy were transmitted
through Minoan-Mycenaean architecture.

Such an impressive list of possible borrowings does not derogate
the achievement of Greek architecture, which adapted them to its
proper genius and taste. This process is, indeed, much more creative
than eclectic, comparable to, though not as original as, the evolution

[17] Dussaud, *Civilisations*, p. 63.
[18] W. F. Albright, *From the Stone Age to Christianity* (New York, 1957), p. 335.

of architecture in early Egypt and Mesopotamia. Directed eclecticism at its best is exemplified in Persian architecture or, with lesser aesthetic value, in Phoenician monuments. Arbitrary eclecticism, which occasionally verges on mere copying, produces still less aesthetic satisfaction in the achievements of the architectural styles of the Levant (North Syria, Phoenicia, Palestine) and Cyprus.

A Chronological Synopsis

Before the Third Millennium B.C.

In the dim dawn of urban organization two sparks cast quite unexpectedly an instant glow on two spots far away from the later cradles of civilization; one was at Haçilar in southern Anatolia (seventh millennium B.C.) and the other, on much more primitive lines, at Jericho. Much later thousands of villages, often surrounded by an enclosure, flourished in northern Mesopotamia between the seventh and the fifth millennia B.C., but these prehistoric settlements did not yet develop any of the urban characteristics found earlier at Haçilar, which had rectangular houses of brick on stone foundations, with painted walls and floors, built-in elements, bins, hearths, and ovens, arranged in an urban layout. It is perhaps significant that plano-convex brick had already been invented in the seventh millennium at Jericho and appears in the later strata at Haçilar (sixth millennium), prior to its regular use much later in Mesopotamia (third millennium B.C.). If the early date of Haçilar is exact, this culture is an isolated phenomenon. We can more easily explain the appearance of the earliest houses on a round plan at Jericho, Orchomenos (Aegean, sixth millennium B.C.), and at Merimde (Egypt, fifth millennium B.C.), of stone (Jericho), mud blocks (Merimde), or even brick (Orchomenos), as the result of an intuitive structural sense akin to that in animal life, a factor that also accounts for early town walls having an oval outline.

The rectangular layout of houses and eventually of town walls is an outcome of the use of tree trunks and wooden rafters as horizontal members of a framework in a house and subsequently also the invention of rectangular brick adapted to the building of straight walls jointed at right angles. The obvious advantages of the rectangular unit in the design and construction of multiple-room structures, or by

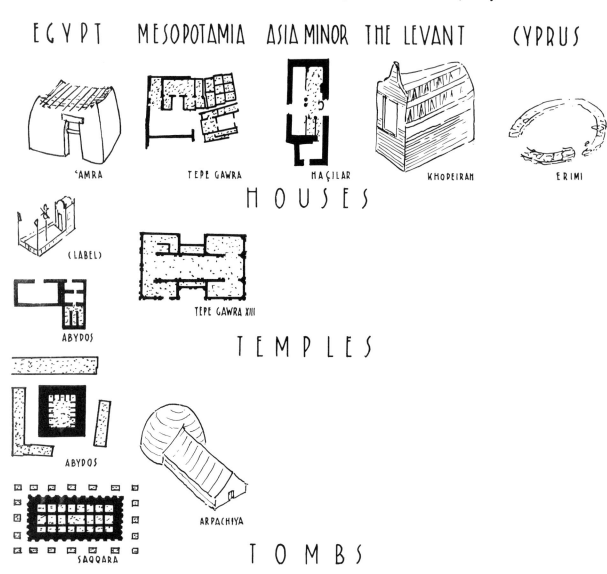

Fig. 35. *Typical structures before the third millennium* B.C.

extension an urban settlement, account for its adoption throughout the ancient world in the fourth millennium B.C. (Maʿadi, El ʿAmra in Egypt; Hassuna IV and Tepe Gawra in Mesopotamia; Mersin and Troy in Anatolia; Ghassul and Khodeirah in the Levant). The rounded shape of the village wall does not affect the orthogonal system of streets, as shown in protodynastic hieroglyphs for "city" in Egypt. The same type of small fortified city on an orthogonal layout surrounded by a square enclosure with buttresses and rounded corners was also represented on protodynastic palettes.

The theory of Frankfort,[1] propounded by some of his pupils,[2] according to which Mesopotamian influences would have found their way into predynastic Egypt either through infiltration[3] or invasion[4] and shaped its earliest culture, has now proved to be grossly exaggerated. The few motifs that are characteristic of early Sumer and occur sporadically in early Egypt, such as the antithetical composition featuring two lions flanking a vertical figure or tree, or the hybrid long-necked animals, could have been introduced through trade relations. Moreover, they were short-lived and did not persist in historic times. As to architecture, the only common stylistic feature, namely the recessed paneling in brick walls, may have originated independently in each country; it never assumes in Mesopotamia the elaboration and emblematic value that it is given in Egypt though it is kept traditionally during later periods[5] and is copied on stelae and sarcophagi. In Egypt it derives from the repetition of the theme of the palace façade, symbolizing the power of Pharaoh, whose Horus-name appears framed within the *serekh*, a schematic representation of the plan and façade of the royal palace. In Sumerian architecture recessed paneling appears only on the doorway of palaces and along the walls or terraces of temples.[6]

Contacts were established between Egypt and Libya to the west and perhaps also with western Asia. Egypt also had trade relations with Sumer through the Wadi Tumilat, but this does not necessarily imply that Sumerians actually reached Egypt in numbers,[7] since wares could have been exchanged from hand to hand along the extensive voyage.

Toward the end of the fourth millennium B.C. Egyptian shrines are built of light materials, such as the vaulted hut to house a god, fronted by a deep enclosed courtyard in which the sacred emblem and two flagstaffs are erected (temple as represented on protodynastic labels). There is even a brick temple that shows the typical

---

[1] H. Frankfort, *Studies in Early Pottery in the Near East* (London, 1924–1927); *The Birth of Civilization in the Near East* (London, 1951).

[2] H. Kantor, "Further Evidence of Early Mesopotamian Relations with Egypt," *Journal of Near Eastern Studies*, Vol. XI (Chicago, 1952), pp. 239 ff.

[3] J. Vandier, *Manuel d'archéologie égyptienne*, Vol. I (Paris, 1952), p. 607.

[4] E. Massoulard, *Préhistoire et Protohistoire d'Égypte* (Paris, 1949), p. 511.

[5] H. Ricke, *Bemerkungen zur ägyptischen Baukunst des Alten Reichs*, I (Zurich, 1944), p. 46, n. 121.

[6] W. Helck, *Die Beziehungen ägyptens zu Vorderasien im 3. und 2. Jahrtausend v. Chr.* (Wiesbaden, 1962), pp. 6–19.

[7] W. Kaiser, *Archaeologia Geographica*, Vol. 6, pp. 69 ff. Helck, *Beziehungen*, pp. 6, 10.

tripartite plan maintained traditionally till the end of Egyptian history in both domestic and religious architecture (temple at Abydos, Dynasty I). In Mesopotamia temples are set on platforms and contain a longitudinal hall, perhaps hypaethral, with four corner rooms (Tell Aqrab). Even at the dawn of history the relative importance of tombs in Egypt is asserted, with well-built underground burial chambers surrounded by storerooms and graves of retainers (Abydos, Saqqara) and surmounted by a superstructure imitating the recessed paneled façade of the royal palace (mastaba tomb). Mesopotamian graves are of no architectural consequence, though occasionally they feature an original compound of a domed chamber with a gabled approach (Arpachiya).

At this early stage the Aegean has not yet entered the picture, and no echo of the momentous architectural achievements in the ancient Orient reverberates from Crete. It is only in the thirtieth century B.C. that influences from the northwest coast of the Delta and from Libya, perhaps even migrations, reach Crete. These influences are responsible for the earliest Minoan architecture, about which only a little can be learned from the shapeless ruins of palaces destroyed by earthquakes and built over.

From Koptos in Upper Egypt caravans reached the coast of the Red Sea through Wadi Hammamat and then the Persian Gulf (toward the 32nd century B.C.). Whether the occurrence of planoconvex brick at Haçilar and Jericho at least two millennia prior to its appearance in Mesopotamia can still be used as a potential clue for the existence of relations between these countries is certainly quite problematic.

Third Millennium B.C.

At the turn of the fourth millennium, architecture evolves in the various countries certain forms, techniques, and styles that can be recognized as the prototypes of the later corresponding elements. As the most essential and concrete expression of culture it enters a phase during which a clear-cut autochthonous typology emerges as a result of both natural and human environments. Materials and methods of construction have passed the test of centuries and are now standardized: sun-dried brick set in clay mortar allied to stone elements in Egypt; sun-dried or baked brick in bitumen in Mesopotamia; sun-dried brick, stone, and wood in Anatolia; stone in the Levant and Cyprus. Some basic features are dictated by geographical conditions, and in both alluvial plains urban settlements grow along the rivers, south and north in the Nile Valley and south on the Euphrates, choosing the highest points above the flood levels. Towns in Egypt are presumably laid out on an orthogonal system within a round enclosure wall, while those in Mesopotamia have oval enclosures parallel to the northwest–southeast course of the river (Ur). In both countries the early invention of irrigation accounts for a sense of order. In Egypt it is coupled with regularity as a result of the regularity of the inundation, which is reflected in the orthogonal town planning and the consistent orientation (north–south) toward

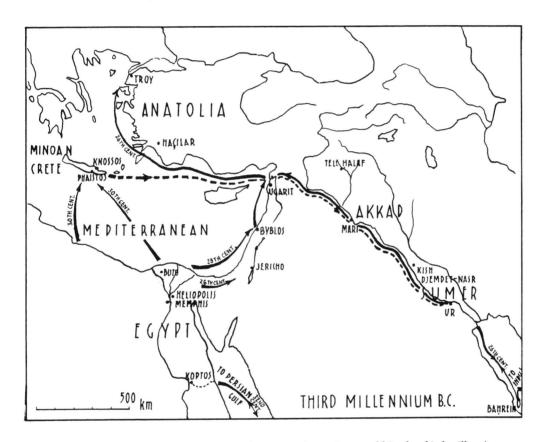

Map 3.   *Cultural relations in the ancient world in the third millennium* B.C.

the prevailing cooler breeze from the north. In the Levant towns aggregate on the top of mounds, and their layouts follow the contour lines in irregular rings within an enclosure wall (Tell Beit Mirsim). The hot climate in both alluvial plains encourages outdoor living, and the plan of the house features a courtyard fronting the north façade of the structure in Egypt (Giza) and a central court protected from sandy winds in Mesopotamia (Tell Asmar). In Cyprus structures are set irregularly in a yard (Alambra). Where the climate is rainy and cold, the courtyard is dispensed with, and the house is a compact

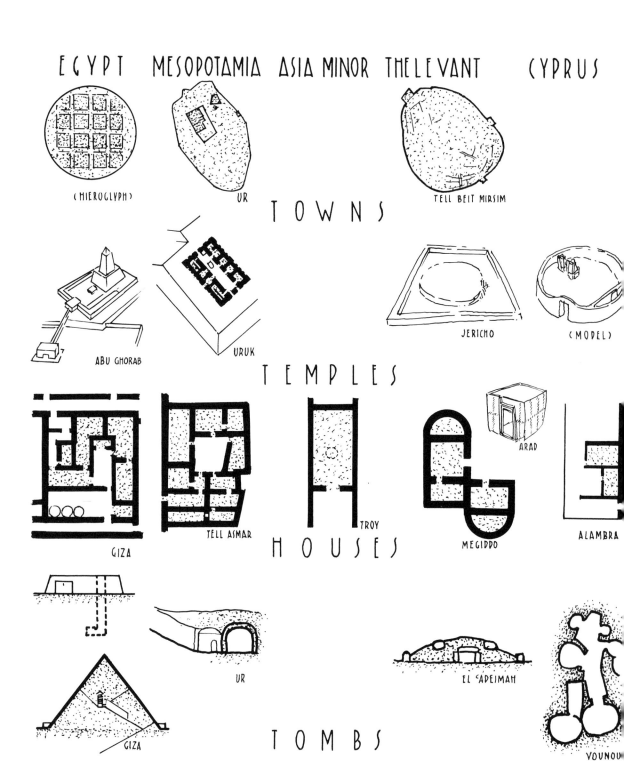

EGYPT   MESOPOTAMIA   ASIA MINOR   THE LEVANT   CYPRUS

(HIEROGLYPH)   UR   TELL BEIT MIRSIM

TOWNS

ABU GHORAB   URUK   JERICHO   (MODEL)

TEMPLES

ARAD

GIZA   TELL ASMAR   TROY   MEGIDDO   ALAMBRA

HOUSES

UR   EL ʿADEIMAH

GIZA

TOMBS   VOUNOU

Fig. 36.   *Typical structures in the third millennium* B.C.

structure protected against the weather by thick stone walls ("mega-ron" in Anatolia, apsidal house in the Levant, and rectangular flat-roofed house at Megiddo).

Cultural development is favorably nurtured in the hothouse of the alluvial plain, and architecture develops to meet the growing re-quirements of social, religious, and funerary ideologies. Here again, Egypt leads in architectural achievement, as to both quantity and refinement, which is further marked by a sense of tradition, perhaps resulting from an innate appreciation of set order and perennial regularity in the natural environment. In early Sumer the ruler lives in the temple precincts, while in Egypt Pharaoh has an elaborate palace built within a fortified rectangular enclosure. Since Pharaoh is of divine descent, everything pertaining to him is divine, and the recessed entrance façade of his palace, or *serekh*, is chosen as an emblematic motif that is repeated on the outside of the enclosures of mortuary temples and tombs, on mastaba tomb superstructures, and perhaps also on city walls. When the Sumerian rulers no longer act as high priests and they leave the temple to reside in a palace, both life and the layout of cities continue to gravitate about their original pole, which is the temple upon its platform (Uruk). It is the abode of the god, who is protector and provider of the community, so that magazines, workshops, and stores are set within the sacred pre-cincts. The Egyptian temple is the "castle of god" and has a tri-partite plan derived from the typical house plan. Adequate scale, symmetry, symbolism, and rich "materials of eternity" contribute to a solemn dignity appropriate to the castle of god. A special temple to the sun-god, with an open courtyard, an altar, and an obelisk, is built in the western desert (Abu Ghorab). A similar open-air cult is performed in the unpretentious nature shrines, featuring an altar within an enclosure in the Levant (Jericho) and Cyprus (as shown by a model of shrine). The concept of an afterlife varies widely in the ancient Near East. While tombs are cut underground in Cyprus (Vounous), a grave at ground level covered by a tumulus suffices in the Levant (El ʿAdeimah). The rulers of Ur I are accompanied in their underground vaults by a number of their retinue along with rich possessions, but there is no evidence of the performance of a regular funerary cult as in Egypt. Here the refined religious concept of a stellar destiny, soon evolving into that of a solar destiny, is the incentive to the creation of mastaba tombs (Giza, Saqqara, Dahshur) and pyramids with chapels and mortuary temples used for a regular funerary cult. Since adequate accommodation of the priests is re-quired, preplanned pyramid towns grow in the vicinity of the necropolises. This interrelated achievement in funerary and domestic architecture in Egypt, contrasted with the relatively unimportant funerary architecture in Mesopotamia, illustrates the creative potentiality of the dynamic Egyptian concept, with its regular funerary cult planned and endowed "for eternity," as compared to a static one. The art of fortification complies with the geophysical environment, resulting in rectangular double enclosures with winding entrances in Egypt (Hierakonpolis, Abydos) and irregular enclosures, some with casemates, adapted to the contour lines of the hills in North Syria and Anatolia.

With the emergence of Egypt and Mesopotamia as the two cultural centers in the ancient world, contacts with neighboring countries develop, mainly to provide Egypt with raw materials from Lebanon (coniferous wood, cedar, and oil from Byblos),[8] from Sumer (lapis lazuli), and from Cyprus (copper?). The trade that flourishes in the Uruk Period between Egypt and Mesopotamia over Aleppo wanes later.[9] The recent discovery of a throne of Sahure^c in Anatolia should be a warning to those who would discount the influence of Egyptian exports. As expected, the eventual impact of trade relations on architecture shows clear stylistic influence on the lesser countries, mainly Egyptian trends at Byblos. Smaller sculptures and jewelry (numerous Egyptian items in Syria) or pottery (Syrian, Cypriote, and Cretan wares at El Lahun and elsewhere in Egypt during the Middle Kingdom) have but little influence, and the alleged Aegean origin[10] of some ornamental patterns in Egyptian murals is debatable. But relations between Minoan Crete, Ugarit, and the Euphrates are attested. To the south, Sumer and the Indus Valley civilization exchanged wares and probably cultural influences through Bahrein in the Persian Gulf. From Ugarit connections between the Near East and Troy were established along the Anatolian coast and others with Egypt through Byblos, which had been the trade center for Lebanese timber since the twenty-eighth century B.C.

Second Millennium B.C.

The great empires of the second millennium B.C. are favorable to a full development of earlier forms and styles and the creation of new ones in architecture. To the autochthonous town growing organically are added more sophisticated preplanned towns on orthogonal plans (artisans' towns in Egypt at El Lahun, ^cAmarna, Deir el Medina) or axial layouts (Egyptian fortresses in Nubia, Borsippa in Mesopotamia). In hilly land the irregular enclosure around a layout with rings following the contour lines, dominated by a citadel (Anatolia,

---

8 Helck, *Beziehungen*, pp. 13–48, 69–78.
9 H. Schmökel, *Das Land Sumer* (Stuttgart, 1956), pp. 54 ff, 87 ff. W. S. Smith, *The Art and Architecture of Ancient Egypt* (Baltimore, 1958), pp. 82.
10 Smith, *The Art*, pp. 115–117.

North Syria), several enclosures (Siyalk in Iran), or a ziqurrat within its temenos (Tshoga Zambil in Iran), still prevails. Houses assume a larger scale and a regular design, though preserving their autochthonous characteristics (tripartite plan in the units at El Lahun or in villas surrounded by small units in a garden at ᶜAmarna in Egypt; central court surrounded by rooms at Ur III in Mesopotamia). Less satisfactory solutions consist of two rooms at the rear of a small court in Anatolia (Boğazköy, Karum Kanesh), or along one long

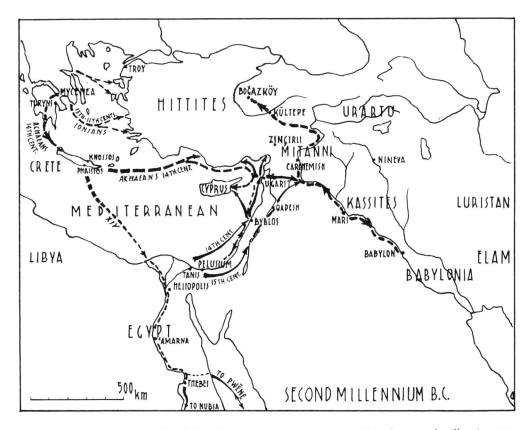

Map 4.   Cultural relations in the ancient world in the second millennium B.C.

side in the Levant (Tell Beit Mirsim), or irregularly around a court in Cyprus (Kalopsida). The bit hilani portico with a column or an atlantas on an animal before a shallow vestibule appears in the entrance of palaces in North Syria and Anatolia.

Architecture attains its fullest expression in the temples, whether in the huge mortuary complexes (Medinet Habu) or cult temples growing by accretion (Luxor, Karnak) and the terraced layout in Egypt (Deir el Baḥari), the deep cella chapels (Uruk) and stepped ziqurrats in Mesopotamia, or the large temples with numerous windows in

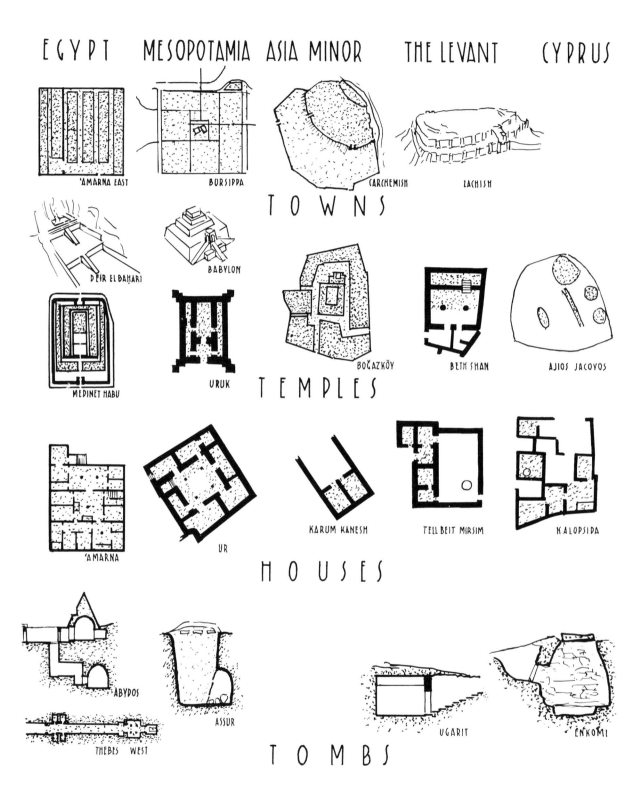

EGYPT MESOPOTAMIA ASIA MINOR THE LEVANT CYPRUS

'AMARNA EAST BORSIPPA CARCHEMISH LACHISH

TOWNS

DEIR EL BAHARI BABYLON BOĞAZKÖY BETH SHAN AJIOS JACOVOS

MEDINET HABU URUK

TEMPLES

'AMARNA UR KARUM KANESH TELL BEIT MIRSIM KALOPSIDA

HOUSES

ABYDOS ASSUR UGARIT ENKOMI

THEBES WEST

TOMBS

Fig. 37.   Typical structures in the second millennium B.C.

Anatolia (Boğazköy). It is noteworthy that the magazines surrounding Temple I at Boğazköy present curious analogies with those of the mortuary temples from the Ramesside Period in Western Thebes (Medinet Habu). The similarity of Chapel No. 2 at Beth Shan to a private funerary chapel at ᶜAmarna may indicate some borrowing from Egypt. This is not impossible, for Egyptian architects built temples in Syria dedicated to local and Egyptian gods at least since Tuthmosis III.[11] In Cyprus shrines remain hypaethral (Ajios Jacovos).

Nothing comparable to the elaborate Egyptian tombs, either in the shape of burial chambers surmounted by pyramid chapels (Abydos) or cut out of the cliff as chambers or corridors (Beni Hassan, Meir, Bersha, ᶜAmarna, Thebes), can be found during the second millennium in the Near East (Assur). An exception should be made, however, of the impressive dromos tombs in the Levant (Ugarit) and Cyprus (Enkomi), both of Aegean origin.

Close contacts between Egypt and Western Asia initiated during the Middle Kingdom (foreign artisans at El Lahun) grow under the Empire into aggressive colonialism. During this period the resettlement of colonies of foreign prisoners around the mortuary temples (Ramses III at Medinet Habu), the amassing of foreign tribute and war booty in the temples' magazines, and the expeditions abroad result in a harvest of objective geographical, botanical, ethnic, and architectural representations on the walls of temples and tombs. While little that is relevant to architecture can be ascribed to the use of foreign craftsmen, this visual education may have had considerable impact, in spite of the screening process of tradition. The design of the elements of fortification in the mortuary temple of Ramses III at Medinet Habu is allegedly inspired by Syrian fortification, many examples of which are represented on the walls of Ramesside temples. There may be more probability of Mesopotamian influence on the planning of the Coronation Hall at ᶜAmarna, which has double ramps set antithetically on both sides of its doorways similar to the device used in Assyrian palaces. Assyrian traders of Karum Kanesh, however, failed to adopt any of their own architecture in Anatolia in their genuine striving for integration. But Egyptian influence is evident in the temples at Byblos, ᶜAmrit, and ᶜAin el Hayyat in the Levant.

While the earlier trade route along the Euphrates that passed through Ugarit to the sea was still the main communication link between Mesopotamia and Egypt to the southwest and the Aegean to the northwest, it was now supplemented by a caravan road along the Jordan Valley. Among the most significant events in the Near East is the appearance of Cyprus as an active melting pot of art influences

[11] Helck, *Beziehungen*, pp. 480–481.

from the Near East and from the Aegean, especially after some of the latter tribes settle on the island in the fourteenth century and relations begin between Minoan-Mycenaean centers and Egypt. Various forms of architectural eclecticism flourish in Phoenicia (Egyptian) and Cyprus (Mesopotamian, Levantine).

The significance of the stimulus received by Crete from Egyptian architecture will, perhaps, be better appraised after its script is fully deciphered, but there is no doubt that the characteristic column with inverted taper (Knossos palace), the general style, and specific motifs in mural painting (monkey, lotus, predatory cat in papyrus) are probably derived from Egypt. The sudden increase in wealth of the Minoan mercenaries and their Mycenaean sailors who transported them to help Egypt against the Hyksos is at the root of the flourishing phase of Mycenaean architecture, which borrowed elements from Crete (inverted taper column) and the Near East (antithetical Lion Gate).

Farther north in the hinterland new ethnic elements settle in new lands (Urartu and Mitanni).[12] The warlike Hittites make their special contribution to the art of fortification and architectural sculpture. Between the thirteenth and eleventh centuries B.C. the Ionians settle along the western coast of Asia Minor, grafting the Greek genius to western Asiatic architecture.

First Millennium B.C.

In the first millennium B.C. Egyptian architecture declines, while in other areas newcomers monopolize creative activity in architecture: Assyrians and Neo-Babylonians in Mesopotamia, Persians in Iran, Phoenicians in the Levant and Cyprus, and Ionians in western Anatolia, and ultimately Thracians in northern Anatolia. This activity is an outcome of various ideologies that borrow elements according to eclectic trends, which are directed in Persia by the king or conditioned in Phoenicia, Ionia, and Cyprus to the law of demand. The Saite revival (Dynasty XXV) in Egypt, stimulated by the earlier Kushite artistic activity in the Sudan, has no effect on architecture.

Although little is known about Egyptian towns except for the growth of a Greek quarter north of the native one, both having a pseudo-orthogonal plan at Naukratis, much is extant of the axial layouts in Mesopotamia (Khorsabad, Babylon) or the perfectly round plan similar to that of the Assyrian camp imitated in the double enclosure at Zinçirli, which is protected by towers at regular intervals and by a central citadel with the royal palaces looming above the city. Several enclosures also surround the early towns of Iran.

[12] E. A. Speiser, *Ethnic Movements in the Near East in the Second Millennium B.C.*

The house plan in Egypt is still tripartite, but in Babylonia a new type appears. This has separate reception apartments and residential ones, based on a unit borrowed from the Assyrian temple with a square court connected at its rear to a broad shallow hall (Babylon). The central court forms the nucleus of houses in the Levant (Tell Beit Mirsim) and North Syria, where separate quarters for summer and winter are arranged, each fronted by its hilani portico (Samʾal). Persian palatial architecture is based upon the harmonic use of the square unit and extensive columniations featuring a hybrid eclecticism (Persepolis). Eclecticism with borrowings from Egypt and Persia characterizes Cypriote domestic architecture (Vuni).

Temples are symmetrical structures, still tripartite and growing by accretion in Egypt (Hibis), with a central court and lateral porticoes or a ziqurrat in Mesopotamia (Assur, Babylon) and a deep antecella and cella fronted by a portico with columns set on animals in Asia Minor (Tell Tayinat). The façade of the Egyptian temple now has an open design with columns, intercolumnar walls, and broken lintels, and a new type of secondary temple, the mammisi, is invented. Religious architecture in Persia, with its fire temples and

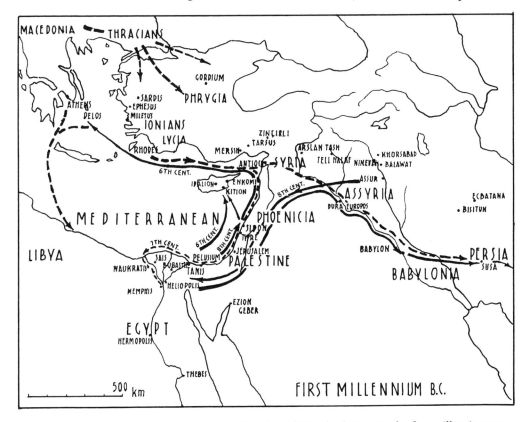

Map 5. Cultural relations in the first millennium B.C.

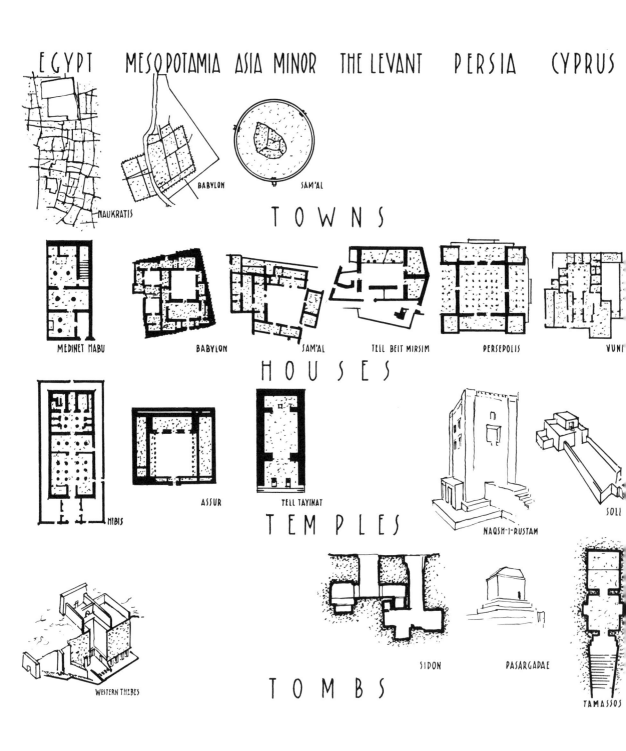

EGYPT MESOPOTAMIA ASIA MINOR THE LEVANT PERSIA CYPRUS

NAUKRATIS BABYLON SAM'AL

T O W N S

MEDINET HABU BABYLON SAM'AL TELL BEIT MIRSIM PERSEPOLIS VUNI

H O U S E S

NIBIS ASSUR TELL TAYINAT NAQSH-I-RUSTAM SOLI

T E M P L E S

WESTERN THEBES SIDON PASARGADAE TAMASSOS

T O M B S

Fig. 38.   Typical structures in the first millenium B.C.

altars (Naqsh-i-Rustam), and in Cyprus is not so monumental and is comparatively insignificant.

In a desperate attempt to obtain safety from tomb robbers, the Egyptians build their huge complexes (Thebes) or massive burial chambers (Saqqara) deep underground with mortuary temples above. Elsewhere only sporadic instances of monumental royal tombs occur: cut underground in Phoenicia (Sidon), as a superstructure in the shape of a gabled house in Persia (Pasargadae), and as underground dromos tombs in Cyprus (Tamassos).

Persian architecture owes its originality to its creative design, even though it is basically eclectic, using elements, materials, and craftsmen from various countries as far west as Egypt and Crete. The Persian system of erecting numerous columns in the squarish apadana hall is reminiscent of the much earlier Coronation Hall at ᶜAmarna. Phoenicians, whose ancestors were in contact with Egyptian art for two millennia, export their own products far across the Mediterranean. Although they send their able master builders to build temples and palaces in Palestine and settle in towns along the south coast of Cyprus and in North Africa, they actually bring little originality to an architecture that is permeated by strong influences from Mycenae, Anatolia, Persia, and Egypt. It is a period of increasing international relations throughout the ancient world, trade carried on between Egypt, the Levant, Cyprus, and even Greece, ethnic shifts with migrations and settling of Greeks in Libya, Egypt, and the Levant and of Thracians in northwest Anatolia, and invasions by military expeditions of Assyrians and later of Persians against Egypt. It is also the period when much constructive work is accomplished, though hardly of original or creative value, by the recruiting of international gangs of artisans from various countries for the construction of the Achaemenian palaces or of Phoenician master builders in Israelite monuments or Cypriote settlements. It is significant that this architectural activity is finally eclipsed by the creation of original styles, of feminine elegance and richness in Ionia, and of clear-cut vigorous design in Greece and Magna Grecia. The achievement of Greek architecture is probably more impressive in terms of its style than for the invention of new elements, for the plan of the temple is derived from the Mycenaean megaron, the Doric order from the proto-Doric Egyptian, the orthogonal system of town plans from Egypt, the peripteral temple from that of Egypt, and probably much of its trabeated architecture and methods of construction in well-dressed stone from Egypt.[13] Although the Greek contribution is outweighed by its borrowings, it resulted in the building, through original interpretation, of a new and dynamic architecture.

[13] H. W. Janson, *History of Art* (New York, 1964), pp. 92–94.

Chart 1

CHRONOLOGICAL APPEARANCE OF VARIOUS ARCHITECTURAL CHARACTERISTICS THROUGHOUT THE ANCIENT WORLD

	EGYPT	MESOPOTAMIA	ASIA MINOR AND NORTH SYRIA	THE LEVANT	PERSIA	CYPRUS	THE AEGEAN
7000 B.C.		Villages (Jarmo)	Rectangular houses of brick on stone foundations, painted (Haçilar)	Stone fortifications (Jericho) Round houses Plano-convex brick Neolithic village (Seyl Aqlat)			
6000 B.C.			Two-storied houses Plano-convex brick Primary urban settlement				Round houses of brick on stone foundations (Orchomenos)
5000 B.C.	Communal urban layout Mud and plant stems (Merimde)						
4000 B.C.	Stone rubble and rectangular plan (Maʿadi) Square town enclosure Circular orthogonal town plan Fortified brick palace	Brick and rectangular plan (Hassuna IV, Tepe Gawra)	Mud architecture (Mersin) Monumental megaron (Troy)	Rectangular houses of brick, painted (Ghassul), gabled (Khodeirah)	Handmade oval brick		
3000 B.C.	Trabeated stone architecture (Dynasty III) Pyramid Age: preplanned pyramid town; geo-metric style	Sumerian city-states Oval towns Incrustation in brick temples, deep cella Urban develop...	Communal urban layout (Thermi) Casemated fortification (Mersin)	Phoenician eclecticism influenced by Egypt ...		Neolithic round houses of stone Shaft or dromos tombs (influenced by Phoenicia)	Acropolis (Mycenae)

	(cont.)	2000 B.C.	1000 B.C.
	Orthogonal town plan (Orchomenos)	Fortified citadel (Mycenae); typical palaces in Crete; apsidal house; megaron; City-states in Greece; Tholos; pillared propylae	Trabeated style; Classical orthogonal town; Axial town (Hippodamian); Greek orders; Peripteral temple
		Tholos with dromos (Mycenaean influence); Mycenaean or Achaean residence (Enkomi); Dromos tomb at Ugarit (Mycenaean)	Phoenician towns in south; Persian types of palace (Vuni) Hittite and Egyptian elements
		Iranian invasion: residence on mound; Double or triple enclosure around town (Siyalk); Oval town, temenos (Tshoga Zambil)	Achaemenian-directed eclecticism; layout with separate units, square apadana, trabeated columnar style, harmonic design
	Apsidal house (Megiddo V)	Underground water system (Palestine); Hittite influences; Chapel similar to ʿAmarnian one	Phoenician builders in Palestine; Proto-Aeolian capital; Phoenician individual eclecticism
		Towns with citadel, jagged enclosure with caissons; stone or brick with wooden reinforcing; Rugged fortification; Gable, hilammar, hilani; Parabolic bay; Nature shrine; well-lit sanctuary surrounded by magazines; Assyrian *karum*	Rounded town enclosure (Samʾal); Atlantas (Mesopotamian); Assyrian palaces (North Syria); Phrygians; Lydians
	Palace near temple; Plano-convex brick (Ur I); Vaults; Houses with central court; Drainage (Ur III)	Ziqqurat; typical centered plan (Dynasty I, Babylon); Monumental plan; Kassite deep cella; Glazed brick statuary; Axial towns; orthostats (Neo-Assyrian)	Assyrian planning unit: square court adjacent to shallow broad hall; Neo-Babylonian processional street; Glazed brick (modeled or flat)
		Classicist style; Orthogonal town of artisans (Dynasty XII); Axial towns (Nubian forts); Terraced layout of mortuary temple; rock tomb separate; Elegant rich style; Cult temple growing by accretion; Osiride pillars; Colossal architectural statuary; deterioration	Saite revival; Greek town (Naukratis); Open façade of temple; Mammisi chapel

Chart 2

SUGGESTED FILIATIONS FROM EGYPT AND THE NEAR EAST TO GREECE

GREECE	INTERMEDIARY	PROTOTYPE
Layout of Towns		
Orthogonal		Egyptian
Axial		Egyptian
Houses		
Prostas-oikos	Rhodian	Egyptian
Pastas		Egyptian
Peristyle court		Mesopotamian
Megaron	Minoan-Mycenaean	Trojan
Stoa	Minoan	Egyptian (?)
Temples		
Megaron (Greek temple)	Minoan-Mycenaean	Trojan
Peripteral temple on podium		Egyptian
Tombs		
Tholos	Minoan-Mycenaean	Mesopotamian
Dromos tomb	Phoenician-Cypriote	Mycenaean
Fortifications		
	Mycenaean	Trojan-Hittite
Elements		
Caryatid-Atlantas		Hittite–North Syrian
Cavetto cornice		Egyptian
Dentils		Egyptian
Doric order		Egyptian
Fluted shaft		Egyptian
Gable	Minoan-Mycenaean	Trojan-Anatolian
Ionic capital	Proto-Aeolian (Levant-Cyprus)	Mesopotamian-Egyptian
Lion gargoyle or spout		Egyptian
Ornament	Minoan-Mycenaean	
Polychromy in architecture	Minoan-Mycenaean	Egyptian
Sphinx (female)	Hittite-Phoenician	Egyptian
Stone technique	Minoan-Mycenaean	Egyptian
Symmetry		Egyptian
Trabeated construction	Minoan-Mycenaean	Egyptian
Harmonic Design		
		Egyptian

Glossary of Technical Terms

Dependencies: subsidiary rooms appended to a residence, such as lavatories, kitchen, storerooms, and granaries.

False-door: a dummy door, an essential element of the Egyptian funerary chapel and the Assyrian temple.

Hilammar: pillared portico stretching along the façade of a vestibule in Hittite architecture.

Hilani or bit hilani: in North Syrian palaces, the broad and shallow entrance hall, accessible from a wide doorway with one or more central columns flush with the façade.

Label: inscribed small plaque of bone attached to vessels in the equipment of Early Dynastic tombs in Egypt.

Mastaba: a type of Egyptian tomb characterized by a massive rectangular superstructure reminiscent of a masonry bench (Arabic, *mastaba*).

Megaron: planning unit in Hittite architecture consisting of a gabled narrow hall with an entrance at one small end and a blind porch at the opposite one.

Orthostat: plinth of carved stone slabs at the bottom of walls in Anatolia and North Syria.

Palette: in protodynastic Egypt, a slab of stone for grinding and mixing pigments, which evolved into a votive type carved with scenes.

Serekh: an Egyptian hieroglyph representing the stylized double gateway of the palace topped with the plan of its rectangular courtyard and inscribed with one of the five names forming the Pharaoh's titulary.

Valley portal: a portal on the edge of the Nile Valley forming the lower approach to the mortuary temple complex of pharaohs.

Window of appearance: a window in the façade of the royal palace at which Pharaoh appeared on festal occasions to his retainers.

Index of Authors

Choisy, François Auguste, 63
Diodorus, Siculus, 15, 97
Fibonacci, Leonardo, 68
Frankfort, H., 188, 213
Herodotus, 3, 4, 6, 75, 182, 185
Hölscher, U., 62

Josephus, Florius, 97
Lloyd, S., 188
Manetho, 8
Strabo, 3, 15, 85, 97, 115, 182
Vitruvius, Pollio, 4

Historical Index

Abu, 101
Aceramic level, 128
Achaeans, 190, 194, 199, 201, 209
Achaemenian Period, 180, 183, 185, 186, 187, 189, 225
Achaemenids, 185
Adad, 78
ʿAdjib, 49
Adonis, 149, 163, 168
Aeolian style, 146, 200
Ahab, 161
Aḥanekht, 70
Ahiram, 150, 171
Ahmes I, 18
Aḥmose, 45
Ahuramazda, 185
Akhenaten, 9, 31, 39, 55, 68, 194

Akhethotep, 50
Akkad, 77, 102
Akkadians, 79, 80, 87, 102, 112, 156
Alexander the Great, 10, 155, 171, 180
Amar-Sin, 111, 119
Amasis, 191
Amenemhat II, 53, 62, 207
Amenemhat III, 37, 53
Amenhotep I, 55
Amenhotep II, 55
Amenhotep III, 27, 31, 38, 61, 67, 70, 162, 208
Amenhotep IV, 31
Ammon, 10
Amonmose, 59
Amorites, 80, 148, 162, 176
Amun, 7, 9, 20, 32, 36, 37, 38, 45, 60, 155

Amun-of-the-Road, 60, 155
Anahita, 185
Anat, 149, 163
Anu, 99, 102, 134
Anu-Adad, 105
Anubis, 33, 44
Aphrodite, 168, 197
Apries, 29, 32
Arabian style, 132
Aramaeans, 80, 122, 138, 148, 150
Asiatics, 9, 36, 222
Assur, 101, 106, 107, 117, 119
Assurbanipal, 80, 180
Assurnazirpal II, 111
Assyrian style, Assyrians, 10, 32, 77, 80,
    81, 84, 85, 92, 103, 105–106, 113,
    118, 121, 122, 123, 127, 128, 132,
    133, 137, 141, 142, 144, 145, 146,
    149, 150, 174, 175, 179, 180, 182,
    187, 189, 201, 221, 222, 225
  New Assyrian Period, 113
  Old Assyrian Period, 117
Astarte, 149
"Astarte-with-Two-Horns," 166
Astarte-Aphrodite, 197
Aten, 7, 9, 39, 40, 67
Athena, 195, 197
Atherat, 163
Attic style, 192
Ay, 32

Baᶜal, 149, 156, 163, 167, 207
Babylonian Period or style, 80, 92, 93, 95,
    97, 103, 105, 107, 108, 111, 112,
    149, 161, 184, 187, 188, 189
  Neo-Babylonian, 80, 84, 89, 105, 107,
    117, 119, 170, 222
Bel, 78, 184
Bes, 31, 134
Bronze, Late, 130

Caliphate, 207
Canaanites, 148, 149, 154, 156, 163, 164,
    166, 174
  pre-Canaanite, 163
Chalcolithic Period, 129, 192
Cheops, 52
"Cheops-is-belonging-to-the-Horizon,"
    49
Chephren, 23, 43, 52, 62
  "Great-is-Chephren," 49
Coptic months, 4
Corinthian capitals, 209
Cretan style, 28, 132, 154, 208, 218
Croesus, 122
Cybele, 136
Cypriote style, 21, 191, 192, 209, 218,
    223, 225
Cyrus, 80, 180, 183, 184, 186

Dagon, 167
Darius, 183, 185, 186, 187, 188, 209

David, Palace of, 161
Decadence, Period of, 8
  Late, 8, 37
  Saitic, 28
Djadjaemᶜankh, 47
Djeḥutiḥetep, 54, 62
Djer, 47
Djeser, 8, 21, 29, 43, 47, 49, 51, 60, 62,
    64, 66, 69, 70
Djet, 49
Doric style, 44, 67, 209, 225
  proto-Doric, 67, 225
Dumuzi (Tammuz), 77, 110
Dur-Ili ("Wall-of-the-God"), 112
Dur-Sharrukin ("Wall-of-Sargon"), 112
Duwanḥor, 50

Ea, 134
Eanna, 106
Edomites, 148
Egyptian style, Egyptians, 84, 85, 106,
    119, 132, 136, 141, 145, 148, 149,
    152, 154, 155, 156, 162, 170, 171,
    174, 175, 177, 178, 184, 188, 189,
    207, 208, 209, 213, 214, 218, 221,
    222, 223
Egyptianizing style, 142, 161, 166, 167,
    168, 171, 178, 191, 195
El, 149, 155
Elamites, 6, 58, 179, 180, 182, 184, 187
Empire (*see* Kingdom, New)
Enlil, 77, 79, 134
Esagila, 107
Esarhaddon, 80
Eshmun, 163
Evagoras, 192

Gasga, 206
Geb, 7
Gem-Aten ("Meeting-Aten"), 40
Greco-Roman towns, 20
Greek style, Greeks, 3, 15, 20, 21, 44, 58,
    67, 71, 75, 85, 108, 146, 149, 151,
    161, 171, 175, 177, 185, 191, 192,
    207, 209, 222, 225
Gudea, 79, 102, 117
Gurgurri Gate, 107, 113
Guti, 79

Hadad, 163
Hamites, 8
Hammurabi, 77, 80, 92, 105, 107, 112,
    121, 180
Haᶜpy, 4
Hathor, 36, 40, 41, 44, 67, 70
Hathoric, 70, 189, 195, 201, 209
Hatshepsut, 37, 38, 44, 55, 62, 63, 67,
    70, 208
Hattusili I, 125
Hebat, 134
Hebrews, 148
Helladic Period, Early, 122

Hellenistic Period, 46, 58, 162, 192, 200
Ḥemaka, 49
Ḥemiwnw, 50
Ḥesireᶜ, 47, 50
Ḥesy, 59
Hiram, 156
Hittites, 9, 79, 121, 122, 125, 127, 130,
    132, 136, 138, 139, 142, 144, 145,
    146, 148, 149, 162, 163, 175, 176,
    177, 188, 191, 195, 208, 222
    Old Hittite era, 129
    pre-Hittite era, 142
Ḥor ᶜAḥa, 49
Ḥorakhte, 39, 40, 45
Horite invaders, 172
Horus, 7, 69
Horus-name, 213
Ḥuny, 51
Hurrian style, Hurrians, 101, 103, 105,
    118, 122, 134
Hyksos, 9, 148, 160, 171, 174, 208, 222

Illushima, 80
Inanna (see Ishtar)
Indo-Aryans, 172
Indo-Europeans, 80, 105, 180, 184
Indo-Germanic people, 121, 145
Ineny, 28, 55
Inpy, 51
Intef I, 54
Intef II, 54
Intefs, 53
Intermediate Period
    First, 8, 25, 53, 54, 56, 66
    Second, 8
Ionians, 189, 222
Ionic style, 146, 209
Iranians, 180, 185, 186, 187
Ishtar, 77, 84, 95, 101, 103, 106, 107,
    110, 115, 119
Isin, 77
Isin-Larsa, 105
Isis, 69
Islam, Islamic style, 6, 85, 127, 207
Israelites, 149, 151, 154, 160, 164, 166, 174,
    225

Jews, 184
Judah, 149, 151

Kaparu, 133
Karaindash, 105
Kar-Ilu-Shamash ("Fortress-of-
    Shamash"), 112
Kar-Tukulti-Ninurta ("Fortress-of-
    Tukulti-Ninurta"), 112
Kassites, 9, 79, 93, 105, 117, 119, 180
Khaᶜsekhemwy, 49
Khentiamentiw, 33, 37
Khentkawes, 16, 21
Kheta (see Hittites)
Khnum, 33

Khnumḥotep II, 54
Khnumit Neferhuy, 207
Khonsu, 38
Kingdom, Middle, 8, 15, 24–25, 37, 38,
    45, 64, 67, 70, 89, 129, 154, 167,
    171
    New, 8, 25–28, 31, 35, 44, 51, 70, 167,
    171
    Old, 8, 15, 21–24, 38, 41, 44, 54, 63,
    70, 154, 155, 167, 178, 207
Kushites, 10, 38, 222

Lebanese timber, 218
Levantine style, 189, 191, 222
Libyan Dynasty, 10
Lipit-Ishtar, 77
Lugalzaggisi, 79
Luians, 145
Lycian sarcophagus, 171
Lydians, 122, 138

Macrinus, 168
Marduk, 79, 107, 184
Maru-Aten ("Sighting-the-Aten"), 40
Maᶜt, 7
May, 32
Medes, 80, 180, 186, 188
Mekal, 163, 166
Meketreᶜ, 25
Melqart, 156, 163
Men, 49
Mentuemḥat, 46
Mentuḥotep, 43, 44, 53
Merikareᶜ, 18
Merneptaḥ, 32, 121
Mesilim, 79
Mesopotamian people, style, 116, 119,
    122, 123, 132, 145, 146, 154, 156,
    160, 177, 180, 184, 187, 188, 189,
    207, 209, 213, 214, 221
Midas, 146
Midianites, 148
Minoans, 16, 154, 156, 190, 207, 208,
    214, 218, 222
Mitanni, Mitannians, 9, 80, 121, 208
Mithra, 185
Moabites, 148
Mursilis, 206
Mut, 38
Mutawalli, 208
Mycenaean style, Mycenaeans, 108, 149,
    162, 171, 175, 176, 190, 191, 194,
    197, 199, 201, 208, 209, 222, 225
Mykerinos, 43
"Mykerinos-is-divine," 49

Nabonidus, 97
Nabopolassar, 80, 95, 107, 111
Nabu, 78, 95, 106, 107, 113
Nannar, 90, 103, 105, 110
Naramsin, 103, 112, 187
Natufian culture, 150
Nebetka, 49

Nebka, 154
Nebuchadnezzar I, 180
Nebuchadnezzar II, 80, 95, 107, 115
Neferhotep, 32
Neith, 33
Neithotep, 49
Nektanebo, 37
Neolithic Period, 5, 8, 10, 13, 15
Neterikhet (see Djeser)
Neuserreᶜ, 39, 64, 68
Ningal, 105
Niqmepa, 132
Nubians, 41
Nut, 7

Omri, 161
Oreia (see Aphrodite)
Orion, 52
Osiride pillars, statues, 67, 68
Osiris, 7, 46, 49
Osorkon, 37

Pabasa, 51
Palestinian style, towns, 59, 150, 151, 154,
     159, 197
Panehsy, 55
Parthian style, 97, 161, 177
Pedamenopet, 51
"People of the Sea," 148, 170, 206
Pepy II, 9, 44
Per-Hai ("House-of-Rejoicing"), 40
Persian style, Persians, 10, 31, 80, 81, 122,
     149, 150, 161, 170, 171, 176, 180,
     182, 184, 185, 186, 187, 188, 189,
     192, 194, 201, 207, 209, 210, 222,
     223, 225
Philistines, 148, 170, 201
Phoenician style, Phoenicians, 21, 147,
     149, 151, 154, 155, 156, 160, 161,
     167, 171, 176, 177, 178, 191, 195,
     197, 200, 201, 202, 209, 210, 222,
     225
Phrygians, 122, 137, 146
Post-Exilic times, 170
Pre-Semitic style, 163
Proto-Doric people, 190
Proto-Elamite writing, 180
Psammetik, 175
Ptah, 32
Ptahhotep, 50
Ptolemaic Period, 37, 38, 70, 192
Ptolemy I or II, 8

Qayᶜa, 49

Ramesside Period, 61, 68, 70, 221
Ramessids, 10, 45, 60
Ramses II, 32, 38, 40, 41, 45, 55, 68, 168,
     171
Ramses III, 27, 32, 33, 38, 45, 59, 60, 68,
     121, 170, 206, 221
Reᶜ, 5, 7, 39, 46, 49

Reᶜ Horakhte (see Horakhte)
Rekhmireᶜ, 62, 208
Remushenti, 54
Reshef, 163, 168
Roman style, period, 6, 18, 20, 37, 38,
     46, 125, 185
Ruaben, 24, 47, 49

Sahureᶜ, 43, 121, 205, 218
Saite, Saitic Period, 28, 222
Sardians, 188
Sargon II, 79, 93, 95, 103, 106, 111, 112,
     113, 121, 161, 163, 191
Sargonids, 77
Sassanian people, 97, 127
Saul, 175
Sehertawy Intef I, 54
Sekhemkhet 49, 51
Seleucid Period, 108
Semites, 147
Semitic culture, 8, 77, 79, 92, 98, 102,
     148
  non-Semitic, 76
Senmut, 208
Sennacherib, 85, 89, 107, 175
Senusert (see Sesostris I)
Senusertᶜankh, 51
Seshemnefer, 50
Sesostris I, 37, 44, 53, 67
Sesostris II, 16, 53, 54
"Sesostris-is-strong," 49
Seti I, 32, 38
Shalmaneser III, 113
Shamash, 106
Shamshi Adad I, 80, 93, 103, 106
Shara, 101
Shulgi, 103, 111, 119
Shusin, 92, 103
Sin, 99, 101, 116, 117, 119
Sin-Shamash, 105, 117, 119
Sirenput I, 55
Snefru, 43, 51, 62
"Snefru-gleams," 49
Sobek, 7
Solomon, 152, 160, 161, 164, 167, 175,
     176, 177, 178
Solomonic Age, 151, 171
Sumerian Period, Sumerians, 15, 77, 78,
     79, 80, 81, 85, 90, 97, 98, 102, 105,
     108, 110, 117, 119, 179, 180, 213,
     217
  Neo-Sumerian Period, 102, 110
Syrians, 16, 45, 56, 59, 122, 132, 133, 139,
     141, 142, 144, 145, 146, 163, 176,
     205, 207, 208, 209, 218, 221

Tammuz (Dumuzi), 77, 110, 149
Tantalus, 138
Teshub, 134
Thebans, 42, 208
Thracians, 222
Thutnefer, 27
Ti, 50

Tiglath-Pileser I, 80, 105
Tiglath-Pileser III, 80, 133, 154
Tudhaliyas IV, 134
Tukulti-Ninurta I, 78, 80, 106
Tuthmosis I, 18, 27, 55
Tuthmosis III, 27, 55, 70, 208, 221

Udimu, 49
Ugaritic writing, 156
Ugme, 110
Unamun, 60, 154
Unas, 62
Urartian, 180
Urnammu, 90, 103, 117

Ur-Ningirsu, 110
Userkaf, 39

Waḥᶜankh Intef II, 54
Waḥka I, 54
Waḥka II, 54
Waḥkareᶜ, 15, 18

Xerxes, 183

Yarimlim, 132

Zimrilim, 92
Zoroastrianism, 185

Geographical Index

Abu Ghorab, 37, 39, 217
Abu Hawan, 175
Abu Matar, 157
Abu Roash, 50
Abu Shahrein (*see* Eridu)
Abu Simbel, 10, 41, 59, 68
Abusir, 37, 64
Abydos, 11, 18, 29, 32, 37, 38, 49, 50, 53,
    56, 112, 208, 209, 214, 218
El ʿAdeimah, 168, 217
ʿAdlun, 162
Aegean Sea, 4, 120, 125, 149, 177, 190,
    205–210, 211, 218, 221
Africa, 6, 225
Aḥmar (*see* Gebel Aḥmar)
ʿAi, 164, 174, 176
ʿAin el Hayyat, 168, 221
ʿAin Mullaha, 168
ʿAin Umm el Darag, 151
Ajia Irini, 195, 201
Ajios Jacovos, 195, 201, 221
Akhetaten, 18
ʿAkka, 147
Akkad, 79, 121
Alaça Hüyük, 132, 136, 137, 142, 145
Alambra, 192, 215
Alasia (*see* Enkomi)
Aleppo, 121, 218
Alexandria, 192, 200
Alishar, 122, 125, 128, 129, 138, 139, 141,
    142, 144, 145
Amanu, 120
ʿAmarna, 5, 9, 18, 20, 25, 26, 27, 28, 31,
    37, 39, 40, 46, 55, 59, 60, 61, 67,
    68, 148, 156, 162, 166, 188, 218,
    219, 221, 225
El ʿAmrah, 13, 14, 15, 66, 212
ʿAmran, 170

Anatolia, 120–146, 190, 205, 206, 211,
    214, 217, 218, 221, 222, 225
ʿAniba, 51, 58
Anti-Lebanon Mountains, 147
Anti-Taurus Mountains, 120
ʿAqaba, Gulf of, 148, 161
Arad, 159, 166, 175
Arbela, 180
Armenia, 76
Arpachiya, 108, 117, 214
Arslan Tash, 122, 128, 141
Asia, 6, 10, 59, 120, 213
Asia Minor, 79, 120–146, 148, 174, 176, 190,
    195, 201, 202, 205, 206, 222, 223
Askut, 18, 58, 60
Assur, 77, 83, 84, 88, 90, 93, 95, 103, 105,
    106, 107, 111, 112, 113, 117, 118,
    119, 175, 197, 221, 223
Assyria, 80, 127, 128, 137, 154, 161, 177,
    180, 189
Aswan, 5, 44, 54, 62
Asyut, 54

Bab edh-Dhraʿ, 164
Babili ("Gate-of-the-gods"), 115
Babylon, 9, 15, 77, 78, 79, 80, 83, 84, 89, 90,
    95, 102, 105, 107, 111, 112, 115, 116,
    117, 118, 119, 121, 184, 191, 222, 223
Babylonia, 80, 183
Badari, 11
Baghdad, 127
Baḥrein, 218
Bard-i-Nishandi, 185
Beersheba, 157
Beni Ḥassan, 44, 54, 58, 67, 221
Beqʿa, 147, 148
Bersha, 44, 54, 62, 70, 221
Berytos, 147

Bethel, 160
Beth Gebrin, 152
Beth Shan, 159, 162, 163, 166, 172, 175, 178, 197, 221
Beth Shemesh, 170, 172, 174
Beth Sur, 152, 174
Beth Yereh (Khirbet Kerak), 159, 164
Black Sea, 80
Boğazköy (Hattusha), 121, 123, 125, 129, 130, 134, 136, 138, 139, 141, 142, 144, 145, 219, 221
Borsippa, 83, 106, 107, 218
Bubastis, 37
Buhen, 18, 58
Burdur, 128
Büyükkale, 125, 139
Byblos (Gublos), 60, 147, 149, 154–155, 157, 159, 162, 163, 167, 168, 175, 178, 190, 205, 207, 218, 221

Cairo, 11, 13
Calah, 117, 118
Canaan, 172
Cappadocia, 185
Carchemish, 122, 123, 128, 137, 138, 139, 141, 142, 144
Carthage, 163
Caspian Sea, 179
Cataract, First, 3
Chemmis, 69
Cilicia, 77, 149
Crete, 9, 67, 121, 145, 146, 154, 156, 171, 195, 207, 208, 214, 218, 222, 225
Cyprus, 79, 149, 156, 161, 171, 177, 188, 190–202, 205, 206, 208, 214, 215, 217, 218, 219, 221, 222, 225

Dahshur, 43, 50, 51, 53, 217
Damascus, 147, 163
Damghan, 180, 184
Daphnae, 175, 209
Da-u-Dukhtar, 186
Dead Sea, 148
Deir el Bahari, 38, 43, 63, 67, 70, 219
Deir el Ballas, 31
Deir el Medina, 18, 25, 27, 28, 32, 46, 53, 56, 218
Delta, 3, 5, 9, 10, 15, 18, 69, 214
Dendera, 37, 38, 51
Deshasha, 56, 209
Diyala, 76, 180
Djemdet-Nasr, 79, 108, 162, 180
Djerablus, 128
Dodecanese islands, 201
Dunbartepe, 122
Dur-Ili, 112
Dur-Kurigalzu, 90, 93
Dur-Sharrukin (Khorsabad), 112, 113

Ecbatana, 127, 182, 183, 185
Edfu, 36, 37, 38
Eflatun Punar, 134

Egypt, 3–71, 78, 85, 87, 89, 90, 97, 102, 108, 112, 116, 118, 121, 123, 129, 134, 138, 147, 148, 154, 164, 167, 170, 180, 183, 184, 188, 191, 194, 199, 201, 202, 205, 206, 209, 210, 211, 212, 213, 214, 215, 217, 218, 219, 221, 222, 223, 225
    Lower Egypt, 14
    Upper Egypt, 77, 214
Elam, 179, 180, 187
Enkomi, 190, 194, 199, 201, 221
Eridu (Abu Shahrein), 76, 90, 98, 99, 111, 112
ʿErq el Aḥmar, 168
Eshnunna (Tell Asmar), 90, 103, 132
Ethiopia, 183
Etruria, 206
Euphrates, 9, 75, 76, 79, 81, 83, 95, 107, 115, 116, 123, 127, 128, 148, 209, 214, 218, 221
Europe, 120, 186
Ezion Geber, 161

Fara, 102
Fars, 186
Fayum, the, 9, 24, 37
Fraktin, 136

Galilee, 148
Gavur Kalesi, 138
Gebel Aḥmar, 5
Gebel Barkal, 41
Geder, 141
Gezbel, 136
Gezer, 144, 151, 167, 172, 174
Ghassul (Teleilat Ghassul), 157, 159, 176, 212
El Gib, 151
Giyan, 187
Giza, 16, 21, 23, 37, 43, 50, 52, 53, 59, 62, 63, 66, 215, 217
Granicus, 180
Greece, 67, 121, 157, 159, 177, 180, 184, 225
Gublos (Byblos), 149
Gülücek, 122
Gur, 127

Haçilar, 121, 122, 123, 128, 144, 157, 205, 211, 214
Hadatu, 128
Ḥalaf, 87
Halys River, 127
Hama, 162, 163, 176
Haraga, 208
Hassuna, 80, 85, 108, 117
Ḥatnub, 5
Hattusha (Boğazköy), 122, 125
Hawara, 50
Hazor, 160, 172, 177
Heliopolis, 5, 39, 49
Hemamiya, 11
Herakleia, 58

Herakleopolis, 9, 43, 56
Hermonthis, 37
Hermopolis, 46
El Hibba, 108
Hibis, 223
Hierakonpolis, 11, 14, 15, 21, 29, 56, 112, 218
Hüyük, 138, 142, 144

Idalion, 171, 192, 195, 197, 200, 202
Ikkur, 18, 58
Indian Ocean, 76
Indus Valley, 218
Ionia, 161, 222, 225
Iraq, 89
Iran, 76, 80, 89, 179, 104, 187, 219, 222
Ishlali, 105
Isopata, 171
Issus, 180
Italy, 192

Jarmo, 78
Jemmeh, 161
Jericho, 150, 151, 152, 157, 159, 160, 163, 170, 172, 174, 176, 192, 205, 211, 214, 217
Jerusalem, 80, 151, 161, 175, 184
Jordan, 147, 148, 168, 221
Judea, 148

El Kab, 16
Kalopsida, 192, 242
Kanesh (see Karum Kanesh)
Karabel, 136
Karatepe, 122, 139, 141, 144
Karim Shahir, 80
Kar-Ilu-Shamash, 112
Karnak, 20, 32, 37, 38, 39, 45, 62, 67, 70, 141, 208, 219
Kart-hadasht, 191
Kar-Tukulti-Ninurta, 78, 83, 93, 106, 112, 117, 119
Karum Kanesh (Kültepe), 122, 127, 129, 137, 219, 221
Khabur River, 187
Khafaje, 81, 101, 112, 116, 117, 119
Khirokitia, 192
Khodeira, 157, 170, 212
Khorsabad, 83, 90, 93, 97, 106, 112, 113, 117, 118, 119, 130, 161, 222
Khoshi, 101
Kish, 76, 79, 90, 103, 108, 110, 111, 112, 117
Kisheshim, 182
Kition, 195, 197, 202
Knossos, 208, 222
Kom Ombo, 38
Kuban, 18, 58
Kültepe (Karum Kanesh), 122, 127, 128, 129, 130, 132
Kumma, 58
Kurdistan, 186
Kurion, 199

Kush, 54
Kypros (Cyprus), 190
Kythera, 197, 202

Lachish, 161, 166, 170, 172, 174, 175, 177, 195
Lagash, 76, 78, 79, 102, 117
El Lahun, 16, 24, 25, 32, 50, 53, 209, 218, 221
Lapithos, 199
Larissa, 136
Larsa, 76, 102
Lebanon, 6, 60, 121, 147, 177, 183, 206, 218
Lejjun, 164
Leontes (Litani), 147
Lesbos, 129
Levant, 147, 178, 188, 190, 205, 206, 214, 215, 217, 221, 222, 225
Libya, 213, 214, 225
Lisht, 50, 53, 62
Lucera, 192
Luristan, 183, 189
Luxor, 4, 20, 38, 67, 219

Maʿadi, 13, 59, 157, 212
Magna Grecia, 225
Mahasna, 11
Malqata, 27, 31, 61, 67
Manisa, 136
Marathus (ʿAmrit), 168
Mari, 79, 92, 93, 95, 101, 103, 119, 174
Maʿsara, 5
Masjid-i-Suleiman, 185
Medamud, 37, 38
Media, 77, 183
Medinet Habu, 25, 27, 28, 32, 45, 59, 60, 61, 68, 219
Medinet Madi, 37
Mediterranean Sea, 3, 6, 76, 80, 120, 144, 145, 149, 159, 162, 200, 201, 206, 225
Megiddo, 151, 154, 159, 160, 161, 164, 166, 170, 172, 174, 176, 178, 197, 217
Meir, 44, 54, 221
Memphis, 5, 8, 15, 20, 29, 31, 32, 50, 208
Merimde, 11, 15, 211
Meroe, 54
Mersin, 122, 129, 138, 139, 141, 142, 212
Mesopotamia, 67, 75–119, 120, 123, 128, 138, 147, 154, 174, 179, 180, 192, 205, 206, 208, 209, 211, 212, 214, 215, 218, 219, 221, 222
Meydum, 51, 61, 62
Miletus, 58
Mina el Beida, 156
Mirgissa, 60
Mitanni, 222
Mount Carmel, 150, 183
Mugharet el Wad, 168
Musasir, 184
Mycenae, 208, 225

Nahr el Fidd, 156
Naqada, 11, 15
Naqsh-i-Rustam, 185, 186, 188, 225
Naukratis, 20, 175, 209, 222
Near East, 68
Negev, 206
Nikolides, 200
Nile River, 3, 4, 7; 9, 11, 13, 15, 16, 18, 20, 26, 31, 33, 35, 40, 58, 60, 209
Nile River Valley, 148, 214
Nimrud, 84
Nineva, 15, 80, 83, 84, 89, 117
Nippur, 76, 79, 81, 102, 103
Nişantepe, 139
Nitovikla, 200, 201
Nubia, 6, 9, 18, 25, 40, 51, 58, 61, 218
Nuzi, 93

Olympia, 159
El ʿOmari, 11, 14
Orchomenos, 157, 159, 211
Orient, the, 20, 81, 177, 190, 205–210
Orontes, 148, 162

Palestine, 80, 147, 164, 174, 176, 177, 178, 188, 192, 201, 205, 206, 207, 225
Pasargadae, 183, 185, 186, 188, 225
Persepolis, 180, 182, 183, 185, 187, 189, 223
Persia, 31, 179–189, 223, 225
Persian Gulf, 81, 179, 183, 214, 218
Petra, 150
Philae, 37
Phoenicia, 106, 134, 145, 147, 151, 161, 162, 171, 177, 188, 190, 197, 201, 210, 222, 225
Polatli, 137
Pwēne (Somaliland), 45

Qadesh, 41, 121, 123, 139, 141
Qasr el Sagha, 38
Qatna, 144
Qaw, 43, 54
Qumm, 180, 184

Ramat Rahel, 161, 177
Ras Shamra (Ugarit), 144, 148, 150, 156, 162, 163, 167, 171, 176, 190, 205, 207, 218, 221
Rayy, 180, 184
Red Sea, 6
Rhodes, 201
Rosetta, 11

Saft el Hennah, 170
Sahara, 3, 230
Sakçagözü, 122, 133
Salamis, 192, 199
Samʾal (Zinçirli), 122, 123, 127, 128, 130, 133, 138, 139, 141, 223
Samaria, 148, 161, 174, 177
Samarra, 108

Saqqara, 21, 24, 29, 47, 49, 50, 51, 62, 69, 214, 217, 225
Sardinia, 149
Sardis, 138, 183
Savah, 180
Scorpion Gate, 130, 133
Sechem, 166, 172, 174
Semna, 18, 58
Sesebi, 20, 25, 39, 59
Seyhan, 136
Seyl Aqlat, 150
Shalfak, 58
Shanidar, 78
Shunet el Zebib, 56
Sicily, 149
Sidon, 147, 149, 151, 155, 162, 163, 168, 171, 178, 191, 225
Sinai, 9
Sippar, 83, 106, 108
Sipylos, 136
Siwa, 10
Siyalk, 180, 182, 184, 186, 187, 219
Soli, 197
Sozuksutepe, 142
Spain, 149
Sudan, 6, 9, 20, 26, 39, 59, 222
Sumer, 76, 77, 79, 92, 130, 176, 213, 217, 218
Surghul, 108
Susa, 58, 85, 180, 182, 183, 184, 185, 187, 188
Susiana, 179
Syria, 76, 79, 80, 120, 121, 122, 127, 128, 132, 139, 142, 145, 147, 148, 152, 156, 171, 180, 191, 201, 206, 207, 208, 209, 218, 219, 221, 223

Tamassos, 200, 202, 225
Tasa, 11
Taurus, 120
Tebtynis, 21
Teleilat Ghassul (see Ghassul)
Tell Ahmar (Tell Barsib), 123
Tell Aqrab, 101, 214
Tell Asmar (Eshnunna), 87, 89, 90, 92, 101, 103, 112, 119, 215
Tell Atchana, 130, 132, 137, 144, 146
Tell Beit Mirsim, 150, 151, 160, 161, 172, 174, 175, 177, 215, 219, 223
Tell Brak, 112
Tell Duweir, 170
Tell el Ajjul, 151, 160, 170, 172, 175
Tell el Farʿah, 151, 159, 160, 161, 170, 171, 172, 174, 177
Tell el Ful, 174, 175
Tell el Hesy, 160, 172, 174, 175
Tell el Nasbeh, 151, 174, 175
Tell el Qadi, 164
Tell el Safy, 175
Tell el Yahudiya, 170, 208
Tell Gemmah, 172
Tell Halaf, 123, 130, 132, 133, 139, 141, 142, 144, 176

Tell Nebesheh, 170
Tello, 88, 89, 110, 118
Tell Taʿnnah, 152, 160, 172, 175
Tell Tayinat, 130, 133, 137, 223
Tell Zakariya, 172, 175
Tepe Gawra, 81, 83, 87, 98, 99, 108, 119, 192, 212
Thebes, 7, 9, 10, 15, 18, 20, 25, 27, 31, 32, 38, 43, 45, 46, 51, 53, 54, 55, 56, 59, 155, 221, 225
Thermi, 122, 129, 139, 141
Thessaly, 159
Thrace, 122
Tigris, 75, 81, 93, 101, 112, 113, 116, 132, 148, 209
Tirzah (see Tell el Farʿah)
Trachonas, 199
Troy, 122, 123–125, 129, 130, 137, 139, 141, 142, 145, 209, 218
Tshoga-Zambil, 180, 184, 187, 219
Tura, 5, 62
Tyre, 147, 149, 155, 156, 160, 162, 163, 171

ʿUbaid, 81, 98, 101, 118, 119
Ugarit (see Ras Shamra)
Umma, 79
ʿUqair, 93, 99, 118, 119

Ur, 76, 78, 79, 81, 83, 84, 85, 88, 89, 90, 92, 95, 101, 102, 103, 105, 108, 110, 111, 112, 117, 215, 217, 219
Urartu, 132, 184, 222
Uronarti, 18, 25, 58
Uruk (Warka), 76, 79, 81, 87, 90, 97, 98, 99, 102, 103, 105, 106, 112, 116, 117, 118, 119, 217, 218, 219

Valley of the Kings, 55
Van, 77
Vounous, 197, 217
Vuni, 194, 197, 223

Wadi ʿAra, 172
Wadi ʿAraba, 148
Wadi Hammamat, 214
Wadi Tumilat, 213
Warka (see Uruk)

Yazilikaya, 134
Yerkapu, 142
Yortan, 137

Zagros, 75, 79, 179, 180, 186
Zawi Chemi Shanidar, 78
Zawiyet el ʿAryan, 49, 51
Zinçirli (Samʾal), 122, 133, 222

Subject Index

Abscissa-and-ordinate method, 63
Accretion, 35, 38, 51, 223
Accuracy, 63
Acropolis, 176
Administration, 8
Adze, 60
Aesthetic value, 66, 67, 70, 116, 117, 178, 209, 210
Aisle, 130, 132
Alabaster, 60
Alcove, 106
Alignment, 20, 113, 117, 119
Altar, 7, 27, 41, 81, 98, 99, 101, 133, 134, 164, 167, 168, 195, 197, 217, 225
Ambulatory, 167
Angle of incline, 51, 63
Annex, 90
Antecella, 103, 105, 107, 164, 167, 168, 223
Apadana, 31, 183, 188, 225
Appliqué, 31
Apsidal, 159
Arch, 14, 117
Archaic Period, 14, 16, 49, 59, 64, 85, 127, 177
Architect, 28, 55, 102
Architecture, 10, 13, 14, 90, 119, 129, 213, 222, 225
  monumental, 133, 145
  problems of, 63
Architrave, 44, 67
Archives, 132, 148
Ark, 167
Art, 5, 8, 9
Artery, 20, 58, 81, 83, 84
Articulation, 66
Artisan, 16, 18, 25, 45
Ascension, 47
  place of, 47

Asphalt (*see* Bitumen)
Asymmetrical layout, 137, 145
Asymmetry, 147
Avenue, processional (*see* Processional street)
Aviary, 40
Awning, 23, 26, 37, 83, 93, 130, 156
Axial layout, 18–20, 35, 55, 83, 84, 95, 99, 101, 105, 106, 171, 184, 209, 218
Axis, 27, 29, 35, 37, 38, 43, 51, 52, 56, 78, 83, 102, 119, 144, 164, 184, 188, 199

Background, 8
Balcony, 56, 58, 88
  of appearance, 32
Balk, 58, 60
Balustrade, 28, 189
Barge, 5, 38, 62
Bark, 37
Barrack, 18, 23, 58, 127, 187
Basalt, 60, 119, 120
Basement, 27
Bastion, 14, 29, 56, 58, 83, 105, 113, 115, 139, 141, 144, 174, 175, 176, 200
Bathroom, 31, 88, 92, 133
Battered wall, 13, 14, 56, 103, 112, 141, 172, 174
Battlement, 29
Beam, 14, 25, 120
Bedroom, 21, 24, 25, 26, 31, 35, 87, 88
Bench, 26, 47
Bent-up approach, 136, 142, 174
Bin, 23, 27, 123, 128
Bitumen, 76, 88, 93, 116, 118, 121, 214
Block, 26, 27, 31, 56
  of clay, 11, 14
Boat, 13, 33, 35, 59, 83, 107, 110, 149
  sun, 39

Boundary, 5
  stelae, 5, 86
Breeze, 24, 128
Brickwork, 6, 49, 76, 120, 121, 176, 182, 214
  invention of, 11, 59, 201, 211
Bridge, 31, 32, 45, 84
Bronze, 106
Brush, 61
Brushwood, 14, 60
Building process, 8, 63
Bull statues, 183, 184, 189
Bundle-shaped elements, 13, 14
Burial chamber, 44, 49, 50, 51, 52, 55, 64, 138, 170, 171, 197, 199, 214, 221, 225
Buttress, 56, 112, 118, 141, 182, 213

Cabin, 13, 15, 59, 64
Caisson, 62, 141, 142, 145
Calendric symbolism, 40
Camp, 84, 123
Campaniform capital, 70
Canal, 4, 5, 15, 27, 39, 84, 112, 138
Cantonment, 122, 129
Capital, 9, 20, 53, 56, 79, 92, 121, 125, 138, 177, 186, 189, 197, 209
  of column, 38, 69, 97
Cardinal point, 16, 18, 37, 81
Casemated construction, 142, 174, 175, 187
Casing, 63, 117
Castle, 7, 28–29, 33, 56
  of eternity, 47
  of the ka, 47
Castrum, 18
Cattle enclosure, 11, 13
Causeway, 39, 62
Cavalier tower, 115
Cavetto, 14, 64, 184, 189
Ceiling, 14, 23, 26, 36, 38, 60, 64, 132
Cell, 39
Cella, 37, 38, 43, 98, 99, 102, 103, 105, 106, 107, 136, 137, 166, 167, 168, 197, 223
Cellar, 27, 28, 97
Cemetery, 14, 138, 182, 186
Cenotaph, 38, 110
Chapel, 7, 37, 38, 40, 43, 44, 88, 92, 103, 105
  mortuary, 45, 46, 221
Chariot, 9
Chimney, 93
Chisel, 60
Circulation, 81, 83, 116
Cist, 110, 137, 168
Cistern (*Bor*), 152
Citadel, 29, 56, 59, 81, 83, 90, 95, 111, 112, 113, 122, 123, 125, 127, 128, 129, 130, 139, 141, 163, 175, 176, 183, 195, 218, 222
Citizen, 77
City (*see* Towns)

City-state, 15, 56, 76, 77, 79, 90, 148
Civilization, 9, 10, 66, 77, 79, 105, 205, 211
Classicism, 67
Clay, 76
Clerestory, 6, 26, 27, 36, 88, 166, 167, 177, 183
Clergy, 9
Closet, 21, 25, 27, 31
Coffin Texts, 53
Collector, 92
Color, 6, 23, 32, 36, 47, 61, 93, 117, 119, 128, 207
Colossi, 7, 37, 40, 45, 67, 68, 78, 97, 146, 167, 178, 183, 207
Columns, 26, 27, 28, 31, 60, 62, 64, 66, 67, 68–70, 90, 97, 132, 137, 146, 162, 166, 176, 177, 183, 184, 185, 222
  bundle lotiform, 23, 25, 44, 67
  Hathoric, 70, 225
  palmiform, 43, 44, 67
  papyriform, 25, 36, 38
  plant-column, 69
  polygonal, 44, 67
  structural, 69, 70
  tent-pole, 70
  wooden, 26
Columned structure (*see* Portico)
Composite capital, 70
Concrete, 61, 68, 200
Construction,
  dummy, 43
  materials of, 8, 23, 26, 52, 61, 116, 128, 145, 176–178, 189, 201–202, 214, 225
  of pyramid, 63–64
Contour line, 18, 123, 218
Copper, 60, 61, 190, 192
Corbel, 49, 51, 52, 110, 117, 144, 171, 176, 207
Corridor, 23, 24, 25, 53, 55
Corvée, 5
Cosmic orientation, 136
Cosmogonic symbolism, 37
Counterscarp, 58, 154
Course of masonry, 62, 63, 141
Court, courtyard, 7, 21, 23, 25, 26, 35, 37, 87, 88, 89, 90, 92, 93, 95, 101, 116, 123, 127, 128, 132, 133, 134, 136, 146, 156, 157, 159, 160, 161, 162, 177, 188, 192, 213, 215, 217, 223
Courtines, 115, 141
Craftsmen, 5, 7, 18, 183, 188, 209, 221, 225
Crenelation, 13, 117, 118, 141, 189
Cross section, 27
Crowbar, 62
Cruciform facade, 186
Crypt, 35
Cubit, 16, 40
Cul-de-sac, 83
Cult, 7, 9, 37

Cult temple, 35–39
Cultivation, 3
Culture, 5, 8, 66, 80, 108
Cupola, 23, 85
Cyclopean masonry, 145, 172, 174, 200
Cyma, 186

Dais, 28, 31, 159
Decoration, 6, 60, 132, 146
Deflection, 63
Dentil, 67, 186, 202
Dependencies, 22, 87, 89, 132
Deities (*see* Gods)
Desert, 7, 16, 26
Design (*see* Harmonic design)
Destiny, 7, 46, 47
Diagram, constructional, 40
Dike, 4, 5, 155
Diorite, 60, 120
Disk, sun, 9
Ditch, 58, 83, 139
Divan, 26
Dolerite, 60
Dolmen, 168
Dome, 11, 13, 14, 23, 60
Doorways, 13, 27, 170, 174, 176, 178, 200
    sliding, 59
Doubling-back layout, 51, 53
Dovetail, 61
Dowel, 61
Drainage, 6, 11, 18, 23, 39, 59, 60, 81, 84,
        87, 88, 92, 93, 98, 103, 116, 118,
        125, 130, 138, 151, 152, 160, 163,
        188
Drawbridge, 58
Dressing, 62
Drill, 62
Dromos, 110, 162, 171, 191, 197, 199,
        201, 207, 221, 225
Dungeon, 29, 31
Dynastic Period, 8, 9, 15, 16, 18, 20, 21,
        23, 24, 79, 80, 112
    predynastic, 15
    protodynastic, 14, 21, 213

Earth, 7
Earthquake, 120, 157, 194, 201, 206, 214
Eclecticism, 177, 184, 194, 206, 207, 209,
        210, 222, 223, 225
Egyptologist, 8
Electrum, 37, 61
Elevation, 68
Enclosure walls, 11, 13, 15, 16, 29, 45,
        49, 56, 112, 113, 115, 116, 123,
        125, 128, 139, 142, 152, 174, 175,
        178, 182, 187, 192, 200, 211, 215,
        217, 218, 222
Entablature, 186
Entasis, 70
Entrance, winding, 101
Epidemic, 230
Estate, 4

Excavation, 53, 101
Exedra, 87

Façade, 35, 36, 40, 41, 47, 85, 87, 92, 97,
        99, 102, 105, 116, 117, 128, 130,
        132, 137, 146, 177, 186, 189, 217
Faïence, 60, 146, 207
False-door, 27, 41, 116, 117, 200, 202
Fence, 56
Finishing or dressing, of stone, 62
Flagstaffs, 36, 60
Flexibility, 119
Floods, 76
Floor, 36, 123, 128, 132
Flue, 88
Foreigners, 18, 45
Foundation, 78, 123, 125, 128, 142, 157
    ceremonies, 63, 78
    deposits, 63
    trench, 63
Fortifications, 106, 111–116, 138–144,
        172–176, 178, 187, 200, 222
Forts, 6, 14, 15, 25, 45, 56–59, 112, 218
Framework, 29, 53
    wooden, 47, 49, 66
Fresco, 146, 208
Frieze, 13, 15, 26, 90, 97, 102, 118, 119,
        146
Frond, 64
Function, 68, 95
Funerary, 7, 108, 217, 218

Gable, 25, 44, 53, 64, 87, 116, 146, 157,
        186, 195, 199, 225
Gallery, 52
Garden, 4, 28, 40
    hanging, 97
Gargoyle, 209
Gateway, 6, 18, 27, 29, 56, 78, 83, 84, 95,
        102, 107, 112, 113, 118, 122, 123,
        125, 127, 133, 136, 142, 144, 145,
        152, 154, 183, 200
    fortified, 45, 59, 142
    water gate, 18
Genii, 84
Geometry, 5
Gerzean Period, 11, 13
Glacis, 58, 172, 174
Glazed brick or tile, 84, 97, 105, 115, 117,
        133
Goddesses, 134, 184
Gods, 6, 7, 33, 36, 77, 78, 79, 81, 83, 90,
        98, 106, 107, 113, 117, 134, 149,
        163, 166, 184, 217
Gold, 61, 111
Granary, 15, 18, 24, 26, 58
Granite, 5, 52, 60, 136
Graves, 11, 14, 49, 111, 171
Griffin, 133
Grotto, 134
Guesthouse, 175
Gum, 61
Gypsum, 61, 88

Hall, 24, 25, 31, 87, 102, 132, 133, 164, 214, 221, 225
  ceremonial, 132
Ḥarim, 21, 27, 31, 32, 92, 183
Harmonic design, 26, 35, 38, 40, 68, 85, 105, 111, 116, 189
Harmony, 5, 67
Hearth, rolling, 130, 133
Heights of ceilings, 41
Hieroglyphs, 4, 8, 15, 18, 21, 28, 39, 56, 84, 121, 134
High priest, 76, 77, 90
Historical background, 8, 78–80
Horror vacui, 68
Horse-drawn chariots, 9
Houses, 15, 16, 18, 21–24, 84, 85–89, 111, 128–130, 137, 138, 139, 144, 145, 157–163, 177, 182–184, 192–195, 211, 215, 223, 225
  attached, 20, 25, 26, 27, 28
  of eternity, 47
  of gold (sarcophagus chamber), 55
Housing unit, 25
Huts, 11, 13
Hypaethral structures, 39, 87, 168, 195, 201, 214, 221
Hypostyle hall, 21, 24, 25, 26, 27, 29, 33, 35, 36, 41, 45, 70, 90, 178, 183

Illusion, 117
Illusionism, 45
Impost, 183, 184, 189
Incrustation, 118
Inlay, 60, 61
Insulae, 89
Intrados, 14
Inundation, 3, 4, 5, 8, 62
Irrigation, 3, 4, 9, 79, 215
Iteration in design, 189

Jagged wall, 174
Joints, 141
  expansion, 118
Jubilee pavilion, 33, 37, 43, 51

Kamares, 16
Kings, 5, 8, 77, 78, 79, 85, 149
  of the city, 76
Kitchens, 26, 31, 87, 128, 194

Labyrinth, 21
Lakes, artificial, 38, 134
Landhouse, 28
Lathe, 61
Latrine, 21, 25, 47, 49, 88, 92, 93, 133, 160
Layers of pyramids, 63
Layout, 16, 20, 39, 77, 81–84, 89, 119, 129, 133, 145, 154, 182, 183, 184, 188, 215
Lighting, 36, 41, 87
Limestone, 5, 60

Lintel, 13
  broken, 68
Lion statues, 137, 176, 209
Living room, 11, 21, 26, 87, 101
Lobby, 23, 95
Location, 7
Loggia, 26, 28
Loophole, 58
Lubricant in construction, 61

Machicolation, 58, 141, 187, 204, 209
Magazine, 13, 20, 23, 28, 41, 92, 136, 161, 163, 194, 221
Magic, 50
Malaria, 206
Mammisi, 37, 69
Mannerist, 84
Mansion, 16, 24, 32, 89, 162, 175, 194
Marsh, 5
Materials, building, 5, 6, 7, 13, 21, 59–61, 62, 67, 85, 87, 90, 132, 188, 214, 217, 218
Mats, uses of, 14, 24, 25, 44, 98
Mausoleum, 138
Medium, 61
Merlons, 15
Metal, 61, 76, 107, 119
Methods of construction (see Techniques of construction)
Military architecture, 45, 174
Mines, 8, 161
Moats, 58, 187
Models, 13, 23, 25, 27, 85, 87, 129, 159
Modular system, 26, 116
Monolithic construction, 167, 189
Monotheist, 4
Month, Egyptian, 4
Mosaics, 90, 99, 101
Mountain, sacred (see Ziqurrat)
Mud, use of, 76
Mummification, 46
Mummy, 7
Murals, 23, 41, 44, 50, 93, 106, 117, 130, 148, 187, 208, 222
Mutules, 44
Myths, 7

Naos, 33, 35
Naturalism, 68
Nature, 7
Nave, 25, 36
Necropolis, 7, 49, 177, 185, 241
Newel, 156
Niche, 44, 49, 53, 54, 98, 105, 106, 136, 171, 188, 195, 199, 208
Nome, 4

Obelisk, 7, 39, 49, 61, 62, 168, 217
Offering table, 39, 40, 41
Offices, 24
Offset, 33, 55
Oracle, 98
Ordinance, 20, 85, 152

Orientation, 26, 35, 63, 76, 78, 81, 83, 89, 92, 99, 101, 116, 128, 129, 130, 136, 151, 161, 183, 184, 188, 215
Ornament (*Kheker*), 13, 61, 93, 98, 146
Orthogonal plans, 5, 7, 15, 50, 87, 119, 151, 155, 180, 201, 209, 213, 215, 218, 225
Orthostat, 95, 118, 137, 145, 163, 176, 194
Osiride pillar, 41, 44, 45
Outline
  geometrical, 139
  rectangular, 139
Oval plan, 128, 211, 215
Ovens, 11, 23, 87, 123

Painting, 13, 27, 31, 32, 45, 61, 64, 93, 118, 128, 157, 182, 211
Palaces, 20, 27, 28–33, 47, 76, 81, 83, 88, 89–97, 103, 106, 113, 122, 127, 130–133, 154, 160, 162, 163, 164, 177, 182–184, 187, 192–195, 209, 214, 217, 225
  façade of, 47, 50, 66, 213
Paleolithic Period, 10
Palette, 14, 15, 237
Palisade, 56
Paneling, 50, 137
Papyrus, 13, 69
Parabola, 142
Parallel plans, 5
Park, formal, 43
Passageway in forts, 144
Pastes, inlaid, 61
Pavilion, royal, 21
Pegs, use of, 60, 76, 98, 102, 106, 118
Peripteral structures, 37, 67, 209, 225
Peristyle court, 32, 43, 45, 194, 209
Pharaohs, 7, 8, 9, 10, 15, 18, 29, 32, 33, 36, 37, 38, 39, 43, 45, 63, 68, 111, 167, 171, 207, 217
Piazza, 137
Pier, 146, 176
Pigment, 61
Pilaster, 117, 118, 200
Pillar, 43, 44, 55, 67, 70, 118, 130, 145, 176, 197, 208
Pisé, 182
Plain, 3, 148
Plan, 15, 24, 68, 225
  centered, 88, 145, 161
  cruciform, 55
  master plan, 20, 84
Planning unit, 6, 93, 97, 111, 145
Plano-convex brick, 76, 90, 123, 128, 150, 157, 176, 205, 211, 214
Plaster, 14, 26, 88, 137
Plateau, 10, 147
Platforms, use of, 23, 76, 78, 81, 89, 95, 98, 99, 103, 106, 134, 183, 185, 186
Plaza, 81
Podium, 28, 37, 98, 197, 202
Pomerium, 18, 58, 59, 127, 151
Pond, artificial, 28

Population of early towns, 11, 84
Porch, 35, 129, 185, 197
Portcullis, 49, 51, 52, 53, 144
Portico, 6, 21, 23, 24, 44, 45, 46, 53, 87, 90, 127, 128, 130, 134, 146, 161, 183, 186, 188
Postern, 113, 127, 144, 175, 176
Posts, wooden, 11, 13, 14, 24, 123, 128, 129
Pottery, 13, 218
Predynastic Period (*see* Dynastic Period)
Prehistoric times, 10–15, 49
Preplanned towns, 6, 7, 16, 129, 150, 217
Priests, 7, 16, 97, 101
  king, 78, 79, 97
  priesthood, 8
Processional street, 20, 23, 37, 38, 78, 84, 95, 107, 113, 115
Project, public, 8
Propylon, 134
Proto-Aeolian style, 161, 177, 197, 202, 209
Proto-Doric style, 44, 67
Protodynastic Period (*see* Dynastic Period)
Protome capitals, 189
Public works office, 61, 85
Pulley, 52, 62
Pylon, 35, 38, 40, 67
Pyramid, 7, 8, 18, 23, 43, 46, 49, 50, 51–54, 63–64, 66, 78, 102, 116, 217, 221
Pyramid city, 16, 21, 23
Pyramidal platform, 208
Pyramidion, 49, 53

Quadrangular plan of city, 128
Quarry, 5, 7, 8, 60, 62
Quarter of city, 16, 18, 32
Quay, 4, 62

Race, Egyptian, 8
Rainy season, 116
Ramp, 47, 62, 106, 110, 142, 144, 221
Rampart, 141, 144, 152
Realism, 68
Reception room, 23, 25
Recessed paneling, 49, 50, 66, 81, 88, 98, 99, 102, 103, 116, 117, 213, 214
Reeds, use of, 8, 13, 14, 21, 60, 61, 64, 87, 98, 106, 110, 116, 117
Relief, 36, 37, 41, 45, 136, 145, 176, 184, 186
  high, 134
Religion, 6, 7, 40, 77–78, 81, 136, 149
Repository for bark of Amon, 37
Reserve, animal, 20
Residence, 20, 32, 33, 132
Rhythm, 5, 66, 117
Ribs, reinforcing, 14, 98, 106
Rite, ritual, 7
River, 3, 4, 5, 45, 78, 81, 112, 139
  bank, 83
Robing room, 27, 31

Rocker, 62
Roof, 13, 25, 87, 139
Rope, 62
Rows of houses, 16, 17, 18
Royal Road, 32
Rugs, 24

Sanctuary, 7, 14, 33, 136, 192
Sand, 101
Sandstone, 5, 60
Sanitary facilities, 6, 156
Sarcophagus, 24, 29, 51, 52, 111, 170, 171,
    186, 202, 213
  chamber, 55
Scaffolding, 62
Scale, 7, 137, 171, 217
Scalloped parapet, 64
Scarp, 58, 141
Scenes, repertory, 44, 50, 93, 117
Science, 8
Scriptorium, 92
Sculpture, 60, 146, 208, 218, 222
Settlement (see Urban centers)
Shaft, 50, 51, 53, 54, 63, 170, 178, 199
  light, 146
Sheaths, metallic, 36
Shelter, early types of, 11, 13
Shrines, 13, 33, 37, 55, 134, 137, 164, 168,
    185, 213
  theriomorphic, 33
Sill, 13
Silt, 5, 10, 14
Sistrum (column), 67
Skyline, 29, 146
Slaves, 8, 77
Sledge, 61, 62
Slot, 27, 41
Soffit, 44
Soul, 7, 41
Soul house, 129
Sphinx, 20, 37, 38, 142, 145, 207, 208
Spiral, 55
Spouts, rain, 25
Stables, 160, 162, 163
Stability in construction, 14
Staircases, 26, 28, 29, 31, 36, 92, 113, 132
  stairway, 47, 98, 99, 102, 103, 128, 176,
    183, 185, 189, 194, 200
Statuary, 41, 66, 68
Statue, 7, 32, 35, 37, 39, 41, 44, 53, 83, 98,
    99, 102, 106, 107, 117, 118, 119,
    130, 134, 136, 137, 138
Stela, 5, 7, 24, 27, 29, 53, 78, 106, 118,
    191, 197, 209, 213
Stoa, 209
Stockade, 21
Stone, 35, 59, 61, 66, 95, 101, 108, 118, 141,
    214, 225
Storeroom, Storehouse (see Magazine)
Stratigraphy, 206
Streets, 6, 15, 16, 18, 24, 50, 56, 78, 81, 84,
    87, 89, 119, 125, 127, 136, 150, 154,
    162, 182, 192, 194

Stronghold, 56, 59
Structure, 4, 64, 128, 137
Stucco, 60, 63
Style, architectural, 15, 64–71, 116–119,
    128, 133, 134, 142, 144–146, 163,
    176–178, 188–189, 201–202, 205,
    213, 214, 225
Stylization, 66, 69
Substructures, 24, 49, 53, 111
Suburbs, 28
Sun, 3, 5, 7, 9, 39, 49, 55, 76, 107,
    184
Sun boat, 52
Sun disk, 9
Sun temple (see Temple)
Superstructure, 14, 41, 46, 47, 49, 53, 54,
    64, 111, 157, 162, 214, 225
Summation series (of Fibonacci), 68
Symbolism, 36, 37, 40, 43, 49, 55, 61, 67,
    69, 70, 78, 98, 101, 106, 107, 110,
    111, 115, 118, 136, 184, 209, 213,
    217
Symmetrical plans or layouts, 33, 35, 41,
    43, 44, 87, 99, 133, 137, 142, 164,
    166, 177, 194, 209
Symmetry, 89, 119, 184, 188, 217

Taper, inverted, 222
Techniques of construction, 61–64, 67,
    189, 207, 214
Temenos, 38, 81, 83, 89, 90, 101, 103, 111,
    182, 195, 219
Temples, 7, 9, 14, 20, 32, 33–46, 67, 77, 78,
    81, 87, 95, 97–102, 116, 130, 133–
    137, 155, 163–168, 178, 184–185,
    195–197, 217, 223
  of appearance, 106
  cult, 35–38
  mortuary, 38, 44, 45, 217, 219
  oval, 101
  palace, 45, 60, 61
  rock-cut, 37, 68, 188
  sun temple, 39
Tent pole, 208
Terraces, 6, 14, 26, 43, 44, 85, 98, 99, 101,
    133, 134, 138, 174, 183, 187, 188
Terra-cotta, 18, 60, 76, 85, 93, 98, 137, 168
Tholos, 209
Throne, throne-room, 27, 31, 92, 93, 95,
    183, 184
Tile, 33, 51, 60, 76, 84, 88
Timber, 60, 76, 120, 177, 189
Tombs, 7, 9, 10, 16, 23, 25, 32, 45, 46–56,
    108–111, 137–138, 168–171, 178,
    185–186, 191, 194, 197–200, 207,
    209
  robber, 10, 50, 53
  rock-cut, 54–56
Torus, 14, 33, 64
Towers, 29, 36, 41, 45, 56, 84, 112, 113,
    122, 125, 132, 139, 144, 145, 152,
    154, 172, 174, 176, 178, 182, 185,
    187

Towns, 4, 6, 15–21, 26, 78, 81, 101, 112, 122–128, 150–157, 175, 180–182, 192, 214, 218, 222, 225
    fortified, 121, 139
    planning, 11, 80–85, 122, 139, 146, 152
Townhouse, 27
Trabeated style, 69, 142, 189, 225
Tracery, 177
Transport, 5
Trap door, 23
Treasury, 183
Trees, use of, 28, 43, 89, 189
    sacred, 97, 106, 161, 177, 208
Triangle, 63, 68
Tripartite plan, 27, 33, 35, 98, 133, 160, 178, 207, 214, 217, 219
Truth (Maᶜt), 7, 67
Tubs, 92
Tumulus, 14, 138
Twist in pyramid construction, 63

Underpass, 16
Unification, 5, 8
Universalist, 187, 188
Urban centers, 4, 10, 13, 15, 20, 29, 78, 80, 83, 84, 85, 89, 123, 125, 150, 151, 152, 154, 155, 157, 179, 182, 187, 192, 201, 205, 209, 211, 212

Vases, 106
Vaults, 13, 14, 23, 25, 33, 47, 59, 60, 64, 87, 97, 106, 117, 144, 176, 189, 199, 201
Ventilator (*Mulqaf*), 6, 25
Vertical doors, 23, 52
Vessels, 105, 117

Vestibule, 35, 37, 55, 132, 134
Villas, 26, 40, 68, 188, 219
Villages, 20, 25, 27, 28, 78, 80, 122, 211
Vista, 78, 84, 105
Volute, 70, 71, 97, 106, 161, 177, 189
Voussoirs, 106, 208

Walls, 16, 18, 20, 21, 81, 92, 93, 113, 115, 116, 118, 127, 128, 129, 130, 139, 141, 172, 174, 192, 211
    party, 14, 29, 49, 146
    retaining, 13, 14, 97
    spur, 18, 58
Water gate, 18
Water supply, 23, 151, 152, 154
Water system, 127
Water tank, 27
Waterway, 58
Wattlework, 5, 6, 51, 116
Wattle-and-daub, 10, 11, 14, 33, 59, 85
Wedge, 60
Wells, 26, 101
White Wall, 31
Wickerwork, 13, 21
Windscreen, 10, 76, 81, 90
Windlass, 52, 62
Window, 5, 13, 23, 28, 85, 87, 130, 134, 171
Window of appearance, 31, 32, 45
Wood, use of, 23, 101, 118, 176, 208, 214
Workshop, 11, 128

Ziqurrat, 78, 81, 90, 98, 102, 103, 106, 107, 116, 118, 184, 219, 223
Zoning, 16, 20, 58, 83, 84, 151

Index of Foreign Architectural Terms

Benben, 39, 49
Berikah ("lake"), 151
Bor ("cistern"), 152
Debir ("Holy of Holies"), 164, 167
Elam ("forecourt, vestibule"), 167
Hekal ("hall, house"), 167
Hesr ("Court"), 167
Hilammar, 136, 145
Hilani, 127, 130, 133, 137, 145, 167, 195, 219, 223
Karum, 121, 127, 145
Lamassu ("Man-headed bull"), 95, 113, 208

Liwan ("rectangular exedra"), 87, 97, 161
Mastaba tomb, 29, 41, 47, 49–51, 111, 170, 214
Megaron, 125, 129, 130, 137, 142, 144, 145, 159, 201
Migdol ("stronghold"), 161, 175
Mulqaf ("ventilator"), 6
Serdab ("closed statue chamber"), 89
Serekh, ("recessed entrance façade"), 213, 217
Sinnor ("tunnel"), 151